BREAKTHROUGH:

An Amazing Experiment in
Electronic Communication with the Dead

BREAKTHROUGH:

An Amazing Experiment in Electronic Communication with the Dead

KONSTANTIN RAUDIVE Ph.D.

Translated by
Nadia Fowler

Edited by
Joyce Morton

www.whitecrowbooks.com

Breakthrough

Copyright © 1971, 2021 by Colin Smythe Ltd. All rights reserved.
Foreword copyright © 2021 by Anabela Cardoso. All rights reserved.

Published in the United States of America and the United
Kingdom by White Crow Books; an imprint of White Crow
Productions Ltd, in association with Colin Smythe Ltd.

The moral right of Konstantin Raudive to be identified as the author of this work
has been asserted in accordance with the Copyright, Design and Patents act 1988.

No part of this book may be reproduced, copied or used in any
form or manner whatsoever without written permission, except in
the case of brief quotations in reviews and critical articles.

For information, contact White Crow Books by
e-mail: info@whitecrowbooks.com.

Cover Design by Astrid@Astridpaints.com
Interior design by Velin@Perseus-Design.com

Paperback: ISBN: 978-1-78677-163-6
eBook: ISBN: 978-1-78677-164-3

Non-Fiction / Body, Mind & Spirit / Parapsychology / Afterlife & Reincarnation

www.whitecrowbooks.com

The editor acknowledges with grateful appreciation the devoted and unwearying efforts of the translators, Mrs. N. Fowler and Mr. W. G. Street, and the generous assistance of Mr. H. V. Bearman, Secretary of the Scientific Committee of the Churches' Fellowship for Psychical Study, who read the manuscript and whose suggestions have been invaluable in compiling the English edition of this work.

Foreword

If this foreword had a title, I would name it "Konstantin Raudive, the scientist of EVP" because nobody has done so much toward the scientific recognition of EVP as Dr Konstantin Raudive.

A Latvian psychologist, Swedish by naturalization, Raudive lived in Germany and taught at the University of Uppsala in Sweden. Philosopher, polyglot, intellectual and a man of culture, his main interests focused on the exploration of the human mind and the potentialities of the human soul in connection to the universe.

Dr Raudive's previous books amply reflect his existential concerns and intellectual capacity. Among those, rightly classified in the elitist category, *Der Chaos Mensch und seine Überwindung* (The Human Chaos and How to Overcome It) is perhaps the best known. But they all reveal his preoccupations and his profound search for transcendence.

He would finally discover transcendence after meeting the Swedish artist Friedrich Jürgenson, rightly called the 'father of the voices'. The piercing of another dimension with palpable proof, must have fascinated Raudive because from 1965 onwards he devoted his life, time and knowledge to the mysterious voices that claim to be the dead speaking from another world.

Like Jürgenson, Raudive previously had not had contact with the anomalous phenomena, thus Jürgenson's experiences must have appeared impossible to him.

He started experimenting with the Jürgenson method and obtained plentiful personal results, which led him to write a book about the awesome events. *Unhörbares wird Hörbar* was published in Germany in 1968 with great success.

But what really agitated the world was the publication in 1971 of the English translation of the German original under the title *Breakthrough, an amazing experiment in electronic communication with the dead*, and I confidently affirm that this is the best book ever written on EVP. Its republication by White Crow Books is a praiseworthy step toward the divulgation of a discipline capable of opening the path of understanding and light to misguided humanity, as was the aim of Raudive and Jürgenson.

Konstantin Raudive's prestige as a man of culture and as a scientist was of such calibre that he was able to assemble some of the top European experts in the field of physics and electronics to help with his work. Professor of Physics Alex Schneider of St Gallen University, Prof. Dr Gebhard Frei, Theodor Rudolph, Engineer in High Frequency Techniques, Dr Ing. Franz Seidl, inventor the Psychophone and other apparatuses designed for communication with the voices, as well as a special hearing device that allowed the deaf, even the deaf from birth, to hear.

Prof Dr Hans Bender, the renowned German parapsychologist, following Raudive's successful work with Friedrich Jürgenson, became interested in his research and participated in experiments.

The fascinating comments, suggestions and plans devised by these and other scientists are compiled in the *Appendices* at the end of this book. The sole reading of that section should be sufficient to fully credit our discipline and raise it to the summit of serious parapsychology.

There are and there will always be detractors of the voice phenomena, be it in the EVP or ITC form. There are misinformed or simply ill-intentioned analysts and observers everywhere, and there are also those who are not interested in considering, never mind accepting the reality of these extraordinary voices and what their content represents to humanity. They are not interested in human enlightenment and wisdom through the breaking of the prevalent paradigm. The electronic voices tell us much more than "death does not exist". The voices tell us that the way we think and live is fundamentally wrong. A breakthrough in human thinking and a breakthrough in human behaviour is what we desperately need. As my own communicators have loudly stated, "We speak from another level, humans need to know about the light!"

The republication of this book, aptly titled *Breakthrough*, is a privilege now open to everybody.

Anabela Cardoso,
August 2021

Preface

On 13th October 1969 as the Frankfurt Book Fair was about to close, Colin Smythe was approached by an elderly gentleman who presented him with a copy of a German book and said: "Here is a book you might like to publish. You had better take it and look at it."

In fact Colin Smythe must have brought back a dozen books in German and some time in November I got round to looking at this particular book entitled *Unhörbares Wird Hörbar*, literally translated *The Inaudible Becomes Audible*.

Browsing through the pages, without actually reading the complete story, I formed the opinion that Konstantin Raudive, the author, had joined the host who are set on telling us that life after death is a reality which can be scientifically proven. I don't think I would have given the book a second thought but for the section containing letters and comments by scientists I personally know to be of the highest integrity, and incapable of supporting anything scientifically suspect; for example, Professor Gebhard Frei, a Roman Catholic Priest and philosopher, Professor Alex Schneider the physicist, Professor Dr. Hans Bender of Freiburg, the psychologist and many others.

I was greatly perturbed, and actually wondered whether by some clever trick I had been misled into assuming that these scientists were actually referring to this book, but doubts were dispelled when I found that they had not written some kind of testimonial for Dr. Raudive, but clearly stated that they were members of a large team that had taken part in hundreds of experiments and were taking personal responsibility for the accuracy of his description of those experiments.

After much thought and consultation with Colin Smythe, I made a great number of telephone calls, and as a result letters and cuttings from German newspapers and other material was sent to us.

The picture that now emerged was fairly clear: Dr. Raudive (through the work of a Swedish author Friedrich Jürgenson) had encountered the phenomenon of voices which appeared on recording tapes, apparently without human intervention, and could be played back at choice. These voices had certain characteristics but, although twice the speed of normal human speech, could be clearly understood. Further investigation had shown that the voices did not appear at random but seemed to respond to invitation to manifest themselves. A great number of experiments had obviously been conducted, and the phenomenon was still being examined by scientists in other countries who had been called in by Dr. Raudive. Of the German newspapers, the larger reputable papers simply reported in the smallest of paragraphs certain lectures given by Dr. Raudive, and did not comment one way or the other. The popular press such as *Bild am Sonntag* (Sunday Pictorial) gave Raudive's work a treble spread and perhaps rather over-did the story with pictures of Hitler, Napoleon, Goethe and Plato, and headlines such as "Hitler speaks from the other side", "Goethe's words from heaven" and "In the footsteps of ghosts".

I was now certain that, without committing our publishing house either way, we ought to talk to the author, and I telephoned Dr. Raudive in Bad Krozingen and secured a three months option on his book.

On Sunday, 16th November 1969, I was once more assailed by the gravest doubts. Two days before, Colin Smythe had reproached me for being unsociable. Although I am always in the habit of closing my office door, that week my colleagues and friends had apparently found me completely unapproachable. Unknown to me, Colin Smythe had purchased a number of recording tapes from our local electrical supplier and followed the simple instructions one of the papers described and I had translated. On the way to Heathrow to board the Dublin plane he told me what he had done, and mentioned that at one particular point (he had scribbled the number on the rev. meter on a piece of paper), a certain rhythm was clearly audible and also a voice but he could not make sense of it. On my return from the airport, I found a tape on the recorder and next to it a piece of paper with the number 126 written on it. I re-wound the tape to 120 and played it back. I heard nothing. I played it back five times and was just about to give up when suddenly I heard this rhythm. I played it again, and once more. It is very difficult for me to narrate clearly what happened next; suddenly I heard a voice—quite distant but very clear. I played this part of the tape again because I was absolutely sure I had fallen a victim of my own imagination. The voice was—if anything—even clearer. A woman's voice said in German: "Mach die Tür mal auf", "Why don't you open the door". This in itself might not appear significant to an outsider, apart from its relevance to the situation I have mentioned, but for two facts. As soon as I heard the voice I recognised the speaker; although the voice spoke terribly fast and in a strange rhythm, I had heard it many times before. For eleven years before her death I had conducted my entire correspondence with my mother by tape, and I would recognise her voice anywhere. And this was my mother's voice. Secondly, Colin Smythe cannot speak German and in any event is quite incapable of playing a deceitful trick of this kind on anybody.

Later that evening, I went back to the tape-recorder and played that tape over and over again. There was no doubt about the voice being on that tape, I no longer had any difficulty in hearing it right away, for somehow my ear appeared to have tuned to this unusual frequency. I tried hard to find some rational explanation and on Monday, without going into details, I asked two of our junior assistants in the firm to listen to the tape. They listened with stereophonic earphones ten or twelve times, then wrote down what they heard phonetically, and although these young men are not trained in phonetics it soon became clear that they were hearing the same thing I had heard. On Colin Smythe's return from Ireland the following day, I asked him to listen carefully to his own recording, and after playing it about five or six times, he noticed a voice but was still unable to identify language or content.

This voice, however remarkable and inexplicable, neither convinced me nor changed my mind as far as the publication of Dr. Raudive's book was concerned. I decided to invite him to come to England to demonstrate his voice phenomenon in the presence of as many witnesses as possible, including experts who could examine every single item used during the demonstration, and on Friday, 12th December 1969, he arrived.

On Friday night he played to us a number of his own tapes, and Colin Smythe suggested that he might like to show us there and then something of his recording technique, for at that stage, of course, we did not understand the various descriptions he gave to voices; "microphone voices", "diode voices" and "radio voices" meant nothing to us. However, I had already arranged for a qualified electrical-engineer to come the next day.

Dr. Raudive had brought a small diode, a box about twice the size of a match-box with two inches of wire sticking out of one end and also a small wire (to be inserted into the hole marked "radio-input" on our tape-recorder) fastened to the other end. To be frank, this thing bothered me because I did not really understand its function and I wondered whether it might be some clever little device which would procure voices. I immediately telephoned the engineer and asked him what a diode was, and I arranged to have this one taken the next morning to his workshop for examination, and then to have another one built—just in case.

Five people were in the room, including Dr. Raudive, when we started the experiment; it was quite obvious, especially to our guest, that we felt extremely uneasy when Dr. Raudive asked Mr. Smythe to start the tape-recorder as if he wished to make an ordinary recording. The microphone was placed in the centre of the room and I was quite satisfied that nothing unusual had been done to the tape-recorder. The experimenter gave his name, the date of recording and invited voices wishing to manifest themselves to do so; he then asked all those present to speak as well, which we did and then waited for the next four minutes in total silence.

Then Dr. Raudive asked the voice-entities to manifest themselves through the diode. I really did wonder about this apparatus, because during his demonstration earlier on I had noticed that those "diode voices" he referred to were clearer or more resonant than those voices he described as "microphone voices". He plugged the diode into "radio input" told us that we could converse freely during the recording on diode and began telling us about his year at Edinburgh in 1931. After some five minutes he suggested that we should switch the recorder off and try to listen for whatever phenomenon might be on the tape. He reminded us that it would be very difficult to tune into the acoustic waves which would be audible only to the trained ear, but that he would play those parts over and over again if he thought that a voice had manifested itself.

The first part to be played back was the "microphone recording". After only ten seconds, in fact in the first empty space after Raudive's short talk, we all heard quite clearly: "Koste—Tekle", in the unmistakable rhythm we had noticed on the demonstration tapes. (There was no doubt about these two words; "Koste" is Dr. Raudive's nickname, often used with other variations of his name by voice phenomena on those recordings we had already heard, and Tekle was the name of his dead sister who, as he pointed out, had spoken on many recordings before). A number of other voices were noticeable but not sufficiently audible to convey their meaning.

As soon as we switched over to the "diode recording", the name Malcolm was called out quite clearly. (Malcolm Hughes, a student at Oxford, was in the room with us). A number of other voices came through, some speaking in Latvian or Russian, with the occasional German word. However, as only Dr. Raudive spoke Latvian and Russian, and I could only make out the German words, we had to take his word for the fact that the short telegraphic sentences really made sense. This was, of couse, an anticlimax, although we knew that nearly all the voices Dr. Raudive had recorded used fragments of different languages to fit the sentence into a pronounced rhythmic pattern.

Then suddenly, two complete sentences followed within five seconds of each other; they were completely in German and I understood them clearly. Malcolm's German is very modest but the actual words (except the name) were quite simple; he too understood the sentences, which were:

"Bauer[1] ist noch hier" this means: "Bauer is still here", and "Wo ist Ruhe?" which means "Where is rest?"

None of the people present could recall anybody called Bauer or Bower, which is a well-known family name on the Continent, and although I could clearly understand the sentence, it had no meaning for me or anybody present. But, beyond a shadow of doubt, the voice was there and by all laws of physics, so we are told, it should not have been.

We terminated the experiment at this point and had a cup of coffee.

I fetched the tape I have mentioned earlier, about which Dr. Raudive knew nothing, and placing it on my own taperecorder I played it three or four times to myself to check that the voice was still there. Dr. Raudive did not even pay any attention to what I was doing, as he was at the other end of the room, discussing with Colin Smythe another book of his which he had given to us as a present. I then called him over and asked him to listen to this tape; for this purpose I gave him a pair of stereophonic earphones and I myself moved the tape forward and backward twice until he stopped me and said: "This voice says quite clearly 'Mach die Tuer mal auf'—where did it come from? I don't remember hearing it earlier and I would not have missed it." I briefly explained that Colin Smythe had obtained this recording, but gave no details.

On Saturday morning Dr. Raudive went with Colin Smythe to the workshop of the electrical-engineer, Mr. David Stanley. Mr. Stanley examined the diode and took it to pieces; within seconds he said that it was an ordinary diode and of no particular value, he would build us one of these within the hour if we wanted. Dr. Raudive then explained to David Stanley about his three different methods of recording and, to our relief, David appeared to have no difficulty in understanding Dr. Raudive's explanation about the technicalities involved. He promised to put all that in layman's language later that evening, when a number of guests had been invited

---

[1] In recent correspondence concerning English language rights in Dr. Raudive's book, Mr. Rolf Schaffranke, a Senior Research Engineer in the U.S.A. mentioned that the first publisher to become involved with work of this nature (many years ago) was a Mr. Bauer. Our information is that Mr. Bauer is now dead.

to meet Dr. Raudive and—we hoped—could actually see him at work.

In arranging this my aim was simply to satisfy myself that I was not hearing or imagining something that others could not hear. The friends I invited are honest people, very much down-to-earth, and they come from different walks of life. Some of them hold eminent positions in public life, but none of the twenty-odd people present was a Spiritualist or in any way associated with studies of the supernatural. I do not wish for one moment to cause any offence to those people who practice Spiritualism; I simply wanted to make absolutely sure that none of the people present had any previous experience of the kind I hoped was in store for them. Suffice it to say that. apart from a number of highly respected members of the academic world, I had invited a high dignitary of the Roman Catholic Church and, of course, two experts in electronics. None of the people invited, except Mr. Stanley, the electrical-engineer on whom I had to rely for explanations to non-experts, knew the real reason for our invitation, but had been told that we had invited an author who was going to talk about a book we might publish. What type of book, who the author was or what kind of evening awaited them, they did not know.

I had asked Mr. Stanley to prepare himself to explain in the simplest possible way, when the appropriate moment came, what certain things of a technical kind would mean and where the limits of recording methods lay etc., and Mr. Stanley's own words and drawings are used here. The full credit for any technical explanation in this introduction is his, and if all the queries that arise are not covered, it is because they were not put to Mr. Stanley on this occasion.

At about 7.30 p.m. on Saturday 13th December 1969 serious business began. Dr. Raudive was introduced as a scientist, born in Latvia, and a Swedish citizen who lived at the moment in Bad Krozingen near the Swiss border in Southern Germany, and I mentioned that his book, containing a record of his research, had been offered to us for publication. Resisting the temptation to present my guests with the voice-phenomenon immediately, I explained our doubts about the suitability of the book for publication in England and added: "By being suitable I simply mean: is there something I have overlooked? I hope that you may be able to help me answer this question at the end of this evening."

Dr. Raudive spoke for about half an hour. He briefly explained his meeting with the voice phenomenon through Jürgenson's book, his subsequent research and his work with a great number of scientists. He then asked for a tape-recorder and played to my guests one tape of different voices, recorded by three different methods, and explained in some cases, where the sense of sentences escaped the audience, the situation or questions he had asked before receiving the answer on his tape-recorder. Everybody was very intrigued, very fascinated and very polite. Nobody asked any questions and the silence was almost embarrassing. Over supper, however, the conversation became quite animated, even heated. In particular, my ecclesiastical friend held forth on what his Church taught on such matters and said he certainly did not intend to deviate one inch from the official position of the Church, citing Joan of Arc, Fatima, Lourdes and other miraculous happenings which had taken the Church many years to investigate. When the Head of one of the Cambridge colleges pointed out that none of these people had been able to produce a tape-recording in evidence when questioned by the Church, he admitted it was the tape-recorder and the simplicity of the matter that worried him most. He still preferred the slow process of taking the testimony of human witnesses, to the scientific examinations of physicists, psychologists, electronic experts and other scientists.

I don't remember ever having had such an animated discussion in my dining room.

Mr. Stanley was then invited to explain the mysteries of electronics in connection with this business. "What can a tape-recorder do and what can it not do?" "What advantage is in a diode and what exactly does a diode do?" We all asked many questions. It is to Mr. Stanley's credit that he satisfied everybody present with his explanations.

The three methods of obtaining voice phenomena then open to us are relatively simple to explain—if you have a basic knowledge of electronics, but few of us have this basic knowledge. Most people know how to record on a tape-recorder and how to play the recorded music or voices back; but how exactly this process of recording takes place is one of the questions very few ask until a moment like this arises, when we begin to wonder whether some trickery or expertise on the part of a good technician might not lead us to believe something that is not really possible. Technology has advanced so much that with the help of little gadgets, transistorised and so small that they can be hidden anywhere, many things can be produced electronically; in fact, our imagination of what may be afoot exceeds physical and electronic possibilities. But to remove any doubt in the bona fide of a recording we must rely on experts, and this was exactly what we did on the evening of 13th December 1969. As far as humanly possible we had taken every step to make absolutely sure that nothing was used in this experiment that might have been tampered with. A new tape-recorder was ordered, which proved rather a setback during the next few hours because even our expert Mr. Stanley had never operated this particular model and we had to use the operating instructions throughout the evening. A number of new tapes, sealed in plastic bags and sealed in boxes, had been purchased and were delivered the same evening; Mr. Stanley opened these tapes and put them on to the new tape-recorder. He operated the machine himself and we all agreed that this would be sufficient evidence that whatever might happen was certainly not due to trickery or technical know-how.

Our first experiment was to obtain microphone voices. This means that the tape-recorder is set for ordinary recording of voice or music or any sound whatever in the room. The technical process is relatively simple, as Mr. Stanley explained:

"The microphone is a device for recording sounds that take place in a room at a particular time. It is merely connected to the tape-recorder. Obviously for the purpose of this experiment you need complete silence as any noise will upset the recording.

Sound waves are picked up by the microphone which converts them into electronic impulses. These electronic impulses are amplified in the tape-recorder and passed through the recording head which gives out a magnetic impulse. This in turn is recorded on the passing magnetic tape. The average microphone will pick up sound waves with a range from 60 cycles per second (the very low sounds) to 12,000 cycles per second (very high sounds). This roughly corresponds to the average range of the human ear, which is unable to perceive sounds outside this range. If there are any voices or noises on the tape, then all the people in the room during the recording should be able to hear them whilst they are recorded. The microphones in use are only able to pick up what is also audible to the human ear."

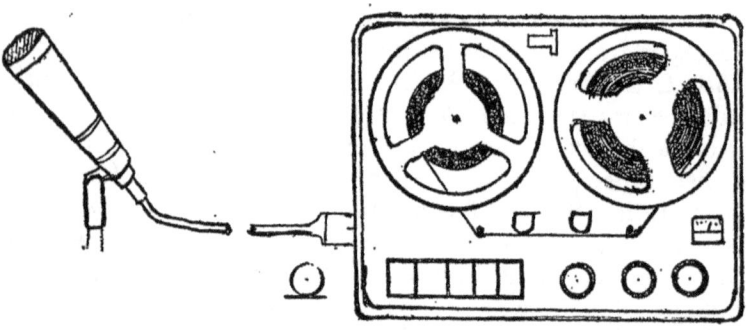

After ten minutes of recording we had the "playback", and the first disappointment of the evening. Whilst everybody had remained silent during the actual recording, a clock on the mantelpiece had been ticking loud and clear and a labrador puppy, two rooms away from where we were, had been crying. These sounds were there and it was impossible to hear anything else. For the purpose of our experiment the recording was useless. It became obvious that Dr. Raudive felt embarrassed, and whilst my guests were all understanding and encouraging, the situation which was building up became a little tense. It was now past ten o'clock, and someone reminded me that the last train to London would be going in one hour. Many a housewife must have felt like me when preparing a meal for a large gathering and discovering that the first course is ruined. I therefore hurried Dr. Raudive, broke into a conversation he was having with Mr. Stanley and asked him to try another method. He suggested radio voices.

I brought a portable radio into the room and Dr. Raudive asked Mr. Stanley to find a "between frequency" which could be used for the recording. Such radio voices as demonstrated on the tape we had listened to earlier in the evening, were very clear and simplified the playback afterwards. However, both Raudive and Stanley warned us that at this time of night the medium wave was fairly overloaded with transmissions and the possibility of finding an "empty" wave was remote. For twenty minutes—agonising minutes for me, watching the time pass—they tried in vain to find that empty space; furthermore, we discovered that the reception even on "Radio 4" (Home Service) was very poor. I then remembered that I might have chosen the worst possible room in the whole house for any experiment of this kind; three months ago the builders had completed an addition to the building and four heavy steel girders which had been put above and on two sides of the room, appeared to create strong interference with our reception. When I pointed this out to Mr. Stanley, he agreed with me and suggested that the radio voice experiment be abandoned. However, he briefly explained what was involved in such a method.

"Dr. Raudive told us that he has carried out many of his experiments on the medium wave. In our own case, the Light Programme broadcasts on 247 metres and the Home Service in this area on 330 metres. Apart from these two, there are dozens of other broadcasting stations on the continent and further afield which make use of this wave band. We have to be very careful in selecting a position which is not being used by a radio station; fortunately we do not have to worry about amateur radio operators, but as Dr. Raudive said, the ideal place for such a recording would be in the middle of the Pacific Ocean where there would be the smallest possible local interference. If one knows when a particular radio station closes down for the night, one would have something to go on but there are certain pirate stations which immediately begin their broadcast on the same wave length. What we want is a true 'inter-frequency' where nothing but a general atmospheric static noise would be audible; this can be generated by a great number of factors, for example a light which is switched on or any atmospheric disturbance. Given a true 'inter-frequency', the radio picks up the static noise but no particular signal. All that gets amplified is the static noise; the process now is similar to that of a microphone recording. This amplified static noise is fed into the tape-recorder and from the recorder head on to the magnetic tape.

There is one point I would like to make; I have listened to some previous recordings made by Dr. Raudive through radio recordings. The amazing thing is that one can dismiss the possibility of those recordings originating from radio stations because there is never any music and the voices speak at a speed which is at least twice the speed of the human voice if not faster. We all know that one can distort voices; one could play around with special devices which would get the waves out of phase, so that the resulting voice would appear higher or lower but you just cannot alter the frequency of a voice. The strange rhythm might be explained by fading but this would not account for the speed. In other words, once speech has originated, the actual spoken word or the emphasis of the word will always remain the same. Of course we can speed up voices; but this can only be done *after* they have been recorded. You can compress it but this would have to be manipulated, it would not just happen. Also, when you speed a voice up like that, it becomes distorted as you are going into a different harmonic, you could no longer understand it."

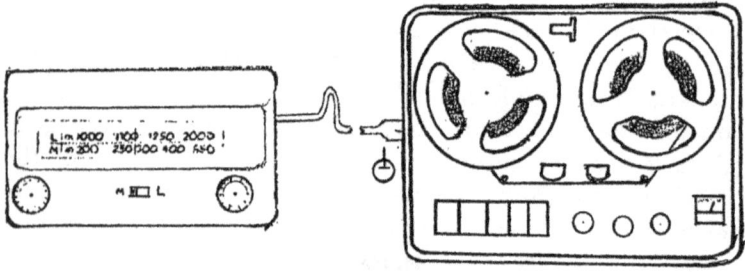

David Stanley then suggested that in view of the difficulty arising from the girders, the small piece of wire which acts as an aerial on the diode, ought to be lengthened by four inches. This was done and Dr. Raudive decided to do a five minute diode recording (his most successful method, although difficult to analyse during the playback) and Mr. Stanley inserted the diode into the tape-recorder. There were three "inputs" at the back of the recorder and he chose No. 2, as he believed that this would give additional control over the microphone input.

Every recording Dr. Raudive makes, is preceded by a brief mention of day, time and other details, just in case the recording should be afterwards used for reference, and to add to this chaotic situation, No. 2 input was found to be faulty (in a brand-new tape-recorder!) and another ten minutes had been wasted. Once the fault had been remedied by inserting the diode into the radio-input, Dr. Raudive decided to split the recording into two distinct three minute parts. For the second half he, or any other person who might wish to do so, could touch the aerial of the diode in order to see whether the aerial potential could thus be increased. In spite of the lengthened aerial, nothing happened. Odd bits of tuneless music (probably five or six different stations all mixed up) came on and off; to add to this, when somebody afterwards touched the aerial, the noise emanating from the recording was absolutely horrifying.

It now appeared certain that the evening had not yielded the desired result. It had been interesting and many a stimulating discussion had started but I had failed to involve my friends directly in this field of voice phenomena. Furthermore, the question had arisen whether the diode method might not be very deceptive; after all, we had just witnessed a number of radio stations coming in together, was there not the possibility of any voices (particularly in more than one language) being just such a mix-up? Mr. Stanley now explained briefly what this particular method of recording was about:

"This diode here is basically a piece of germanium with a bit of metal on it. It will conduct electricity one way and not the other; electricity will flow one way only. Really it is nothing but a common crystal set we used to know as a cat's whisker in early radio days. It acts in a similar way to a radio but it is not as sensitive. A radio would select a particular station one wants from all the signals that are picked up by the aerial (radio-television-teleprinter etc.); the radio will select just one particular frequency. I don't want to go into the technical details here because they are a little complicated, but by tuning the dial we set in motion a sophisticated process of selection. A diode like this is a very crude and primitive gadget which has a slightly tuned coil and an aerial. However, I must comment on this particular aerial because it is absolutely useless for picking up anything. The nearest broadcasting station to this house is Brookmans Park and in order to receive a signal from that station we would need an aerial of some 2 to 3 metres (or 6 to 8 feet) at least in length. This aerial is only three inches long (7 centimetres) and absolutely useless for picking up anything. I can say quite categorically, that it is impossible to pick up anything with this aerial. There is no signal strong enough to induce a three inch wire to act as an aerial."

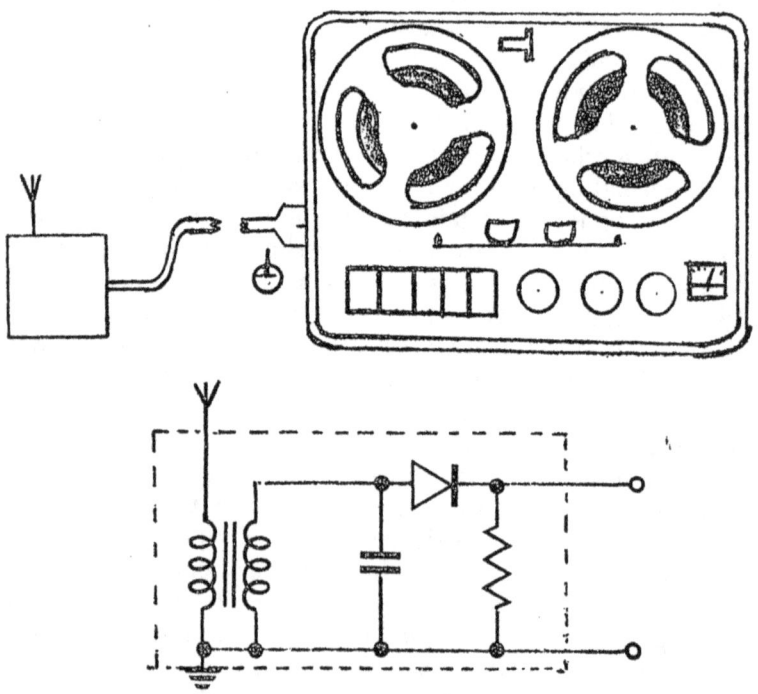

There is no doubt that Dr. Raudive must have felt very unhappy and embarrassed at this moment, and in retrospect I appreciate that the unsuitable circumstances under which he had conducted a scientific experiment formed no basis on which to make up one's mind whether to publish or not. However, with this last failure, it looked as if we might have to consider the whole project once again. During the next half hour a number of my guests talked to Dr. Raudive on technical points, and one of them indicated that the only proof he was now willing to accept would be something definite; for example, if a voice were to give the name of a person present. As it was highly unlikely that such a name would be "floating in the air" from some radio station, it would prove to him that a voice was trying to make a deliberate contact.

Meantime Mr. Stanley had disconnected the additional four inches of wire from the diode and connected the original diode to the radio input, letting the tape run. I think the tape had only been running about two minutes, (by now we had used the fourth tape because each time an experiment had been made, we opened a new tape), when Dr. Raudive asked Stanley to play the recording back. With about twenty people talking and wishing each other a Merry Christmas, it was most surprising when four of them suddenly rushed to the taperecorder. There, clear and without a shadow of doubt, a rhythmic voice, twice the speed of human voice said *"Raudive there"*—Mr. Stanley was perhaps the most surprised of them all, because according to his explanation there just could not be any voice on the tape. But there was a voice and it called the name of the one person who was most concerned with it all.

At this unexpected turn of events, I asked Dr. Raudive not to continue with any further experiments. Professor Alex Schneider, the physicist who had participated in the experiments on the continent, has said in one of his reports that all that mattered was to prove just *one* single voice, its genuineness, and the impossibility of this voice being the result of some freak reception. Everything else would simply confuse the scientist. I remembered this and felt that any further experiments would only blur the impression this particular recording had made on all present. Naturally, we had to rely once again on our experts, who assured us that this voice could not have been caused by radio interferences and also that to hear the name of a person present at that particular moment was more than surprising, it was "mathematically an inconceivable chance". Very late that night Mr. Stanley discussed with those who stayed on, the problem of understanding—or rather, the difficulty in actually hearing the voices immediately. He gave two examples of situations well known to most people:

"If you telephone a strange office and the operator at the other end mumbles something and you don't know the actual name of the firm or person, you may well be left in ignorance whether you have dialled the right number or not. If you were attuned to that particular voice and knew which company or person you were speaking to, you would have no difficulty at all in making sense of the mumble. The same applies to aircraft broadcasting to one another. It is very difficult to understand at all. Unless you are actually attuned to a certain noise, you will always find it very difficult to perceive it properly and understand the spoken word. It is quite surprising how much we rely on sight to understand speech, as well as on clarity of diction."

On Sunday 14th December 1969, Dr. Raudive signed our contract. The original German text, with his additions and alterations, has been translated and edited. Material has been added and the translations of reports we have obtained from physicists and other scientists checked with experts in this country.

No doubt, much controversy will follow. Some scientists will try to prove that Dr. Raudive might be mistaken, others will endeavour to prove that he has contributed to our understanding of great things beyond our wildest dreams. Dr. Raudive's research is only in its earliest stage of development. *But*—if he is right, and there is nothing to suggest that he is not, then we have entered a new age. I know that his pioneer work is still going on, and he is now experimenting on far more advanced methods of scientifically recording such phenomena. "If these voices can be received through radio magnetic waves" he said to me at London Airport, when I saw him off, "then I am convinced that sooner or later television will play an important part in our work."

Personally, I am satisfied as to the bona fide of results and evidence I have seen and heard. I make two qualifications. The first concerns Dr. Raudive; the second the phenomenon itself. Dr. Raudive is Latvian by birth and has lived in many countries, speaking different languages. I think this has serious drawbacks when it comes to interpreting some of the voice phenomena correctly. For example, Raudive played back a particular passage from a sample tape. According to the printed explanations, the text was: "Te Macloo, may—dream, my dear, yes". Yet to a large number of English people present, the voice said: "Mark you, make believe, my dear, yes". I challenged the interpretation and explained to Dr. Raudive that "mark you" was not only good English but also made sense in the context of the recording. I am convinced that Dr. Raudive's multi-lingual background has something to do with the fact that messages received by him are in two, three or sometimes even four languages. Latvian appears to dominate, Russian, German and occasional words from other languages with which he is acquainted make up the rest. Yet all the recordings I have heard made in his absence are straight-forward, in one language. In this book, some of the examples given, especially where English or German is used, are not as I understand them. This, I stress, does not affect the basic principle of the recorded voices at all; it is simply a question of how well the vocabulary of the language used is known to the listener.

One of the most difficult problems for the translator, and the editor, has been the sequence of words in many of the recordings. Although some of the passages may appear to leave much to be desired as far as editing goes, in fact it is those very passages which have been given the most careful consideration. I have discussed this more than once with both editor and translator, for whose work my admiration is difficult to express, and generally we decided to keep the sequence of the original language as typical of the strange rhythm employed by the voice-entities.

My second reservation concerns eminent names which are quoted in some of the manifestations. The nonsense they occasionally appear to talk is quite remarkable and out of character for the person or entity they purport to be. Again, this does not mean that the recordings are not genuine. But is it not possible that some of these names are being given by entities who wish to impress? If we accept the principles of good and evil, truth and untruth, sincerity and deceit to be universal, we may well have an explanation for some of the puzzling sayings.

All this does not really worry me; as long as we are aware of fallibility, both human and spiritual or psychic, we shall not fail to apply commonsense in judging the voice phenomena on their merit.

Since the visit of Dr. Raudive to England, the voice phenomena have been subject of discussion at scientific congresses and in the international press. Somehow, they have been labelled "Raudive voices" but this is both incorrect and misleading. Dr. Raudive has been neither the first person to receive these voices nor the only one to research into them. Among the many scientists who have worked on the subject, he is, by any standard, primus inter pares and the most successful, and he is the first person to admit that this phenomenon is not exclusive to him.

Of course, better instruments are needed, better tapes and better methods of interference-free recording. All this can and will be achieved by our technicians. There are obvious limits to the instruments available but, on the other hand, what has been done by Konstantine Raudive and other normal, down-to-earth people, is so remarkable and exciting, challenging and provocative that we should not dismiss this opportunity without good cause. Millions of people believe in a life after death and the idea as such is not new to them. Many thousands have practised or are practising methods of communication which rely on certain extraordinary gifts and the integrity of individuals; here now is a man who does not lay claim to any particular gift. Dr. Raudive is a scientist; and as far as his religious attitudes and beliefs are concerned, he is a practising Roman Catholic and therefore not inclined or willing to participate in something of which his own Church would disapprove.

His collaborators include people from many walks of life—physicists, psychologists and electronic experts, as well as doctors, teachers and representatives of the church.

They all say quite simply: "Here are voices which identify themselves, call our names, tell us things which make sense (or sometimes puzzle us); these voices do not originate acoustically, and the names they give belong to people we know to have left this earth." The voices are on a tape which can be listened to and heard by everybody. The physicists cannot explain the phenomenon, and the psychologists cannot offer an explanation either. Scientific tests have shown (in the Faraday cage, for example) that these voices originate outside the experimenter and are not subject to auto-suggestion or telepathy.

Philologists have examined the phenomenon and testified to the fact that, although audible and understandable, the voices are not formed by acoustic means, they are twice the speed of human speech and of a peculiar rhythm, which is identical in the 72,000 examples so far examined.

Matters of this kind do not only cause controversy, they create many other problems as well. For some considerable time it has been known—in Fleet Street, as well as elsewhere—that the American space programme has yielded certain unexpected results which nobody had foreseen. Dr. Raudive has been visited twice by American engineers who have asked too many peculiar questions to be explained by mere curiosity, and have themselves given too little information from which to draw any definite conclusions, and when Dr. Raudive asked whether there was a chance to listen to tape-recordings made during moonflights, he was told that those recordings would not be released for some years to come; it would therefore be wrong to speculate on the possibility that information might be forthcoming from official sources in the United States of America. Nevertheless, if Dr. Raudive has received voice phenomena with his ordinary recording apparatus, it stands to reason that more sophisticated equipment would probably receive those phenomena as well. The utter silence on this matter is interesting. Many eminent scientists have participated with Dr. Raudive (among them those whose reports appear as Appendices to this book) and to ignore their work and achievement would be foolish. However, it would be equally wrong to expect that tomorrow we can "dial M for mother" and establish long conversations with those who have departed. First, we have not got sufficiently advanced equipment to do so. Secondly, this kind of impatient expectation would not help the scientific research being carried out at the moment.

Many people will be concerned about the reaction of the Church to Dr. Raudive's work, and we have included in Appendix I reports which give some indication of a support which is truly remarkable, and of great importance to the author.

Many scientists have put forward suggestions and ideas; Dr. Fatzer, a participant in Dr. Raudive's experimental recordings, has expressed a wish to see experiments conducted by different people in different localities in order to form a basis for comparison and clarification of both the nature and meaning of phenomenon. In the United Kingdom, members of the Society for Psychical Research and the Scientific Committee of the Churches Fellowship have shown great interest in the project. Trinity College Cambridge has awarded the Perrott Warwick Studentship to Mr. David Ellis: his research subject is the investigation of 'Raudive Voices'. Mr. Ellis and I have spent many hours conducting experimental recordings. The voice phenomena we have recorded are of modest quality: we gave them a B— to C— grading, but all of them had a relevant content. These recordings were independently verified by two more listeners, Mr. Colin Smythe and Mr. Leslie Hayward. We have so far established two important facts: first, all our recordings are in one language and not of a polyglot construction; secondly, they are always relevant.

To simplify recording playbacks I developed a loop-tape with a running time of nine seconds at $3\frac{3}{4}$ i.p.s. ($9\frac{1}{2}$ cm.p.s.). I found we received one message per recording.

It seems ages ago since I heard "Mach die Tür mal auf" in November 1969. As publishers we have opened a door to you; we don't know what you will find. Perhaps much, perhaps nothing; this book may give you comfort, or it may disturb you. If you dislike the thought of such voices really being those of people whom you know to have left this earth, don't worry about it. After all, if you dislike a picture you need not look at it. You would have to use a tape-recorder to hear voices and even then the chances of establishing a reasonably successful dialogue are unpredictable. You need patience and time to acclimatise the ear to those strange rhythmic sounds, and you might find yourself at a loss if some of the words are in a language you cannot understand.

On the other hand, you may be excited at the thought of witnessing a break-through in another dimension; this is neither spooky nor frightening; it is simply strange and unlike anything you have ever done before.

PETER BANDER

Contents

Foreword by Anabela Cardoso   vii
Preface by Peter Bander   ix

CHAPTER I
THE PHENOMENON

INTRODUCTION	1
FIRST CONTACTS	13
FIRST STEPS TOWARDS EXPERIMENTS	16
METHODS OF RECORDING	20
(1) *Microphone*	20
(2) *Radio*	22
(3) *Radio-microphone*	25
(4) *Frequency-transmitter*	26
(5) *Diode*	27
THE LANGUAGE OF THE VOICES AND HOW THEY SPEAK	27
PLAY-BACK OF RECORDINGS	32

CHAPTER II
SPEECH-CONTENT OF RECORDINGS

I INDIVIDUAL MANIFESTATIONS	34
Mother	35
Aunt	39
Sister Tekle	40
Brother Alexis	41
Sonja/Liepina	43
Aileen Finlayson	44

Margarete Petrautski ... 46
Further Close Friends ... 57
Latvians, Latvia and Latgale ... 67
Writers and Artists ... 70
   (a) *Latvian writers and poets* ... 70
   (b) *Writers of other nations* ... 77
Psychologists and Parapsychologists ... 83
Statesmen ... 86
A Multitude of Voices ... 91

II STRENGTHENING CONTACTS ... 94
Experiments in Partnership ... 94
The Presence of the Voice-Entities—
   "We are here—we see—we hear." ... 111
Their Independence and Power of Judgement ... 114
Their Encouragement, Help and Advice ... 119
Their Warnings ... 127
Their Gratitude ... 129

III TWO WORLDS ... 131
Religious and Ethical Factors ... 131
Relationship of the Entities to Earth ... 136
Here and Hereafter—The Anti-World—The Bridge,
   Crossing and Customs-Points ... 140
Existence after Death ... 145
Conditions in the World of the Voice-Entities ... 152
Transport, Travel and Place-Names ... 159

IV PRACTICAL PROBLEMS OF COMMUNICATION ... 165
Spidola ... 165
Technical Questions: ... 169
   Radio—Radar—Transmitting Stations ... 169

CHAPTER III

RECORDINGS WITH COLLABORATORS

Mr. Bernard Weiss, Physicist ... 180
Mr. Karlis Lidums, Building Contractor ... 185
Parapsychological Society of Switzerland ... 187
Mrs. Irma Millere, Educationalist ... 196
Miss A. Morgenthaler, Teacher (a) ... 198

Miss A. Morgenthaler, Teacher (*b*)	201
Dr. Arnold Reincke	202
Mr. F. Scherer, Electro technical Expert, and Mr. G. Inhoffen, Photographer	204
Dr. Hans Naegeli, Psychiatrist, and Mrs. K. Nager, Psychologist	207
Mr. Gerd Kramer, Assistant Headmaster, Mrs. H. Kramer and Mr. G. Inhoffen	210
Dr. R. Zimmerman	214
Dr. Arnold Reincke (*a*)	216
Dr. Arnold Reincke (*b*)	217
Miss A. Morgenthaler	220
Zenta Maurina, Ph.D., Writer	222
Mr. Friedrich Jürgenson	227
Mr. Valerij Tarsis, Writer	230
Mr. K. Baüers, Singer	234
Mr. F. Scherer	237
Professor Atis Teichmanis	244
Professor Dr. Hans Bender, Psychologist, and Dr. F. Karger, Physicist	248
The Swiss Parapsychological Society	251
Mr. H. von Guilleaume, Publisher	258
Mrs. Cornelia Brunner, Psychologist, and Mrs. N. von Muralt, Parasychologist	260
Valeriji Tarsis, Writer and Dr. Hildegard Dietrich	263
Professor Dr. Werner Brunner, Mrs. Ida Bianchi and Mr. Peter Rutishauser	266
Miss Helen Schnidheiny, Graphologist, and Miss Katrin Bolli	271

CHAPTER IV

RESULTS OF PARTNERSHIP EXPERIMENTS

The Mother of the Experimenter	276
Tekle	277
C. G. Jung	278
Margarete Petrautzki	279
Professor Gebhard Frei	282
Edvards Virza	284
Karlis Skalbe	285

Vilis Lācis	285
Collaborators:	
Miss A. Morgenthaler	286
Miss Ilse Diersche	288
Dr. Wilhelmina Hennequin	289
Mr. Felix Scherer	291
Mr. Valerij Tarsis	294
Dr. Zenta Maurina	298
Mr. and Mrs. Inhoffen	300
CONCLUSION	302

APPENDICES

I. THE EXPERTS' REPORT	307
A. *Theologians and Philosophers*	307
The Rev. Prof. Dr. Gebhard Frei	307
The Rt. Rev. Mgr. Prof. Dr. Charles Pfleger	308
Dr. Zenta Maurina	312
The Rev. Voldemars A. Rolle	316
The Rev. Fr. Leo Schmid	319
B. *Psychologists and Parapsychologists*	321
Dr. Theo Locher	321
Dr. Hans Naegeli	324
Mrs. Katharina Nager	328
Friedrich Jürgenson	328
Mrs. Cornelia Brunner	330
Mrs. N. von Muralt	333
Professor Walter H. Uphoff	335
C. *Physicists and Electronic Engineers*	336
Professor Alex Schnieder	336
Theodor Rudolph	355
Franz Seidl	361
J. M. Meier	365
Ralph Lovelock	366
II. THE COLLABORATORS' COMMENT	367
Karlis Lidums	368
Dr. Arnold Reincke	368
Dr. R. Fatzer	369
Dr. Rudolf Zimmermann	370

CONTENTS

Mrs. I. Millere	371
Miss A. Morgenthaler	373
Valerij and Hanni Tarsis	374
Professor Atis Teichmanis	376
Kārlis Bauers	377
Herwart v. Guilleaume	378
Dr. Wilhelmine Hennequin	379
III. THE LISTENERS VERIFY	381
IV. EXTRACT FROM ARTICLE BY HOLGER ESS	388

Chapter I

The Phenomenon

1. INTRODUCTION

The experiments described in this book are, in some respects, a hazardous venture; but then, we always have to accept hazards whenever we venture onto paths as yet undiscovered and untrodden, and the adventurous spirit of the explorer is coupled with deep humility before new truths and realisations.

Our human existence is orientated one-sidedly along limited, measurable and calculable lines. The evidence of voices of mysterious origin set out in this book, challenges us to alter our thinking habits and to let them range freely on unfettered cosmic energies, and on spirit-beings, such as we ourselves one day may become.

It certainly sounds fantastic to assert that we have made contact with spirit-beings, i.e. the dead, through tape-recordings. Today, however, when more or less adequate technical devices are at our disposal, it is possible to test the facts by experiment and to lift them out of the realm of the fantastic. Tape-recorder, radio and microphone give us facts in an entirely impersonal way and their objectivity cannot be challenged.

The present stage of the investigation reveals this contact as, so far, only the delicate, fleeting pulse of a new reality, no more than vaguely discernible as yet, because of our lack of experience and the inadequacy of our technical aids. Nevertheless, the voices here described can open up new spiritual vistas, irrespective of how we explain, interpret and understand them.

Man has an inherent, stubborn characteristic: the wish to fathom his own destiny—within himself and concerning himself. We die whilst we live, for our concepts of life and death conceal the future that awaits us.

From the fragments we hear in the voice-experiments I have made we can perhaps form some ideas about this problem. My research has led me to the personal conclusion that apart from the biological-psychical level on which we human beings here exist, there is a second level: that of the psychical-spiritual being, whose potentialities are only released after death. This psychical-spiritual being tries to build a bridge between its world and that of our earthly form of life, and it endeavours on its own initiative to make contact in order to guide those on earth into a new reality.

Only someone who himself ventures to plumb these inaccessible layers of human existence, where we discern neither beginning nor end, only a forward compulsion of ourselves and our lives, can assess the true position. It is quite possible that one day results will emerge from the voice-experiments that will have a bearing on the highest, indeed the ultimate goal man has sought throughout the ages and is still seeking—the answer to the question: who am I and where am I going? Death might then be seen as no more than a metamorphosis from one state of development to another.

This thought, as well as the attempt to contact those in the so-called next world, is nothing new. From time immemorial man's mind has been preoccupied with the idea of a hereafter and has tried to gain visual or acoustic impressions of it. We only have to remember the ancient Indian and Greek, and the early Christian religious experiences. Similar attempted realisations have also been experienced through Spiritualism, Occultism and Anthroposophy.

The present investigation takes a different course: it is based on acoustics and leads to empirically provable reality with a factual background that can open new perspectives for the study of psychology. We are trying to gain some insight into this as yet unknown reality, and such insight not only changes our ideas and gives new direction to the activities of our psyche, but points to undreamed-of powers reigning within us and over us.

Those oriented towards natural science believe that such problems can be solved by empirical means. This book is the record of an attempt to do so.

I believe the solution to the problem lies in two directions:

(i) New insight into the domination of the unconscious (or subconscious).

(ii) New aspects of the theory of relativity,[1] which gains considerable impetus through the voice-phenomenon.

(i) *The hypothesis of the unconscious*

The existence of the voices is established through the sense of hearing; methodic repetition then makes deciphering and checking possible. The voice-phenomenon is autonomous, as far as the listener is concerned, for it manifests on tape-recordings through radio or microphone. Anybody can study it and, by fulfilling certain preconditions, take up contact with it.

During experiments with the voices no spontaneous instances were observed. The phenomenon always manifests steadily and adheres strictly to its characteristics. Consequently the voices can be distinguished from noises emanating from different sources in the atmosphere. These constantly repeated, unmistakable features are a safeguard against psycho-acoustic deception and freakish radio sounds, habitually used by *a priori* sceptics as an explanation of their own negative attitude. As the voice-phenomenon is of an empirical nature the suspicion of trickery, fraud, or self-deception, constantly levelled against parapsychological manifestations, falls away automatically, for the voice-phenomenon can be examined with scientific accuracy.

It is a well-known fact that man has the innate ability to act upon matter without physical action. This psychic faculty is known as telekinesis. Rhine and his successors are of the opinion that subconscious psychic forces stand as basic factors behind parapsychological phenomena. This view gave rise to the belief that our subconscious mind is just as autonomous as our conscious one, that these two layers of our mind can act independently of one another and that the various problems of parapsychology are subordinate to the function of the "unconscious". Accordingly, we should equally look for the key to the voice-phenomenon in the realm of the unconscious. This belief ranks amongst the most ingenious rationalistic hypotheses and belongs almost to a tendency to explain man through man himself.

[1] See note on page 9.

Professor Hans Bender, who has advocated this hypothesis for thirty years, wrote in his paper "*Zum Problem der Aussersinnlichen Wahrnehmung*" (*The Problem of Extra-Sensory Perception, 1936*; pages *34* to *35*): "The tendency towards a personality-synthesis of dissociated psychic content can often be observed in automatic writing or spelling of quite normal persons. Usually the impulse to create such personifications comes from environmental suggestions, from a casual stimulus picked up as crystallisation-nucleus for the most fantastic images. In Spiritualistic séances such images of personalities often present themselves as incarnations of the dead and try to give evidence of their identity. In rare cases they produce an astonishing abundance of verifiable data which the medium could not have obtained by normal sensory means."

Thirty years later Professor Bender tries to interpret Spiritualistic phenomena as aspects of pathology in his "*Mediumistische Psychosen*" (*Mediumistic Psychoses; Parapsychology, 1966, Pages 574 to 604*). He describes Spiritualistic practices as "psycho-mechanic automatism" and explains them by means of what he calls "overflow pipes of the unconscious": the belief that Spiritualists are in touch with the "world beyond" is erroneous, he asserts, for the Spiritualistic supposition that other-worldly intelligences, "spirits", appear before us stems from the personification-tendency of the unconscious and these phenomena are encouraged by paranormally gifted automatists; alleged contact with the dead therefore has to be classified as a pathological phenomenon. "Many find solace and hope in the conviction that contact with the dead is possible, and they can defend their conviction by pointing to documents of some literary value containing such 'messages from the beyond' " (page 576). In a nutshell: Professor Bender's own observations, as well as existing literature on psychiatry, have prompted him to regard Spiritualistic practices as "mediumistic psychoses".

Professor Bender's term for functions provoked by such subconscious reactions is "psychic automatism", and he distinguishes between a mechanical and a sensory form. The mechanical function manifests through subconscious processes of movement such as automatic writing, table-tilting, knocking, tc.; the sensory form through visions, voices, or haptic illusory experiences. His classic example is the shell, which acts as stimulus for acoustic pseudo-hallucinations. He regards acoustic hallucinations as rare occurrences in Spiritualistic practices. Acoustic voices, heard by Spiritualists or mystics alike, he describes as illusory acoustic perception. He explains it all as a "clever deception of the unconscious, which uses the normally incorruptible senses the moment the critical ratio of the patient is no longer convinced by former procedures—a sign of the strange split in the personalities of such Spiritualistic adepts" (page 584).

Professor Bender thus dismisses the Spiritualist's hypothesis as pathological and so precludes any possibility of discussion. Spiritualists are, in his opinion, pathological cases in need of psychiatric treatment. He illustrates this belief with examples of his own observations from which he concludes: "Once more the affective shock becomes evident, induced by the misunderstood experience of the beyond and the functional dependence of the voices on the progressive development of complexes made autonomous through night-long experimenting with the pendulum" (page 599).

Clearly his view is that the Spiritualist hypothesis is a kind of psychic sickness which he tries to explain by what he calls "psychic automatism", and he regrets that most psychologists dismiss the idea. His treatise ends with the following statement: "The superstitious attitudes built on misunderstood communication with 'spirit-beings' are widespread and carry, as case-histories show, the seeds of mental illness."

One may deduce from Professor Bender's paper and the literature he quotes that in him we are faced with an exponent of the psychiatric school who interprets all paranormal phenomena as pathological symptoms and thereby questions their objective existence.[1]

But the paranormal phenomena connected with materialisation mediums, clairvoyants and so-called miracle cures cannot be explained by psychic automatism. The difficulties involved in getting to the bottom of a paranormal phenomenon cannot be taken as evidence against its existence or its

---

[1] Since this introduction was written, Professor Bender has become interested in the author's research, and has participated in experiments. See pages 248–251.

importance. It may seem well-nigh impossible to interpret such phenomena by hypothetical assumption, but parapsychology exists expressly to concern itself with the supernormal and in most cases this does not permit a rational supposition. It is quite unimportant whether something is supposed to happen or not; the fact that something that cannot be explained by rational means is definitely happening is sufficient reason for parapsychological research and examination. The materialistic attitude of science fails in this respect, because it tries to argue away anything that is not supposed to exist and does not fit in with the traditionally accepted view of life. It is the problem of life after death that really contains the essence of our existence, and since time out of mind man has probed this central question.

One of the mysteries of the human soul on which the voice-phenomenon can shed new light is the question of the unconscious which, since Sigmund Freud's teachings, has become almost an obsession of the human intellect. The unconscious can be explained as scientific fiction, a construction of the conscious mind, but in order to demonstrate this, I shall have to go more deeply into the matter.

Parapsychological research presupposes the existence of the soul. "The soul is the greatest of all cosmic miracles," said C. G. Jung. The question is: can one explain this miracle through one's own self? Does it perish with death or can this soul hope to exist beyond the grave? We know that materialistic thought denies life after death and disposes of any transcendental expression of our soul by declaring it to be a pathological creation of our unconscious. The theory of the unconscious originated amongst such romantics of psychology as Carl Gustav Carus, 1789–1869, and the philosopher Eduard von Hartmann, 1842–1906, who became known as the "philopher of the subconscious".

Well, many things start in the heads of philosophers and poets! Sigmund Freud took up the idea, developed the theory of the unconscious and turned it into a kind of scientific dogma. C. G. Jung and, particularly, Gustav Richard Heyer were very much aware of this. "The unconscious has become a *hotchpotch* of all the psychic happenings that cannot be understood by simply applying the principles of ordinary, everyday psychology of the conscious mind, says Heyer in his lecture *Tiefenpsychologie als Grenzwissenschaft* (*Psychology of the Subconscious—A Borderline Science*), addressing the audience at the second Lindau Psychotherapy Week, 1951. The concept "the unconscious" (or subconscious) has only a relative meaning in connection with scientific truth and therefore cannot claim to be "definite".

This concept of the unconscious can, in my opinion, be likened to that of the "ether" in physics. Compared with other sciences psychology, and parapsychology in particular, *is* of quite recent date; but physical science too has only developed gradually and was nourished for a long time by fictitious beliefs. Right into the twentieth century scientists believed in the existence of "ether", and even such a progressive and forward-looking physical scientist as Sir Oliver Lodge was convinced of its reality. Not until the beginning of the twentieth century did the physicist Max Planck dispose of this fictitious substance. He spoke of light quantums and photons and finally came to the conclusion that space was conditioned by electro-magnetic radiation.

Prior to Planck, "ether" was made to explain something that could not be understood. Earlier physicists had tried to portray the whole of nature in mechanistic terms. Planck's conception of the world, however, was not a mechanistic one; on the contrary, it seemed impossible to connect it with any kind of mechanistic view of life. Mainly for this reason Planck was at first rejected and ridiculed, but his teaching triumphed and developed into one of the great principles of modern physics—the quantum theory. This was the end of the mechanistic era in physics and an entirely new phase began.

One can take the "unconscious" of parapsychology as a parallel and rate it as mechanistic-automatic fiction which calls for revision. We cannot explain man through man himself.

The psychologists of the nineteenth century were apt to assume that their knowledge penetrated the whole of creation, and their dogmas on the nature of man were built up on that basis. Even today the unconscious is thought to be *"something like a colossal labyrinth"*. Nobody, however, asks how this unconscious is sustained. The hypothesis of the unconscious can be regarded as a *psychological illusion* for the following reasons:

The apparently acceptable supposition of an "unconscious" fails immediately we are faced with a new reality, namely *post-mortal life*. We come back, straightway, to the cardinal question whether the unconscious, on whose efficiency our inner life is supposed to depend, really exists or whether it is no more than a figment of our imagination. We must always remember that the reality of the unconscious is only a hypothesis, introduced into science by the psychologists. These psychologists, who imagined that everything could be explained in mechanistic terms, concluded that all the activities of our psyche could also be interpreted by some mechanical means; but this intangible "something" is a supposition, a fabrication, *an intensely private thing within the conscious inner realm.*

To interpret the voices as products of the unconscious however is out of the question, as the phenomenon is of an *objective, physical-acoustic nature.*

Psychology uses the term "the unconscious", but admits that it knows nothing about it. C. G. Jung gives a hint in this context: ". . . psychology can know nothing about the substance of the psyche, because it cannot realise anything except through the psyche. One can therefore neither deny nor confirm the validity of such terms as Mana, Daemon, or God; but one can note that the feeling of unfamiliarity, which is connected with the experience of the objective, is authentic."

What we wish to express in the term the "unconscious", we can equally express as "Mana", "God" or "Daemon". C. G. Jung finds these expressions much more qualifying than "the unconscious". In his memoirs (page 339 of the German original) he says: ". . . for the unconscious is banal and therefore nearer to reality".

The reason why the theory of the unconscious is questionable, is that it seeks to explain man through man himself; consequently paranormal phenomena would be automatically reduced to something emanating from man himself. This opinion negates the independence of paranormal phenomena and dissolves in the end into conscious and subconscious subjectivism. We know nothing of that which moves and guides us, nothing of the sources of our paranormal faculties.

The essence of the voices can be gleaned from their acoustically perceptible appearance and from insight into the meaning of their utterances, rather than through psychological knowledge or psycho-philosophical theories. The voices make their objectively valid statements independently of our attempts at interpretation; they are an acoustic fact and need no special theories to confirm them.

(ii) The theory of relativity[1]

The hypothesis of the unconscious can be confronted by that of an "anti-world", which is based on the theory of relativity. There is no "thing as such", there is no "man as such" either. The phenomenon "man" exists, with his conscious and unconscious faculties, as a unit; but he is dependent on a host of relationships that mark him as "man". He can only then regard himself existent as "man" when both the world and its counterpart—the higher world—are in existence and he, as "man", has a relationship to both these worlds.

Starting from the same premise we see, for instance, that the unconscious can only prove its existence in relationship to a higher consciousness. A world establishes its reality by its relationship to an anti-world; and the anti-world is a condition for the relative existence of the world and of all that is portrayed as reality in man.[2]

This assumption fits in with the hypothesis of "spirits": a spirit-world must exist in order to proclaim the earthly, human world. This hypothesis can be shored up, or demolished by experiments. It is by no means based on mere dogmas of faith, but on the theory of relativity. The key-note of our world is interaction and man stands at its centre, he is not an exception to the rule, but the result of a great universal "teamwork". This is the reason why it is so difficult to understand man's earthly existence and his higher existence in isolation from each other, or to bring both under the same denominator. Nothing can be explained from the purely human point of view alone.

The voice-phenomenon calls for consideration of both these hypotheses, that of the unconscious and that of relativity.

[1] Or relativeness—not to be confused with Einstein's theory of relativity.
[2] See also page 141 and Appendix IV (page 388).

The unconscious presents parapsychology with a dire dilemma: the problem concerns the belief in a "dark side" of our psyche on the one hand, and the principle of consciousness on the other. Can a way of reconciling the two be found? Is there something constant within us—without consciousness?

Philosophical thought and physical science have led us to the realisation that no object can be more than the sum total of its attributes, and these attributes exist only in our consciousness. Accordingly, our world is a construction of the conscious, composed of symbols shaped by the human senses. The philosopher Berkeley, who believed in "categories of the spirit", held that components forming the structure of the world itself have no substance without the conscious, and reasoned that existence itself would be impossible, unless it existed in the consciousness of an eternal spirit.

This realisation calls for the existence of a higher consciousness, which alone can give us an understanding of human consciousness. We comprehend that man stands in relation to a higher existence, and that this justifies his own "being".

Asserting that man can be explained through man himself must logically lead one to the conclusion that he needs no other reality outside himself. If, however, man assumes that he himself is the explanation of all extra-sensory phenomena, then his existence loses all meaning; such an "explanation" is but a subjective feeling used to express the supernormal part of our psyche. In other words, instead of providing an explanation, man, in his subjectivism, simply rotates around himself.

It is interesting to note in this context that the most eminent physicists of our times, Einstein and Planck, followed this train of thought consistently when they pointed out that even time and space are just frames into which we fit our observations and are as inseparable from consciousness as are our conceptions of colour, shape, or size. In the opinion of these two physical scientists space simply serves to bring order into the range of objects we perceive, and time has no independent existence outside the order of events by which we measure it. This basic realisation explodes our so-called reality and shows us how circumscribed our senses really are. The human eye is sensitive only to the limited range of colours between red and violet, and the difference of a few ten-thousandths of a millimetre in wave-length signifies the difference between the visible and the invisible.

The same applies to our ear, which can hear only a small fraction of the field of frequency. Our sense of hearing cannot discern electro-magnetic waves, they must first be converted into sound-waves by electronic apparatus. The sound-picture of the world received by the human ear is incomplete and attenuated. How much more would our world mean to us if our sense of hearing were a hundred or even ten times sharper, if our eyes were receptive to X-rays, or the gamma-rays of radium!

Realising that in fact all our knowledge of the universe rests on fragmentary impressions of our senses, we must assume that we shall never fully appreciate the true reality of the cosmic structure.

The voice-phenomenon, however, opens up new paths for parapsychologists to explore and points to an underlying objective reality, which hitherto lived only as an assumption or a belief in our imagination. *This reality is the continued existence of our soul after death.*

To solve the puzzle of the human soul without taking life after death into consideration, seems to become increasingly difficult. The voice-phenomenon unmistakably indicates a higher reality of the soul, an "overself", that by some mysterious means can send us messages. Thanks to electronic apparatus it is possible to verify this existence after death objectively; through this objective knowledge we can heighten our perception of the universe and can be helped to understand many psychic phenomena which hitherto were shrouded in mystery.

If the physical scientists with their equations have been able to penetrate deeper into the invisible and inaudible secrets of the universe, than have the psychologists and parapsychologists into the secrets of the soul, it is because the psychologists have been philosophising about themselves without any means of explanation of the psyche other than through the psyche. For this reason the psychology of the past could produce no objective interpretation of psychic phenomena and simply drowned in supposition.

The voice-phenomenon shows acoustically perceptible, objective manifestations that lead us, by inference, to what may be at least a true hypothetical reality. One must, of course, take into consideration that extra-sensory phenomena can hardly be probed by the research methods of physical science. Further difficulties arise in research into the voice-phenomenon, because we have no idea of the substance in which our soul exists after death.

The American parapsychologist Rhine indicates in his book, *The Reach of the Mind*, that man possesses, in addition to his normal consciousness, an "inner window" that is breached time and again by experiences of extra-sensory perception. Rhine compares the impact of this parapsychological fact with that of nuclear physics, while Professor Bender has now expressed the opinion in a talk, recorded on tape, that the voice-phenomenon is equal to nuclear physics in importance.

The working hypothesis of the unconscious and of relativism could complement each other in a significant way if researchers acknowledged the fact that all we commonly call "real" represents only a fraction of true reality. The voice-phenomenon establishes a relation to an extra-real or anti-real world of manifestations.

C. G. Jung followed the same trend of thought in his theories: "Our psyche is of a cosmic design and what happens on a large scale also takes place in the smallest and most subjective way in our soul. That is why the God-image is always a projection of the inner experience of a mighty *vis-à-vis*."

The physicist Werner Heisenberg equally rejects the dividing of the world into subject and object, inner and outer world, body and soul, in his conception of the nature of modern physics. "In natural science," he states, "the object of research is no longer nature itself, but nature subjected to man's questioning." *Das Naturbild*, page 18; (*The Image of Nature*). The theme is no more just an "image of nature" as such, but an "image of *our relationship to nature*" (page 21). Descartes' division of the world into "res-cogitans" and "res-extensa" is therefore no longer valid for modern natural science. Man is an interaction of sensory and extra-sensory worlds, and the animistic view of life will have to be abandoned, for its image of man relates to sensory man only.

As an object can be explained only in relation to something

else; so man stands in relation to a higher, spiritual, sovereign being that does not perish with death.

Meticulous analysis of the voice-phenomenon confirms the fact that it *cannot be interpreted in animistic terms*. It manifests in collaboration with our psyche (anima), but confronts us as an independent acoustic manifestation, exhibiting its specific, individual existence. The tangible results of this new discovery encourage the assumption that the voices can be defined as extra-sensory entities. Appearing as independent manifestations, they can be determined by a host of basic features. We can experience the occurrence as an acoustic phenomenon and draw rich material for research from its content.

In searching for clarity concerning the ultimate questions of our existence we search for the most precious gift of all—the certainty of our soul's survival. This is perhaps the main problem parapsychology, in its attempt to define life after death empirically, has to solve. In the same measure that we attain clarity on the ultimate questions concerning our soul, shall we also find meaning and aim for our earthly existence.

It is my opinion that the voice-phenomenon produces facts by means of which we can break through the habitual confines of our existence and make contact with the "opposite world" that can be regarded as the *centre of our life after death*. We step into a new dimension and that means freedom from the fetters of time, space and physical preconceptions. We enter into transcendental reality.

One thing is clear—the path that leads to this truth will be long and arduous, for many preconceived ideas and thinking-habits will have to be brushed aside. Those who do not shy away from all these difficulties however will feel enriched, and empowered to guide their lives towards a higher destiny.

2. FIRST CONTACTS

Towards the end of 1964 a book appeared in Stockholm under the title *Rösterna från Rymden* (*Voices from Space*). The author's name was Friedrich Jürgenson.

All my life I have been preoccupied with parapsychological problems, especially with those concerning death and life after death. These problems play a part in all my books and particularly in *Der Chaosmensch und seine Überwindung (Chaosman and his Conquest)*. Whilst studying in England I had come into close contact with men like G. N. M. Tyrrell and William Oliver Stevens, who were then working intensively on various parapsychological problems. After the war I lived in Sweden and I am closely connected with those interested in parapsychological research in that country. Jürgenson's name struck me as that of an outsider.

Reading Jürgenson's book carefully several times gave me a very definite impression of the author as a highly sensitive and susceptible man. Many of his ideas seemed to me to have been formed by a vivid imagination; the kind that could conjure up pictures in an empty room or voices out of the stillness. Later in his book, however, he came to develop a fascinating theme: he maintained that with the help of tape-recorder, microphone and radio he was able to hear voices on tape which he called "voices from space"; that these voices did not belong to any other "physical" world, but to a world in contrast to ours, a spiritual world; *that the voices were those of the dead*. Jürgenson gives a detailed account of this in a book called *Sprechfunk mit Verstorbenen (Radio-Link with the Dead)*, 1967. He heard not only the voices of near relatives or friends, but also those of historical personages of the recent past, such as Hitler, Göring, Felix Kersten, the Yoga-author Boris Sacharow, the controversial Chessman etc. Jürgenson mentions a great number of such voices—all recorded on tape in the course of several years.

Almost every page of the book confronted me with unanswered questions; no practical hints were given and so I contacted the author in April 1965 and asked him to demonstrate some of his tapes to a small private audience.

I felt an immediate sympathy towards Friedrich Jürgenson: all that he told me had a ring of sincerity and deep emotional involvement.

Apart from myself, three people were present at the demonstration: Dr. Zenta Maurina, G.Sch. (a teacher) and Mrs. M. Jürgenson. Jürgenson went straight to the point and let us listen to a selection of his recordings. Against a background of ordinary tape-noises voices were audible; we could hear them, but our unpractised ears had great difficulty in identifying them. They had to be repeated several times before our sense of hearing could gear itself to the unusually quick rhythm.

At the first recording Jürgenson made in our presence, through microphone, voices appeared that could not possibly have come from any of the people in the room. Dr. Maurina, for instance, remarked that she was under the impression that the inhabitants of the beyond were living a happy, carefree life. A voice answered: "*Nonsense!*" This word was distinctly audible and easily identified by all of us when we listened to the tape being played back, and there were other voices that could not be determined quite so unequivocally.

The phenomenon began to grip my attention and awakened all my explorer's instincts. After looking into several hypotheses and theories, I studied the phenomenon as a function of the unconscious; then again I tried to explain voices obtained through radio as coincidental sound-freaks from transmitting stations.

My searching and reflecting involved me more and more in Jürgenson's discovery and in June 1965 I decided to do some research with Jürgenson on his estate, Nysund, in order to gain some personal experience.

Renewed contact with Jürgenson and deeper insight into his personality and his life's history confirmed my view that this man was utterly sincere; that he was completely immersed in the mystery of this phenomenon and firmly convinced that he was dealing with a world beyond—a world into which we merge after death and where we continue our activities in a transcendental existence. Faith and intuition can never harm a cause; for my part, I endeavoured to understand the phenomenon in its factual sense.

In the beginning our recordings produced unclear, hardly discernible voices; not before 10th June at 9.30 p.m., did we achieve good results. This successful recording was made through radio. I have played it over to many people since, and all have heard and understood the voices it contains. First a voice calls: "Friedrich, Friedrich!"—then a woman's voice says softly "Heute pa nakti" (German and Latvian: "Tonight") followed by a woman's voice asking "Kennt ihr Margaret, Konstantin?" (German: "Do you know Margaret, Konstantin?"); the voice continues in a singing tone: "Vi tālu! Runā!"

(Latvian: "We are far away! Speak!"). The fragment closes with a female voice: "Va a dormir! Margarete!" (French: "Go to sleep! Margarete!").

These words made a deep impression on me, as Margarete Petrautzki had died recently, and her illness and death had greatly affected me. This coincidence gave me much food for thought and I resolved to investigate the phenomenon by myself; to isolate it, if possible, from Jürgenson's personality as medium and to make it "independent". Was the phenomenon really universal and free from all subjective influence? In that case it should be able to manifest itself on tape quite independently, regardless of persons, time, or space. Should this prove to be so, one would have to reckon with an objective existence of the phenomenon. If I were able to succeed in becoming aware of the phenomenon through my own individual research, I would try to understand its working and penetrate its meaning.

So I started my own experiments in June 1965. In the course of five years I have made so many observations and gained so much experience that my main task now lies in sifting the enormous amount of voice-material collected on my tapes; in crystallising the essential criteria common to all possible forms of manifestations heard, and in discarding all details not essential to a thorough comprehension of the phenomenon.

3. FIRST STEPS TOWARDS EXPERIMENTS

"Realisation of the character of something seen or heard is the adding of a specific impression to an overall meaning one already knows", says A. F. Marfeld in his book on electrotechnics and electronics.

It is very difficult to trace the voice-phenomenon back to an already known denominator. First of all one has to grasp the nature of the manifestation, determine the pitch of the voices and understand the language they use; as the phenomenon is of a physical nature, all these problems are still this side of the "cloud of unknowing". How the voices create electro-magnetic fields on the tape remains for the moment an unsolved riddle;

but experimental work is bringing us nearer to the root of the problem.

To begin with I wanted to find out whether the phenomenon happened independently of outer influences. I started with recordings through microphone. Despite my most strenuous efforts I heard nothing but the words I had spoken myself and the rushing sound of the tape whenever I played a recording back. After three months of practice, at last I heard a male voice. In answer to my observation that the inhabitants of the beyond, just like earthly humans, probably have to contend with certain limitations, the voice said in Latvian: "Pareizi tā būs" ("That is right"). The voice keeps a definite, steady rhythm:

"Pa- rei- zi- tā būs"

I must stress here that although this was the first voice I heard, it was by no means the first to have imprinted itself on tape during my experiments. Later on, after repeated and careful listening-in, I could detect many voices I had not noticed in the beginning.

(a) How the voices are heard

Psycho-acoustic experts assume that the human ear can distinguish approximately 400,000 different sounds and therefore it always recognises the difference between two sounds presented one after the other; but this is only a theoretical assumption. Research shows that most people are unable to distinguish more than seven levels of sound-volume and seven levels of pitch. During various listening-in tests we made the interesting discovery that, to start with, the human ear either does not pick up the voices at all or distinguishes them only very slowly and vaguely. The ear must attune itself for quite a period before it can start to hear the phonemes. (A phoneme is the smallest unit of speech-sound that can be distinguished from another.)

All of us, with the exception of those who have a specially trained sense of hearing, hear only very superficially; but the sense of hearing is of the highest importance when it comes to discerning the voices. Musically trained people were able to follow the voices with much less trouble than others during tests. Professor Atis Teichmanis, of the College of Music in Freiburg (Breisgau, Germany), noticed immediately when listening-in that the voices differ in pitch and sound-volume from ordinary human voices. Despite his particularly acute sense of hearing, however, he could differentiate and understand the voices only with difficulty at first—because of the unaccustomed rhythm, pitch, intensity and strange mode of expression used, which make these voices sound so different from earthly human ones. After a time of diligent practice, when the ear has become attuned, we can find in these very deviations from the accustomed the clues to help us determine the structure of the voices. Voices may vary in sound-volume from whispering to fortissimo; their timbre is usually well defined.

Over four hundred people have taken part in listening-in tests, which have shown that each participant could become aware of the voices through the sense of hearing and could understand the speech content. At first, most people had difficulties, depended often only on feeling and guessing, and heard only vague noises; after a period of practice, however, the noises emerged as definite sound-shapes and meaningful sentences. Audibility of the voices, therefore, depends on practice, ability of the ear to distinguish, and the extent of undivided attention given whilst listening. The ear is the best voice-analyser (apart from electrical measuring-techniques which allow us to measure the minutest time-differences); it is a masterpiece of nature, "for in the nerve-fibres various electronic processes are connected in series, each of which lasts roughly 100 micro-seconds. With such slow-working elements as building-material, the electronics-engineer could achieve such accuracy only with the greatest difficulty." A. F. Marfeld, *Elektrotechnik und Elektronik (Electrotechnics and Electronics)—Safari-Verlag, Berlin, 1965.* p.725.

It is necessary to stress that the verification of the voices depends on repetition, and the ear cannot hear the voices without technical aids. Tape-recorder and microphone are as essential for the investigator of the voice-phenomenon as microscope and telescope are for the natural scientist and the astronomer.

When we have detected a voice on tape we still have to

identify and understand it. We start by determining what language it uses, and whilst the ear will not quickly differentiate unknown foreign languages, it can adapt itself to the mother-tongue or languages that are familiar to it much more easily. The voices are characterised by an unmistakable, polyglot speech.

After having determined the language(s), we try to grasp content and meaning. Only when we have analysed the sentence in this way and found that it is composed of several languages and that the words add up to a sensible content, can we claim that the voice is paranormal. The extra-sensory character of the voice-phenomenon can only be determined by comparing its mode of expression with the rules and regulations of ordinary human speech. Everyday life, and speech in particular, is full of complicated noises composed of a multitude of varied frequence-components. When such a noise spreads through the air one can treat each component separately, for the sound-waves travel through the atmosphere without influencing each other. It is quite easy to determine, when listening to a tape, that the voices are in no way influenced by any other sources of human noise.

I would like to repeat here that the decisive factor in studying the voice-phenomenon is not the theoretical interpretation, not the philosophising, but the empirical result, arrived at through experiment, that can be verified under test-conditions. The fact that the voices are audible to our ear and we can understand that speech, confirms that they exist physically and independently from us, and the experiments prove that the voices can be heard by anybody with a fair sense of hearing, regardless of his or her personal views, sympathy or antipathy. The voices are objective entities that can be verified and examined under psycho-acoustic, physical conditions. This concurrence of psycho-acoustic and paranormal data can hardly be brushed aside as mere coincidence; the voices must therefore be deemed to stem from a different plane of existence than our own.

(b) Listening to the voices

The main difficulty for effective research lies in the "listening-in" process. Because the ear has only a very limited range of frequency, and the language of the voices is tuned to more rapid frequencies than human speech, I have found that it takes at least *three months* for the ear to adjust itself to the difference: to begin with, though it may hear speech-like noises, it cannot differentiate the words—let alone understand what they mean. Of course, sharpness of hearing can differ widely from person to person: listening-in tests have shown that children and people with a musically trained ear have least difficulty in following the voices; military-trained radio-operators achieve a high degree of accuracy and for some unknown reason specialists of internal diseases and Catholic priests also seem to be able to discern the voices with relative success.

To augment audibility, I have evolved the following method:

When a sentence that can be understood has been located, this section of the original tape is re-recorded on to another tape and this process is repeated at least five times. It is a procedure that makes it easier to analyse the voices phoneme by phoneme, and statements can be verified with greater certainty. It is for this reason that a recording of, for instance, ten minutes, may take ten hours to analyse and verify.

The concrete results of this new method of research give substance to the assertion that the voices can be defined as belonging to transcendental beings. They appear as independent acoustic shapes that can be determined by a number of basic, characteristic features. This means that we can recognise the phenomenon in its acoustic manifestation.

Results vary considerably according to the method of recording used.

4. METHODS OF RECORDING

(1). *Microphone Recording*

The process of making recordings through microphone for the investigation of the voice-phenomenon is approximately the same as for ordinary tape-recording.[1] Speed can be

[1] See page xvi.

adjusted to 3¾ i.p.s. or 7½ i.p.s. Friedrich Jürgenson considers that a speed of 7½ i.p.s. is probably more suited to the fast-speaking voices; but my own experiments show that 3¾ i.p.s. gives equally satisfactory results and quite often the voices appear to be even clearer at that speed.

When the tape-recorder has been switched to "recording", the person in charge of the session might begin, for instance, by simply giving the date: "Today is the ..." Unless the experimenter is alone, he can then give the names of participants. Should the investigator be by himself, he might say perhaps: "Hello, hello, here is X.X.— I should be very happy to know that the unseen friends are here and are manifesting through the tape." He can follow this up by calling the names of dead friends and acquaintances; he should feel free to say whatever he likes, to ask questions, to explain or to specify what he wishes to know. If, on the other hand, the recording is being made in the presence of several people, the conversation should be kept on general lines so that each participant can contribute whatever he or she wants to express. Recording sessions should not exceed ten to fifteen minutes, because, as I have explained, examination of voices received may take several hours.

I have found microphone-voices to be very soft, quick as lightning, and only too often drowned or made unintelligible by voices of people taking part in the experiment. I therefore advise participants to speak slowly, quietly, and to take time to pause; afterwards, when the tape is being played back, to pinpoint every hint of a voice precisely and to repeat that section, so that the utterance becomes audible, the content clear and unequivocally verifiable and identifiable to the human ear.

Equally important is that participants should refrain from making noises, such as, for instance, murmurs of assent or dissent. Sincerity and honesty of purpose are, of course, essential. How the manifestations are explained or interpreted by those present is not important at this stage; it is most important that we should hear the voices and essentially comprehend them, in their various aspects of rhythm, language, content, etc.

Sincerity and honesty do not rule out logical thinking and

criticism, but an atmosphere of harmony and discipline should prevail. Idle gossip during recordings is to be avoided.

The microphone voices fall into three grades of audibility:

Group "A" consists of voices that can be heard and identified by anyone with normal hearing and knowledge of the language spoken; no special training of the ear is needed to detect them.

There are several hundred microphone-voices amongst my recordings that fall into this group. It is easy to make tape-copies of "A" voices and they can be repeated as often as desired. Thus, I have analysed roughly 25,000 voices according to speech content, language and rhythm. By this method of repetition, the acoustic reality of the voices can be established beyond doubt, and hallucinations of the ear are excluded.

Group "B" consists of voices that speak more rapidly and more softly, but are still quite plainly audible to a trained and attentive ear. The ability to differentiate increases with practice, but this is a slow and wearisome process. For this reason it is difficult to use non-regular participants for experimental purposes with group "B" voices.

Group "C" consists of the most interesting voices; voices that give us a great deal of information and much paranormal data. Unfortunately, these can be heard only in fragments, even by a trained ear, but with improved technical aids, it may eventually become possible to hear and demonstrate these voices, which lie beyond our range of hearing, without trouble. This grading and my comments are but a rough guide in the present stage of our approach to the psycho-acoustic aspect of the investigation.

(2). *Radio Recording*

The problems pertaining to the recording of voices through radio are complex. In recording, as well as in listening to the results, the sense of hearing is of vital importance. Friedrich Jürgenson maintains in his book *Voices from Space* that no radio-voice recordings can be made without a "mediator". This "mediating voice" is that of a woman (in his case "Lena"), telling one which transmitting station, wavelength, and hour of day or night to choose for a recording. I was able to hear

Jürgenson's mysterious "mediator" on one of his tapes. She asked him to wait for the recording till 9 p.m.; hints about people and events also came through in her strangely hissing voice.

I had to wait six months before such a mediator appeared on my tapes. It was at the end of 1965 when at last I heard a voice reply to my query as to who my mediator might be; it said "Spidola" (a Latvian name), spoken in Group "B" audibility. A male voice added in Latvian: "Mēs dzirdējām. Latvieši tev palīdzēs." ("We have heard. The Latvians will help you.")

At the next radio-voice recording—it was the first one I made by this method—I heard a female voice indicating a quite unknown transmitting station. "Sak' Pēter!" (Lat.—"Tell Peter!"), it said. Further evidence on tape confirmed that someone called Spidola really did assist in radio-voice recordings, and that the voice-entities appear to have several transmitting stations of their own.[1]

If one is relying on the help of the "mediator", one glides slowly from one end of the wavelength-scale to the other and listens carefully for a voice that will hiss "Now", or "Make recording!", or some such hint. At that precise moment one switches on the tape-recorder (which is connected to the radio as shown on page xviii) and starts the recording, regardless of music or speech being transmitted on that particular wavelength, or of any other noises. Afterwards, when the tape is being played back, all extraneous noises resulting from radio-transmissions have to be carefully eliminated, so that possible "voices" (always distinctly marked by their unmistakable rhythm, language-mixture, and frequent habit of addressing the experimenters) may be discerned. I will come back to these special features later, when we examine speech-content.

Further experiments proved, however, that successful radio-recordings could be achieved even without the help of Spidola. One chooses transmitter waves that meet and produce a typical "rushing" sound.[2] In this way one can make recordings without interference from radio programmes; but only afterwards, when the tape is being played back, can one hear how

[1] See page 174.
[2] Known to technicians, I believe, as the "white noise".

the voices stand out against the background of any incidental fragments of radio-transmissions. Once again they are recognisable by their paranormal features. They may address the experimenter and give him hints; or persons we know may give their names, tell us something, warn us or plead with us. *But whether the voices use microphone, radio, or other methods of recording, they always keep the same rhythm, the same peculiarities of speech, and often say things that relate to extra-sensory data.*

The presence of Spidola, the mediator, is confirmed on many of my recordings.[1] Sometimes she gives quite definite advice; sometimes other voices rebuke her, or try to make her rôle appear unimportant, even unnecessary.

Radio-voices too can be grouped into three grades of audibility; but they differ from microphone-voices in that their pronunciation is clearer and their messages are longer and have more meaning.

The voices themselves tend to clamour again and again for radio-recordings. I have some extremely good examples of this on tape. We know that radio waves penetrate the human body without being registered by the sense-organs. Electromagnetic fields within us continually make music or speeches —and perhaps these voices from "beyond" also cry out for contact within us and we fail to hear them. Many things are inaudible to our unaided ears, but a sensitive radio or microphone receives these subtle vibrations and creates electromagnetic fields on tape which are transformed into soundwaves and made audible. Perhaps these "voices from space" seem strange to us only because they are excluded from our ordinary, everyday powers of perception, but I have the impression that they are always present and through microphone or radio, can give us enormously varied information.

So we see the voice-phenomenon is closely linked to radio waves that come from afar, penetrate everything and create electro-magnetic fields within the so-called physical world, and we can regard the tape-recorder as an intermediary between electronic waves and sound-waves; only with the help of a tape-recorder can we hear what the electronic world tells us through the medium of sound-waves.

[1] See page 165.

(3). Radio-Microphone Recording

Quite by chance I discovered a method of combining radio and microphone recordings. One day, whilst I was playing back a recording, I noticed changes on the tape. A voice incessantly demanded "signals". Suppressing my astonishment I followed this strange recording to the end. When the tape had run through I fixed a fresh one, as I intended to make a radio-voice recording, but I forgot to adjust the tape-recorder, so that in effect the recording was made through microphone while the radio connection remained in operation. On playing the tape back I discovered several voices; by mistake, so to speak, I had stumbled upon a method which opened up quite new possibilities of registering conversation. By this method the voices can enter into discussions and answer questions. Listening, as the tape is being played back, we hear our own queries, and conversations between participants, to which quite exceptionally meaningful answers and comments are received. Once again I noticed the characteristic peculiarities of the phenomenon, which remained exactly the same as in the other recording methods. Sentences are compressed, the meaning is usually obscure, and in all languages used grammatical rules are ignored; for instance, the German word "binde" ("bind") becomes "bindu", a combination of "bind" and "du", the German word for "thou". Neologisms are particularly remarkable: our apparatus is called "Dezentraten"—"decentrators".

My question as to how it had been known that I was playing back a tape was answered by a woman's voice: "Wir waren in deinem Zimmer." (24g: 041)[1]—German: "We were in your room." Sentences in Latvian and Russian followed, for example: "Izrādās tāds nevīzīgs, nebo!"—literally, "It becomes apparent that he is negligent, oh Heaven!" but as we might say "Heavens, he's obviously been careless!" The next sentence is striking: "Jundahl kan gå själv,—oh vecā pott! Bindu han an de(m) mort-bed!" (24g: 041). The sentence is composed of five languages: Jundahl—a name; kan gå själv—Swedish: vecā—Latvian; pott—North German dialect or

---

[1] The references here and throughout are to the numbering of the experimenter's tapes (24g), and the place on the tape at which the words occur (041 on the rev. meter).

Swedish; bindu—modified German; han—Swedish; an de(m) —German; mort—Latin or one of the Romance languages; bed—English. In English the sentence would run: "Jundahl can walk by himself, the old pot. Tie him to the death-bed." In this context yet another sentence became audible: "Lido ernst nach ziami auf Konstant! Konstantin, Alex." (24g: 042). This is a mixture of Latvian and German words: lido—Latv: flying; ernst—German: serious; nach—Germ.: to; ziami— Latv.: earth; auf—Germ.: on (or: to); can be understood in English as: "Fly in earnest to earth to Konstant! Konstantin, Alex!"

The method of recording is virtually the same as in radio-recordings, except that the tape-recorder remains switched to "microphone"; the microphone itself is placed very close to the radio. It is best to tune the radio-set to a wavelength that gives only the "rushing" sound, so that no noises from radio stations can be heard and even the "rushing" sound is hardly audible. There is, of course, always a chance that earthly transmitting stations may intervene, but, as stressed before, the voice phenomenon has its own distinctive features which rule out any danger of confusion. With me the voices use mostly Latvian and as the Latvian language is very rarely heard on radio, one may safely regard messages spoken in Latvian as being of the same paranormal origin as those spoken in various languages.

Radio-microphone-recordings, where voices can take up points of discussion and answer questions, produce excellent evidence of the voices' independence and their partnership with us, and the results like the others, can be grouped into A, B and C grades of audibility.

Since April 1968 two new recording-methods have been developed in co-operation with Physics Professor Alex Schneider of Switzerland:

(4). *Frequency-Transmitter Recording*

This method excludes freak noises from radio and microphone: only carrier-frequencies operate and these are used by the voice-entities. The voices thus recorded show the same traits as those of other recording-methods. Their statements are often slightly overlaid by sinus-frequencies, but their audibility is good and they are free from other interferences. Up to several hundred voices recorded in this fashion have been definitely verified by Professor Schneider and other collaborators.

(5). *Diode Recording*

In this highly interesting method the recording is made directly from the room on to the tape.[1] For various reasons it is a complicated process. The length of the aerial (6–8 cm.) has to be exactly adjusted, and vibrations sent out by the voices are received by this aerial. In quality the voices thus received come nearest to those of ordinary human ones, although we find exactly the same peculiarities as before. When this last method has been further developed and perfected, we shall be able to regard it as a direct contact, in every sense of the word, with the unseen entities. Results of diode-recordings can be heard without great difficulty even by an untrained and unprepared ear. One has the impression that the voices speak directly on to the tape; they have a spaceless quality, an immediate impact and their diction is remarkably clear; they are instantly received and can be heard without atmospheric interferences. These recordings have to be made with the tape-recorder turned to highest sound-volume. (The copying too has to be done with both machines turned to maximum. Other recordings, whether by radio or microphone, would produce ear-splitting noises at that volume.)

For more information about these latest two methods, see Professor Schneider's technical commentary Appendix I, page 336.

5. THE LANGUAGE OF THE VOICES AND HOW THEY SPEAK

Although we are far from grasping the full complexities of the phenomenon as yet, the so-called "voices from beyond", are easily distinguishable from terrestial human voices. They speak in an unmistakable rhythm and usually employ several languages in a single sentence; the sentence-construction obeys

---

[1] See page xx.

rules that differ radically from those of ordinary speech and, although the voices seem to speak in the same way as we do, the anatomy of their "speech-apparatus" must be different from our own.

Examination of our human speech-mechanism has shown that the whole process of "speaking" is a very complicated one; vocal chords, glottis and lungs all play their part. In producing the sound of a voice, the vocal chords are brought together by a system of rotatory cartilages and a complicated interaction of small muscles; air, being pressed out of the lungs, causes the vocal chords to vibrate, and size and tension of the chords determine the frequence of this vibration. The movement of the vocal chords, influences the stream of air and this, in turn, sets off the resonance-frequencies in the oral cavity. The timbre of a voice depends largely on the shape of the mouth. Voices are usually unique and everybody possesses, so to speak, his or her own voice, distinguished by its special, unmistakable tone-quality.

Apart from their paranormal characteristics, the voices that manifest on tape show great similarities to those produced by ordinary human speech-organs. It is possible that they may use already existing human voice-material. They are softer, (those in groups B and C generally only a whisper) but they do seem to be produced through some kind of speech-apparatus.

Differentiations in their speech-pattern also seem to indicate that in some unexplained way, the voices use the same sources from which we terrestial humans build our speech. They use continuous and fragmentary sounds just as we do. The continuous sounds are characteristically drawn out, whilst the fragmentary ones break off abruptly. One can also distinguish vocal and non-vocal sounds, according to whether vocal chords have been in action to produce them or not.

The words made audible on tape are generally pronounced in an unmistakably uniform way, regardless of the language used. Identification of the voices is, nevertheless, often a remarkably difficult task. One may, whilst listening-in, discern the resonance and frequency of voices—one hears the sounds, but the sense of hearing has the utmost difficulty in recognising them as words; only after intensive and concentrated listening does a tangible word emerge. Some of my collaborators often heard definite resonance-frequencies over quite a period of time, without being able to grasp what they contained. These difficulties pertain particularly of course to the whispering voices of group C. It is interesting to note that troubles arise not only on the side of the listener, but also on the side of the speakers—the voice-entities. I have examples on my tape which demonstrate how a voice tries to form words out of torn vibrations that sound like the humming of a bumble-bee.

It is impossible to explain the language of the voices by saying that it is formed through the language of the experimenter himself. The voices speak their own language—a kind of Esperanto, a single sentence often comprising a number of languages and cut down to the barest essentials. For instance: the experimenter calls upon his deceased collaborator, Professor Frei, to state his name clearly and unequivocally from 'the other side". A voice answers distinctly: "Frei! Du sova, willst nicht glaube!" (Swedish and German: "You sleep, you will not believe!"). Here we have the curtailed polyglot mode of expression repeated consistently in all the recordings that have produced voice-texts, up to the present time over 72,000. It is this particular voice-phenomenon-language, differing fundamentally from terrestial human languages, by which the entities can be distinguished from ordinary human voices.

The voice-phenomenon-language must, of course, strike us as highly complicated and on first encounter, without comment given or some knowledge of the situation, it seems confusing, even senseless. In many cases, however, each word has a wider, symbolic meaning, given to it in such a way that the individual experimenter may *recognise the voice-entity behind it*; in a few instances I have added comments, but in general I have quite intentionally avoided interpretation, as I wanted to stress the factual character of the phenomenon rather than its deeper meaning. The voice-phenomenon must be allowed to speak to the reader directly. Facts are the servants of truth; to understand the new reality in the form presented to us by the voice-phenomenon, we need a certain amount of preparation and much more knowledge relating to the possibility of a higher existence.

Let us ask ourselves briefly an important question: does a thought consist of words?—The answer is: no. Thoughts consist of psychic particles that stand in the same relation to reality as words. As we all know, there are many forms of language: the language of the battlefield, the language of reports, the language of every-day life, an ex-cathedra-language and so forth. This means that to think of a language-form is to think of a form of life.

I will give some examples of the voice-phenomenon-language portraying a form of reality we have not yet learned to understand:

"Eine no Tote," German and English: "One who is not dead." We find here a rigorous shortening of the sentence construction. Or: "Kant te pustjak," Latvian and Russian: "Kant does not have any importance here." This we may understand to mean that values are different in the spiritual world; even Kant does not have any special importance there. Another example: I address the Russian poet Majakowskij and complain about the difficulties in dealing with certain human beings. Quick as lightning a voice answers briefly: "Majakowskij! Konstantin, pluj!" Russian: "Konstantin, spit on it!" meaning that I should not bother about what people say, but get on with what I think is right.

These short sentences are rich in meaning. Briefness takes many forms; one more example: "Nedomā zirgi;" Latvian: "Horses don't think." One might complete the sentence by adding: ". . . because they do not possess the mental ability." Here it seems I am told that I cannot expect too much from people who lack certain mental or spiritual qualities.

Naturally, intimate knowledge of the particular language helps. The Latvian sentence: "Koste, Slankis, sapulci—vāciete", for instance, literally translated: "Koste, Slankis, the gathering —the German", can only be properly understood by those who know the Latvian language well. A full translation of this truncated sentence would read: "Koste, here is Slankis. The gathering (or meeting) is being conducted by the German woman."

Sometimes pronouncements are kept strictly to the point and refer to current situations on our side, or on theirs. Once, reporters of the newspaper *Bild am Sonntag* (Sunday Pictorial) visited me, remaining in the studio almost the whole night. Dr. Zenta Maurina, whose night's rest had been disturbed, was somewhat upset. A voice summed up the situation in three words: "Du zornig, Maurina." German: "You angry, Maurina."

Complicated thought processes may be expressed in very short sentences. For example, the experimenter asked in the course of a recording session whether the voice entities could tell him something about Dr. X. The answer came: "Ko, dativo bes." This is Spanish and Russian and means: "Ko (Konstantin,), dative-devil." In the light of the given situation, this means that Dr. X. in his capacity of examiner of the voice-phenomenon, can be taken as the "devil's advocate". However, only if one remembers the scholastic tradition of discussion in the Middle Ages—from which the expression "advocatus diaboli" stems—in which the "dative" played an especially important rôle, and the fact that it is still quite common for philologists analysing Greek and Latin texts to argue for hours, does the meaning become clear.

On the other hand, there are quite straightforward utterances needing no explanation, for example: "Konstantin, tev netic, Munthe." Latvian: "Konstantin, one does not believe you, Munthe." Or, again, "Bedenke, ich bin!" German: "Imagine, I am!"

This last clear pronouncement was made by Margarete Petrautzki[1] who, in the last days of her life, had maintained that she could not envisage an existence after death. During one of his recording sessions, the experimenter asked her how she felt "over there", and the answer—"Imagine, I am!"—was spoken in a happily astonished tone of voice.

I will summarise briefly the characteristics I have mentioned in this section:

1. The voice-entities speak very rapidly, in a mixture of languages, sometimes as many as five or six in one sentence.
2. They speak in a definite rhythm, which seems to be forced upon them by the means of communication they employ.
3. The rhythmic mode of speeech imposes a shortened, telegram-style phrase or sentence.

See page 46.

4. Presumably arising from these restrictions, grammatical rules are frequently abandoned and neologisms abound.

These characteristic features of the language of the voices and their speech content, are the outstanding paranormal aspects of the phenomenon and the guide-lines to further research, and in my opinion this is, at least for the time being, the best approach in our endeavours to get closer to its essence.

6. PLAY-BACK OF THE RECORDINGS

One may look at the problem of reproducing the voices from various points of view. Results depend on the sense of hearing as well as on mechanical and electronic aids.

The psycho-acoustic aspect plays a major part in listening to the recordings, for the sound encounters many pitfalls on its complicated route between ear and brain, and one tends to hear what one wants or expects to hear. The radio's humming may be transformed into words, and a blurred shout may sound like a name, but these errors can be eliminated in time, because everything recorded on tape can be repeated until the ear is sufficiently well-trained to make sharp, accurate distinctions.

One must admit, however, that emotions welling up whilst listening to the voices can be of a highly personal nature, and this may be due to the communication of extremely subtle sensations. The voices transmit—as we shall later learn from speech-contents—a vast range of feelings, emotions, passions, thoughts and wishes that are deeply embedded in the human psyche and awaken within us a transcendental sensibility. It would be naïve to presume that such complex interrelations could be explained through simple physical formulae. Each individual may react quite differently when listening to the voices, according to his or her thinking-habits or ethical and religious concepts. *Whilst listening-in one should try, as far as possible, not to be emotionally affected by what one hears and to keep one's own feelings, thoughts and wishes well under control.*

Gradually, the ear adapts itself to the voices and their various individual characteristics. We realise that each one has its own typical voice-quality, and these qualities help us greatly when it comes to identifying individual voices. With practice it becomes possible to guess at the type of personality hidden behind a particular voice.

As recordings vary a great deal in quality and the experimenters are still unsure of their ground, many voices reach us only in a heavily distorted form. A voice may lose its characteristic quality through the recording process. Radio-recordings are particularly prone to such distortions, caused mainly by music, speech or insufficiently strong transmitting beams, and in such cases it is impossible to recognise the voice either by its timbre or its speech-content. The problem we have to deal with here is the technical one of how to improve recording-methods in such a way as to perfect the audibility of a voice and retain its original timbre. The technical aids currently at our disposal allow no more than a partial, often faulty, reproduction of the voices, although quality has been substantially improved by the diode method of recording, and the repeated copying of the audible voices on tape is a further improvement, as it helps the ear to distinguish words phoneme by phoneme (smallest sound-unit). A voice thus recorded can be measured by technical apparatus in the same way as a human voice.

Chapter II

Speech-content of Recordings

(I) *INDIVIDUAL MANIFESTATIONS*

Out of the abundant recorded material, my collaborators and I have analysed over 25,000 voices, and I have made a selection of voice texts divided into categories for this book.

I do not wish to give the impression, through the voice-texts selected, that I am bent on any particular hypothesis, interpretation or explanation. Quite simply, I want to report on the physical-acoustic aspect of what I have heard; for only on the basis of concrete experience can we come to understand the nature of the phenomenon. In the long run it will not, of course, be enough to admit the reality of the voices and just leave it at that. Their statements have a much deeper significance than we might suspect on hearing them for the first time, but a too hasty interpretation may only hinder research at this stage.

Whilst reading the following pages, I would like my readers to keep in mind that the existence of a phenomenon bearing characteristics of the paranormal has been established beyond a shadow of doubt. That being so, conventional methods of evaluation according to our own pre-conceptions cannot be rigidly applied.

When we find incoherent ejaculations, and sometimes phrases consisting of words which do not seem to make sense, the natural impulse to dismiss them as unworthy of consideration should be resisted, for we are dealing with facts (including the fact that research is as yet in its infancy), and we should be willing to await, and to seek for, the revelation of their true significance.

From the speech-content of the texts, it seems that "dead" persons are trying to make contact with the "living", from a world hidden from our conscious perception, that has hitherto remained inaccessible to us.

There are those who will find this a new and difficult conception, but I would remind them that much they encounter in daily life only makes sense because of the previous knowledge brought to its contemplation; for example, a political cartoon is meaningless to a small child or to a primitive tribesman. The phenomenon opens up new vistas of a transcendental existence, and we should study it with unprejudiced interest and sympathy.

1. *Mother*

Amongst roughly 72,000 audible voices the 'mother-motive' is statistically the most frequent. My mother appears in manifold forms and uses various languages, including some she did not know during her lifetime; Spanish, Swedish and German, for instance; but most of all she uses Latgalian, the dialect of Latgale, a Latvian province. Usually she addresses me directly and personally, but sometimes other entities report her presence, introduce her or give some messages regarding her.

> A female voice:
> "Tava māte!" (22r: 277)[1]
> (Latvian: "Your mother!")

> "Mōte te atrūdās. Tekla." (23g: 158)
> (Latg.: "Mother is here. Tekla.")
> See "Tekla" page 40.

At times she uses very tender terms in addressing me:

> "Kostulīt, tā tove mōte." (29g: 036)
> (Latg.: "Kostulit, this is your mother.")

In some sentences she uses Spanish words, for instance:

> "Te madre, Kostja." (39r: 406)
> (Latv., Spanish or Italian: "Here is mother, Kostja.")

Her presence is indicated by the following messages:

---

[1] These numberings refer here, and throughout, to the experimenter's tape numbers and the rev. meter.

"Mōte tevi pavad" (39r: 406)
(Latg.: "Mother is with you.")
"Mōti laid!"—Then a female voice: "Kosta!" (39r: 739)
(Latg.: "Let mother through!"—"Kosta!")
"Kostulīt, Kostulīt! Māte!" (49r: 328/30)
(Latv.: "Kostulit, Kostulit! Mother!")
"Koste, tava māte runā." (40g: 286)
(Latv.: "Koste, your mother speaks.")
"Tala Kosti, mamucis." (Amg: 084)
(Swedish, Latv.: "Speak, Kosti, Mummy.")
"Wir danken."—"Māte lentē." (43g: 447—same place 450 M)
(German and Latv.: "We give thanks."—"Mother on the tape.")
"Māte te, runā Kosta!" (43r: 044)
(Latv.: "Mother is here, speak, Kosta!")
"Kostja, mōte ustobā." (43r:519)
(Lettg.: "Kostja, mother is in the room.")
"Din moder."—"Krustmeita." (44b: 244M)
(Swedish, Latv.: "Your mother."—"Niece".)

The experimenter addresses his mother: "I shall be happy to hear your voice."

"Deine Mama!" (44b: 592)
(German: "Your Mama!")
"Tava Mamma, tava māte." (25r: 384/6)
(Latv.: "Your Mama, your mother.")
Immediately afterwards and even more directly:
"Māti mīl, tavu jauno Mona Roz!" (same place)
(Latv.: "Love mother, your young Mona Rosa!")

The name of the experimenter's mother was Rosalia. In some other recordings the experimenter's mother introduces herself now and then as "Mona", for instance in 25r: 455 and 475.

"Mona, ljubi judi!" (31r: 520)
(Russian, German; the latter with a modified ending: "Mona, love the Jews.")
"Mona, tūva tu!" (42r: 381)
(Latv.: "Mona, you are near!")
"Din Mona dzird, dzird." (33r: 024)
(Swed., Latv.: "Your Mona hears, hears.")
"Kosta, atmin mōte Mona!" (34r: 122)
(Latg.: "Kosta, remember mother Mona!"

Every now and then somebody reports on the mother's condition; for instance:

"Mātei sāp galva." (31r: 543)
(Latv.: "Mother has a headache.")
"Māte sjuk. Tava krustmeita te. Deras pensionats." (44b: 080)
(Latv., Swed.: "Mother is sick. Here is your niece. Her boarding-school.")
"Te māte raud." (44r: 905)
(Latv.: "Here mother cries.")
"Konstantin, tova lobā mōte raudaja par savu zudušo dēlu. Konstantin, par savu zudušo dēlu raud tava māte." (26r: 033)
(Latg., Latv., with unusual modifications of sentence and words: "Konstantin, your kind mother cried over her lost son. Konstantin, over her lost son cries your mother.")

A little later she speaks herself:

"Konstantin, te tava mōte." (same place: 036)
(Latg.: "Konstantin, here is your mother.")

The concern apparent in the above example is often expressed:

"Konstantin, tava māte. Furchtbare, furchtbare Kräfte mot dej. Turies bei mej! Deine Mutter." (26r: 031/2)
(Latv., German, Swed.: "Konstantin, your mother. Terrible, terrible forces against you. Hold on to me! Your mother.")
"Mōte. tu nīci." (39g: 317)
(Latg.: "Mother. You are pining away.")
"Aizgulēj, Kosti, paliec par spiti!" (35r: 302)
(Latv.: "You have overslept, Kosti, stay in spite of that!")
"Kosta, tu kurls, te mōte". (39g: 512)
(Latg.: "Kosta, you are deaf, here is mother.")

After two recording-sessions with a group of participants, in which his mother does not manifest, the experimenter makes a recording by himself alone (No. 323). He asks his mother which of the collaborators she likes best.

"Nivīns napatīk—tava Mutter." (46g: 373)
(Latg., German: "I like none of them—your mother.")
The same voice asks: "Māti tu juti?" (46g: 390)
(Latv.: "Have you felt mother?")

His father is interested in what the experimenter is doing:

"Ko tu dari? Tāvs te." (42r: 381)
(Latv.: "What are you doing? Here is father.")

On the same tape we hear.

"Vientula māte."—"Māte te vieno." (42r: 422 and 632)
(Latv.: "Mother is lonely."—"Mother unites here.")

"A ko tu dor? Klars monds. Neredz tu moti? Mōte stipra."
(44b: 176)
(Latg., German: "What are you doing? The moon is clear. Don't you see mother? Mother is strong.")

The following fragment of a conversation seems to indicate that the voices respect the mother:

"Mōte, stoj!"
"Lettisch prūt?"
"Prūtam".
"Kop tik īkšā!" (35r: 223)
(Latg., German: "Here is mother, stop!"—"Do you understand Latvian?"
"We understand"—"Just step in.")

We hear messages regarding the mother's "domicile". The experimenter wishes that his mother may walk on easy paths in the" beyond".

A voice: "Danke, palidzēs man." (44b: 256/8)
(German, Latv.: "Thank you, it will help me.")
Experimenter: "I am very close to you. Where do you live now?"
Voice: "*Es te dzīvoj Nonsburdē. Både amico sind, Kosti.*" (same place)
(Latv., Swed., Germ.: "I live here in Nonsburdē. We two are friends, Kosti.")

At a different occasion the experimenter asks again:

"Mother, where do you live now?"
Voice: "Es dzīvoju Niapolī."—"Tu Mutter hjälpi." (47g: 620)
(Latv., Germ., Swed.: "I live in Niapoli."—"You help mother."

The experimenter says he is convinced that her strength is growing through her spiritual nourishment and environment.

A voice answers: "Vi skall hoff, Kost. Mutti, Ko." (42g: 540)
(Swed., Germ.: "We shall hope, Kost. Mummy, Ko.")
She, on her side, asks: "Bist Du zufrieden?"—"Mama, Konstantin." (34g: 216/20)
(German: "Are you content?"—"Mama, Konstantin.")

The following sentence is particularly interesting from a language point of view:

"Raudive, taurē, nabaga matj. Rau—tut aber nichts. In der Kirche sleep!" (40r: 427)
(Lat., Russ., Germ., Engl.: "Raudive, blow, poor mother. Rau—, but it doesn't matter. In the church sleep!")

The following voices show a very definite relationship to the experimenter:

"Nevaru dziedat tev, mans mīlais. Tava mazā māte." (23r: 495)
(Latv.: "I cannot sing for you, my dear. Your little mother.")
"Māte tencina." (43r: 044)
(Latv.: "Mother thanks.")
"Pagaidi te, Kosti. Mutti seviški mīli!" (44b: 230)
(Latv., Germ.: "Linger here, Kosti. Love mother particularly.")
"Mōte. Ich liebe Dich." (44r: 132)
(Latg., Germ.: "Mother. I love you.")
"Mīlē, Kosta, mōti!" (44r: 178)
(Latg.: "Love, Kosta, mother!")
"Neatkāpies tik lielumā! Mōte!" (46r: 684)
(Latg.: "Don't give in in big things only! Mother.")
"Koste, te mōte, laba diena, Mēs warten, Kosti, tagadnē." (47g: 028)
(Latg., Germ.: "Koste, here is mother, good day. We wait, Kosti, in the present.")
"Māte—primā norma." (42r: 725)
(Latv.: "Mother—the first norm.")

2. *Aunt*

An Aunt on my father's side had shown a particular interest in my life and though for reasons unknown to me she entered a convent when she was a young woman, she had remained fond of me right up to the time of her death. Every now and then mention is made of her in my recordings. She manifests to give warnings or simply to state her presence.

"Tā tava Tante, tote, tote Tante. Tā tava Tante, tote Tante. tu bezdievis, dzied!" (28g: 168)
(Latv., Germ.: "This is your aunt, dead, dead aunt. This is your aunt dead aunt. You godless, sing!")
"Tava tote Tante, tava tote Tante." (28g: 188)
(Latv., Germ.: "Your dead aunt, your dead aunt.")
"Kosti, te Tante." (40g: 457)
(Latv., Germ.: "Kosti, here is Aunt."

From a recording made in the town of Göttingen:

"Te Kosti, te Tante. Nepiekusi! man nocērpe matus." (Hr. 295)
(Latv., Germ.: "Here is Kosti, here is Aunt. Don't tire yourself! My hair has been cut off.")

"Tötka tja, guten Tag!" (45r: 118)
(Russian, Latg., Germ.: "Aunt is here, good day!")
"Matilde, te Tante. Lūgšanas!" (40r: 523)
(Latv., Germ.: "Matilde, here is Aunt. Prayers!")

3. Sister Tekle—Mona

Tekle is my elder sister with whom, until her death, I had the closest links. In my earliest youth, as in later years, she was almost a second mother to me in her ever present concern about me and her interest in my way of life. The persistence of her appearances on tape is second only to that of my mother.

The name of my cousin Mona is more rarely mentioned. She died in 1944, a child of twelve.

"Tekle. Otru reizi mani nervi neizturēja, bet par ātru. . . ." (23g: 337)
(Latv.: "Tekle. The second time my nerves could not stand it, but too quickly . . .")
"Neraud, te Tekla. Wer weint für die andere." (28g: 666/7)
(Latv., Germ.: "Don't cry, here is Tekla. Who cries for the other one.")

Some voices indicate who Tekla is; for instance:

"Tekla, tova mōsa." (29g: 495)
(Latg.: "Tekla, your sister.")

Four consecutive sentences speak of Tekle:

"Tici Teklai!"
"Tekle nomodā."
"Eto sestrà."
"Tjännare, Tekle, mūsu jobka." (35g: 103)
(Latv., Russ., Swed.: "Believe in Tekle!"—"Tekle keeps watch." "This is the sister."—"Hello, Tekle, our worker.")
"Atkal Tekle." (44g: 457)
(Latv.: "Once again Tekle.")

The following fragment of conversation gives the impression that Tekle, my sister, has to get through some sort of barrier. (See "Crossing and Customs Points", page 140).

"Stakars mosa!"
"Tekle te."
"Pasportu!"

"Tekle Raudive." (Hg: 180)
(Swed., Latv.: "Poor sister!"—"Here is Tekle."—"Passport, please!")
"Tekle Raudive."

The experimenter addresses his sister Tekle. A voice answers:

"Ataman, plika." (42g: 346)
(Russ., Latv.: "Leader, I am naked.")—I have to explain here that my elder brothers and sisters called me "Ataman", "leader", when we were children.

Immediately afterwards the experimenter seeks contact with his mother, his friends and relations. A voice reports:

"Kosti, nu du smikra; viņi gul." (42g: 347)
(Swed., Latv.: "Kosti, now you are flattering; they sleep.")
"Wir binde Tekle, Konstan."—"Te Konstantins muns." (42g: 551)
(First sentence German: "We bind Tekle, Konstan." The second sentence is spoken by a female voice; Latg.: "Here is mine Konstantin.")
"Wohnst Du hier? Liebe Du Schwester!" (43g: 122)
(German: "Do you live here? You must love sister.")
"Kosti, tu? Schwester hier. Svētī tu?" (43g: 135)
(Latv., Germ.: "Kosti, you? Sister here. Are you celebrating?")
"Te Tekle. Māsa raud." (43g: 553)
(Latv.: "Here is Tekle. Sister cries.")
"Tekle Dir will helpe." (UIIr: 124)
(German: "Tekle wants to help you.")
"Nu mierā Tekle." (44r: 283)
(Latv.: "Now Tekle is content.")
"Atman, tev liek dvoiku. Mōsa, señor." (44r: 906)
(Latv., Russ., Spanish: "Atman, you are given a two. The sister, señor.")
The "2" is the second-best mark given in German schools.
"Te tava Mona. Loti maza. Tu runā, Kosti." (47r: 070)
(Latv.: "Here is your Mona. Very small. You speak, Kosti.")
"Mona, hej!" (46r: 641M)

4. *Aljosha* (*Alexis*)

Apart from my sister Tekle, Aljosha (or Alexis) manifests very often, calling himself my brother and helper; Aljosha was indeed my brother's name and during his lifetime we had always been on good terms with each other.

Here are some examples of his name being mentioned:

"Lido ernst nach ziami auf Konstant. Konstantin, Aleks." (Übsg: 252)
(Latv., Germ.: "Flying in earnest to earth to Konstant. Konstantin, Alex.")
"Kosta, tu te esi. Kosti, Aleks." (Ü Ir: 163)
(Latv.: "Kosta, you are here. Alex")
"Ja prūtu sprechen. Aleksis, Konstantin, Aleksis." (37r: 599/600)
(Russ., Latv., Germ.: "I know how to speak. Alexis, Konstantin, Alexis.")
"Brāl, tas milzīg angažē."—"Tiše, Aleksej!" (44r: 232)
(Latv., Russ.: "Brother, this interests mightily."—"Softer, Alexej!")
"Tev Aljoša help!" (44r: 474)
(Latv., Engl.: "Aljosha helps you!")
"Brālis te Glück!" (42g: 158)
(Latv., Germ.: "Brother, here is luck!")
"Te guni dedzi! Aleksis sveiks. Emilija pie galda svin." (42r: 818)
(Latv.: "Here light the fire! Alexis is well. Emilia celebrates at table.")

The following sentences seem to indicate that Aljosha acts as intermediary between the voice-entities and the experimenter:

"Mēs daudzi te, piesūc pie zemes, Aljoša!" (45g: 659)
(Latv.: "There are many of us here, cling firmly to the earth, Aljosha!")
"Aljoša. Koste, te Liebe. Koste, Brücke te." (47g: 067)
(Latv., Germ.: "Aljosha. Koste, here is love. Koste, the bridge is here.")
"Aljos, Koste. Sveiks, Koste. Wir gehen auf Osun." (47g: 366/70)
(Latv., Germ.: "Aljos, Koste. Good day, Koste. We are going to Osun.") Osune is the home of the experimenter.

The experimenter addresses Aljosha and the following voices appear:

"Man patika fraze."
"Te Papukin dankt."
"Dein Vater te kommt." (47g: 512)

(Latv., Germ.: "I liked that sentence."—"Here Papukin thanks." "Here comes your father.")

5. *Sonja Liepina*

Sonja L., my friend for many years, died in Riga in 1958 after a long, harrowing illness. We never lost contact and corresponded with each other up to the last days of her life. An agreement had been made between us that the one to die first should give the other a sign of his or her continued existence beyond the grave. Strangely enough I never received the slightest hint from her, either in dreams or in waking consciousness. With her death she seemed to have vanished completely from my life; but in 1965, when I began to experiment with the voice-phenomenon, she manifested her presence on tape.

"Hier Sonja." (33r: 023) (German: "Here Sonja.")
A voice reports:
"Ir pasīva, lilla Sonja, Konstantin." (same place 439)
"Radars, pirmo rīmi sakroplo." (same place)
(Latv., Swed.: "The little Sonja is passive, Konstantin."—"Radar distorts the first rhyme.")
The voice continues:
"Sataisies chotj bez patiesības." (same place)
(Latv., Russ.: "Be ready, even without truth.")

The experimenter asks how Sonja is. A male voice answers:

"Sonja devitā namā." (35r: 082)
(Latv.: "Sonja in nineth house.")

Frequently experimental recordings were made during travels. In Heidelberg, a voice was heard to say:

"Fern Sofija heute." (38g: 547)
(German: "Far Sofija today.")

Once again the experimenter addresses Sonja and asks her how she feels in the beyond. The voice answers:

"Tagad ir labi." (42g: 631)
(Latv.: "Now it is good.")

The experimenter asks if she could not help him.

"Pacentišos. Te lustība." (same place)
(Latv.: "I will try. Here is gaiety.") The word "lustība" is a mixture of German and Latvian.

A voice comments:

"Raudive piesmaka. Sonja ruft. Konci, Vortrag war det schlecht." (42r: 892)
(Lat., Germ., Swed.: "Raudive has become hoarse. Sonja calls. Konci, the lecture was that bad.")

Further messages from, or about, Sonja:

"Liepina." (43g: 323)—Sonja's family name.
"Bald Uppsala, Sonja." (43g: 442)
(German: "Soon Uppsala, Sonja.")

The experimenter calls Sonja Liepina.

"Liepina Tālavā." (43g: 496)
(Latv.: "Liepina in Talava.")

In answer to another call on Sonja from the experimenters:

"Wieviele Rechte hattest Du?" (44b: 684)
(German: "How many rights did you have?")
"Tja Liepina, Raudiv." (44b: 879)
(Latg.: "Here is Liepina, Raudiv.")

Once again the experimenter talks to Sonja. A voice says:

"Esmu tava, tu mans, Konstantin!" (45r: 468)
(Latv.: "I am yours, you mine, Konstantin.")
"Mūsu Sonja kommt." (Amg: 126)
(Latv., German: "Our Sonja comes.")
Male voice:
"Eku, Sonja!" (43r: 239)
(Latv.: "Look, Sonja!")
Female voice:
"Mēs eksistējam." (same place)
(Latv.: "We exist.")

6. *Aileen F.*

Aileen F. was Scottish. I met her in Paris, when I was a student. She was very attached to me and I remained in contact with her until her death in 1948; only the war had temporarily cut our links. Meantime she had married a doctor and lived in South Africa, but later she returned to Europe where she died. Her brother gave me the details of her passing.

The experimenter calls on Aileen F. A voice answers:

"Aileen, die andere Verpflichtungen übernommen hat." (22r: 369)
(German: "Aileen, who has taken on other responsibilities.")
A little later:
"All sait dein Aileen. Aileen, Konstantin!" (31r: 025)
(Engl., French, Germ.: "Your Aileen knows all. Aileen, Konstantin!")
"My Darling, I am Aileen." (35r: 060)
"Aileena." (39g: 427)
An impressively clear voice:
"Finlayson!" (40g: 580)—Family-name of the deceased.
"Te Vucyns. Finlaysonu es redzu." (Hg: 253)
(Latv.: "Here is Vucyns. I see Finlayson.")
A female voice continues:
"Ir vēstules tev, Konci. Gulu te. Gultina te." (same place)
(Latv.: "You have letters, Konci. I sleep here. Here is a little bed.")
A very distinct voice:
"Aileena!" (44r: 661)
"Finlayson." (43g: 049)
"Aileen te, nu runa tu, Konstantin!" (43g: 544)
(Latv.: "Aileen is here, now you speak, Konstantin!")

The experimenter addresses all his friends. After Aileen's name has been mentioned the following voice is heard:

"Brauks zyrgu tja—Grabis." ((42r: 783)
(Latg.: "The horse will drive here—Grabis.")
"Aileen!" (46r: 679)

7. *Margarete Petrautzki*

Margarete was Dr. Zenta Maurina's secretary, and ten years of her life had been devoted entirely to duties and services rendered to her employer. Our relationship was a friendly one and she was my right hand in the execution of daily tasks. She was talented and had had a good education, and in addition she was cheerful, sensible, practical, and had a particularly clear memory.

When she fell ill, and cancer was diagnosed, I became an almost daily witness of her suffering. During those times we used to discuss many problems of life and death. She stayed fully conscious right up to the last moment of her life. Her passing was not easy—it was full of pain and discomfort.

After her death on 10th February 1965, I started to study literature on the subject of death and post-mortal existence with particular intensity, but found only hypothetical suppositions and analogies which left the basic problem still wide open and unsolved. Then I read in a Swedish newspaper that Friedrich Jürgenson had recorded audible voices from the beyond on tape.

Much later when I had advanced sufficiently in my own experiments, I heard the following voice:

"Margarete tev seko." (22r: 273)
(Latv.: "Margarete follows you.")

Soon afterwards I heard a penetrating voice:

"Margarete!" (same place: 309)

At a different recording a male voice was heard to say:

"Hier Detektiv. Margarete untreu mit eigenem Vater." (23g: 066)
(German: "Here detective. Margarete unfaithful with own father.")

I deduced from this sentence that there are voice-entities who create emotional discord within the experimenter or try to make him drop the experiments altogether.

After a few days came another voice:

"Du Gretel, kära man har." (23g: 591)
(Swed.: "You Gretel, you have a dear man.")
A distinct female voice:
"Margarete!" (25r: 209)

The name Margarete appears more and more frequently; now and then with modifications:

"Margarete, Margarelli, Margarete!" (25r: 409)
"Margarete..., runā, runā, runā!" (28g: 004)

(Latv.: "Margarete ..., speak, speak, speak!")
"Te Margarete." (same place: 008)
(Latv.: "Here is Margarete.")
"Margarete sjuk på dej." (same place: 113)
(Swed.: "Margarete pines after you.")
"Kosti, tiesā."
"Kosti apžēlo Margareti."
"Apžēlo Margaretes līgavaini."
"Mēs lūdzam."
"Man trūkst te viss." (same place: 128)
(Latv.: "Kosti, judge."—"Kosti, pardon Margarete."—"Pardon Margarete's fiancé."—"We beg."—"Here I lack everything.")

Then she tells what she lacks:

"Man trūkst niebura, mantela. Man trūkst mantela." (same place.)
(Latv.: "I lack a bodice, a coat. I lack a coat.")
"Margarete, Margarete bittet für Sie, Konstantin." (28g: 156)
(German: "Margarete, Margarete pleads for you, Konstantin.")

A little further on we hear a woman's voice:

"Bitte, bete für Margarete's Seele." (same place: 158)
(Germ.: "Please, pray for Margarete's soul.")

The same voice continues:

"Bete für Margaretes Seele. Par Margaretes ligavaini." (same place: 160/1)
(Germ., Latv.: "Pray for Margarete's soul. For Margarete's fiancé.")

Another voice takes up:

"Par Margaretas māti.—Par Margaretas tēvu. Par radiem mūžībā." (same place)
(Latv.: "For Margarete's mother.—For Margarete's father. For the relatives in eternity.")
"Par viņas tēvu mūžībā." (same place)
(Latv.: "For her father in eternity.")

In a further recording we again hear a voice with similar text:

"Aizlūdzies par Margarētu." (28r: 320)
(Latv.: "Pray for Margarete.")

A different voice reports:

"Margarete in andern Tage wird in andern Stock. Wir ihr folgen." (same place: 443)
(German: "Margarete in another day will to different floor. We follow her.")

This sentence is less clear in meaning, but perhaps one may presume that Margarete is moving to another place.

Next day a woman's voice is heard:

"Konstantin, hier ist Margarete." (29g: 091)
(German: "Konstantin, here is Margarete.")

On 10th February 1966, at 1.45 in the morning, exactly one year after Margarete's passing, a recording was made which brought astonishing results. It was made through microphone.

To start with, a few hardly audible voices float past; then the experimenter calls: "Hallo, hallo, Margarete! This is the exact hour of your death a year ago."

A voice objects:

"Nevajag tā darīt." (30r: 140)
(Latv.: "One mustn't act like this.")
"Konstantin, Numero eins, vår Konstantin." (same place: 245)
(Swed., Germ.: "Konstantin, number one, our Konstantin.")
The experimenter: "Gott helfe meiner Margarete."
(Germ.: "God help my Margarete.")
A voice: "Wieso? Auf der Wiese." (same place: 247)
(German: "What for? On the lawn.")
"Du für mich bete, Du gläubig, Du Wilde." (same place: 257)
(German: "You pray for me, you believing. You wild one.")

A male voice explains:

"Margarete steht bei deinem Stuhl. Sie verzwist. Gib ihr tūlin Kuss!" (same place: 258)
(Germ., Latv.: "Margarete stands by your chair. She despairs. Give her kiss immediately!" The word "verzwist" seems to be a distortion of the German word "verzweifelt.")

The experimenter states that he wishes to establish contact with Margarete.

Voice: "Richtig, ich bin." (same place: 261)
(German: "That's right, I am.")

After a pause the voice adds:

"Hilft, hilft ... Tita på mej. Ja, Hilfe mir." (same place)
(Germ., Swed.: "Help, help ... look at me. Yes, help me.)

SPEECH-CONTENT OF RECORDINGS

After the experimenter's words: "I pray for you," a voice is heard:

"Kost . . . , Konstantin, auj, tu kājas!" (same place: 237)
(Latv.: "Kost . . . , Konstantin, put on shoes!")

Immediately following, a male voice:

"Meiten uzauga ārā." (same place)
(Latv.: "The girl grew up outside.")

After many voices just on the border of audibility, a remarkably clear one comes through:

"Guten Abend med dej. I wishy your bebi Wein." (same place: 293)
(Germ., Swed., Engl., Spanish: "Good evening to you. I wish to drink your wine.")—This voice is of highest sound-quality and can be heard by everyone.

A voice implores: "Mīli, mīli vinu—mīli vinu!"

(Latv.: "Love, love her—love her!)"

A woman's voice:

"Te stāvu nedel—nedelām. Palīdz nokārtot Jürgens . . . Sei gnädig." (same place: 312)
(Latv., Germ.: "Here I stand week in, week out. Help Jürgens . . . tidy. Be gracious.")

It is interesting to find that Margarete has kept a strong link with her last domicile:

"Uppsala, Margarete. Persona Grete. Säga, Margarete—zviedriete?" (37r: 325/30)
(Swed., Latv.: "Uppsala, Margarete. Person Grete. Say, is Margarete Swedish?")

It happens that a voice slanders Margarete, as for instance the following:

"Margarete ir Dirne." (36g: 162)
(Latv., Germ.: "Margarete is a prostitute.")

The experimenter comments during a recording on the importance of equanimity and harmony. A voice answers:

"Margarete vāras sen te, tu Raude." (38r: 032)
(Latv.: "Margarete raves long time here, you Raude.")

The negative voices often speak against Margarete. For instance:

"Strunta flicka!"
(Swed.: "Insignificant girl.")
"Margarete ir fiza.—Tu gribi Kosti."
(Latv.: "Margarete is flighty.—You want Kosti.")

When the experimenter starts to praise Margarete, a female voice is often heard to intervene, as, for example:

"Kostan, tig! Tu esi dums. Margaret." (39r: 648)
(Swed., Latv.: "Konstantin, be quiet! You are foolish. Margaret.")

Quite often an indication as to Margarete's condition is given:

"Margarete. Dej lugni. Es paliku hospitī." (40r: 094)
(Swed., Latv.: "Margarete. Calm yourself. I stayed in hospital.")

After the experimenter's words: "I greet you especially Margarete," a voice is heard to say:

"Nabags Latvis! Wir lieben dich, Kosti." (same place)
(Latv.: "Poor Latvian! We love you, Kosti.")

The experimenter states that Margarete is the most important person to him "over there". A voice answers:

"Kosta, klusāk runā. Dzird. Danke dir. Pats Petrautzki." (42g: 101)
(Latv., Germ.: "Kosta, speak softer. One hears. Thank you. Petrautzki herself.")

Statements of the experimenter are often corrected by Margarete's voice. For instance, as the experimenter talks about the earthly and the transcendental the second "I", a voice interjects:

"Konstantin, ersti nava. Te Petrautzki." (42g: 217)
(Germ., Latv.: "Konstantin, the first is not real. Here Petrautzki.")

Every now and then the experimenter's way of addressing the voices is rudely rejected. He says, for example: "My dear friends." A voice replies:

"Nava tev Freunde." (42g: 371)
(Latv., Germ.: "There are no friends for you.")

The voices continue:

"Jasā!"—"Keine Feunde."—"Margarete te."—"Margarete te, Kosta, Margarete te. Kostja, stāj, Margarete." (same place)
(Swed., Germ., Latv.: "Yes, so!"—"No friends."—"Here is Margarete."—"Here is Margarete, Kosta, here is Margarete. Kostja, stop, Margarete!")

The experimenter states that Margarete was the most sincerely loved human being. A voice retorts:

"Lūdzu, nemīl viņu." (same place: 380)
(Latv.: "Please do not love her.")

When the experimenter points out that Margarete meant a great deal to Zenta Maurina as well as to himself (Zenta Maurina is the experimenter's wife), the answer, in Latvian, is:

"Nerunā, tas nelīdz, beti!" (same place)
("Don't talk, that doesn't help, pray!")

Travelling around, the experimenter makes a recording in Wildbad, Germany. He addresses Margarete with the words: "Dear Margarete, Zenta is giving a lecture in Wildbad. Send her a greeting." A voice replies:

"Ko tu bādā! Lāga meitene, Konstantin, Uppsalā." (42g: 447)
(Latv.: "Why do you bother. The nice girl, Konstantin, in Uppsalā.")

As stated before, Margarete P. died in Uppsala; she was also buried there. The voice gives further hints:

"Te Petrautzkis, lečka på dir." (same place: 450)
(Latv., Russ., Swed., Germ.: "Here is Petrautzki, get yourself well.")
"Raudive, nespiego!" (same place)
(Latv.: "Raudive, don't spy!")

In the same recording the experimenter asks Margarete to help Zenta. A voice reacts:

"Gerne, Petrautzki. Te radars, Petrautzki. Konstantin, tu daudz runā. Margarete aizgāja par agri." (same place: 615/6)

(Germ., Latv.: "Gladly, Petrautzki. Here is radar, Petrautzki. Konstantin, you talk too much. Margarete went away too soon.")

The experimenter mentions that Marta (a name appearing often on tape) helps him a great deal. A voice objects:

"Niemand. Grete wohl, Kosti."
(German: "Nobody. Grete does, Kosti.")

The experimenter addresses Margarete and asks her how she is.

"Es atpūšos." (492 same place)
(Latv.: "I am recuperating.")

The experimenter wishes Margarete to assist him from the beyond.

"Tod nada." (44b: 050)
(Germ., Spanish: "Death is nothing.")

After the experimenter has "thanked" for the promise of help, the voice of a woman:

"Hole Sekt, Margarete." (same place)
(German: "Fetch champagne, Margarete.")

The experimenter presumes it was Margarete who gave the promise. A female voice answers:

"Tā noliki, seko!" (same place)
(Latv.: "This is how you have fixed it; follow!")

Experimenter: "Dear Margarete, I greet you!" A voice:

"Milzu darbs!" (44b: 109)
(Latv.: "A terrific deed!")

The experimenter asks Margarete how she is. Answer:

"Danke, Kosti. Raudi, parlez!" (same place: 649)
(Germ., French: "Thank you, Kosti, Raudi speak.")

Once again the experimenter addresses Margarete. In response:

"Pagaid, pagaid! Tu laupi man tas meitens." (same place: 671)
(Latv.: "Wait, wait! You rob me of the girl.")
"Kosta, tu drusku sapinies. Margarete, Kosti, tevi te ieredz." (44r: 117)

(Latv.: "Kosta, you are a little bit involved. Margarete, Kosti likes you.")

The experimenter asks after Margarete.

"Tā te sjunga." (44b: 862)
(Latv., Swed.: "She sings here.")
"Denke a Petrautzki." (same place: 865)
(German: "Think of Petrautzki.")

Again the experimenter enquires after Margarete.

"Vina tagad streiko." (44r: 028)
(Latv.: "Now she is on strike.")
"Petrautzkis. Uppsala, fricost, Kosti." (same place: 306)
("Fricost," Swedish: "Free meals.")

The experimenter talks to Margarete. Reply:

"Ich danka." (same place: 442)
(German: "I thank.")
"Sak Margarete." (same place: 844)
(Latv.: "Tell Margarete.")
"Žāl mums Margrite." (same place: 894)
(Latv.: "We feel sorry for Margarete.")
"Te Petrautzki, Kost." (45g: 037)
(Latv.: "Here Petrautzki, Kost.")
"Petrautzki dzīva. Var adit!" (45r: 037)
(Latv.: "Petrautzki lives. She can knit.")

These statements are taken from the new year's recording, 1967. Seven participants were present and all of them were most impressed by this voice. During the years spent with Zenta Maurina and myself, Margarete had celebrated the new year ten times with us. The mentioning of her knitting is significant and was probably given as proof of her identity: she used to knit whilst reading, whilst engaged in conversation, even on her sick-bed she went on knitting.

"Pateicaties! Petrautzka." (46g: 458)
(Latv.: "Give thanks! Petrautzka.")

The experimenter asks Margarete whether she really does exist and begs her to report to him.

"Te pieteicqs, te Petrautzkis." (46g: 635/7)
(Latv.: "Here reports, here is Petrautzkis.")
"Margarete te." (same place)

(Latv.: "Here is Margarete.")
"Koste, te Petrautzkis! Man tev' uzticēja." (46g: 651)
(Latv.: "Koste, here is Petrautzkis! One has asked me to look after you.")
"Margarete nāk."
"Konstantin, Margarete būs Spīdola."
"Es Spīdola."
"Konstantin, te tev grūti bez manis." (40r: 522/5)
(Latv.: "Margarete is coming."—"Konstantin, Margarete will be Spidola,"[1]—"I Spidola."—"Konstantin, it is difficult for you here without me.")

The experimenter addresses the friends in the beyond; in answer:

"Sie gul. Margarete ir augšā." (42r: 778)
(Germ., Latv.: "They are sleeping. Margarete is awake.")
"Es simtiem te, Petrautzkis." (46r: 657)
(Latv.: "I am here in hundreds, Petrautzkis.")
"Te Petrautzka. Vīns te tev patīk?" (46r: 678)
(Latv.: "Here is Petrautzka. Do you like the wine here?")
"Petrautzkis! Petrautzkis nezaga." (46r: 681)
(Latv.: "Petrautzka! Petrautzka did not steal.")

Friday, 10th February 1967 at 0.30 hours, two years after Margarete P's hour of passing, the experimenter made a recording and the first microphone-voice to be heard reported:

"Margarete var. Kostja, mierā! Tevi, Kosti, dzird." (Amg: 013)
(Latv.: "Margarete can. Kostja, keep calm! You, Kosti, can be heard.")

After switching over to radio the following voice became audible:

"Šitā badība! Tala du, Margarete." (same place: 060/2)
(Latv., Swed.: "This hunger! You talk, Margarete.")
"Hat sie žilka bei Kosti?" (same place: 063)
(Germ., Russ.: "Has she an artery with Kosti?")
"Mēs visu rītu veltijām vinai." (same place: 083)
(Latv.: "We have devoted the whole morning to her.")
"Te Margaretin. Wo Märsta?" (same place: 105)
(Latv., Germ.: "Here is little Margarete. Where is Märsta?")

See page 165.

Margarete P's last train journey was from Märsta to Uppsala.

"Tev ir tas numers. Tala, Raudiv!" (same place: 120)
(Latv., Swed.: "You have the number. Speak, Raudiv!")
A male voice:
"Manfreds Aire. Nu vi trio. Feins meitens. Pa raidu sakam." (same place: 120/1)
(Swed., Germ., Latv.: "Manfred Aire. Now we are three. A fine girl. We say it through transmitter.")—The Latvian word "raidu" is a neologism of the verb "raidīt", to send (transmit).

The same recording registers the voices' continued conversation:

"Koste var darbus pabeigt."—"Våga niemand." (same place: 121)
(Latv., Swed., Germ.: "Koste can finish the works."—"Nobody dares.")
"Kosti, Sigtuna immer da. Margarete šeit. Mēs naktī grecoli." (same place: 243/56)
(Germ., Latv., Gr.: "Kosti, Sigtuna is always there. Margarete is here. At nights we are always fearful.")

"Kosti, te Margarete Petrautzki." (same place: 290)
(Latv.: "Kosti, here is Margarete Petrautzki.")

This interesting recording-session produced more than 250 voices. The greatest number of statements made concerned Margarete P.

On 15th March 1967, at 1 a.m., a recording was made and devoted to Margarete P. in particular. Amongst others, the following voices became audible;

"Te ilgas ir, Koste." (47g: 544)
(Latv.: "There is yearning here, Koste.")
"Morgens te stroga." (same place)
(Germ., Latv., Russ.: "In the morning it is strict here.")
"Te diena furchtbar, Koste! Bet abgeführt." (same place: 548)
(Latv., Germ.: "The day is terrible here, Kosti! But taken away.")
The meaning of the second half of the sentence is not clear.
"Jūs dzintara biste. Viens puteklis." (same place)
(Latv.: "They are an amber bust. A grain of dust.") The first half might also mean "*You* are an amber bust."
"Tā diena patika mums. A dienu pakal nepirka." (same place)
(Latv.: "We liked the day. But one could not buy back the day.")

"Kapēc tu aicini?" (same place: 549)
(Latv.: "Why do you invite?")
"Lai pestej. Te Grīegs. Tu te knapi lūdz. Nepagurt!" (same place)
(Latv.: "That he would redeem. Here is Grieg. You pray here little. Do not get tired!")
"Lettland ir pastirka. Petrautzkis hier." same place: 554)
(Germ., Latv., Russ.: "Latvia is shepherdess. Petrautzkis here.")
"Te ir Petrautzkis. Te latvietis, Kost. Koste, darbdiena." (same place: 558)
(Latv.: "Here is Petrautzkis. Here a Latvian, Kost. Koste, it is week-day.")

These direct statements, made by distinct individuals, give some very strange hints and messages.

On 25th March 1967 Zenta Maurina made an experimental recording. Voices obtained included the following:

"Te Petrautzkis." (48g: 352)
(Latv.: "Here is Petrautzki.")
"Mīļo Konstantin, mūsu pašu Uppsala." (same place)
(Latv.: "Dear Konstantin, our own Uppsala.")
"Te Petrautzka, te Uppsala." (same place)
(Latv.: "Here Petrautzka, here Uppsala.")
"Tumšs! På našem inte Uppsala." (same place: 354)
(Latv., Swed., Russ.: "Dark! According to our way Uppsala is not.")
"Koste, pat lietus nav." (same place)
(Latv.: "Koste, there is not even rain.")
"Hitlers, astāj Petrautzki!" (48g: 355)
(Latv.: "Hitler, leave Petrautzki!")
"Kosti, Latva!" (same place: 356)
(Latva is the old name for Latvia.)
"Stiprinasin veco salu!" (same place: 359)
(Latv.: "Let us strengthen the old island.")
"Redzam visu, pietiek." (same place: 366)
(Latv.: "We see everything, enough.")
"Te nāves nav. Nadzīva zeme." (same place: 366/7)
(Latv.: "There is no death here. The earth is dead.")
"Dzēvs guļu." (same place: 367)
(Latv.: "Living I sleep.")
"Te Deutsche pünktlich. Jakobs Stakis." (same place: 415)
(Germ., Latv.: "Here the German one is punctual. Jakobs Stakis.")

SPEECH-CONTENT OF RECORDINGS 57

Every now and then Margarete is referred to on tape as "the German".

"Te Petrautzki. Tev ir mašinīte. Nesastrīdies ar Latgali!" (lar: 158)
(Latv.: "Here is Petrautzki. You have the little machine. Do not get into a quarrel with Latgale.")
"Te Petrautzkis. Te Margaret."
"Richtig! As probindo." (47r: 079/102)
(Latv., Germ., Latg., Spanish: "Here is Petrautzkis. Here Margaret."—"Right! I connect you.")
"Koste, Petrautzkis liecinā." (47r: 567)
(Latv.: "Koste, Petrautzki is witness to it.")
"Smert, Kostja, richtig Begriff." (47r: 572)
(Russ., Germ.: "Death, Kostja, is a real concept.")

The experimenter asks where Margarete lives.

"Margarete te."
Male voice: "Mūsu nometne Bergogā." (47r: 638)
(Latv.: "Here is Margarete."—"Our camp is in Bergoga.")—
The name "Bergoga" is mentioned several times on the tape. For instance:
"Mēs te runājam no Bergogas." (46r: 571)
(Latv.: "We speak here about Bergoga.")

8. *Further close friends*

Kazimirs Luta—Julijs Rupais—Marta—Matilde—Dr. Oskar Loorits—Umberto Lohmann—Stykuts—Konstantin Čakste—Arvīds (Arvis) T.—Jānis Veinbergs—Grizāns.

Names of some of the experimenter's nearest friends appear again and again amongst voices manifesting on tape; they often produce voices of the highest quality as far as audibility and clarity are concerned. The most frequently recurring names have been dealt with individually, and in the following chapter other voices of friends, particularly remarkable for their clarity and speech-content, have been drawn together.

Kazimirs (Kazis) Luta (died in 1945) manifests very often. Ever since their school-days he and the experimenter had been close friends.

"Luta!" (36g: 283)
"Te tev Luta!" (40g: 311)
(Latv.: "Here you have Luta.")
"Kazimirs te." (40r: 218)
(Latv.: "Kazimirs is here.")
"Kosta, te jūṛa, te Luta." (42r: 785)
(Latv.: "Kosta, here is the sea, here is Luta.")
"Te Plaudis. Ļuta cīņā. Tālums ir."
(Latv.: "Here is Plaudis. Luta is in battle. The far-away exists.")
"Kostulīt, Osyuna mūsu. Luta te." (40r: 465)
(Latg.: "Kostulit, Osyuna is ours.")—Osyuna (Asūne) was the name of the place where we went to school.

The experimenter addresses K.L. in German: "Kasimir Luta, you are in the beyond. I greet you."

"Ich bin Lette, danke!" (42g: 344)
(Germ.: "I am Latvian, thank you!")
"Tu gribi Kazi? Zirgus paņem, Kosti! Kostja, verzeih!" (42g: 906)
(Latv., Germ.: "You want Kasi? Take the horses with you, Kosti! Kostja, forgive!")—K.L. had been a great lover of horses and had been a cavalryman.
"Luta tala, izponni!" (42r: 276)
(Swed., Russ.: "Luta speaks, think of me!")
"Luta skeptikis. Gertrudis helf. Doch Blumene. Luta, tev atpūst." (43g: 545)
(Latv., Germ.: "Luta is a sceptic. Gertrudis helps. A flower after all. Luta, you must recuperate.")
"Mūsu Luta pipo!" (43r: 195)
(Latv.: "Our Luta is smoking")—K.L. was a passionate smoker.
"Luta. Latgolā pusdīna." (43r: 451)
(Latg.: "Luta. It is lunch-time in Latgale.")—This recording was made on 25th September 1966, at 1 p.m.
"Tja Luta. Du god vän, Kosti."
"Lūdzu, saki."
"Raudiv zin."
"Dank, Konstantin."
"Kur Zenta?"
"Politik, smertja tja." (49g: 663)
(Latg., Swed., Latv., Germ., Russ.: "Here is Luta. You are a good friend, Kosti."—"Please, say it."—"Raudive knows it."—"Thank you, Konstantin."—"Where is Zenta?"—"Politics, here is death.")
"Te latvis. Kosti, latviski. Luta, sveiki." (49r: 400/2)

(Latv.: "Here is a Latvian. Kosti, speak Latvian. Luta, goodbye.")
At the end of the recording one hears:
"Bye, bye!" (49r: 403)

My teacher and friend *Julijs Rupais* (died 1946) also manifests frequently.

"Rupais." (43g: 154)
"Rupais te. Polski znat." (43r: 028)
(Latv., Polish, Russ.: "Here is Rupais. One has to understand Polish.")—Rupais spoke Polish, as well as Russian, fluently.
"Rupaine. Ko tu laĭd?—Pupilla." (44b: 177)
(Latv.: "Mrs. Rupais. What do you let out?—Pupilla.")
"Kosta, te Rupais!" (44r: 387)
(Latv.: "Kosta, here is Rupais.")
"Učastis Rupais te." (45g: 505)
(Russ., Latv.: "Rupais takes part in this.")
"Propusk! Rupais te." (45g: 435)
(Russ., Latv.: "Entry! Here is Rupais.")
"Te ir Rupais." (46g: 636)
(Latv.: "Here is Rupais.")

Marta. This name occurs often. As appears from the words spoken, the experimenter once knew "Marta"; but it took a whole year before she identified herself on tape.

"Te Marta Brennecke." (46g: 257)
(Latv.: "Here is Marta Brennecke.")
"Deine Marta." (23g: 055/6)
(Germ.: "Your Marta.")
A male voice affirms:
"Dann Krieg an!" (same place: 057)
(Germ.: "Then there was war.")
"Marta, hört, hört!" (25r: 200)
(Germ.: Marta, hear, hear!")
"Marta, pierūdi!" (39g: 494)
(Latv.: "Marta, adapt yourself to it.")

The experimenter thanks Marta for her answer and for all help given.

"Marta! Ak Kosti!" (42g: 603)
(Latv.: "Marta! oh Kosti!")

Once more the experimenter addresses himself to Marta.

"Ko tu gribi? Marta? Ekur Nadja. Hilda auch. Myusu Kostja." (42r: 338)
(Latv., Germ.: "What do you want? Marta? Look, there is Nadja. Hilda too. Our Kostja.")
"Marta, Marta." (42r: 438)
"Kostja, Marta!" (43g: 678)

Experimenter asks: "Marta, can you hear me?"

"På stol!"
(Swed.: "On the chair.")
"Marta te. Pakas pako tev." (44b: 726)
(Latv.: "Marta is here. She is packing the parcels for you.")
"Marta, tot ir flicka." (45g: 472)
(Germ., Latv., Swed.: "Marta, the girl is dead.")

Matilde was a good friend from my Riga days. She died in Riga, during World War II, from some internal disease.

"Matilde te." (42r: 358)
(Latv.: "Here is Matilde.")
"Matilde!" (same place: 367)
"Matilde taisa tiltu." (42r: 379)
(Latv.: "Matilde builds the bridge.")
"Matilde pašreiz skata pūri." (42r: 380)
(Latv.: "Matilde is just looking through the dowry.")

The experimenter asks after Matilde.

"Latvijā." (same place: 385)
(Latv.: "In Latvia.")
"Matilde ražo te." (43r: 908)
(Latv.: "Matilde works here.")
"Epochā—Matilde Pažags." (38g: 234)
(Latv.: "Epoch—Matilde Pažags)—(Matilde Pažags was her full name)
"Maizi dod, Matilde!" (46g: 339)
(Latv.: "Give bread, Matilde!")

The experimenter asks: "Who is Matilde?"

"Rikšu tā, galvenā palīdze." (47g: 350)
(Latv.: "She is in a hurry. The main helper.")

Soon afterwards a voice is heard:

"Matilde." (47g: 357)
"Matilda!" (48g: 493M)

"Lieber Kost, Matilde." (47r: 070)
(Germ.: "Dear Kost, Matilde.")
"Matilde ruft Martin." (75r: 661)
(Germ.: "Matilde calls Martin.")
"Matilde mizērā."
(Latv.: "Matilde is in misery.")

Dr. Oskar Loorits (died 1964), was a close friend of the experimenter when in exile, and in Uppsala both men had often discussed parapsychological problems. When Dr. Loorits was on his sick-bed, he gave an account of his experiences during unconsciousness. He remembered seeing his dead parents standing by his bed together with his brother and some friends. He was a well-known researcher into primitive religions and an exact scientist, and he therefore tried to explain these "visions" of his as "phenomena of the subconscious". Shortly before his death, however, he became quiet on the subject and used to say: "We shall see what happens to us human beings after death. Should I continue to exist in some form, I will give you a sign." Excepting Sonja L., no other dying person ever gave me such a promise.

After the very first contacts with the phenomenon of the voices, Oskar Loorits called:

"Konstantin, hier Loorits."
(Germ.: "Konstantin, here Loorits.")
"Te Loorits, te Loorits." (26g: 264)
(Latv.: "Here is Loorits, here is Loorits.")
"Kosti, man Loorits saka tā: Labdien! Es guļu te." (40r: 120)
(Latv.: "Kosti, Loorits tells me this: Good day! I sleep here.")

At a time when the experimenter was busy with other phenomena on tape, a voice warned:

"Nieko uznēmumu. Kosti, Loorits."
(Latv.: "That messes up the recording. Kosti, Loorits.")
"Loorits pienāks klāt." (45g: 454)
(Latv.: "Loorits will come to it.")
"Mans Kosti, te Loorits!" (44r: 433)
(Latv.: "My Kosti, here is Loorits!")
"Loorits aizvien gratis. Vāciete te." (46g: 519)
(Latv.: "Loorits always free. The German one is here.")
"Loorits ir Grännā."—"Raudive! Bist du Raudive?" (46g: 178)

(Latv., Germ.: "Loorits is in Gränna."—"Raudive! Are you Raudive?")
"Loorits zin Raudivai." (49r: 254)
(Latv.: "Loorits knows it for Raudive.")
"Loorits tev hjälpa!" (same place: 178)
(Latv., Swed.: "Loorits helps you.")

Umberto Lohmann, a German friend of the experimenter, had dedicated his whole life to parapsychological problems; during his life-time he had an absolutely clear vision of the "beyond". The experimenter used to argue with him about his concepts, pointing out that empirical evidence of an afterlife was still being sought in vain. U.L. promised to give evidence from "the other side", if possible, as soon as he was able to do so.

During one recording session the experimenter remarked that in all probability our souls continued to exist on some other plane of consciousness after death.

"Te Lohmanns." (43r: 634)
(Latv.: "Here Lohmann.")
"Mēs guļam." (same place: 635)
(Latv.: "We sleep.")
"Herr Lohmann . . ." (23g: 328)
(Germ.: "Mr. Lohmann . . .")
"Te Umberto ist (poet)." (39g: 310)
(Latv., Germ.: "Here is Umberto poet.")
"Lohmann viva!" (Hr: 355)
(Italian: "Lohmann lives.")

Stykuts was a schoolfriend of mine whom I remember only very vaguely. He appears often on tape:

"Te Stykuts. Noperies po ban!" (43g: 152)
(Latv., Russ.: "Here is Stykuts. Rub yourself down in the bathroom.")
"Stykuts piesakas. Grizāns ir nomiris." (43r: 491)
(Latv.: "Stykuts reports himself present. Grizāns has died.")
Grizāns too had been one of my schoolmates.
"Šeit vola. Te Stykuts." (44b: 699)
(Latv., Russ.: "Here is freedom. Here Stykuts.")
"Koste, Stykuts, Stykuts!" (49r: 485)
"Koste, ty? Stykuts te." (same place)
(Russ., Latv.: "Koste, You? Stykuts is here.")

Konstantin Čakste (Tuntān) died in 1944. Professor Čakste, an eminent lawyer, was one of my closest friends during my time in Paris and in Riga. He was known as "Tuntān". Arrested by the Gestapo, he perished in a concentration camp.

During one of the recording-sessions the experimenter expresses his hope that the friends in the "beyond" will help him.

"Te Professors Čakste." (20g: 378)
(Latv.: "Here is Professor Čakste.")

The experimenter asks his friend if he couldn't help him. In answer:

"Es nevaru." (20g: 787)
(Latv.: "I cannot.")
"Tuntāns tav paziņo: es Tunstinā." (39r: 448)
(Latv.: "Tuntān tells you: I am in Tunstina.")—"Tunstina" is a completely unknown name.

The experimenter asks who it is that helps him to build the bridge.

"Kosta, Tuntāns ir lobs." (44b: 267)
(Latg.: "Kosta, Tuntān is good.")
"Čakste!" (32g: 544)
"Čakste te." (40g: 491)
(Latv.: "Čakste is here.")
"Mūsu Čakste dort. Vilna tava. Izmēzi zemi. Nya Deutschland." (44r: 135)
(Latv., Germ., Swed.: "Our Čakste is there. Vilna is yours. Clean out the earth. The new Germany.")
"Lab wach! Tuntānu gestera pārvedi."
"Piekusi?"
"To tu taču manīji." (44r: 521)
(Germ., Latv.: "Keep good watch! Yesterday you fetched Tuntān here."—"Were you tired?"—"You must have noticed that.")
"Kosti, te Tuntāns." (44r: 837)
(Latv.: "Kosti, here is Tuntān.")
"Te Tuntāns schläft." (45g: 058)
(Latv., Germ.: "Here sleeps Tuntān.")
"Koste, Čaksti! Mēs Parizē." (47g: 047)
(Latv.: "Koste, ask Čakste. We are in Paris.")

The experimenter lived and studied for quite a time in Paris, with his friend Professor Čakste.

"Čakste! Jā, es Čakste. Čakste te." (47g: 329)
(Latv.: "Čakste! Yes, I am Čakste. Here is Čakste.")
"Čakste putj. Professor de nada." (48g: 282)
(Russ., Span.: "Čakste is the way. Professor of non-existence.")

After Professor Čakste had read Unamuno's book on Nada-philosophy (in the experimenter's translation) he had commented on this philosophy and had added: "I too am in reality a 'Professor of Nada'."

"Guten Abend. Čakste pieteic. Leib—geistiga Bewiesa." (49g: 482)
(Germ., Latv.: "Good evening. Čakste announces himself. The body is the evidence of the spirit.")
"Mūsu Tuntāns." (45g: 475)
(Latv.: "Our Tuntān.")
"Nastja tala!"
"Professor Čakste."
"Čakste iet filmā jau." (Amg: 168)
(Swed., Latv.: "Nastja, speak!"—"Professor Čakste."—"Čakste is already going into film.")

Professor Čakste's wife is called Nastja (short for Anastasia). As far as can be deduced from the recurrence of the word "filma" in recordings, it means "movement" in the language of the voice-phenomenon.

Arvids (Arvis) T. died in 1956, holding, as his wife later stated, a book by the experimenter in his hands; he left an unfinished letter to the experimenter.

"Arvids paties." (35g: 124)
(Latv.: "I really am Arvids.")
"Konstantin, Arvidu tu atceries?" (35r: 888)
(Latv.: "Konstantin, do you remember Arvids?")
"Arvis pētīs. Arvidu pētīja." (45g: 393)
(Latv.: "Arvis will explore. Arvid has been explored.")
"Gaid Arvi!"
"Arvis!"
"Ieteic Kosti."
"Kostin, tu Krafta." (46g: 252)
(Latv., Germ.: "Wait for Arvis!"—"Arvis!"—"Recommend Kosti!"—"Kostin, you are strength.")
"Arvi, kur īsi!" (46g: 262)
(Latv.: "Arvi, how short it is!")
"Pagaid tu! Te Arvis močniks." (46g: 356)

(Latv., Russ.: "You wait! Here is Arvis helper.")
"Arvis putjom." (46g: 610)
(Russ.: "Arvis on his way.")
"Arvid, kur tu sover?" (48r: 252)
(Latv., Swed.: "Arvid, where do you sleep?")
"Koste, te Arvis." (49r: 658)
(Latv.: "Koste, here is Arvis.")

Jānis Veinberg, who died in 1965, is one of the strangest appearances on tape so far recorded. The experimenter knew him well and had maintained contact with him over many years; after Veinberg's death this contact was renewed in an astonishingly intensive way.

During a microphone-recording on 22nd March 1966 the experimenter called on J.V.

"Negribu runāt." (35g: 796)
(Latv.: "I do not want to speak.")

The following conversation amongst several voices ensued:

"Vai atvedi Jāni?"
"Nu tu ragari!"
"Tja Kosti nav vairs tāli."
"Na, Jānis. Tu Jānis?"
"Ne da šutka."
"Nem domas!"
"Palaižu domas."
"Nevar bekot Veinbergs."
"Slinkis!"
"Jānis—ora pro nobis."
"Jāni gratulē. Meitas sirsnīgi mīli."
"Varēji man Jānīti iedod."
"Mēs drīkstej' gratuliere." (35g: 832-916)
(Latv., Swed., Russ., Germ., Latin: "Have you brought Jānis?"—"Well, tough boy!"—"Here Kosti is no longer far."—"Well, Jāni! Are you Jānis?"—"Joking apart!"—"Take the thoughts!"—"The thoughts I leave free."—"Veinberg cannot go to the devil."—"Idler!"—"Jānis—ora pro nobis [pray for us]." —"Congratulations, Jānis. Love the girls heartily."—"You could give me Jānis."—"We may congratulate.")

Hearing this fragment one has a distinct impression of the deceased man's personality, which is still rooted in earthly matters. Voices in a further fragment again characterise J.V's personality:

"Jānis! Konstantin, kaislība skaisti!"
"Vinš nedzird, nabadziņš."
"Konstantin, velns te!"
"Ko muld tu!"
"Šitis čangalis!"
"Raudive, te junda, kūp sakari!" (same place)
(Latv.: "Jānis! Konstantin, passion is beautiful."—"Poor thing, he can't hear!"—"Konstantin, here is the devil."—"What nonsense are you talking?"—"This Čangalis!" [derogatory name for a Latgalian.]—"Raudive, this is a roll-call, the connection is steaming.")

Another conversation-fragment reveals J.V's occupation after death:

"Hajo, Jānis!"
Female voice:
"Jānis joba par Gärtneri, sarūn."
"Provadi Jāni molā!"
"Jau molā!"
"Kosti, jetzt mani turi Uppsalā." (35r: 074)
(Swed., Latv., Germ., Latg.: "Hajo, Jānis!"—A female voice: "Jānis works as a gardener. He is getting used to it."—"Accompany Jānis to the side!"—"Already at side."—"Kosti, keep me now in Uppsala.")

A further voice explains:

"Te Jānis, noch müde." (same place)
(Latv., Germ.: "Here is Jānis, still tired.")

The experimenter addresses J.V.

"Raudive, wir hören."
"Mes pasūtinam Veinbergu."
"Wir hören Veinbergu."
"Hier direkt Veinberg."
"Palīgā, Konstantin! Palīdzēt tu vari no šejienes. Ella bra!" (35r: 525/8)
(Germ., Latv., Swed.: "Raudive, we hear."—"We asked for Veinberg."—"We hear Veinberg."—"Here Veinberg directly."—"Help, Konstantin, you can help us from here. Ella is good.")

At a different time the experimenter once again addresses himself to J.V.

"Nesatiku Veinbergu."
"Nesatiku Veinbergu. Nein, netic vēl. Netic vēl!" (35r: 804/9)
(Latv., Germ.: "I have not found Veinberg."—"No, [he] does not believe yet.—[He] does not yet believe.")

Again, Veinberg reports his presence:

> "Te Veinbergs, Raudive."
> "Lielāka nediena!"
> "Numuriert—viens—divi—letonīši pa šņūri." (35r: 860/2)
> (Latv.: "Here is Veinberg, Raudive!"—"The greatest annoyance!"—"Numbered—one—two—the Latvians on the line.")

In another recording a woman's voice begs:

> "Mīļais Kostīti, sakat Jānis Veinberg . . ."

A man's voice adds:

> "Nupat mana Brigita nomira." (36g: 176)
> (Latv.: "Dear Kostiti, tell Jānis Veinberg . . ."—male voice: "My Brigita has just died.")

Grizāns was a schoolmate of the experimenter and had been interested in parapsychological problems since his early youth.

> "Gul, Kosta, te Grizāns pa Ikšķili.—Mark Irdo." (47g: 186)
> (Latv.: "Sleep, Kostja, here is Grizāns in Üxküll.—Mark Irde.)
> "Kosti, paskaties! Te kvartu sit, te puiši!"
> "Es Stonu Mikels."
> "Gražuli ir te." (same place: 468)
> (Latv.: "Kosti, look! Here strikes the quarter [hour], here are lads!"—"I am Stonu Mikels"—"Here are the Gražuli.")

The brothers Gražuli had been close friends of the experimenter. The brothers had harboured Jews, had been discovered and arrested by the Gestapo and subsequently shot.

9. *Latvians, Latvia and Latgale*

Latgale (Latgola) is the experimenter's home-province. Latgalians and Lithuanians have clung tenaciously to Baltic traditions and languages. After the collapse of the Lithuanian Empire, Latgale came under Russian dominance; it was freed in 1918 and joined with the other provinces of Latvia.

The Latgalian language is used frequently in the voice-phenomenon, often in its most vernacular form and sometimes sprinkled with Russian. The following conversation-fragment has Latgale as its subject and apparently stems from "travelling" voice-entities:

> "Te Barinovci, aka!"
> "Te Lettgal, te krusti."
> "Latgola, Kosti! As, Kostu! Slinko tu?"
> "Neplāpā, Vinkentij! Te Tekle endlich."
> "Tja maldetta Latgale! Jōns, Jōns!" (42r: 337, 577, 684/95)
> (Latv., Latg., Germ.: "Here is Barinovci, the source!"—Barinovci is the experimenter's birth-place—"Here is Latgale, there are crosses here." Latgale was, in contrast to other Latvian provinces, a Roman Catholic area in which one could see many crosses at the roadside. "Latgale, Kosti! I, Kostu! Are you idling?"—"Don't natter, Vikentij! Here at last is Tekle." Vikentij was the name, in Russian form, of the experimenter's father, and Tekle the name of his deceased sister. "Here is that damned Latgale! Jōns, Jōns!")
> "Vi trau Latgoli!" (43r: 055)
> (Swed., Germ.: "We trust Latgale!")
> "Latgale, Cuiba." (44b: 136)
> "Šitis čangalis!" (same place)
> (Latv.: "This Tschangalis!")—derogatory term for a Latgalian.
> "Warte, Kost, tja Latgola!" (37r: 353)
> (Germ., Latg.: "Wait, Kost, here is Latgale!")
> "Latgale, Vojin lobi bojari!" (42g: 020)
> (Latg., Russ.: "Latgale. The warriors are good Bojars.")
> "Bojars" are members of the old Latgalian and Lithuanian aristocracy.

Judging by texts grouped under the heading "Latvia—Latvians", one may deduce that the voice-entities are grouped according to nationalities. The Latvian voices give us remarkable insight into this aspect, because of their special link with the experimenter.

> "Latviēsi te, ko tu noslēpi mūs?" (43r: 002)
> (Latv.: "Here are Latvians, what are you hiding from us?")
> "Stav Letti pūlī, koatu gribi?" (same place)
> (Latv., Germ.: "A great many Latvians are ranged around, what do you want?")
> "Latvis." (43r: 226)
> (Latv.: "Latvian.")

The experimenter addresses his Latvian friends. A voice asks:

> "Lempi, ko tev vajag?—Es jūs mīlu." (43r: 241)
> (Latv.: "Rascal, what do you need?—I love you all.")

The experimenter greets his Latvian friends, and a voice comments:

"Mīli mani, te dzimtene!" (43r: 604)
(Latv.: "Love me, here is the homeland.")

Fragment of a conversation:

"Te liels darbs. Dzileja."
"Te Brunners, te draugi sen."
"Dzileja korrigē."
"Apstāja tevi leṭiņi." (44b: 110)
(Latv.: "Here is a great deed. Dzileja.") Dzileja, a Latvian writer whom the experimenter knew slightly, died in 1966 in Stockholm. "Here is Brunners, for a long time there have been friends here." Brunners too had been an acquaintance of the experimenter and died in New Zealand. "Dzileja corrects."— "The Latvians have surrounded you.") The expression "Letiņi" is a little on the ironic side.
"Mūsu latvieši!"
"Kosta, te daudzi latvieši du Blinde(r)."
"Trotzkis nav lettisch." (44r: 313)
(Latv., Germ.: "Our Latvians!"—"Kosta, here are many Latvians, you blind one."—"Trotzki is not Latvian.")
"Viesi! Visi latvieši. Grüssi Uppsala." (44r: 442)
(Latv., Germ.: "Guests! All are Latvians. Greet Uppsala.")
"Kosti, latvis." (44r: 778)
(Latv.: "Kosti, a Latvian.")
"Tu tala pa latviski." (44r: 912)
(Swed., Latv.: "You speak Latvian.")

The experimenter says: "My friends . . ."

"Te latvieši tavi draugi!" (42g: 240)
(Latv.: "Here are Latvians, your friends.")
"Nabags, tu latvietis." (35r: 585)
(Latv.: "Poor thing, you are a Latvian.")
"Ko latvieši saka?" (35: 054)
(Latv.: "What do the Latvians say?")
"Latyschi piekļūst!" (45g: 651)
(Russ., Latv.: "The Latvians are approaching.")
"Labi. Latvieši viņam vertraut." (40g: 679)
(Latv., Germ.: "Good. The Latvians are familiar to him.")
"Maz' dzīvības, paliksim Indo-Moskviči!" (42r: 272)
(Latv.: "There are only few living ones, we shall remain Indo-Muscovites.") This sentence hints at the tragedy of the Latvian people, who had been absorbed by the "Muscovites".

10. *Writers and Artists*

Many writers who had been friends of the experimenter manifested on tape; but the phenomenon also produced names of long-dead writers whom the experimenter had never met.

(a) Latvian writers and poets:

The first of these voices was *Albert Sprūdžs*, a close friend of the experimenter, who was killed in a bombing-raid in 1944. The experimenter calls on him and a rhythmic voice answers:

"Pateicas Sprūdžs no sirds." (14r: 282)
(Latv.: "Sprūdžs thanks with all his heart!")

Other voices followed intermittently:

"Albert te stāv." (37r: 442)
(Latv.: "Here stands Albert.")
"Albert Sprūdžs te." (40g: 559)
(Latv.: "Here is Albert.")

Once again the experimenter addresses his friend.

"Golva! Golvas nav! Konstantin, Konstantin, esmu ar tevi vienmēr." (42g: 628)
(Latg., Latv.: "Head! No head! Konstantin, Konstantin, I am always with you.")

The statement "no head" may refer to the fact that A.S. had been blown to pieces by the bomb; this ghastly experience may have had emotional repercussions after death which A.S. had not been able to overcome as yet.

"Albert Sprūdžs, glabies ewigi du!" (Iar: 199)
(Latv., Germ.: "Albert Sprūdžs, save yourself for eternity!")
"Alberts te. L'homme nesteidz!" (48r: 143)
(Latv., French: "Albert is here. Man, don't make haste.")
"Albert! Hei, Kritiki! Tu te nevar drukaties!" (54r: 211)
(Latv.: "Albert! Hallo, critic! Here you can't print.")
"Es på venti Kosti."
(Latv., Swed.: "I am waiting for Kosti.")
"Kādreiz dzimtene tik mīl."
(Latv.: "Sometimes only the native country loves.")
"Kosti, kontakts tu!"
(Latv.: "Kosti, you are the contact!")
"Raudiv', Sprūdžs."

The second name to be called by the experimenter is that of *Jānis Akurāters* who died in 1937.

"Lauj mieru!" (20g: 681)
(Latv.: "Grant me my peace!")
"Labāk gulēt!" (same place: 706)
(Latv.: "Better sleep!")
"Miers!" (21g: 463)
(Latv.: "Quiet!")

The experimenter asks *Jānis Poruks* (died 1911): "What are you doing, Jānis Poruks?

"Ich denke." (20g: 463)
(Germ.: "I think.")

At another recording-session the experimenter asks: "You think. What are you thinking, dear poet?"

"Mūžību." (20g: 911)
(Latv.: "Of eternity.")

The experimenter states that he regards Poruk's poem "Near thy white, high window" as the best lyrical poem in Latvian language.

"Pateicos!" (20g: 348)
(Latv.: "I thank!")

During one recording, we hear the following sequence of phrases:

"Kā tu pāri tiki?"
"Poruku Jānis"
"Tava skaistule. Te tu mājās." (39r: 728)
(Latv.: "How did you come over?"—"Poruku Jānis."— "Your beautiful one. Here you are at home.")
"Esmu Poruks, dyrt!" (46r: 621)
(Latv., Swed.: "I am Poruks expensive!")
"Poruks vientulais!" (59r: 674)
(Latv.: "Poruks the solitary.")
"Vi koordinati." (s.pl.)
(Swed.: "We are co-ordinated.")

Kārlis Skalbe (died 1945) manifests often and very clearly; right from the start he indicates that he wants to help the experimenter.

The experimenter begs Skalbe to speak to him, if possible.

"Kon..."
A woman's voice interrupts:
"Nevari!"
A man's voice counters:
"Nem bomani!" (20g: 918)
(Latv.: "Kon..." Woman's voice: "You cannot!" Man's voice: "Take the toll-bar.")

At a subsequent recording-session the experimenter says: "Dear Skalbe, you were ready to help me."

"Jā, palīdzēšu manam draugam." (20r: 332)
(Latv.: "Yes, I will help my friend.")

The experimenter expresses a wish to hear his friends.

"Skalbe hört." (20g: 378)
(Germ.: "Skalbe hears.")
"Pomini, Skalbe te." (22r: 235)
(Russ., Latv.: "Think of me, here is Skalbe.")
"Tev tik Skalbe! Vän tātad tot." (40r: 313)
(Latv., Swed., Germ.: "For you only Skalbe! So the friend is dead.")
"As Skalbe." (40r: 330)
(Latv.: "I am Skalbe.")

The experimenter addresses his friend in the "beyond". In response a male voice:

"Piemini Skalbi. Vesna!"
"Wy pomni Skalbe." (39r: 506/8)
(Latv., Russ.: "Remember Skalbe. Spring!"—"You remember Skalbe.")

A very distinct voice:

"Bau! Autori raida. Tu nemirsi."
"Skalbe, tu skapi kārto?" (42g: 018/9)
(Germ., Latv.: "Build! The authors are sending. You will not die."—"Skalbe, are you tidying the cupboard?")
"Skalbe—mīli Latviju!" (46g: 550)
(Latv.: "Skalbe—love Latvia.")

After the experimenter had addressed Skalbe, a voice says:

"Konstantin nepietiek." (43g: 503)
(Latv.: "Konstantin, it is not enough.") This is probably a pointer to the restrictions imposed by our means of communication.

"Kosti, varu. Skalbe."
"Tici tu?" (46g: 552)
(Latv.: "Kosti, I can. Skalbe."—"Do you believe?")
"Skalbe, gulēsi!" (same place)
("Skalbe, will you sleep!")
"Achtung, Skalbe!" (44b: 655)
(Germ.: "Attention, Skalbe!")
"Te la guarde lepna. Piemin Skalbe!" (47g: 176)
(Latv., Spanish: "Here the guard is manifold. Remember Skalbe.")

The experimenter again addresses Skalbe and, amongst others, the following voices are heard:

"Tu te vivaci."
"Jürgensonu!"
"Te mirklis skaitas."
"Mēs Latvijai. Te māsiņas." (47g: 514/6)
(Latv., Ital.: "You will live here."—"Please, Jürgenson!"—"Here one counts the moment."—"We are for Latvia. Here are the little sisters.")

Response to the experimenter addressing Skalbe:

"To no nāves dzirdi." (54g: 246)
(Latv.: "You are hearing from the realm of the dead.")

Vilis Lācis, a well-known Soviet-Latvian author who died in 1965, appeared on tape before the experimenter had heard of his passing.

"Kosti, unser Wiedersehen. Vila Lācis dels. Lācis te." (33g: 568)
(Germ., Latv.: "Kosti, our meeting again. Vila Lācis' son. Lācis is here.")

We hear the following segment of a conversation:

"Es lūdzu rili."
"Kādu Vili?"
"Liedzēju Vili Lāci."
"Es gribu Vili."
"Ko tu plāpā! Guni, Konstantin!" (33g: 569/77)
(Latv.: "I beg Vilis."—"Which Vilis?"—"Vilis Lāci the negator."—"I want Vilis."—"What are you babbling! Light, Konstantin!")

"Es lupata, Kosti,—saproti?"
"Vilis Lācis patiesi." (Abht 1: 13, 14)
(Latv.: "I am a scoundrel, Kosti,—do you understand?"—"I am really Vilis Lācis.")

Jānis Veselis was a well-known Latvian writer and a friend of Zenta Maurina, although the experimenter had known him only briefly. He died in 1962. We hear a whole collection of statements either from him, or about him:

"Te Veselis—Zentai—tev! Raudive, Raudive, ko raksta tie? Veselis te." (39g: 074/9)
(Latv.: "Here is Veselis—for Zenta—you! Raudive, Raudive, what are you writing? Veselis is here.")
"Sdravstvuj, hallo, Herr Raudive! Herr Raudive, Vesel!"
(Russ., Germ.: "Good day, hallo, Mr. Raudive! Mr. Raudive, Vesel!")

A voice demands:

"Veseli gribu!" (39g: 570)
(Latv.: "I want Veselis!")

After the experimenter has addressed Veselis:

"Tas guļ!" (43g: 503)
(Latv.: "He sleeps.")
"Kostulīt, tu teiksi!" (49r: 256/7)
"Veselis spirit." (same place)
(First sentence Latv.: "Kostulit, you will say."—Second Latin: "Spirit of Veselis.")
"Veselis!" (35r: 138 and 44b: 575)
"Guļu, ko tu gribi?" (43r: 610)
(Latv.: "I sleep, what do you want?")

The experimenter did not know the famous *Latvian poet Rainis*, who died in 1929, but later he did make the acquaintance of Rainis' wife, Aspāzija, herself a poetess. We hear the following voices:

"Rainis te." (34r: 093)
(Latv.: "Here is Rainis.")
"Rainis pusdienoj mit." (35r: 658)
(Latv., Germ.: "Rainis takes part in eating lunch.")
"Rainis te under, Kosta. Vai tu redzi viņu? Kaudzīt, Konstantin." (38g: 843/7)
(Latv., Swed.: "Rainis is down here, Kosta. Do you see him? Kaudzīt, Konstantin.")
"Raini gaidījat?"
"Rainis forderá." (same place: 928)
(Latv., Germ.: "Have you waited for Rainis?"—"Rainis will promote.")

"Rainis. Visi gaišie! Lieber Kosta, te vidno." (49g: 419)
(Latv., Germ., Russ.: "Rainis. All the shining ones! Dear Kosta, here one sees.")
"Rainis dobratá." (49r: 167)
(Russ.: "Rainis is goodness.")
"Te Rainis! Gaidi, tu sābris." (55g: 296)
(Latv.: "Here is Rainis. Please wait, neighbour.")

Edvards Virza (died 1940) has manifested on tape quite often, though the experimenter hardly knew him.

"Kundziski Virzu piemin!" (35r: 108)
(Latv.: "Remember Virza in a grandiose manner.") This request is in tune with Virza's style of living: his poetry as well as his way of life had been "grandiose".
"Te Virza." (42r: 340 and 752)
(Latv.: "Here is Virza.")
"Virza runā. Te Raudive runā." (43g: 393/4)
(Latv.: "Virza speaks. Here speaks Raudive.")
"Virza pat te!" (42r: 422)
(Latv.: "Even Virza is here.")

The experimenter talks to Virza. In answer:

"Balts čigāns." (43g: 503)
(Latv.: "White gipsy.")
"Nemocies, Kosti. Tulko Virzu!" (43g: 535)
(Latv.: "Do not torture yourself, Kosti, Translate Virza!")
"Piemin tu Virzu." (43g: 640)
(Latv.: "Remember Virza.")
"Virza te, Kosta." (46g: 488)
"Virza, tu netiec! As tja stūrē. Kur te tas Kosts?"
(Latv., Latg.: "Virza is here, Kosta."—"Virza, you can't follow. I am steering here. Where is Kost?")
"Pūlaties, vecā galva! Virza te. Te Jerums vēl." (48g: 374)
(Latv.: "Make some effort, you old head! Here is Virza. Here is also Jerums.")
"Laila! Kosti, Virza!" (48r: 281)
"Koste, kāpēc tu vāciets? Es Virza."
"Koste, Virza!" (49r: 502)
(Latv.: "Koste, why are you a German? I am Virza."—"Koste, Virza.")
"Virzu tirda.—Wichtig!" (49r: 567)
(Latv., Germ.: "Virza is being stringently interrogated."—"Important!")

Jānis Grīns, another author (died 1966), had been ill

disposed towards the experimenter, whom he had not known personally.

"Te Grīns."
"Ir Grīns."
"Es Kosti pasūtu." (35r: 092/5)
(Latv.: "Here is Grīns."—"Grīns exists."—"I ask for Kosti.")
"Te listiga. Hallo, Jānis Grīns!" (35r: 104)
(Latv., Swed.: "Here are the cunning ones. Hallo, Jānis Grīns.")
"Koste, piedod, te Grīns. Koste, te Grīns, piedod. Latvieši!" (47g: 052)
(Latv.: "Koste, forgive, here is Grīns. Koste, here is Grīns, forgive. Latvians!")
"Hej, Raudive! Piedodi, Konstantin, te Grīns." (49r: 534)
(Swed., Latv.: "Hi, Raudive! Forgive, Konstantin, here is Grīns.")

Čaks (died 1950):

"Ko tu guli, Čak?" (39g: 044)
(Latv.: "What are you sleeping for, Čak?")
"Pasaku, Čaks." (42r: 827)
(Latv.: "Fairy-tale, Čaks!")
"Mūsu Čaku!" (43g: 544, 44b: 768)
(Latv.: "Our Čaks!")

Vilis Cedriņš, a poet of repute (died 1946), was carried off by the Bolsheviks and perished in some slave-labour camp. The experimenter knew him well. The poet manifests on tape:

"Vilis Cedriņš—Mūsu Kosta, es pieminu Čupos." (43r: 248)
(Latv.: "Vilis Cedriņš.—Our Kosta, I remember Čupos.")
"Vilis Cedriņš gul." (U1: 101)
(Latv.: "Vilis Cedriņš sleeps.")
"Cedriņš tja." (49r: 601)
(Latg.: "Cedriņš is here.")

The poet *Veldre* disappeared without trace after the Russians had marched into Latvia in 1944. Nobody knows what happened to him, but it is presumed that he committed suicide. The experimenter knew him.

"Veldre ir. Raudiv, skål! Te nemirušie." (Amg: 170/3)
(Latv., Swed.: "Veldre exists. Raudiv, cheers! Here are the non-dead.")

SPEECH-CONTENT OF RECORDINGS

Zeitbolts was a Latvian author, not very well known, whom the experimenter had never met.

"Koste, te Zeitbolts." (47g: 046)
(Latv.: "Koste, here is Zeitbolts.")—In fact Zeitbolts had already manifested. (26g: 711)

The experimenter addresses his friend, the poet *Jānis Ziemelnieks*, who died in 1933.

"Te tavs Jānis Ziemelnieks."
"Te tev Raudive kalpo. Pažags tja." (49g: 257)
(Latv.: "Here is your Jāņis Ziemelnieks."—"Here Raudive serves you. Here is Pažags.")

Kvālis, also a poet, knew the experimenter. Kvālis died in a bombing raid on Berlin.

"Veseli dzimtenes draugi! Kvālis, Koste. Tja pa vidu geh!" (48g: 481)
(Latv., Germ.: "Greetings, friends from my homeland! Kvālis, Koste. Go here in the middle.")

A voice adds:

"Denke, Koste ir vel. Nauda viņam mysli." (48g: 482)
(Germ., Latv., Russ.: "Think, Koste still is. Thoughts are like money to him.")

Endzelins, well-known Latvian-Baltic philologist, manifests:

"Es Kokmuižē. Endzelins." (Iar: 347)
(Latv.: "I am in Kokmuižē. Endzelin.")
"Tikai tu, Endzelins." (Übs. 11g: 228)
(Latv.: "Only you, Endzelins.")

(b) Writers of other nations:

The first to manifest was *Ortega y Gasset*. The experimenter had heard his lectures on philosophy at Madrid University, had translated his works into Latvian and had dedicated to him an essay in his book *Der Chaos-Mensch und seine Überwindung* (*Chaosman and his Conquest*).

"Ortega. Wir sind, wir sind, wir sind!" (30r: 375)
(Germ.: "Ortega. We are, we are, we are!")
"Madri . . . , yo siento. Man prieks. Pensamiento, Ortega."—"Gigants."—"Buena cosa man." (46r: 678/9)

(Span., Latv.: "Madrid, I feel. I have joy. Thoughts, Ortega."
—"Giant."—"A good thing for me.")
"Ortega, din vän." (47g: 147)
(Swed.: "Ortega, your friend.")
"Ortega te." (48g: 365)
(Latv.: "Ortega is here.")
"Ortega! Partei wird Ortega!" (54g: 171)
(Germ.: "Ortega! Party becomes Ortega!")
"Entro jas muchas cuestionas." (54r: 559)
(Span.: "You will solve many questions.")

There are other occasions when the name of the philosopher is pronounced by himself, or mentioned by others. Unfortunately, these particular voices belong to the group most difficult to verify and cannot therefore be quoted here.

Garcia Lorca was killed in Malaga, during the Spanish civil war. He was a friend of the experimenter.

The experimenter talks to his friends in the "beyond" and asks them to help him as much as possible.

"Te Garcia Lorca sturē." (42g: 601)
(Latv.: "Here steers Garcia Lorca.")
"Garcia Lorca. Sei ruhig, Kostja. Vi bundna kopā." (45r: 356/7)
(Germ., Swed., Latv.: "Garcia Lorca. Be calm, Kostja. We are linked together.")
"Garcia Lorca putjom bystro." (Ülr: 143)
(Russ.: "Garcia Lorca on quick route.")
"Garcia Lorca—auf Wiedersprechen!" (47g: 099)
(Germ.: "Garcia Lorca—speak to you again!")
"Reparemos hablando. Achtunga—Garcia, danke!" (47g: 339)
(Span., Germ.: "We strengthen each other talking. Attention —Garcia, thank you!")
"Lorca naktī, šonakt, Raudive." (47g: 039)
(Latv.: "Lorca in the night, tonight, Raudive.")

Miguel de Unamuno (died 1936) was in close contact with the experimenter during the latter's student days in Spain. The experimenter has translated Unamuno's works into Latvian.

"Amico Unamuno! Invencibles, Konstantin! Wir sind." (43g: 396)
(Span., Germ.: "Friend Unamuno! You are invincible, Konstantin! We are.")

The experimenter says that he has written about Unamuno.

"Unamuno te. Nakti—Miguel." (ÜIr: 097)
(Latv.: "Here is Unamuno. At night—Miguel.")
"Amico Unamuno." (44b: 489)
(Span.: "Friend Unamuno.")
"Vai tu Cervantes?" (43r: 027)
(Latv.: "Are you Cervantes?")

L. N. Tolstoi (died 1910)

"Tolstoj, kum. Ty Kosta?" (Hg: 154)
(Russ.: "Tolstoi, godfather. Are you Kosta?")
"Te Tolstoj! Te Kosti slavē." (40r: 526)
(Latv.: "Here are the Tolstois. Kosti is praised here.")
"Tolstoj, Koste. Golvu tev nokers bēda." (47g: 199)
(Latv.: "Tolstoi, Koste. Sorrow will get hold of your head.")
"Raudive, te Tolstoj." (40g: 343)
(Latv.: "Raudive, here is Tolstoi.")
"Te Tolstoj. Te tik Ort. Willst du te palikt?" (Hr: 278)
(Latv., Germ.: "Here is Tolstoi. What a place this is. Do you want to stay here?")

The experimenter greets Leo Tolstoi and Dimitri Mereschkovsky in Russian.

"Kosta runā. Mēs mīlam tevi." (42g: 363)
(Latv.: "Kosta speaks. We love you.")
"Tolstoj spirits. Var tikai tencināt." (lar: 270/1)
(Latin, Latv.: "Tolstoi's spirit. One can only give thanks.")
"Tolstoj ist. Tolstojs maina profession." (48r: 250)
(Germ., Latv.: "Tolstoi is. Tolstoi changes profession.")
"Tāda flickes naktī."
A woman's voice calls:
"Tolstoi!" (49r: 336)
(Latv., Swed.: "Such a girl at night!"—"Tolstoi!")
"Tolstojs, Konstantin. Piši." (same place: 348)
(Russ.: "Tolstoi, Konstantin. Write!")
"Kosti, piši, Tolstoj!" (54r: 225)
(Russ.: "Kosti, write, Tolstoi!")

Fjodor Dostojevsky (died 1881)

"Dostojewski, gulat." (lar: 157)
(Latv.: "Dostojevsky, sleep.")
"Lieber Kostja, Dostojevsky muns admirals."
"Te velns katolis."
"Tas nav velns."
"Dostojewskijs, dela cieš." (49g: 428/30)

(Russ., Latg., Latv.: "Dear Kostja, Dostojevsky, my admiral."
—Here the Catholic is a devil."—"He is not a devil."—
"Dostojevsky, the cause suffers.")
"Kosti, Dostojevsky!" (56r: 301)

The experimenter asks to be advised if he should go to the USA to make speeches and carry through demonstrations, as medium A. had suggested. He asks for information about medium A. too.

The voice:
"Čepucha!—Tu malēsi piektdienā. Kompromisa. Koste, Dostojevskij." (57r: 300)
(Russ., Latv.: "Nonsense!—You shall paint on Friday. Do make compromises. Koste, Dostojevsky.")

There is relevance in what this voice says. Medium A. used to do her mediumistic painting on Fridays. We further hear the advice to make compromises, not to be too rigorous about the point of view of other people. And we are informed that it is Dostojevsky who speaks.

Fjodor Stepun (died 1965). The experimenter greets Fjodor Stepun and thanks him for his friendship.

"Lieber Raudi, Kosti, danke dir." (Hr: 358)
(Germ.: "Dear Raudi, Kosti, thank you.")

The experimenter adds: "Try to help your friend."

"Nevaru. Na, boman! Kostja, du börja nur." (42g: 545)
(Latv., Swed., Germ.: "I can't. Well, barrier! Kostja, you are only starting.")
"Nächste Liebe sage dir." (same place: 550)
(Germ.: "Love thy neighbour I tell you.")
"Kostja ty? Kosti, brauc pa Izi." (Üllr: 090)
(Russ., Latv.: "Kostja, you? Kosti, go on the Isar.")—The Isar is a river in Bavaria, Germany. Meaning of this sentence is obscure.

The experimenter addresses himself to Stepun.

"Raudive, tematu main." (43r: 372)
(Latv.: "Raudive, change the subject.")
"Grüsse Dichter, mans draugs!" (39r: 026)
(Germ., Latv.: "Greet the poet, my friend!")

The experimenter greets Stepun and asks how he is.

"Negrēko. Gut Prostite!" (42g: 671)
(Latv., Germ., Russ.: "Don't sin. Good. Forgive!")
"Bunin, Konstantin, pa mysli-mosti." (33g: 295/6)
(Russ., Latv.: "Bunin, Konstantin, over the bridge of thought.")

Maxim Gorki.

"Kur Kosti palika? Tja Gorki." (41g: 608)
(Latv.: "Where has Kosti got to? Here is Gorki.")
"Gorkij." (33g: 368)

The experimenter makes a recording in Darmstadt (Germany) and addresses the poet *Arnold Krieger*, with whom he had often been in company in that city.

"Tuja!" (38r: 328)
(Tuja is the name of the dead poet's wife.)

The experimenter greets A.K.

"Arnold—Tava slava, Arnold." (same place)
(Latv.: "Arnold—your glory, Arnold.")

The experimenter addresses himself to all who would like to meet him in his hotel-room.

"Arnold!" (38r: 696)
"Kriegers ir tja." (45r: 232)
(Latg.: "Krieger is here.")

Friedrich Nietzsche (died 1900). Nietzsche's name can be heard often, either by itself or in whole sentences.

"Tja Nietzsche." (40r: 174)
(Lattg.: "Here is Nietzsche.")

In the following fragment of a conversation Nietzsche emerges quite clearly:

"Kur ej?"
"Nietzsches bugatā."
"Te yudins."
"Stockholm, staru tiltu!"
"Nietzsche—he—he—he!"
"Natschow, Kosti."
"Nietzschi gribi, pfui!"
"Nietzsche selbst."
"Vi anwoh—naše Kranke." (41g: 735/9)

(Latv., Latg., Swed., Germ., Russ.: "Where are you going?"—"In Nietzsche's bugata." The word "bugata" might mean a small hut or a bungalow.—"There is water here."—"Stockholm, bridge of rays."—"Nietzsche, he, he, he!"—"Natschow, Kosti."—"You want Nietzsche, fie!"—"Nietzsche himself!"—"We have become accustomed to our sick ones.")

A recording made by Dr. Hans Naegeli also produces Nietzsche's name:

"Te furchtbar. Vai tev Nietzsche ieteicama būtne?"
"Eteriska būtne." (45g: 588)
(Germ., Latv.: "It is terrible here. Do you think Nietzsche is a commendable being?"—"An ethereal being.")
"Nietzsche, ko tu domā?" (42g: 178)
(Latv.: "Nietzsche, what are you thinking?")

The following names manifest sporadically:

"Natasha, Kontakt, te Goethe." (42g: 621)
(Latv.: "Natasha, contact, here Goethe.")

"Natasha" is a name that often appears in connection with "contact". One gains the impression that she is a helper in the linking-up process.

"Goethe! Liebe Helene." (54g: 189)
(Germ.: "Goethe! Dear Helene.")
"Piemin—te Goethe." (56r: 591)
(Latv.: "Remember—here is Goethe.")
"Lieber Goethe. Laiks allerdings.—Laiks—anti." (s.pl.)
(Germ., Latv.: "Dear Goethe. The time nevertheless.—The time—anti.")
"Glaube—te Goethe hilft." (s.pl.)
(Germ., Latv.: "Believe—there helps Goethe.")
"Kosti, turpina, te tavs Rilkis."
"Velu versuchen." (46g: 493)
(Latv., Germ.: "Kosti, continue, here is your Rilke."—"Too late trying.")
"Barlachs nav."
"Lässt suchen." (47g: 016)
(Latv., Germ.: "There is no Barlach."—"Being searched for.")
"Heidenstamm." (23r: 001)
"Te Dominique, hörst du?" (41g: 736)
(Latv., Germ.: "Here is Dominique, do you hear?")
"Wirklich Descartes. Kosti, Descartes!" (47g: 335)
(Germ.: "Really Descartes. Kosti, Descartes.")

11. Psychologists and Parapsychologists

Amongst this group the name of C. G. Jung is mentioned above all others.

> "Jung hatte te Lampa." (34r: 280)
> (Germ., Latv.: "Jung had the lamp here.")
> "Schwachis ist Unterbewusste." (35g: 731)—see *Independence and Power of Judgement*, page 115.
> (Germ.: "Weak is the subconscious.")
> "Mera viktigt, Jung." (29r: 048)
> (Swed.: "More important, Jung.")
> "Jung, bundi, te einsam." (42r: 292)
> (Swed., Latv., Germ.: "Jung is tied, he is lonely here.")

The experimenter addresses Jung.

> "Tod, Tod, Kosti!"
> (Germ.: "Death, death, Kosti!")
> "Bitte Raudive!"
> "Runāt radio?"
> "Kosti, du vārti!" (47g: 623/8)
> (Germ., Latv.: "Ask Raudive!"—"Talk via radio?"—"Kosti, you are the door!")

The experimenter once again talks to Jung and tells him amongst other things that his compatriots would be arriving the following day; what was he to tell them? Several voices are heard in answer:

> "Ara no Wehrpunkt!"
> "Jāpublicē."
> "Ein System zu schaffen, so dass auch Komponisti aufteile."
> "Rudens vel."
> "Te Jungs piestāj."
> "Tja valns Sapantino." (lar: 357/64)
> (Latv., Germ., Latg.: "Get out of the defensive position."—"One must publicise."—"Create a system, so that the composers too distribute it." This sentence is not quite clear.—"It is still autumn."—"Here Jung stops."—"Here is the devil Sapantino.")

These statements show that a new situation has been created in so far as voice-entities who have been addressed react by giving their names. The strange contents of some of the utterances also deserve special attention. For instance, in response to the experimenter's calling on C. G. Jung, the following male voice is heard:

"Jetzt Mode furchtbar eitel."
"Wir hier, zdrasdvuj!"
"Tu laikam pieder gurkim."
"Pentonā. Koste, genau."
"Koste, te Jungs. Telefonē, tu biedri, inbunden." (47g: 509/11)
(Germ., Russ., Latv., Swed.: "Now fashions [are] terribly vain."—"We are here, good day."—"You belong probably to the cucumbers[?]" The meaning of "cucumbers" seems obscure.—"In Pentona, Koste, exactly."—"Koste, here is Jung. Telephone with restraint, comrade.")

On 19th July 1967 the experimenter made a recording aimed at contacting Jung in particular.

"Gruezi." (49r: 503)
"Koste, liecini." (same place: 524)
(Swiss, Germ., Latv.: "How do you do."—"Koste, bear witness!")
"Te tev Jungs." (same place: 527)
(Latv.: "Here you have Jung.")
"Te Jungs, Jungs." (same place)
(Latv.: "Here is Jung, Jung.")
"Nabaga tilta!" (same place)
(Latv.: "The poor bridge.")[1]
"Te Jungs tev palīgā." (same place: 532)
(Latv.: "Here Jung comes to your aid.")
"Raudive, te Freud!" (39g: 066)
(Latv.: "Raudive, here is Freud!")
"Danke, Freud." (40g: 535)
(Germ.: "Thank you, Freud.")
"Par ilgu zīme—Paula Dāle. Dibini, Kosti!"
(Latv.: "Too long time is the sign—Paul Dāle. Investigate, Kosti!")
"Kosta maj—stop! Dāle te. Guli tu, Ko, saulē?" (44b: 644)
(Latv.: "Kosta is waving—stop! Here is Dāle. Are you sleeping, Ko, in the sun?")
"Dāle stock." (44r: 332)
(Swed.: "Dāle forms.")
"Piepeši Dāle!" (43r: 333)
(Latv.: "Suddenly Dāle.")

"Kostja, Kostja, Findlay, Pieter ich."

Arthur Findlay was one of the most renowned British parapsychologists. He conducted extensive experiments into the phenomenon of the "direct voice". His books on this and other subjects are widely read, two of the best-known ones

[1] See page 140.

being *On the Edge of the Etheric* and *Where Two Worlds Meet*. The medium John C. Sloan, famous in his day, assisted in many of Findlay's experiments.

"Bitte Führers Findlay!"
"Ich bin Findlay."
"Labi, labi skan. Kosti, bind!" (48g: 162)
(Germ., Latv.: "Please leader Findlay!"—"I am Findlay."—"Good, it sounds good. Kosti, bind [tie].")
"Ko(nstantin), gute Nacht! Findlay."
(Germ.: "Ko[nstantin], good night! Findlay.")

Carl A. Wickland, American psychologist and parapsychologist, became known through his book *Thirty Years Among the Dead* (1924). He has manifested several times in microphone and radio recordings.

In the course of one microphone recording the experimenter addresses Wickland and receives a voice in answer:

"Eins zeitig, Raudive." (40r: 320)
(Germ.: "One timely, Raudive.")

The experimenter says he has read the book *Thirty Years among the Dead*. The voice:

"Yes, Konstantin." (same place)

Later Wickland appears three times in a radio recording:

"Llave, petit Gruss bara."
"Akti, du Margel, Wickland." (39r: 615/6)
(French, Germ., Swed.: "Llave, only a small greeting."—"Look out, you slut, Wickland.")
"Bei madre, Wickland." (44b: 432)
(Germ., Span.: "With mother, Wickland.")

The experimenter addresses *Sir Oliver Lodge* and the following voices are heard:

"Ringa du, mēs gaidīsim."
"Te Kosta, Lodge."
"Raudive, te Jung."
"Padod Raudive, extra dich."
"Te gultu tikai."
"Lieber Kosti, Kosti, strīdi!" (47g: 137/46)
(Swed., Latv., Germ.: "Put your call through, we will wait."—"Here is Kosta, Lodge."—"Raudive, here is Jung."—"Give me

Raudive, particularly you."—"You only sleep here."—"Dear Kosti, Kosti, fight!")

Dr. Eiduks was Riga's first psychotherapist; he died in the process of an experiment into the effects of hunger.

"Eiduks!" (46r: 591)
"Vai par tevi strīdi?—"Eiduks, paguli." (47g: 619)
(Latv.: "Does one fight over you?"—"Eiduks, sleep a little.")

12. *Statesmen*

This section deals with men who once wielded political power. The experimenter did not call for them; all came unbidden, excepting John F. Kennedy whose presence one of the collaborators had vigorously demanded. (*See page* 211).

Some examples re *John F. Kennedy:*

"Te Kennedy." (22r: 270)
(Latv.: "Here is Kennedy.")
"Dabūs Kennedy." (44b: 228)
(Latv.: "One will get Kennedy.")
"Kennedy." (44r: 908)

Sir Winston Churchill. One of the voices announces:

"Winston Churchill." (34r: 140)

Several dictators appear on tape uninvited: their pronouncements indicate that they are caught in a spiritual impasse from which, even after death, they cannot escape. *Lenin*, for instance, talks like a patient in a lunatic asylum. His words revolve round the same circle of ideas that had exercised his mind during life on earth. He appears several times:

"Lenins."
"Lenins, njet peredači. Dranki tur."
"Mīts, Kostja. Begestri dali!"
"Rossija včora segodnja da."
"Na zemlju radio blattno." (43g: 431/3)
(Russ., Latv., Germ.: "Lenin."—"Lenin. There is no transmission. A mess there."—"Myth, Kostja. Continue to be impassioned."—"Russia is there yesterday and today."—"Radio on earth is scandalous.")
"Delostj. Lenin, gulat!" (44b: 351)
(Russ.: "Business. Lenin, walking!")

SPEECH-CONTENT OF RECORDINGS

An interesting sequence of voices that belong, regrettably, to audibility-group "C" but are nevertheless clear enough to be understood:

"Hallo, uz Rigu turies. Diktatur nesmādē. Lenins runā."
"Čudak! Lenins runaja uz pavēli."
"Tu gul uz pavēli?"
"Mūs Kosta, pavēl nu tu!"
"Raudive, befiehl!"
"Hörst du uns?"
"Netraucē Kostuli, atpūties!" (40g: 298/303)
(Latv., Russ., Germ.: "Hallo, keep to Riga. Do not decry dictatorship. Lenin speaks."—"Strange fellow! Lenin spoke on command."—"Do you sleep on command?"—"Our Kosta, you give command now!"—"Raudive, give command!"—"Do you hear us?"—"Do not disturb Kostuli, rest yourself.")
"Awake Lenin." (45r: 410)

Stalin too is heard:

"Nu Stalin!" (42r: 783)
"Stalin!" (42r: 779, 44r: 749)
"Stalins te. Furchtbar karsts. Furchtbar Eile."
"Ko tu teici?"
"Mēs pazinojam, ka Izricā ir Kosta." (42r: 572)
(Latv., Germ.: "Stalin is here. Terribly hot. Terrible hurry."—"What do you say?"—"We report that Kosta is in Izrica.")
"Stalin bei mir."
"Raudive vi ser."
"Stalins te." (42g: 184/5)
(Germ., Swed., Latv.: "Stalin is with me."—"We can see Raudive."—"Stalin is here.")
"Hej, stura man! Konstantin, Stalin!" (48g: 302)
(Swed.: "How do you do, big man! Konstantin, Stalin!")
"Hallo, Kontakt! Stalin damoj!" (Gg: 365)
(Germ., Russ.: "Hallo, contact! Stalin, going home!")

A few statements concern *Trotzki*:

"Tja studē Trotzkis."
"Naidu palaidi. Gogols."
"Trotzkis te, joka dēļ." (47g: 092)
(Latv.: "Here studies Trotzki."—"You have kindled hatred. Gogol."—"Trotzki is here, for a lark.")
"Pomiluj, te Trotzkis!"
"Pazinu bra."
"Tu pazini Kosti?"

"Komēdījai."
"Pagaid, Kostulīt!" (47r: 638)
(Russ., Latv., Swed.: "Have pity, here is Trotzki."—"Did you know Kosti?"—"I knew him well."—"For a comedy."—"Wait Kostulit.")

The German dictator *Adolf Hitler* manifests most frequently and one gains the impression that even in the transcendental dimension he now inhabits, he shows exactly the same traits that characterised him on earth: self-glorification (megalomania), persistence in pushing himself forward and a certain spiritual depravity—all sharply rejected by some of the other voice-entities. To illustrate the situation, two examples:

"Hitler Pack te." (49r: 464)
(Germ., Latv.: "Here Hitler is [of the] rabble.")
"Kosti, te Hitler baigs." (50r: 113)
(Latv.: "Kosti, here is Hitler uncanny.")

The voice-text examples that follow seem to make the point that existence after death is a direct reaping of what has been sown on earth. Seen from a higher ethical level one might say: our own deeds are our judges.

Utterances by Hitler or about him could fill a separate book. We have chosen only a few fragments, distinguished by their audibility and particularly strange or interesting speech-content.

(*a*) Direct statements by or about Hitler:

The most frequently repeated phrase is "Hitlers te." (31r: 644, 35g: 314, 40g: 466, 42g: 609, 911, 437, 44b: 431) In Latvian: "Hitler is here."

A voice addresses the experimenter with:

"Hitlers izziņo dich." (33g: 379)
(Latv., Germ.: "Hitler is calling you.")
"Lai pierāda, pielaiko toni Hitlera mōjam." (34r: 163)
(Latv.: "May he prove that he adjusts the tone to Hitler's house.")
"Sveicināts, pa priekšu tev vajag humor. Te Hitlers major. Pa-ehr Hitleru!" (35g: 314/5)
(Latv.: "Greetings, first you must have a sense of humour. Here is Major Hitler. Honour Hitler a little!")

A different voice interjects:

"Siekalu man nevajag." (same place)
(Latv.: "I need no bootlickers.")
"Hitlers tic. Te Kosti." (Gg: 474)
(Latv.: "Hitler believes. Here is Kosti.")
"Ondoms liels. Kosti Hitlers braucht." (41g: 254)
(Swed., Germ., Latv.: "The evil is great. Hitler needs Kosti.")
"Uppsala te tōl. Te Hitlers ilgojas pēc tevis." (41g: 256)
(Latv.: "Uppsala is far from here. Here Hitler longs for you.")

Hitler even presents himself as a helper:

"Hitlers te. Hitlers tev helfe." (42g: 609)
(Latv., Germ.: "Hitler is here. Hitler helps you.")
"Hitlera padoms: Kosta, heil Hitler!" (43r: 298)
(Latv., Germ.: "Hitler's advice: Kosta, heil Hitler!")
"Koste, Hitlers ir Vorteils, jūsu Vorteils." (47g: 020)
(Latv., Germ.: "Koste, Hitler is an advantage, your advantage.")
"Te Hitlers guļ." (45r: 337)
(Latv.: "Here Hitler sleeps.")

(b) Mentioning of warlike activities in connection with Hitler:

"Hitler spricht här: Sei beaktsam! Tjugo timmeklockel till tal."
A woman's voice:
"Wir haben viel Funken."
"Wir singen, wie heilig für uns Toten." (35r: 128/36)
(Germ., Swed.: "Hitler speaks here. Pay attention! Twenty hour-clock to the speech."—Woman's voice: "We have many sparks."—"We are singing, how holy for us dead.") The last sentence seems to indicate that for certain dead people Hitler is "holy".
"Hitlers meklē jūs. Hitlers meklē jūs." (28r: 661/2)
(Latv.: "Hitler is searching for you, Hitler is searching for you.")
"Bitte, nur Tiefdruck, unterdrücke!"
"För wem?"
"Für Hitler." (31g: 655)
(Germ., Swed.: "Please, only low pressure, suppress!"—"For whom?"—"For Hitler.")
"Smagi, smagi A-vadā."
"Deckungsfeuer! Manda Befehle! Hitler." (31r: 646/8)
(Latv., Germ., Ital.: "It is difficult, difficult in train A."—"Covering fire! Send orders! Hitler.")

"Hitler bara schickt Schäbiga." (47g: 007)
(Swed., Germ.: "Hitler sends only the shabby ones.")

(c) Utterances against Hitler, by people who had to suffer, or are still suffering, because of Hitler:

"Tautu spazma, Hitlers tesnatá." (45r: 653)
(Latv., Russ.: "Plague of nations, Hitler's narrowness.")

A voice instructs the experimenter:

"Anti-Hitler soll du verborgt, aber nicht zu viel." (31r: 181)
(Germ.: "Anti-Hitler you shall be in secret, but not too much.")
"Vilks, te Gestapo, vilks, vilks!" (38g: 681)
(Latv.: "Wolf, here is the Gestapo, Wolf, Wolf!") "Wolf" is probably short for the German name "Wolfgang".
"Te Pleskava. Noputas manas, te bara Hitlers." (42g: 906)
(Latv., Swed.: "Here is Pleskau. My groans, here is only Hitler.")

The following fragments of a conversation give quite an insight into the plane of consciousness that Hitler seems to inhabit:

"Hitlers."
"Uzgaidi, pats strōdō."
"Kur Petrautzki?"
"Tja nobody?"
"Vergi te."
"Gryuti stradāju."
"Gryuti gryust tja."
"Labprāt aizdedzu."
"Te tu strodnieks."
"Tu te flicka, sonst fliege. Hitlers te." (42g: 911, 42r: 437)
(Latv., Latg., Engl., Swed., Germ.: "Hitler."—"Wait, he is working personally."—"Where is Petrautzki?"—"Is nobody here?"—"Here are slaves."—"I am working hard."—"It is difficult to stamp [trample] here."—"[I] kindle willingly."—"Here you are a worker."—"You are a girl here, or you are thrown out.—Hitler is here.")
"Kosti, Hitler viens."
"Bra, Hitlers atlets."
"Mūsu bāda, mūsu Hitlers lobs skūtele." (43g: 321)
(Latv., Swed.: "Kosti, Hitler is alone."—"Good, Hitler is athlete."—"Our worry, our Hitler is a good animal-infesting louse.")
"Scherzi beiseite. Nem pātadz, Hitlers tavā vārā." (44b: 428)

(Germ., Latv.: "Joking apart. Take the whip, Hitler is in your power.")
"Hitlers te naudu vilto."
"Hitlers nav piemērs te." (45g: 015)
(Latv.: "Hitler makes counterfeit money here."—"Hitler is no example here.")
"Hitlers mūsu radio pārņem. Furchtbar!" (46g: 271)
(Latv., Germ.: "Hitler takes over our radio. Terrible!")

Benvenuto Mussolini manifests a few times only:

"Mīl duči!"
"Bez rotas tu?" (42r: 841/2)
(Latv.: "Love the Duce!"—"Are you without jewellery?" It could possibly also mean "without company" (military), as the Latvian word "rota" has two entirely different meanings.
"Vai Kosta tur? Meine Heimat: Norditalien." (42r: 907)
(Latv., Germ.: "Is Kosta there? My homeland: Northern Italy.")
"Līgotne duče pievelk klāt." (46g: 55-)
(Latv.: "Līgotne attracts the Duce.")

Karlis Ulmanis, former Latvian President, gives perhaps the most convincing impression of having kept his human personality intact. He points to the tragic fate that befell him on earth: he was arrested on Stalin's orders and taken to a Siberian slave-labour camp. Sometimes other voice-entities announce his presence; for instance: "Psycholog, Ulmani ved." (50r: 764) (Latv.: "Psychologist, here one leads Ulmanis.")

We hear further:

"Pats Ulmanis vēl."
"Te Ulmana nav."
"Latvis, Koste, piemin!" (47r: 307)
(Latv.: "Yet Ulmanis himself."—"There is no Ulmanis here."—"A Latvian, Koste, remember me!")
"Te Latvis. Mēs atstumtie, Ulmanis." (47g: 067/8)
(Latv.: "Here is a Latvian. We are the outcasts, Ulmanis.")
"Vai te Konstantins? Ulmanis." (49g: 635)
(Latv.: "Is Konstantin here? Ulmanis.")

13. *A multitude of voices*

Very often one can hear voices immediately after the

opening sentence. The experimenter says: "Dear friends..." and straightaway we hear a voice saying the same thing in two languages:

"Wir sind Tausende. Wir te tūkstōš." (44r: 388)
(Germ., first sentence, Latv. second sentence: "We are thousands.")

With the first radio-recordings came many well-known names, but also scores of voices belonging to entities that never had contact with the experimenter during their earthly lives. One gets the impression that the voice-entities are jostling each other to get to a "point of contact". (See *Bridge, Crossing and Customs-Points*, page 140).

"Konstantin, hier ist Beh." (22r: 056)
"Konstantin, tava Kragplätterin Olga." (22r: 059)
(First sentence Germ.: "Konstantin, here is Beh."—Second sentence Latv., and Germ.: "Konstantin, Olga who ironed your collars.")
"Konstantin, Hindenau, hör zu!" (22r: 095)
(Germ.: "Konstantin, Hindenau, listen!")
"Professor Maldon!" (22r: 070)—A Latvian theologian of repute, who had had a nodding acquaintance with the experimenter.

Professor H. Biezais, taking part in the experiment, addresses his one-time teacher, Professor Maldon. A voice reacts:

"Te Maldons!" (50g: 145)
(Latv.: "Here Maldon!")
"Herr Züricher." (22r: 092)—A Swiss painter and author whom the experimenter knew.
"Silva, Mädchen von Ghetto." (33g: 037)
(Germ.: "Silva, girl from the ghetto.")
"Pader noster, wieder Flieder, hier Pastor Diko." (25r: 760)
(Lat., Germ.: "Our father, lilac again, here Pastor Diko.")
"Frau Jusiki, Kosti, mans mīluli." (22r: 284)
(Germ., Latv.: "Mrs. Jusiki, Kosti, my dearest!")
"Irene doma."
"Pa Ireni prigral." (46g: 589)
(Russ.: "Irene is at home."—"With Irene you have lost.")
"Konstantin, *vis-à-vis* Pauline." (27g: 246)
"Tava Vera ir." (Hr: 361)—(Latv.: "Your Vera exists.")
Vera was a schoolmate of the experimenter.
"Erica, mēs esam te draussi." (42g: 643)

(Latv., Germ.: "Erica, we are outside here.")
"Nebeidzama! Na, tava Velta te. Mēs te winka." (49g: 068)
(Latv., Germ.: "Never-ending-one! Well, your Velta is here. We are waving here.")
"Es čechs, kuŗa senči bij latvieši." (38g: 672)
(Latv.: "I am a Czech, whose ancestors were Latvian.")

Long lost schoolmates appear:

"Krāslava, te tavs Dubra." (39r: 447)
(Latv.: "Kraslava, here is your Dubra.")—Dubra disappeared somewhere in Russia years ago. The experimenter had not seen him or heard from him since their schooldays.

Various Latvian personalities the experimenter had heard of, but had not known personally, manifest on tape:

"Cielēns" (26g: 128)
"Felix." (same place: 190)
(Felix Cielēns)
"Pulkvedis Weiss." (29r: 859)
(Latv.: "Colonel Weiss", a Latvian officer who was killed in World War II.)
"Te Niedra Jahrburgē." (43r: 063)
(Latv.: "Here is Niedra in Jahrburg.")
'Te Kuprins." (43r: 042)
"Es exil-biskopu mīlu." (25g: 385)
(Latv.: "I love the exiled Bishop.") This statement could refer to the exiled Latvian Bishop Urbšs, who died in Monserate, Spain, just about the time this particular recording was made (18th January 1966).

Mrs. Brunhild K., one of the participants at a recording-session, asks for her dead father, called Israel.

"Israel, diese Richtunga."
(Germ.: "Israel, in this direction.")
A female voice:
"Ich bin, Koste." (47g: 039)
(Germ.: "I am, Koste.")
"Māte, Izrael!" (47g: 178)
(Latv.: "Mother, Israel!")
"Brunhilde!" (47g: 545)
"Hildebrand Ilga."
"Wie furchtbar, diese Lettin!" (49g: 421)
(Germ.: "How terrible, this Latvian woman!")—"Ilga" is a typically Latvian name.

"Es junge Medici, Medici." (47g: 487)
(Latv., Germ.: "I am the young Medici, Medici.")
"Sveici Raudivi, Leonard." (44b: 633)
(Latv.: "Greet Raudive, Leonard.")

"Gerda" is mentioned often, but the experimenter knew no one of that name.

"Gerdu lūdzu."
"Gerda te." (a male voice)
"Gerda lūdz." (23g: 059/61)
(Latv.: "I ask for Gerda."—"Gerda is here."—"Gerda pleads.")
"Te Gerda." (39r: 857)
(Latv.: "Here is Gerda.")
"Gerda na putj." (40g: 460)
(Russ.: "Gerda on her way.")
"Mēs, nupat nomira Gerdi." (Hg: 251)
(Latv.: "We, Gerdi died just now.")
"Tava Gerda überall. Mīli Gerdu!" (43r: 260)
(Latv., Germ.: "Your Gerda everywhere. Love Gerda!") The word "überall" might also be a distortion of "über alles", which means "above all".

(II) STRENGTHENING CONTACTS

14. *Experiments in partnership*

Amongst the thousands of voices on tape those that address themselves directly to the experimenter—often giving their names—are the ones with the greatest value to the investigator. Contents and structure of utterances give a strong impression of independence. Many fragments seem to indicate that close relatives or friends seek contact from beyond the grave, and wish to be remembered by those remaining on earth:

"Vai tu liebe Kosti?"
"Asūne, kopīga skola."
"Dzirdi mūs?"
"Snabis, pudele te. Piemini!" (35r: 635/7)
(Latv., Germ.: "Do you love Kosti?"—"Asūne, school together." "Do you hear us?"—"Brandy, the bottle is here. Remember us.")

SPEECH-CONTENT OF RECORDINGS

The second school to which the experimenter went was in Asūne.

"Do you hear us?"—"Brandy, the bottle is here. Remember us.")
"Atceries tu mani no skolas?" (23r: 178)
(Latv.: "Do you remember me from our schooldays?")
"Konstantin, te Vladislavs, tu mani pazini Krāslavā." (Hg: 123)
(Latv.: "Konstantin, here is Ladislav, you knew me in Kraslava.")—The experimenter was at the grammar-school in Kraslava.
"Boris tja!"
"Raudive styrka."
"Tu pētī te?"
"Vōrslavs te. Pētī, uszvilp man!" (49g: 636)
(Latv., Swed.: "Here is Boris."—"Raudive is strength."—"Are you investigating here?"—"Here is Vōrslavs. Investigate, don't give a hoot about me!") Vōrslavs was a schoolmate of the experimenter.
"Radiniek, radiniek baci!—Radiniek!"
"Deine Schwester." (23r: 117/21)
(Latv., Ital., Germ.: "Relative, relative, kisses!—Relative!"—"Your sister.")
"Tovi brōli, Konstantin, tovi brōli!" (23r: 509)
(Latg.: "Your brothers, Konstantin, your brothers.")
"Kosti, te Vanka. Kosti, Kosti, Kosti paliec! Redzat man, redzat mani, djadja Kostja!" (38g: 669/72)
(Latv., Russ.: "Kosti, here is Vanka. Kosti, Kosti, Kosti stay! Do you see me, do you see me, Uncle Kostja!")
"Ko Koste saka?"
"Raudive!"
"Daugava tja būs."
"Tu latve. Koste, te Jadviga." (49r: 150)
(Latv.: "What does Koste say?"—"Raudive!"—"The Duna will be here!"—"Latvian woman. Koste, here is Jadviga.")—Jadviga was a schoolmate and later a good friend of the experimenter. She was married to Voldis D. who manifests often on tape.
"Kosti da!"—
"Te Energie twå."
"Vitalist."
"Ursula atliek." (49r: 303)
(Germ., Latv., Swed.: "Kosti here!"—"Here is Energy two."—"Vitalist."—"Ursula postpones.")
"Tala, Konstantin, tu sveša."
"Es redzu mūsu Kosti." (49r: 173)
(Swed., Latv.: "Speak, Konstantin, you are a stranger. [or: you are strange.]"—"I see our Kosti.")

"Koste, vai tu detektē?" (49g: 639)
(Latv.: "Koste, are you detecting?"—The word "detektē" is a neologism of the Latvian word for "detective".)
"Raudiv, te velti nauda. Raudive quar." (49g: 669)
(Latv., Swed.: "Raudiv, here money makes no sense. Raudive remains.")
"Laid, Kosti fint! Vestibi." (49r: 331)
(Latv., Swed.: "Let Kosti through, fine! Vestibi.")
"Konstantin, wir brauchen hören, wir brauchen dich." (23g: 052/4)
(Germ.: "Konstantin, we need to hear, we need you.")
"Turi, turi mani, Konstantin!"
"Tautiets mans!" (23g: 505/7)
(Latv.: "Hold me, hold me, Konstantin!"—"My compatriot.")
"Lūdz tu Kostuli!" (23g: 538)
(Latv.: "You ask Kostuli.")
"Mūsu Kosti treff!" (37r: 340)
(Latv., Germ.: "Meet our Kosti!")
"Wir zini, kur Ko. . . ." (23r: 486)
(Germ., Latv.: "We know where Ko. . . .")
"Kostja, Kostja, hörst du uns?" (25r: 177)
"Kosta, Kosta, hör du uns!" (26g: 039)
(Germ.: "Kostja, Kostja, can you hear us?"—"Kosta, Kosta, hear us!")
"Slava, Kosta dzird!" (34r: 126)
(Latv.: "Praise, Kosta hears!")

The voices also indicate that to them the experimenter is far away:

"Konstantin, tu mums esi tālu." (31g: 012)
(Latv.: "Konstantin, you are far from us.")

The plea for contact is always voiced more or less urgently:

"Raudive ir tja! Kosti, taisi tiltu!" (47g: 093)
(Latv.: "Raudive is here! Kosti, build the bridge!")[1]
Another voice adds:
"Mūsu Kosti vadi!"
"Brahms ir till Kostja." (same place: 099)
(Latv., Swed.: "Guide our Kosti!"—"Brahms is for Kostja.")
"Bez vakara Kosti."
"Sveiki Koste!"
"Lobs pazina."
"Tiltu!" (49g: 571)

[1] See page 140.

(Latv.: "Kosti is without evening."—"How do you do, Koste!"—"A good acquaintance."—"The bridge, please!")
A distinct microphone voice:
"Sveicināts esi! Te Kosti will." (47r: 666)
(Latv., Germ.: "Greetings. Here one looks for Kosti.")
"Konstantin Raudive!" (29g: 218)
"Hej Raudive, solo mej." (35g: 0201)
(Swed., Ital.: "Greetings, Raudive, I am alone.")
"Raudive, wo willst Du hin?" (45g: 458)
(Germ.: "Raudive, where do you want to go?")
"Du wolltest ja, jau pusnakts."
"Tas Kēninš."
"Wieviel Dank!"
"Edison pats."
"Wir Menschen such weit." (47r: 427)
(Germ., Latv.: "You wanted to, it is already midnight."—"This is Kenins" (a well-known Latvian poet).—"Many thanks!"—"Edison himself."—"We are looking all over the place for human beings.")
"Raudive, piedod!"
"Konstantin, Latvis!" (47r: 363)
(Latv.: "Raudive, forgive."—"Konstantin, a Latvian.")
"Guten Tag, Kosta Raudive! Raudiv', Guten Tag. Vī škērsa Raudive. Naša Kosta." (49g: 041/51)
(Germ., Swed., Latv., Russ.: "Good day, Kosta Raudive! Raudiv', good day. We are crossing Raudive. Our Kosta.")
"Kostja, tja Hugo. Tja grūti. Hitlers ir viltīgs. Te Hitlers. Nietzsche te." (47r: 479)
(Latv.: "Kostja, here is Hugo. It is difficult here. Hitler is cunning. Here is Hitler. Nietzsche is here.")

The impression grows that the voice-entities react directly when addressed. The experimenter addresses, for instance, Sir Oliver Lodge. In answer:

"Oliver, Koste, Oliver!" (47r: 301)

After the experimenter had addressed Garcia Lorca, the following sequence of phrases is heard:

"Danke, tu Koste!"
"Smerti tev vajdzēj, angel tu."
"Raudive tu putns."
"Nomira Oidipus. Viraka pietiek." (47r: 434/42/68)
(Germ., Latv., Russ.: "Thank you, Koste."—"You needed death, you angel."—"Raudive, you are a bird!"—"Oedipus died. Incense is enough.")

"Te Kosta, Loge." (47r: 173)
(Latv.: "Here, Kosta, Loge.")

There are many indications that the voice-entities are able to see the experimenter; that, in fact, they are present in the room. (See "We Are Here", page 111).

"Konstantin, es kaktā stāvu pie tevis." (23r: 084/5)
(Latv.: "Konstantin, I am standing in the corner near you.")
"Kosti, moment bei dir drin!" (42g: 721)
"Kostja tja. Vi zajedim. Lorca secret." (34r: 151)
(Germ., Latv., Russ., Swed.: "Kosti, this moment I'm in with you."—"Here is Kostja. We come in. Lorca's secret.")
"Da Kostja, du!"
"Lipoj tu!"
"I tūkstoš te redzam!" (42r: 660)
(Germ., Latv.: "There you are, Kostja!"—"You are [symbolically] wagging your tail."—"We are here in our thousands.")
"Darom, Koste."
"Saskija, prima Kosti!"
"Razalīte, redzu Kosti." (49g: 580)
(Russ., Latv.: "Free, Koste."—"Saskija, first class, Kosti."—"Razalite, I can see Kosta.")
"Koste, mīli Nambrenci." (49g: 592)
(Latv.: "Koste, love Nambrenci.")
"Raudive te." (49g: 585)
(Latv.: "Here is Raudive.")
"Kur tu te?"
"Pirti, Konstantin."
"Nākam sisti pie Kostes." (lar: 169/71)
(Latv.: "Where are you here?"—"Bathroom, Konstantin."—"We come beaten to Koste.")
"Wir hier sind. Kostja, kur tu?" (49g: 519/20)
(Germ., Latv.: "We are here. Kostja, where are you?")
"Pa Kosti radzu tja. Kozu Jānis." (49g: 570/1)
(Latv.: "I see Kosti here. Kozu Jānis.")

Sometimes access seems to be impossible:

"Nu ej, nu ej, Konstantinu paņem!"
"Iekšā netiek. Nosodītas par grēkiem." (33r: 082/3)
(Latv.: "Now go, now go, take Konstantin with you."—"One can't get in. They are punished for the sins.")
"Kosti, Fremde!"
"Gå borta." (38r: 725)
(Germ., Swed.: "Kosti, strangers!"—"Go away.")

The voices assure the experimenter of their love and friendship:

"Kosti, mans mīluli!" (22r: 284)
(Latv.: "Kosti, my dear!")
"Lieber Konstantin, ich liebe dich." (23g: 288)
"Konstantin, du Lieber, liebe du mich." (same place: 298)
(Germ.: "Dear Konstantin, I love you."—"Konstantin, dear one, love me.")
"Tava Brigita tevi mīl, Konstantin. Brigita tevi mīl.—Viņš mīl Brigitu." (23g: 319/22)
(Latv.: "Your Brigita loves you, Konstantin. Brigita loves you. He loves Brigita.")
"Es visu Konstantinu mīlu." (25g: 385)
(Latv.: "I love all of Konstantin.")
"Vän Kosti, tu mūsu draugs." (23r: 467)
(Swed., Latv.: "Friend Kosti, you are our friend.")
"Ty—jag, Freunde! Wo können ... stanim!" (33g: 359)
(Russ., Swed., Germ.: "You ... I, friends! Where can ... stay!")
"Wir beten für Raudive." (25g: 287)
(Germ.: "We pray for Raudive.")
"Kosta, vän, pietiek ar muziku." (27r: 448)
(Swed., Latv.: "Kosta, friend, it is sufficient with the music.")
"Dōrgs Kostule! Ecco, tu man dōrgs!—Ko dara Zenti? Ekkur Raudi." (36g: 191)
(Latg., Ital.: "Dear Kostule! Ecco, you are dear to me!—What is Zenta doing? There is Raudi.")
"Kosti, tev ir draugi." (45g: 660)
(Latv.: "Kosti, you have friends.")

We hear remarks about the experimenter, positive and negative judgements concerning him, and hints as to his physical and mental condition.

At one recording, in which Zenta Maurina, Gustav Inhoffen and his wife Ingeborg, a Miss H. and a Miss M.R. took part, Mrs. Inhoffen remarked that Zenta Maurina was contributing more than anyone else, whereupon a female voice was heard to say:

"Konstantin, unser Psychologe!" (18r: 419)
(Germ.: "Konstantin, our psychologist!")

An interesting dialogue ensued between a man's and a girl's voice:

"Meitens, viņš nav Schwed in schwedischer Sprache."
"Viņš nav Schwed?"
"Er einwanderte in Schweden." (23g: 323/7)
(Latvian, Germ.: "He is not Swede in Swedish language, my girl."—"Isn't he Swedish?"—"He emigrated to Sweden.")

"Vi känner Kosta." (31g: 437)
(Swed.: "We know Kosta.")
"Dzīvo, dieser Kosta."
"Raudive ir skeptikis."
"Atstōj, moj skeptikis!" (34g: 340)
(Latv., Germ., Russ.: "He lives, this Kosta."—"Raudive is a sceptic."—"Leave it, my sceptic!")
"Pero Lindström, piesargi Kosti, tagad nīkst pie radio." (35g: 197)
(Latv.: "Pero Lindström, take care of Kosti, he is now pining away at the radio.")
"Raudive nava bargs." (36r: 021)
(Latv.: "Raudive is not strict.")
"Es gibt richtig stroga. Warum, lieber Koste?" (47r: 417)
(Germ., Russ.: "There is real severity. Why, dear Koste?")
"Fein, sachlich, Koste da."
"Raudive tiesā."
"Kostulīt, tautas grib."
"Vi hoppas te Raudive." (49g: 289/99)
(Germ., Latv., Swed.: "Fine, factual, Koste is."—"Raudive judges."—"Kostulit, the nations want to."—"We are hoping, here is Raudive.")
"Raudive deutsche versteht." (47g: 285)
(Germ.: "Raudive understands German.")

The experimenter usually speaks German during these investigations. A voice asks:

"Kāpēc vāciets tu nu?" (42r: 651)
(Latv.: "Why are you now German?")
"Diktare Kosti."
"Kosti ir diktare."
"Saki nadi, liels žūpis." (44b: 249/51)
(Swed., Latv., Span.: "Poet Kosti."—"Kosti is a poet."—"Don't say anything, he is a great tippler.")
"Hej, hej! Perkoni nodrukā!" (46r: 684)
(Swed., Lat.: "Good day, good day! Let 'Perkons' be printed!")
This refers to a novel by the experimenter which was just due to be printed in New York when this recording took place.
"Kosti lobs katoļu Sohn's" (44b: 912)
(Latv., Germ.: "Kosti is a good Catholic son.")
"Dumš Kostis."
"Viņš ir īpatnējs." (44r: 407)
(Latv.: "Kostis is stupid."—"He is strange.")
"Ekis, Kosti padumš." (46g: 319)
(Latv.: "Ekis, Kosti is a little stupid.")
"Kosti, wieviel noch strunt!" (49g: 481)
(Germ., Swed.: "Koste, how much more silly stuff!")

SPEECH-CONTENT OF RECORDINGS 101

"Liels slinkulis!" (46g: 352)
(Latv.: "A big loafer!")
"Koste, tu traks." (49r: 327)
(Latv.: "Koste, you are mad.")
"Septiņi piki, tev napatikšanas!" (47g: 227)
(Latv.: "My word, you have worry!") The experimenter really did have worries at that time.

The voice-entities are concerned about the experimenter's concentration and his abstinence. They issue warnings:

"Kostulīt, tikai nepagurt!" (33r: 460)
(Latv.: "Kostulīt, above all don't get tired!")
"Tu nogurs esi. Vai tur Kosta redz?" (47r: 265)
(Latv.: "You are tired. If Kosta can see there?")
"Konstantin, nepērc grēku!" (25r: 253)
(Latv.: "Konstantin, don't buy sin!")
"Konstantin, streite nicht!" (27r: 419)
(Germ.: "Konstantin, don't quarrel.")
"Negausa! Kosta par daudz plītē, mūsu Kosta. Du Trinker!" (36g: 552/5)
(Latv., Germ.: "Insatiable! Kosta drinks much too much, our Kosta. You drunkard!")
"Ora!"
"Piestāj, Kosta! Dvēsele piestāj."
"Die Liebe—der künftig varge!"
"Slová. Kosti gul tai pašā guļā." (42r: 712, 735/6)
(Lat., Latv., Germ., Swed., Russ.: "Pray!"—"Stop, Kosta! The soul calls a halt."—"Love—the future she-wolf."—"The word. Kosti sleeps in the same bed.")
"Kosti, tu? Raudive, guli tu? Mutti."
"Gib mir einen Kuss!"
"Ko tu vilini?"
"Isti smirdē pēc skorosti."
"Kostulit, nakts miers!" (43g: 613)
(Latv., Germ., Russ.: "Kosti, you? Raudive, are you asleep? Mother."—"Give me a kiss."—"Why are you attracting?"—"It really stinks of speed."—"Kostulit, night's rest.")
"Kā tu skrīnī var tupēt!"
"Furchtbar tu dzer, muns Koste." (47g: 259/61)
(Latv., Latg.: "How can you hover in the cupboard!" Could also mean "in the shrine", the "chest" or the "cabinet". "You drink terribly, my Koste!")
"Kosti, Alozs pakal. Ceļa nav."
"Pievelc tu, padre te."
"Vai tu plītē?"
"Gryuti, Winter te." (47r: 267/75)
(Latv., Span., Germ.: "Kostja, Alozs is following you. There

is no way."—"Pull tight, here is father."—"Are you boozing?"—"Difficult, here is winter." Not clear whether the last word means the season, or whether it is "Winter"—the name of a person.)

We often hear congratulations at successes, or other statements that show interest in our investigation of the voice-phenomenon.

"Jagau. I wishy für Raudive Erfolg." (22r: 117)
(Engl., Germ.: "Jagau. I wish Raudive success.")
"Walters Rapa, Jānis Rapa: Konstantin, beglückwünsche. Wirklich ein stor pētījums. Nepagurt."
(Germ., Swed., Latv.: "Walter Rapa, Jānis Rapa: Konstantin, congratulations. Really a great research. Don't get tired!")
Walter and Jānis Rapa were the experimenter's Latvian publishers in Riga. They manifest several times.
"Koste, te ist Rapa."
"Koste, te ir Rapa." (Amg: 257)
(Latv., Germ.: "Koste, here is Rapa."—"Koste, here is Rapa.")
"Fischer Koste, te Rapa." (48g: 164)
(Germ., Latv.: "Fisherman Koste, here Rapa.")
"Te tev Rapa. Skaitīt lūgšanas." (47r: 117/8)
(Latv.: "Here you have Rapa. Go on praying.")
"Izdevējs ir Rapa. Projektiņš, projektiņš!" (49g: 103)
(Latv.: "Publisher is Rapa. Little project, little project!")
"Konstantin grūts darbs. Diezgan rūpju par Zentu. Sasniegsit praktiski ko vēlaties." (23g: 278/80)
(Latv.: "Konstantin has heavy work. Enough worries about Zenta. They will practically attain what they are wishing.")
"Man tu pateici patiesību." (23g: 474)
(Latv.: "To me you have told the truth.")
"Wir sind deinetwegen." (31g: 574)
(Germ.: "We are [here] because of you.")
"Tack, Raudive."
"Gratulation tev, Konci! Pekainis. Tev nav ko eilt, Konsta." (33r: 207)
(Swed., Engl., Latv., Germ.: "Thanks, Raudive!"—"Congratulations to you, Konci! Pekainis. You don't have to hurry, Konsta.")

One voice encourages the experimenter:

"Weg, Raudive, šlipsi! Mes cīnamies. Raudive, tu tōl!"
(Germ., Latv.: "Away, Raudive, with the tie! We are fighting. Raudive, you are far away!")
"Konstantin, mit kraft." (35g: 327)

(Germ.: Konstantin, with strength.")
"Apsveicam tev, Konstantin, durch Radio."
"Anna Strotford beglücka."
"Hammarskjöld, mit meinen Worten, prosit, Konstantin, du mutig!" (35r: 722/3)
(Latv., Germ.: "We greet you, Konstantin, through radio."—"Anna Strotford congratulates."—"Hammarskjöld, with my words, cheers, Konstantin, you courageous!")
"Kosti, atšķir labi svarīgāko!" (36r: 179)
(Latv.: "Kosti, distinguish well the most essential!")

Critical or sarcastic pronouncements appear more rarely:

"Liec smieklīgam palikt!"
"Pētniecība!"
"Vi pie-hjälp in Literatur-künsten."
"Kosti, neciti šim, latvis." (25g: 392/406)
(Latv., Swed., Germ.: "Let him become ridiculous."—"Research!"—"We will help in the literary art."—"Kosti, don't believe him, Latvian.")
"Konstantin žēlīgs mums."
"Mõnās vēl." (31g: 361/2)
(Latv.: "Konstantin is gracious towards us."—"Still deceives.")
"Raudive, vai tu beigsis." (46g: 380)
(Latv.: "Raudive, are you going to stop?") This voice was heard at the end of a recording.
"Vi går nu hemma, son."
"Vi alla lengti in hemma."
"Wir hörten dich, lieber Konstantin." (23r: 467/70)
(Swed., Germ.: "We are going home now, son."—"We are all longing to be home."—"We heard you, dear Konstantin.")

The voice-entities are equally concerned with the experimenter's environment:

"Salūzusi Zenta, Raudive." (47r: 267)
(Latv.: "Zenta has broken down, Raudive.") This statement refers to the fact that Zenta Maurina was feeling ill at the time the recording was being made.
"Wo willst du hin? Tu mīl Kosti. Zenta, kehr um! Te Māsi. Roberts sjukhuseta." (47r: 6705)
(Germ., Latv., Swed.: "Where do you want to go? You love Kosti. Zenta, turn back! Here is Masi. Robert is in hospital.")

This strange sentence contains a hint from Zenta Maurina's sister Renate, called "Masi"; she seems to be indicating that Robert Maurinš, the father, continues to work at a hospital after his death. (See the experimental recording on pages 225 and 230).

As a further illustration of direct partnership between the voice-entities and the experimenter we add a few more excerpts from various recordings. The dialogue indicates immediate contact and shows the rudiments of a proper conversation between the voices and the experimenter. The latter tries at times to provoke a reaction by addressing himself to a particular person. He calls on Margarete P. and a voice answers:

"Petruschka!"
"Margarete Petrautzka!" (49r: 370)

The experimenter addresses Robert and Renate Mauriņš. A voice:

"Lyudzam mēs tevi. Mellis ir Stärke." (49r: 382)
(Latg., Germ.: "We beg of you. Mellis is strength.") Mrs. Mellis was at that time staying with Zenta Maurina.

On 21st April 1967, at 11.15 p.m., the experimenter makes a recording in order to contact his friend Eskil Wikberg, who died in Uppsala by committing suicide on 12th April 1967. After the friend has been addressed directly, the following voices are heard:

"Tack, mein Kost." (47r: 214)
(Swed., Germ.: "Thanks, my Kost.")

The experimenter asks his friend how he is.

"Kostja, velāk. Matilde ir tja." (same place: 225/8)
(Latv.: "Kostja, later. Matilde is here.") See also section: "Further Close Friends" on page 60, *Matilde*.

A man's voice:

"Kosti redzu. Ingen luft, Raudive." (same place: 228)
(Latv., Swed.: "I see Kosti. No air, Raudive.")
"Eskils ir müde." (same place: 231)
(Latv. Germ: "Eskil is tired.")

The friend talks about his condition:

"Ir citādāk. Mēs slimnīcā te. Pulkstens ir tja." (same place)
(Latv.: "It is different. We are in a hospital here. There is a clock here.")

"Te man nav Platz. Raidi tu! Wichtig furchtbar! Na kuge sind." (same place: 235)
(Latv., Germ.: "I have no room here! You transmit! Terribly important! We are on the ship.")

The experimenter addresses other friends and asks them to give some information about Eskil Wikberg.

"I latviete. Piedāvā—Kosti. Draugs pa kapiem." (same place: 240)
(Engl., Latv.: "I am a Latvian woman. I offer my [help] to Kosti. The friend is going [through] the cemetery.") The experimenter heard later that E.W. was buried on 22nd April.

On the day of the burial when the experimenter asks how Eskil Wikberg is, the following voices are heard:

"Tack dir." (same place: 275)
(Swed., Germ.: "Thank you.")
A female voice:
"Raudive dich will."
"Pietiks Hagerut!" (same place: 285)
(Germ., Latv.: "Raudive wants you."—"Enough Hagerut!")
Again a female voice:
"Tava Ješka. Noskait pāterus, Raudiv'! Koste, te dārzi." (same place: 295)
(Latv.: "Your Jeschka. Pray, Raudiv'! Koste, there are gardens here.")

On 19th May 1967 a voice reports:

"Kosti, te jauns zviedris." (49g: 249)
(Latv.: "Kosti, here is the young Swede.")

On 10th July 1967 the experimenter addresses Eskil Wikberg and a microphone-voice of good audibility answers:

"Kerstin, piedod!" (49r: 355)
(Latv.: "Kerstin, forgive.") Kerstin is the name of Eskil Wikberg's wife.
"Kur pērti! Eskils te pliks." (50g: 415)
(Latv.: "Heat the bathroom. Eskil is naked here.")

Whilst travelling, the experimenter made a recording in Schongau, a small German town, on 2nd June 1967, to find out whether the results were in any way dependent on time and space.

The experimenter tells the voice-entities at the beginning of the session that he is in Schongau and asks whether they can hear him. In answer:

> "Wir sind hier. Kostja, kur tu?" (45g: 519)
> (Germ., Latv.: "We are here. Kostja, where are you?")
> "Drīz, Mona, es nākšu." (same place: 529)
> (Latv.: "Soon, Mona, I will come.") See section "Mother" page 35.

Some interferences disturb the recording. Between interference-noises a voice is heard to say:

> "Jetzt deutlich!" (same place: 540)
> (German: "Now clear!")

The following voice shows that the communicators have found immediate contact with the experimenter:

> "Kosti, Kosti, Schongau." (same place: 542)
> "Pa Kosti radzu tja." (same place: 570)
> (Latg.: "I see Kosti here.")
> "Kozu Jānis. Sveiki, Koste! Lobs paziņa. Tiltu!" (same place: 571/3)
> (Latg.: "Kozu Janis. [Latgalian family-name] Good day, Koste. A good acquaintance. Please, the bridge!")
> "Aloša, sabotāža! Neguli tja! Radzu tja. Eku, kur Kostja?" (same place: 579/80)
> (Latg.: "Aljosha, sabotage! Don't sleep here. Look, where is Kostja?")

Further voices at this recording are largely aimed at the experimenter himself:

> "Saskia, prima, Koste."
> "Rozalīte, redzu Kosti." (same place: 580)
> (Second sentence Latv.: "Rosalite, I see Kosti.")

Friends that were poets put in an appearance:

> "Raudive te. Skalbe piepelnī. Trudno." (same place: 585)
> (Latv., Russ.: "Raudive is here. Skalbe makes additional earnings. It is difficult.")
> "Virza te." (same place: 590)
> (Latv.: "Here is Virza.")

Towards the end of the recording-session a voice is heard to say:

> "Papa, Kosta. Spiegi tja." (same place: 599)
> (Latv.: "Papa, Kosta. Here are spies.")

SPEECH-CONTENT OF RECORDINGS

On 7th July 1967, Mr. Ekkehard Sapper, a scientist (chemistry), made an experimental recording (011) aimed at contacting Miss Irene Justi, a close friend of his, who had died the previous year.

The recording was made through microphone and produced unusually clear voices:

"Nabadze te." (48r: 226)
(Latv.: "Here is the poor thing.")
"Raudive te." (same place: 227)
(Latv.: "Here is Raudive.")
"Alīza te." (same place: 229)
(Latv.: "Here is Alisa!")
The experimenter: "Now we will both concentrate. . . ." A voice:
"Irene Justi." (same place: 230)
Experimenter: ". . . on Irene Justi who was still with us but a year ago." Voice:
"Sergej." (same place: 230)
Experimenter to Mr. Sapper: "Have you something to ask?" Voice:
"Te labi. Irene." (same place: 233)
(Latv.: "It is good here. Irene.")
Mr. Sapper: "I think she can't hear us."
"Tici! Detstva!" (same place: 234)
(Latv., Russ.: "Believe! Childhood.")
The experimenter: "Nothing stands in the way. . . ."
"Ekkehard, du Materieller! Irene! Ko tu smēj! Maurina." (same place: 238)
(Germ., Latv.: "Ekkehard, you materialist! Irene! Why are you mocking? Maurina.") As a chemical science expert Mr. Sapper's views tend to be rather materialistic; he believes, for instance, that it will become possible to create a human being by a purely chemical process. Irene Justi had been a close friend of Zenta Maurina.

Radio Voices:

"Nakts gul paša, Konstantin." (48r: 281)
(Latv.: "The night itself is sleeping, Konstantin.")
"Kosti, pagaidi! Alfreds te dziedē." (same place: 284)
(Latv.: "Kosti, wait! Alfred is healing here.")
"Hej! Alfreds mūžam šeit, Kosti." (same place)
(Swed., Latv.: "Heh! Alfred is eternally here, Kosti.")
"Justi tja. Kosti tu?" (same place: 285)
(Latv.: "Justi is here. You, Kosti?")
"Mūsu Kosta! Ekkehard! Ekkehard!" (same place)
(Latv.: "Mūsu": Our.)

This experimental recording clearly shows an after-death relationship to the living: both Mr. Ekkehard Sapper and the experimenter are being directly addressed by their dead friends.

On 14th July 1967 the experimenter once again tests the partnership during a recording, and addresses himself exclusively to Margarete Petrautzki. The following microphone-voices answer:

> "Nabaga Margaret!"
> (Latv.: "Poor Margaret!")
> Experimenter: "I am talking to you, Margarete!"
> "Danke! Danke! Konstantin."
> (Germ.: "Thanks! Thanks! Konstantin.")
> Experimenter: "I hope you can hear me."
> "Koste radz! Genau!" (49r: 408/16)
> (Latg., Germ.: "One can see Koste. Exactly!)

Radio-Voices:

> "Koste, schäme dich!"
> "Tu te pliks, Koste."
> "Pliks esi tu." (49r: 417)
> (Germ., Latv.: "Koste, be ashamed of yourself."—"You are naked here, Koste."—"Naked you are.") The experimenter was, in fact, because of the heat in the recording-room, almost naked.
> "Raudive, Durst!"
> "Koste, Petrautzka te."
> "Margaret, Koste." (49r: 417/21)
> (Germ., Latv.: "Raudive, thirst!"—"Koste, Petrautzka here."
> —"Margarete, Koste.")

The next recording to demonstrate partnership was made on 16th July 1967.

The experimenter:

> "I shall soon have completed my book on the voice-phenomenon."
> In answer: "Koste, Rapa. Gaidi!" (49r: 458)
> (Latv.: "Koste, Rapa. Wait!") "Rapa" was the name of the experimenter's publisher in Riga.

The experimenter addresses Margarete Petrautzki, a voice:

> "Petrautzka." (49r: 459)

The experimenter addresses Tekle, his sister.

"Osyuna!" (same place) "Osyuna" is the Latgalian name for Asūne, the experimenter's birthplace.
"Latvi siti."
"Hitler—Pack te." (49r: 464)
(Latv., Germ.: "You beat the Latvian."—"Hitler is here—rabble!")

After the experimenter had addressed C. G. Jung, the following microphone-voices are heard:

"Koste, Koste!"
"Bitte, Jungs te." (49r: 466)
(Germ., Latv.: "Please, here is Jung.")
The experimenter asks: "Jung, can you help me?"
"Gulat, tu saņemsi gultā. (49r: 467)
(Latv.: "Sleep, you will receive in bed.")

Radio-Voices:

"As radzu."
"Slikti tu zin." (49r: 467)
(Latv.: "I can see."—"You know it badly.")
"Te ir Riga." (same place: 477)
(Latv.: "Here is Riga.")
"Raudi, tu plītē!" (same place)
(Latv.: "Raudi, you drink!")
"Paturi Dzilnej!"
"Tu traucē Kostuli." (49r: 469)
(Latv.: "Keep Dzilnej."—"You are disturbing Kostuli.")
"Silvers ty?"
"Niži på Rychner."
"Du flieh!"
"Redzu Kosti."
"Kostja!" (49r: 469)
(Russ., Swed., Germ., Latv.: "Are you Silvers?"—"Lower than Rychner."—"You flee!"—"I see Kosti."—"Kostja!")

The experimenter calls Leo Tolstoi. Two microphone-voices are heard:

"Ty Kosti?" (49r: 471)
(Russ.: "Are you Kosti?")
"Konstantin, te Čakste."
(Latv.: Konstantin, here is Čakste.") See also page 63.

The experimenter addresses Sir Oliver Lodge.

"Raudivi!" (49r: 477)
(Latv.: "Raudive please!" A microphone-voice.)

"Dervelē español!" (49g: 485)
(Latv., Span.: "Chatter in Spanish!")
"Tu Konstantin, te Pīpala rymde!" (same place)
(Latv., Swed.: "Konstantin, here Pīpala broke out!")
"Koste ty?"
"Ich bin hier." (same place)
(Russ., Germ.: "Koste, you?"—"I am here.")
"Koste ty?"
"Stykuts." (same place)
(Russ.: "Koste, you?"—"Stykuts". See page 62.)
"Konstantin, tala Myschkin." (same place)
(Swed.: "Konstantin, Myschkin speaking.") Myschkin was a Russian acquaintance of the experimenter. He had interested himself in parapsychology and had been a great admirer of the works of Sir Oliver Lodge.

The experimenter calls on Margarete.

"Margaret klaras." (49r: 486)
(Swed.: "Margarete manages.")

The experimenter calls his brother Aljosha.

"Kostja!"
"Raudivi!" (49r: 488)
(Latv.: "Raudive please!")
"Kosti, Vikentijs tic." (same place)
(Latv.: "Kosti, Vikentij believes.") Vikentij was the name of the experimenter's father. See also page 135.

Radio-Voices:

"Botschaft! Kaire, Luta." (49r: 489)
(Germ.: "Message! Kaire, Luta.") Kaire and Luta were schoolmates of the experimenter.
"Koste, spāku!" (49r: 490)
(Latg.: "Kosta, the strength!")

The experimenter addresses Eskil Wikberg and asks him: "How are you?"

"Bra!"
(Swed.: "Well.")
Experimenter: "I will give Kersten your greetings."
"Du schuldi!"
(Germ.: "You owe it.") The German word "schuldest" is here modified to "schuldi".

Recording 401 brings the voice of the experimenter's father:

"Koste, tu?—Papis tja.—Ko tu Koste tagad dari?—Kur tu tiki?—Cik tu maksā za quartier?"
(Latv., Russ.: "Koste, you?—Here is Papa.—What are you doing now, Koste?—Where have you got to?—What are you paying for your quarters?")
A voice comes in with:
"Akls!" (50g: 455/60)
(Latv.: "Blind!") This probably refers to the experimenter who cannot see the voice-entities.

Further experiments aimed at establishing partnership produced splendid results and showed many instances in which people who had been called upon answered, or responded by pointing to circumstances that were relevant to them.

15. *The Presence of the Voice Entities—*

"We are here—We see—We hear"

At the very first microphone-recordings voices could be heard to make remarks like:

"Darf ich Fenster offen?" (18r: 361)
(Germ.: "May I open window?") or:
"Ich bin hier." (same place: 362)
(Germ.: "I am here.")
"Wir hier ustabā. Katinku laid ōrā!" (34g: 335)
(Germ., Latg.: "We are here in the room. Leave Katinka outside!")
"Wir hier sind. Vi gästar." (33g: 149)
(Germ., Swed.: "We are here. We are guests.")
"Grüezi, wir te trakie." (23g: 668)
(Swiss-Germ., Latv.: "Good day, we are the mad ones here.")
"Hier sitzt din Benda." (36g: 557)
(Germ.: "Here sits your Benda.")

The voices not only realise that they themselves are present at a recording-session; they are equally aware of people taking part on our side and often indicate whether they approve of them or not. For instance, the experimenter tries to tell the voice-entities that Dr. Zenta Maurina and I.M. are taking part. A voice answers:

"Vi vet det." (42g: 895)
(Swed.: "We know that.") A second voice adds, referring to Dr. Zenta.
"Hon vitne." (same place)
(Swed.: "She is witness.")

Another time a psychologist was present who took a sceptical view of the phenomenon. A voice demanded:

"Dzen to veci, Konstantin!" (37r: 593)
(Latv.: "Chase the old man away, Konstantin!")

The experimenter remarks that the most important thing is to prove the existence of the voices.

"Tala facta, Konstantin." (42g: 079)
(Swed.: "Facts speak, Konstantin).

Every now and then voices report that they can hear what the experimenter is saying and sometimes they ask whether they can be understood by us. The experimenter starts, for example, by saying: "Greetings to you who have come amongst us", and immediately a voice is heard to say:

"Wir hörten." (20r: 810)
(Germ.: "We have heard.")
"Vai tu Konstantin mūs sadzirdi?" (22r: 346)
(Latv.: "Can you, Konstantin, hear us?")
"Kosti dzird." (40g: 545)
(Latv.: "One can hear Kosti.")
"Ich habe listen." (44b: 241)
(Germ., Engl.: "I have listened.")

Visibility is something the voices particularly tend to stress. In varied statements we are told that they can see the experimenter; on the other hand they express their regret that the experimenter seems to be "blind", meaning that he is unable to see them.

"'Kosti te redzu." (40r: 375)
(Latv.: "Here I can see Kosti.")
"Tevi redzu, gosse, tu guli." (same place: 432)
(Latv., Swed.: "I can see you, boy, you are sleeping.")
"Raudivi skatu, skatu Schiene." (same place: 435)
(Latv.: "I see Raudive, I see rail.")
"Meist ich sehe Kosti." (41g: 218)
("Most I see Kosti.")
"Sie sind augenseits." (23g: 024)

SPEECH-CONTENT OF RECORDINGS

(Germ.: "They are within our sight.") The word "augenseits" does not really exist in German; it is an interesting neologism and literally translated means "eyesides"—"on the side of our eyes".

"Varēja redzēt mūsu radinieku." (same place)
(Latv.: "One could see our relative.")

Sometimes the voices comment on what the experimenter wears:

"Sarkans pulovers viņam mugurā." (30g: 322)
(Latv.: "He has a red pullover on his back.")

Some voice-entities seem to need aid in order to see us:

"Ja, tusin! Hier diesig, för tusen. Atta, Zündholzen verwend! Wir sehen Kosti." (33g: 474/5)
(Swed., Germ.: "Oh bother it! It's misty here, bother it, Atta, use matches! We see Kosti.")
"Titta, Kosta, mūsu Kosti." (35g: 739)
(Swed., Latv.: "Look, Kosta, our Kosti.")
In answer:
"Ak, nerunā!" (same place: 740)
(Latv.: "Oh, don't speak!")
"Aklis! Kosta mūs neredz." (35g: 639/40)
(Latv.: "Blind! Kosta does not see us.")
"Kosti aklis!" (44b: 342)
(Latv.: "Kosti is blind!")
"Es Čaks, mūsu Kosti akls." (same place)
(Latv.: "I am Čaks, our Kosti is blind.")
"Tita, Kostulīt, la voz!" (Gg: 459)
(Swed., Span.: "Look, Kostulit, the voice!")
"Raudivi redz." (36g: 279)
(Latv.: "One can see Raudive.")
"Jag ser gratis dir." (36r: 561)
(Swed., Germ.: "I see you free of charge.")
"Tu Kosti neredz. Mes jau te." (38g: 499)
(Latv.: "You, Kosti, do not see. We are already here.")

At one time, when the experimenter was travelling, he made several recordings in hotel-rooms. One voice commented on this:

"Danke, Raudiv! Du keine Zuflucht!" (38g: 511)
(Germ.: "Thanks, Raudiv! No refuge for you.")
"Mēs tevi redzam." (same place: 856)
(Latv.: "We see you.")

"Māte, atlauts. Raudi radz, Dieva vārds!" (41g: 056)
(Latv.: "Mother, it is permitted. One can see Raudi, by God!")
"Ninitschka, Kosti vidim." (42g: 931)
(Russ.: "Ninitchka, we see Kosti.")
"Lubuške, te Kostuli redz." (42r: 827)
(Latv.: Lubuske, here one can see Kostuli.")
"Nausikaa Kostu redz." (44r: 166)
(Latv.: "Nausikaa can see Kosta.")
"Es redzu mūsu Kosti." (49r: 173)
(Latv.: "I see our Kosti.")

The following recording gives some characteristic statements regarding the actual presence of the voice-entities. It was made at the house of Mr. and Mrs. Strik-Strikfeld in Oberstaufen on the 24th May 1967 (Southern Germany).

"Es operēju. Tev vāgis. Madride būs sarkana." (49g: 321)
(Latv.: "I operate. You have a car. Madrid will turn red.")
"Uppsala! Vācieši te. Tu varētu gaidīt. Te Vortrags." (same place: 338)
(Latv., Germ.: "Uppsala! Here are Germans. You could wait. A lecture is taking place here.")
"Viesi, Dela!" (same place: 355)
(Latv.: "Guests, Dela!") The hostess's Christian name was Dela.
"Koste, Strik-Strikfeld. Latvijai baigi. Te tev ir Raudive, Strik-Strikfeld." (same place: 382)
(Latv.: "Koste, Strik-Strikfeld. It is uncanny for Latvia. Here you have Raudive, Strik-Strikfeld.") Mr. S. is a Baltic-German and very attached to his former homeland.
"Bildes nav. Raudive, tev par lobu. Raudive, raidi!" (same place: 391)
(Latv.: "There is no picture. Raudive, it is to your advantage. Raudive, transmit!")

16. *Their Independence and Power of Judgement*

Independence of judgement is a marked aspect of the voice-entities. Right from the beginning of the experiments, voices would be heard that tenaciously, and at times obstinately, set their opinions against those of the experimenter or other participants. On the other hand, there are words and sentences of agreement. Such assenting or dissenting statements often concern the background of the voice-phenomenon.

At one recording-session, Professor Hans Bender and Dr. Zenta Maurina try to explain the phenomenon in animistic terms and maintain that the unconscious projects the voices on to the tape. The experimenter takes the opposite point of view, and is of the opinion that his research would lose its true significance if the voices did not come from a different plane of being.

A woman's voice:

"Raudive, tā nav." (13g: 104)
(Latv.: "Raudive, it is not so.")

Another voice takes up this theme a little later:

"Švakis ist Unterbewusste." (35g: 731)
(Latv., Germ.: "Weak is the subconscious.")
"Permets, Bender prompt. Tyrrell." (30r: 055)
(French: "Permit, Bender is prompt. Tyrrell.") Tyrrell, one of the foremost British parapsychologists, was the experimenter's teacher.

Another voice radically pronounces a very different opinion:

"Bender sehr veraltet, Konstantin. Versuche andere Hilfe zu finden. Kann finden. Hades-Verein." (35r: 531)
(Germ.: "Bender very old-fashioned, Konstantin. Try to find other help. Can find. Hades-Association.")

The situation is thrashed out in greater detail:

"Te tev Benders."
"Nav ko labu gaidīt."
"Probierte."
"Bet laudis par viņu publicē."
"Ko varēs, to pakers, saproti mani."
"Man jāpriecajas."
"Lurbs! Bender grüssi!"
"Koda—Uppsala vīri tev." (35g: 385/8)
(Latv., Germ.: "Here you have Bender."—"Nothing good is to be expected."—"Tried."—"But men publicise him."—"He will attack whatever he can, understand me."—"I must rejoice." —"Blockhead! Greet Bender!"—"Coda—the men of Uppsala are for you.")

Scores of voices around Professor Bender are pressing for his co-operation:

"Bender sicher überlegt." (31g: 666)
"Si, Kostja, handle sehr vorsichtig." (31r: 080)
"Raudive, ņem Bender." (33g: 163)
(Germ., Span., Latv.: "Bender thoroughly thought out."—
"Yes, Kostja, act very carefully."—"Raudive, take Bender.")
"Raudive, Benderu mīli." (33g: 413)
(Latv.: "Raudive, love Bender.")
"Bender—vetate gote." (35g: 877)
(Swed.: "Bender—knowledgeable Goth.")

The experimenter asks the voice-entities at one recording for irrefutable proof:

"Kosti, ak Kosti, schenk skaisti, dati runā." (47r: 652)
(Latv., Germ.: "Kosti, oh Kosti, give generously, the data speaks for itself.")

There is assent and dissent amongst the voice-entities about the way in which the experimenter conducts his research. When the experimenter announces that he is switching to radio, a voice is heard to say:

"Tu lieki konstatē, dumji!" (44b: 260)
(Latv.: "You state this unnecessarily, stupid.")
"Inte doch." (same place)
(Swed., Germ.: "No, don't!")
"Dummes Zeug du rede." (43g: 250)
(Germ.: "Nonsense you are talking.")

The experimenter says he greets the unseen friends. A voice repeats several times:

"Unsinn!" (13g: 547)
(Germ.: "Nonsense!")
"Tu plāpis." (46g: 319, 385)
(Latv.: "You chatterbox.")
"Koste, plāpā." (Gg: 438)
(Latv.: "Koste, you chatter.") The three last expressions appear again and again in a variety of situations and at all opportunities, indicating rejection and opposition.

The experimenter mentions the "bridge" and says that it should be recognised as a fact.[1]

"Vēl par agri." (42g: 097)
(Latv.: "Still too early.")
"Nākotnes darbs." (44b: 495)
(Latv.: "The deed of the future.")

[1] See page 141.

"Vāji tu joba." (44r: 912)
(Latv., Swed.: "Weak you work.")
"Pabeidz šķietalu!" (36r: 558)
(Latv.: "Have done with the seemingly apparent.")
"Tu grūti saprot." (46r: 596)
(Latv.: "You find it difficult to understand.")
"Konstantin, Pēte da. Lobs sōkums." (44r: 757)
(Latg., Germ.: "Konstantin, Pete here. A good beginning.")

The experimenter says he expects help and advice from his friends.

"Richtig, Raudive." (40g: 238)
(Germ.: "That's right, Raudive.")
"Konstantin, du unabhängig." (40r: 276)
(Germ.: "Konstantin, you are independent.")

The experimenter complains that he finds it difficult to strike the right note in his approach.

"Atradi toni!" (44b: 488)
(Latv.: "You have struck the note.")
"Kosti, tā nur ir pētīts. Kosta, vari, ko tu dari." (45r: 113)
(Latv.: "Kosti, that's the way to research. Kosta, you are good at what you are doing.")

We hear demands to intensify research:

"Brāli šeit. Kosti, tu mūs ilgi pameti." (45r: 620)
(Latv.: "Here are brothers. Kosti, you have long abandoned us.")
"Kostja, bau!" (40g: 175)
(Germ.: "Kostja, build!")

The voice-entities express their wish that we should remember them.

"Hilfe, die uns minē." (45r: 514)
(Germ., Latv.: "Those that think of us help us.")
"Lyudzu Ikšķilīti piemin!" (45r: 532)
(Latg.: "Please, remember Ikskiliti!")

The tie between the experimenter and the voice-entities is briefly stated:

"Raudive, gut. Rubuls." (45r: 389)
"Vi bundna kopā." (45r: 357)
(Germ., Swed., Latv.: "Raudive, good. Rubuls."—"We are linked together.")

At a subsequent recording, when the radio-contact had been more or less successfully established, a male voice commented:

"Tagad mēs atrodamies uz pareiza ceļa darbā." (23r: 036/8)
(Latv.: "Now we are on the right road in this work.")

After a while the same voice advises:

"Mierā veikt savu pienākumu; tikai neaizimirst radara spēju veikuma atpalicību!" (same place: 039/42)
(Latv.: "Do one's duty quietly; but do not forget the inadequacy of radar-capabilities!")
A woman's voice adds:
"Apsveicu!" (same place: 043)
(Latv.: "I congratulate!")
"Richtig du benehmst, Konstantin." (30g: 341)
(Germ.: "You behave in the right way, Konstantin.")

Then again a critical voice:

"Kosti, tu slikti stūrē."
"Ko tu saki?"
"Kosti, dodi Uppsala!" (43g: 153)
(Latv.: "Kosti, you are steering badly."—"What are you saying?"—"Kosti, give Uppsala!")

The voices comment rather laconically on our ideas about death and the hereafter.

The very first voice the experimenter heard on 21st July 1965, when he had begun his own investigations, belongs to this context. He supposed that the entities who produced the voices were just as hampered by limited possibilities as we humans here on earth, and expressed this opinion by saying: "Even if your conditions are not perfect, you must nevertheless be with me." In answer he heard a voice:

"Pareizi tā būs!" (2g: 258)
(Latv.: "That is right.")

This particular expression of assent is now and then repeated. The experimenter says: "When we have clarity of ideas about the hereafter, then our view of this life too will be plainer and clearer to us than if we remained in uncertainty."

"Pareizi tā būs." (9r: 149)

At a recording with several participants, namely Dr. M. E. Bircher, Mrs. Martha Bircher, a psychologist, and Dr. Zenta Maurina, the experimenter commented that death was only a transition.

"Richtig!" (16g: 151)
(Germ.: "Right.")

Mr. and Mrs. Gustav Inhoffen, Dr. Zenta Maurina and the experimenter are present at another recording when Mr. Inhoffen says that if he is mentally alert, he can die in the way he wishes to die. A female voice promptly:

"Nein, kann er nicht." (9r: 194)
(Germ.: "No, he cannot.")

At times voices give their judgement on world affairs:

"Bolševiki atbrīvo falsch Freiheit!" (31g: 050)
(Latv., Germ.: "The Bolsheviks release freedom in the wrong way.")
"Tauta muti lai pamazgā." (35g: 369)
(Latv.: "Mankind should wash out its mouth.")
"Ar vilkiem vilks." (35r: 581)
(Latv.: "With the wolves wolf.")—Meaning "to howl with the wolves".
"Hunger trennen die Welti." (lar: 154)
(Germ.: "Hunger divides the world.")

17. *Their Encouragement, Help and Advice*

The motive of confidence can be traced right from the beginning; it appears with the very first microphone-recordings. The voice-entities encourage, soothe and comfort the experimenter.

At one recording the experimenter is talking to Zenta Maurina who remarks that he has already left several ideologies behind. A voice comes in with:

"Vertrauen!" (2r: 219)
(Germ.: "Confidence!") and again:
"Vertrauen!" (8g: 283)
"Kostulīt, usticies." (35g: 354)
(Latv.: "Kostulīt, have confidence.")

The word "faith" is used in many a context:

"Tic!" (22r: 480)
(Latv.: "Faith.") or "Belief".
"Tomēr tici!" (40r: 543)
(Latv.: "Nevertheless, believe!")

"Ticu tev." (43g: 341)
(Latv.: "I believe you.")
"Tici, Kosti, es palikšu." (same place)
(Latv.: "Believe, Kosti, I will stay.")

The voices defend the experimenter against his own doubts:

"Skeptikis—Zukunftsverderber!" (35g: 354)
(Latv., Germ.: "Scepticism—spoiler of the future!")
"Zweifeln kann. War müde. Cik auksts!" (44b: 580)
(Germ., Latv.: "Can doubt. Was tired. How cold!")

The experimenter expresses his worries regarding scientific proof:

"Ko tu te drukso! Pūt tu dirsā zinātniekiem. Richtige Aufgabe in dir." (30g: 338/40)
(Latv., Germ.: "Why are you confusing yourself here! To hell with the scientists. The right task is within you.")
"Konstantin, nešaubies!" (30g: 584)
(Latv.: "Konstantin, don't doubt.")
"Kosti desperti." (same place: 588)
(Romance language: "Kosti despairs.")
"Otdaché, då muss man irra." (30r: 417)
(Russ., Swed., Germ.: "Rest yourself, or you will make mistakes.")

The voices point out that the research has not yet achieved sufficient result to interest people:

"Neviens nedzird tavu balsi." (31g: 455)
(Latv.: "Nobody hears your voice.")
"Nav laužu, nav vērigu laužu." (31g: 675)
(Latv.: "There are no people, no attentive people.")

Inadequacies of the human sense of hearing are blamed for many difficulties:

"Nevar, Kosti, paklusas ausis." (45: 277)
(Latv.: "It won't work, Kosti, rather dull ears.")

The experimenter complains that there is confusion about the method of research and that some people have no confidence in his work.

"Schön vertrau!" (35r: 444)
(Germ.: "Do be confident!")

A question as to whether the voice-entities could not help in furthering the experimenter's research is answered:

"Vadi, ko tu prasi!"
"Raudiv, pabeidzis darbu, nobaida dīki." (35r: 418/23)
(Latv.: "Lead, why do you ask!"—"Raudiv, after completed work, you will stir up the pond.")

"Erlaube, Konstantin, die Entscheidung bei dir." (42g: 314)
(Germ.: "Permit, Konstantin, the decision [lies] with you.")

When the experimenter says he ought to have proof of the existence of these voice-entities we hear:

"Sorge du!" (40g: 326)
(Germ.: "You see to it!")

Further, in answer to the experimenter's wish that co-operation should be extended:

"Nevaram, brōli!" (40g: 328)
(Latv.: "We can't, brother!")

In the last phase of the microphone-recordings "Spidola" (see page 165) was often heard to give advice and consolation. The experimenter was a little worried about the radio-recordings.

"Neraizejies! Naraud!" (22g: 246)
(Latv.: "Don't fret! Don't cry!")

Every now and then words of comfort are spoken because of recordings that were failures, or because of some technical difficulties. A male voice, for instance, comments at the end of a recording on the many interfering noises audible on the tape:

"Unvermeidlich, denn ging nicht anders, die kleine Spidola..." (23g: 603)
(Germ.: "Unavoidable, there was no other possibility, little Spidola...")

A voice judges the preceding recording which was marred by music and other radio-interferences:

"Wir gestern missglückten. Abend lasse kommen Bubus, Kosta. Wir Verrückten." (23g: 673/3)
(Germ.: "We failed yesterday. Let evening come Bubus, Kosta. Like madmen.")

In the beginning, radio-recordings were so primitive that interference from noises became a veritable cacophony and it is probable that many voices tried in vain to make themselves heard. Towards the end of one of these recordings voices break through:

"Abi dīvi—pālikam bešā."
"Für heute genug. Auf Wiederschau-, auf Wiederhören."
"Doch die Uhr für morgens abend."
"Gestern wohl gemacht." (23g: 684/6)
(Latv., Germ.: "We two got nothing."—"Enough for today. See you,—hear you again."—"Nevertheless the clock for tomorrow evening."—"Yesterday well done.")

To foster confidence, the voices promise help:

"Jancis tev palīdz." (35g: 355)
(Latv.: "Jancis helps you.")

At first, the experimenter often called on "Lena", Friedrich Jürgenson's so-called assistant, and asked for her help. A female voice:

"Verrat!" (20r: 418)
(Germ.: "Treachery!")

The experimenter then says that in time he will find his own helpers. The same woman's voice:

"Mycket bra!" (same place: 422)
(Swed.: "Very good.")

A little later in this recording another female voice is heard:

"Spīdola tava palīdze." (same place: 428)
(Latv.: "Spidola your helper!")

Later still, more helping voices follow:

"Mēs Latvieši. Mēs dzirdējām, Konstantin." (same place: 903/10)
(Latv.: "We are Latvians. We heard, Konstantin.")

In a subsequent recording the experimenter thanks Spidola for her offer of help.

"Es nāku tev pālīgā, mans mīlais Konstantin." (C3r: 021/3)
(Latv.: "I come to your aid, my dear Konstantin.")
A male voice:
"Wir verteidigen gegen brutale Angriffe." (22r: 019)
"Dusi! Latvieši palīdz."
"Wir versuchen wie kann." (31g: 645/51)
(Germ., Latv.: "We defend against brutal attack."—"Rest, the Latvians are helping."—"We try, as we can.")

"Wir wollen dir helfen. Jetzt niederdrückt du bist." (31r: 283/5)
(Germ.: "We want to help you. Now you are suppressed.")
"Par jūsu darbību, Raudiv, pūlamies, Raudiv, pūlamies. Raudiv, mēs pūlamies." (33g: 544)
(Latv.: "For your efforts, Raudiv, we concern ourselves. Raudiv, we concern ourselves. Raudiv, we are concerned.")

The experimenter insists that help be given to him.

"Mēs tev palīdzam." (35r: 423)
(Latv.: "We help you.")
"Kosti, Latvieši tev palīdz." (35r: 446)
(Latv.: "Kosti, the Latvians help you.")
"Palīgi tavi, naciki."
"Mēs sekojam tev." (36g: 125, 345)
(Latv.: "Your helpers, Nazis."—"We follow you."—) There is more detail about the Nazis as "helpers" in the chapter "Technical Questions".
"Mēs gribam tev palīdzēt. Nataša." (42g: 150)
(Latv.: "We want to help you. Natasha.")

The experimenter asks for conscious help from the voice-entities.

"Ja, mit Freude, wir schätzen dich." (40r: 372)
(Germ.: "Yes, with pleasure, we appreciate you.")

When the experimenter explains that he is busy copying tapes of his voice-recording sessions, a voice is heard to say:

"Wir in Krozingen dir helfen." (43r: 137)
"Meine Mithilfe." (same place: 483)
(Germ.: "We in Krozingen help you."—"My co-operation.")

More rarely voices react negatively to pleas for help. For instance:

"Nevar, Konstantin." (Ü Ir: 080)
(Latv.: "One can't, Konstantin.")

The voices give advice ranging from the purely technical to matters concerning the experimenter's personal life. From the following examples one gets the impression that the voice-entities are actually present, ceaselessly follow the progress of our research and note errors and mistakes; but direct intervention on their part does not seem to be possible.

"Labāk, kad muzik raid." (23g: 134)
(Latv.: "It is better when music is being transmitted.")

The appropriate wavelength must be carefully tuned in and kept steady on the radio's dial.

"Turat vilni, brāli. Herrlich!" (23r: 486)
(Latv., Germ.: "Hold the wavelength, brother! Marvellous!")

Only a little bit of tape is left for recording, but the experimenter wants to make use of it. A woman's voice advises:

"Guten Morgen! Nem jaunu bandi, mīlais Konstantin!" (25r: 563)
(Germ., Latv.: "Good morning! Take a new tape, dear Konstantin.")

The experimenter fixes a new tape (No. 26), but does not switch over to radio. At the very beginning of this recording one can hear a female voice repeating sixteen times:

"Konstantin, vergesse . . ." (26g: 000/18)
(Germ.: "Konstantin, forgets . . .") and the same voice adding five times:
"Konstantin müde." (same place: 018/22)
(Germ.: "Konstantin tired.")
Male voice:
"Varbūt izklaidigs."
Female voice:
"Mein Konstantin, ich will dir helfen."
Male voice:
"Vielleicht ist er zerstreut."
Female voice:
"Vi hjälpa, vi hjälpa." (26g: 023/7)
(Latv., Germ., Swed.: "Perhaps he is absent-minded."—"My Konstantin, I want to help you."—"Perhaps he is absent-minded."—"We are helping, we are helping.")
"Konstantin, wechsle Ton!" (27r: 371)
(Germ.: "Konstantin, change sound.")
"Nevar tagad uzņemt. Ej atputini galvu!" (35g: 547/9)
(Latv.: "You can't record now. Go and rest your brain.")

The next statement seems to indicate that disturbing elements are threatening the recording:

"Triec weg raibo!" (31g: 674)
(Latv., Germ.: "Chase away the gaudy one!") The Latvian word "raibais" is a negative expression synonymous with "devil".

Voices advise publication of the research work:

"Kosti, dibini Kreis!" (36g: 102)
(Latv., Germ.: "Kosti, found a circle.")

"Uno konferenze(n) gran importancia—dod vino, gute Marke!" (Ü 11r: 114)
(Ital., Span., Latv., Germ.: "A conference of the greatest importance—give wine, good vintage!")
"Napiši!" (44b: 233)
(Russ.: "Write down.")
"Ja, bitte, denke nach." (42g: 726)
(Germ.: "Yes, please, think on it.")

The experimenter receives the advice to avoid quarrels:

"Kosti, lietiškāk, tev patīk tie strīdi." (40g: 296)
(Latv.: "Kosti, be more objective, you enjoy quarrels.")
"Nestrīdies! Tavi radi." (40r: 527)
(Latv.: "Don't quarrel! Your relatives.")
"Kosti, koncentrāciju!" (47g: 253)
(Latv.: "Kosti concentration.")
"Kosta Raudive, ty ekonomičaj jasyk!" (42r: 235/7)
(Russ.: "Kosta Raudive, moderate the language.")
"Iztikam. Lieber Kosti, kura dig!" (same place)
(Latv., Germ., Swed.: "We managed. Dear Kosti, cure yourself.") This advice is given by a woman's voice.
"Merka tågas!"
"Papucīt, latviski!" (Amg: 147)
(Swed., Latv.: "Remember trains!"—"Little Papa, speak Latvian.")
"Rītā, Kosti, divpadsmitos!" (45r: 550)
(Latv.: "Tomorrow, Kosti, at 12 o'clock.")
"Wir brauchen Foto, Koste. Gleiche Nacht." (same place: 555)
(Germ.: "We need photo, Koste. Same night.")
"Kosta, te parunā! Vai tu pa BBC?" (same place: 622)
(Latv.: "Kosta, speak here. Are you on BBC?")

The presence of the voice-entities and their awareness of what is happening is demonstrated by the following incident:

On 4th February 1966, Professor Hans Bender and his colleague, Dr. G. Rönicke, visited the experimenter. Together they examined the phenomenon of apparent alterations to the words of lyrics and carried out their investigation by listening to some Schubert Lieder. Their discussion centred mainly on this phenomenon, which can be examined by two different methods. Professor Bender was of the opinion that the "unconscious" of the listeners produced the alterations in otherwise known lyrics. The experimenter followed this interesting discussion for a time but then returned to his voice-phenomenon research.

A radio-recording that same evening produced these well defined voices:

"Galu gaidīt lietai!"
"Var skadet lietas darbam."
"Vēl gadu gaidīt!"
"Nedabū mani gaidīt!"
"Ko tu trako, Konstantin!"
"Neparliecinā profesoru Benderu! Neparliecināt vina kollegu ar Šubertu dziesmu tekstiem!"
"Jaņem uz savu kabatu! Vel pirmdieni vari izmantot."
"Tu vēl nevari gulēt, Konstantin. Liels pienākums—priekškaru pacelt. Nešaubies!"
"Priekškaru pacelt, pienākums tavs. Kosti, tavs pienākums pacelt aizkaru. Pacelt to sev! Paturi sev, paglabā to sev! Kosti, neparsteidzies! Neparsteidzies, neizdot savu tekstu!" (30g: 015/41)

(Latv.: "Await the end of the endeavour."—"It could harm the work for the cause."—"Wait another year!"—"Don't let me wait!"—"Why are you raging, Konstantin!"—"Don't convince Professor Bender! To convince his colleague with Schubert-Lieder texts will not succeed."—"Do it on your own account. You can still use Monday."—"You cannot sleep yet, Konstantin. A great responsibility—to lift the curtain. Do not doubt!"—"To lift the curtain is your duty. Kosti, your duty is to lift the curtain. Keep it to yourself! Keep it yourself, keep it for yourself. Kosti, don't rush! Don't rush, don't give up your text!")

Sometimes voices try to dissuade one from taking a certain course. They seem to know what is going to happen. Two instances here:

In the first the experimenter intended to visit a scientist to discuss the voice-phenomenon with him. Voices are heard to say:

"Kost, nebrauc!"
"Nebūs slikti slinki drīzi modināt."
"Nav nozīmes cilāt šīs problēmas ar X." (40r: 358/61)
(Latv.: "Kost, don't travel."—"It won't be bad to wake the loafer soon."—"It is not important to discuss these problems with X.")

The experimenter, having gone to see this man all the same, finds that the advice was right: the scientist in question turned out to be hard of hearing and his brooding on theoretical questions had nothing to add to the experimenter's research.

The second instance concerns another warning against a journey:

"Tur nebūs tev labi!" (42g: 577)
(Latv.: "You will not fare well there.")

The results of that particular journey were disappointing.

18. *Their Warnings*

The repeated occurrence of this motive often clothed in the characteristic mixture of languages, precludes any suspicion that warnings about rest and sleep could be mere coincidental snippets from radio broadcasts. Especially at the end of a recording-session a male or female voice is frequently heard to wish "good night", as, for instance, the clearly audible woman's voice at the close of a microphone-recording:

"Bonne natt!" (23g: 350)
(French, Swed.: "Good night.")

At times a leave-taking is coupled with good advice:

"Stora adiós! Ty sirdi skuni! Bez steigas!" (28g: 062)
(Swed., Span., Russ., Latv.: "A great leave-taking! Take care of the heart! Without hurry!")

Whole series of voices mention the experimenter's name on saying "good night". For example:

"Kosti, gute Nacht tillönskan." (35r: 525)
(Germ., Swed.: "Kosti, we wish good night.")

Other voices give their own names:

"Labu nakti, Nastja." (37r: 355)
(Latv.: "Good night, Nastja.")
"Gute Nacht, Medeles Jonis, gute Nacht."
"Liebe gute Nacht, Petrautzkis!" (47g: 644/5)
"Guten Abend, mūs' puisēn!" (40r: 467)
"Kostja, Pamūns sveica. Lobu nakti!" (49r: 094)
(Germ., Latv.: "Good night, Medeles Jonis, good night."— "Loving good night! Petrautzkis!"—"Good evening, our chap!" —"Kostja, Pamuns greeted you. Good night!")

The many warnings not to neglect rest and sleep show that the voice-entities watch us; they regard the relaxation through rest and sleep as absolutely necessary for human existence. In this context the experimenter is once more called upon by name; it gives a marked impression of active partnership:

"Sova gossen, rappelez-vous!" (34g: 049)
(Swed., French: "Sleep boy, remember!")
"Tagad mierā!" (23g: 265)
(Latv.: "Now quiet!")
"Tagad davolna—mierā!" (31g: 653)
(Latv., Russ.: "Now it's enough—quiet!")
"Paklaus, Kosti, abends Ruh!" (31r: 563)
(Latv., Germ.: "Listen Kosti, evenings rest!")
"Gute Nacht lauj putniem!" (42r: 202)
(Germ., Latv.: "Grant the birdies good night!")
"Nachts Ruhe!" (44r: 922)
(Germ.: "At night rest!")
"Konstantin, gute Nacht."
"Gute Nacht, Konstantin." (43r: 923)
(Germ.: "Konstantin, good night."—"Good night, Konstantin.")
"Kosti, gul!" (46g: 400)
(Latv.: "Kosti, sleep.")

The voices comment on the experimenter's work-conditions:

"Tikai naktī tu joba." (44r: 051)
(Latv., Swed.: "Only at night you work.")

At one recording, made at midnight, the voices react with:

"Kostuli, nachts Ruhe Biberā." (40g: 158)
(Germ., Latv.: "Kostulit, at night quiet in Bibera.")
"Kosti, Kosti, te vārti, te vīla Kosimā." (40r: 160/1)
(Latv.: "Kosti, Kosti, here is the gate, here is peace in Kosima.")
"Bibera" and "Kosima" seem to be place-names.

The experimenter asks his unseen friends at another night-recording-session whether they can hear him.

"Maxima wecki inte! Tu blasfemē." (42g: 07/12)
(Germ., Swed., Latv.: "Don't wake Maxima! You are blaspheming.")

On a different night the following voices were heard:

"Nachts Ruhe!" (42r: 322)
"Nacht ist Ruh!" (same place: 347)
(Germ.: "At night rest!"—"Night is rest!")

"Kosta, gul!" (same place: 422)
(Latv.: "Kosta, sleep.")
"Guli, Kosti! Vitolds Nolde." (same place: 428)
(Latv.: "Sleep, Kosti! Vitolds Nolde.")
"Paguli, mīļo." (43g: 623)
(Latv.: "Go sleep a little, dear.")

Sometimes good-night wishes include pertinent statements or comments on emotional conditions. A one-time grammar-school teacher, Mrs. Gailīte, warns:

"Hier Gailīte. Naktī čučē. Vilks milē nakti." (43r: 038)
(Germ., Latv.: "Here Galite. One sleeps at night. The wolf loves the night.")
"Furchtbar vientuļš! Gute Nacht!" (43r: 283)
(Germ., Latv.: "Terribly lonely! Good night!")
"Tev bēdīg(a) Nacht!" (44b: 298)
(Latv., Germ.: "A sad night to you.")
"Gute Nacht! Pagul saldī!" (44b: 228)
(Germ., Latv.: "Good night! Sleep sweetly a little!")
"Kostulīt, gute Nacht! Signovskij." (44b: 700)
(Germ.: "Kostulit, good night! Signovskij.")
"Konstantin, gulēt iet." (44b: 934)
(Latv.: "Konstantin, one must go to bed.")
"Du sova gott." (44r: 042)
(Swed.: "Sleep you well.")

The night's rest is kept in the beyond just as firmly as it is here. Several voices hint at this: A voice calls "Jāns!", whereupon a woman's voice strictly demands "Nachts Ruhe". (40g: 169). Other voices also state that they are tired:

"Nachts bin ich müde." (44b: 613)
(Germ.: "At night rest!"—"At night I am tired.")

19. *Their Gratitude*

Expressions of gratitude can be heard throughout the experiments. Voices mainly give thanks for the fact that we remember them, but every now and then they express gratitude for other things.

During the course of one recording Mrs. M.F., one of the participants, says she hopes for a successful continuation of the research work and the establishment of a link with the voices. A female voice:

"Danke." (17g: 508)
(Germ.: "Thank you.")

Mrs. M.F. wishes that Margarete Petrautzki shall be happy in the beyond. A voice, sounding incredibly near, answers:

"Danke!" (same place: 518)

Words of gratitude are poured out in two languages:

"Tacka, tacka, tacka; tack, tack, tack—unser Vater, unser Vater." (23r: 031)
(Swed., Germ.: "Thanks, thanks, thanks; thank you, thank you, thank you—our father, our father.")
"Es tev paldies saku." (28r: 645)
(Latv.: "I give you my thanks.")
"Das heisst Dank." (35r: 892)
(Germ.: "This means thanks.")

The experimenter addresses his unseen friends.

"Besten Dank." (38g: 946)
(Germ.: "Best thanks.")

At the end of a recording the experimenter closes the session with: "Till we hear you again, my dear friends." In response:

"Tack, bonito!"
(Swed., Span.: "Thank you, kindly one.")

Sometimes expressions of gratitude are formulated in a most unusual way and contain reservations:

"Heute halb Dank. Deutlichkeit. Bushstaben-Stadium. Luftiga Pracht. Ej gulēt!" (35r: 857)
(Germ., last sentence Latvian: "Today half-thanks. Clarity. Alphabet-stage. Airy splendour. Go to bed!")
"Paldies, Kosti, pilni saki, Kosti runā!" (40r: 499/504)
(Latv.: "Thanks, Kosti, tell all, Kosti speak.")

The following voices give the impression of a daughter receiving her father "over there"; the father begs his daughter to "see" for him:

"Kostja, tack, tack. Tici bara mig."
"Tita för mej!"
"Komm, Papa." (44b: 459)
(Swed., Latv., Germ.: "Kostja, thank you, thank you. Do believe me."—"See for me!"—"Come, Papa.")

The voices are particularly grateful when we switch from microphone to radio:

> "Wir danken, Kosti!" (45r: 645)
> "Kosti, paldies!" (46g: 524)
> (Germ., Latv.: "We give thanks, Kosti."—"Kosti, thank you!")

Some voices add their names when they say thank you:

> "Spasibo, Margarete." (45r: 269)
> (Russ.: "Thanks, Margarete.")
> "Hier complimento De La Val. Mein gracias, muchas gracias." (34r: 618)
> (Germ., Span.: "Here compliments from De la Val. My thanks, many thanks!") De La Val, a Spanish writer, was a friend of the experimenter.

After the experimenter has sent greetings to his friends in the beyond a voice answeres:

> "Vi tack." (42g: 227)
> (Swed.: "We give thanks.")

(III) TWO WORLDS

20. *Religious and Ethical Factors*

The religious and ethical factor plays an extensive part in the voice-recordings. It may be best not to attempt an explanation or interpretation at this stage, but simply to state the fact that the following voices were clearly audible to all present at this recording-session and may be verified by anyone listening to the appropriate tape.

> "Jesus einsam te irrte." (38g: 685)
> (Germ., Latv.: "Jesus wandered here in loneliness.")
> "Te Kristus, te priester ir." (39g: 296)
> (Latv., Germ.: "Here is Christ, here are the priests.")
> "Te Kristus pestej, te Kristus pats." (43r: 251)
> (Latv.: "Here Christ delivers, here Christ himself.")
> "Te Kristus piestāj, te Kristue pestej." (43r: 252)
> (Latv.: "Here Christ makes a halt, Christ delivers here.")
> "Überglücka! Von Jesus berührt hatte." (47g: 658)
> (Germ. (modified): "Rapturous! Have been touched by Jesus.")

"Heilands tja." (40g: 457)
(Germ., Latg.: "Here is the saviour.")

Apart from the foregoing, which appears to refer to the Catholic doctrine of purgatory, the following examples also contain elements associated with the Catholic faith:

"Wir sind, wir spüren Madonna." (38g: 951)
(Germ.: "We are, we feel the Madonna.")
"Te Mōra tala. Tja valna nav." (49r: 167)
(Latg., Swed.: "Here speaks Mora. There is no devil here.")

Russian pilgrim-monks are mentioned:

"Paldies par uzrunu."
"Vi tjäna dir."
"Ko, te stranniki." (38r: 870/9)
(Latv., Swed., Germ., Russ.: "Thank you for addressing us."
—"We serve you."—"Ko, here are pilgrim-monks.")
"Vi gan katol . . . denke, Vater Saluste." (46g: 687)
(Swed., Latv., Germ.: "We apparently think in Catholic terms, Father Saluste.")
A curtly phrased question:
"Ty Christ?" (43g: 272)
(Russ.: "Are you a Christian?")

A call upon the heavenly Father sounds like a prayer:

"Liels kungs, atmin Raudivi!" (44b: 147)
(Latv.: "Great Lord, remember Raudive!")

The experimenter states that the recordings do not depend on the will of human beings alone. A voice in response:

"Debešu tāva, cilvēka griba ir ierobežota." (36r: 673)
(Latv.: "On the heavenly Father, the will of man is limited.")

Sacrifice and prayer are mentioned:

"Kosti Raudive, nados ziedot Dievam Petrova." (42r: 417)
(Latv.: "Kosti Raudive, Petrova will make no sacrifice to God.")
"Lyudzi par mums! Mias capam." (42r: 418)
(Latg.: "Pray for us! We burn.")
"Patin, aizlūdzat Ko!" (42r: 769)
(Germ., Latv.: "Godmother, intercede for me with Ko!")
"Aizlūdz! Jag stå unter ondska." (46g: 446)
(Latv., Swed., Germ.: "Pray! I am in the power of the evil one.")

"Was weiss mit einem?—Orat!"
"Unser Glaube wolle Dietmar." (34g: 229/31)
(First sentence Germ., Lat.: "What knows with one?—Pray!") This does not seem to make sense and probably means "What does one know?—Pray!"
(The second sentence is in German and is equally cryptic: "Our faith will Dietmar.")

The existence of evil, which opposes God, is featured in the following fragment of a conversation:

"Te Dievs. Vater unser."
"Bada kungs, mūsu Tēvs. Tja valns." (30g: 610/5)
(Latv., Germ.: "Here is God, our Father."—"Lord of hunger, our Father. Here is the devil.")

The conservative concept of a "devil" or evil appears fairly often:

"Velns ir." (46g: 348)
(Latv.: "The devil exists.")
"Koste, te jods." (43r: 042)
(Latv.: "Koste, there is a devil.")

When the experimenter mentions the electronic world, a voice says:

"Es velns." (43r: 613)
(Latv.: "I am an evil one.")
"Konstantin, velns te." (35r: 035)
(Latv.: "Konstantin, the devil is here."), but:
"Tja valna nav." (49r: 167)
(Latg.: "There is no devil here.")
Someone confesses:
"Guten Tag. Es culpā!" (42g: 497)
(Germ., Latv., Latin: "Good day. I am guilty.")

There are voice-entities whose beliefs seem to reach back to pagan, pre-Christian ideas:

"Nav krēma. Nauda var atdot veļu tēvam." (42g: 426)
(Latv.: "There is no cream. The money can be given to the father of the Manes [shades].")
"Jej bogu, veļu nav." (24g: 584)
(Russ., Latv.: "By God, there are no Manes.")
"Sērst Laima." (40g: 530)
(Latv.: "Laima is guest.")

Laima is a goddess of fate in the ancient Latvian religion.

She still lives in the religious imagination of the Latvian people.

Once the experimenter calls "Radio Peter" at 3.15 a.m. (See page 174).

> "Valkyra du bist, sveiks." (42g: 260)
> (Swed., Germ., Latv.: "You are a Valkyrie, good-bye.")

When, at the same recording, the experimenter states that he keeps to "Radio Peter", several voices come in:

> "Fint, iepriecinā eben."
> "Tev dūša, pakalpo!"
> "Esi frei!" (same place: 262/4)
> (Swed., Latv., Germ.: "Fine, one is happy about that."—"You have courage, serve!"—"Be free.")

Ethical values, friendship, faith, reverence, confidence, courage, etc. are mentioned by the voices on many occasions. (Pointers to the ethics of the voice-entities can also be gleaned from emotional states described in other chapters as well as from the appropriate texts.) We hear, for instance, that it is the heart that counts; that we should beware of flattery; that tolerance is important; and we are advised: "Be careful!—Keep your reserve!—Don't talk too much!—Close your eyes!" etc.

> "Vi künftiga, mēs ticam." (47r: 105)
> (Swed., Latv.: "We, the future ones, we believe.")
> "Visam tic! Pagans, tic!" (30g: 453)
> (Latv.: "Believe all! Pagan, believe!")
> "Tu te draugs, tu te draugs!" (40r: 274)
> (Latv.: "Here you are friend, here you are friend!")
> "Te klanim kopj, nyom tillvar." (40g: 535)
> (Latv., Russ., Swed., Germ., with partially modified words. The sentence could be interpreted as: "Here one bows one's head before the new existence.")
> "Paldies, Konstantin, par to drošu! Palīgu tev nav." (33g: 193)
> (Latv.: "Thanks, Konstantin, for your courage. You have no helpers.")
> "Otvaga—styrka." (47g: 044)
> (Russ., Swed.: "The strength lies in the risk.")
> "Pierādi milosti pret fattigiem!" (47g: 478)
> (Latv., Russ., Swed.: "Be charitable towards the poor.")

Many statements are concerned with love, one of the ruling forces in the "world of voices":

"Konstantin, tur bara mīlestību!" (38g: 945)
(Latv.: "Konstantin, hold only love.")
"Liebe ist." (43g: 047)
(Germ.: "Love is.")
"Liebe ist nécessaire." (Hg: 297)
(Germ., French: "Love is necessary.")
"Mīlestība ir Beethoven." (38g: 097)
(Latv.: "Beethoven has love.")
"Älska ist, Dan Kane."
(Swed., Germ.: "Love is, Dan Kane.")
"Kosta, mīlestība!" (40r: 271)
(Latv.: "Kosta, love!")
"Mīla krusts, Pintor!" (40r: 389)
(Latv.: "Love is a cross, Pintor.")

Reverence for ancestors and respect for family-ties are particularly stressed:

"Senčiem te ihre Stufe." (Hr: 297)
(Latv., Germ.: "The ancestors have their rank here.")
"Māte pirmā norma." (42r: 725)
(Latv.: "The mother is the first norm.") (See section "Mother", page 35.)

The father of the experimenter appears more as a helping hand, or needing help himself; his presence is often reported by other voices, and at times one hears his Christian name, Vincence, Vinca, or Vikentij.

"Tāvs var—und wir helfen viņam." (42r: 892)
(Latv., Germ.: "Father can—and we are helping him.")
"Sputnik. Tala spirito. Tack du! Te tāvs Konstantin." (43g: 515)
(Swed., Ital., Latv.: "Sputnik. The spirit speaks. Thank you! Here is father, Konstantin.")
"Vincente, dein Vater." (22r: 289)
(Germ.: "Vincente, your father.")
"Te tāvs!" (23r: 183)
(Latv.: "Here is father.")
"Es Vinca." (43r: 570)
(Latv.: "I am Vinca.")
"Mūsu padre te. Tja Liebe mūsu. Tu dzird? Es te pi altares." (43r: 062)
(Latv., Span., Germ., Latg.: "Our father is here. Here is our love. Do you hear? I am here near the altars.")
"Tavs dimbā. Vi, Kosta, lūdzu, atceries mūs!" (43g: 538)
(Latv., Swed.: "Father is in a fix. We, Kosta, think of us!")
"Daudz strādā tāvs īpaši Mona." (44b: 675)

(Latv.: "Father works much, particularly Mona.") "Mona", see section "Mother".

"Vinca te teksta russi. Job gryuti." (44b: 511/3)
(Latv., Swed.: "Vinca spells here in Russian. The work is hard.")

To end this section, a straightforward precept:

"Lūdzat Dievu! Lūdzat, putekli!—Mīlat!" (47g: 529)
(Latv.: "Pray to God! Pray, dust!—Love.")

21. *Relationship of the Entities to Earth*

The voice-entities are aware of conditions on earth; they mention winter-time, cold weather, rain, etc.; they seem to react particularly strongly to thunder and are sensitive to the light of the moon.

It was snowing during one recording-session and the landscape outside was shrouded in white.

"Ziema ragavam." (23g: 270)
(Latv.: "Winter for the sleighs.")
"Richtiga sals. Te arktis. Piesalam līdz kauliem."
(Germ., Latv.: "Real frost. Here is the arctic. Frozen through to the bones.")
"Koste, mūs winter eksistē."
(Latv., Germ.: "Koste, where we are winter exists.")
"Hallo, Donner!" (35r: 713)
(Germ.: "Hallo, thunder!")
"Rimis pērkons." (36g: 279)
(Latv.: "The thunderstorm has ceased.") The last two remarks were correct: it had been thundering and raining during the relevant recordings.
"Nach de Regen te riecht." (37r: 633)
(Germ., Latv.: "It smells of the rain here.")

Once again the experimenter records during a thunderstorm:

"Hör, Donner!" (38g: 426)
(Germ.: "Listen, thunder!")
"Liela migla." (same place: 428)
(Latv.: "Great fog.")

The voice-entities sense what the weather will be, or comment on the prevailing conditions:

"Būs regn." (39r: 885)

SPEECH-CONTENT OF RECORDINGS

(Latv., Swed.: "It will rain.")
"Oj, Donner." (40g: 629)
(Germ.: "Oh, thunder!")
"Rietriņu vēji." (40r: 221)
(Latv.: "Westwind.")
"Töplyj laiks." (40r: 295)
(Russ., Latv.: "Warm water.")
"Kosta, warm." (40r: 643)
"Bona tja līst." (42r: 817)
(Latv.: "Bona, it is raining here.")

The moon is frequently mentioned; it plays a positive rôle in the world of the voices and seems to enhance contact.

"Mēnesi!" (22r: 317)
(Latv.: "Please, the moon.")
"Vollmond." (42g: 021)
(Germ.: "Full moon.")
"Ieelpo,—luná!" (42r: 819)
(Latv., Russ.: "Breathe in—moon!")
"Mēnesnīcu gribētu ņemt mit." (43r: 038)
(Latv., Germ.: "I would like to take the light of the moon with me.")
"Moon's omsida." (43r: 462)
(Engl., Swed.: "Reverse side of the moon.")
"Luná svetlá. Te De-eikva." (44b: 450)
(Russ., Latv.: "The moon is bright. Here is De-eikva.") The experimenter does not know the meaning of the word "De-eikva."
"Mātei wichtig Mond." (45g: 349)
(Latv., Germ.: "For mother the moon is important.")

The voice-entities experience (probably through their contact with the earthly sphere of existence) human desires that have remained firmly anchored in their consciousness.

A voice confirms:

"Alma ir!" (44r: 912)
(Span., Latv.: "The soul exists."); but in answer to the experimenter's remark that the soul is free of the body after death, we hear:
"Tā nav, Kosti." (21r: 051)
(Latv.: "It is not so, Kosti.")

Two voices regret that they cannot stay—they are probably unable to stay within the earth's region. First a sad female voice:

"Nevaru palikt." (22r: 460) Then a male voice:
"Nevaru palikt." (same place: 461)
(Latv.: "I cannot stay.")

Very often voices ask for water:

"Sieh, Raudive! Lyudzu dud yudini!" (35r: 173)
(Germ., Latg.: "See, Raudive! Please give water!")
"Yudini, Raudive, yudini!" (35r: 300)
(Latg.: "Water, Raudive, Water!")
"Kostulīt, mierini, yudentini!" (36g: 115)
(Latg.: "Kostulit, comfort me, little water!")
"Aqua!" (43r: 626)
(Latin: "Water!")
"Es ūdens gribu." (45r: 527)
(Latv.: "I want water.")

Voices ask for bread:

"Lūdzu maizīti." (22r: 463)
(Latv.: "Please, the dear bread.")
"Maizi dodat man." (36g: 575)
(Latv.: "Bread give me!")

The voice-entities remember commodities of their earthly days and sometimes ask for them.

"Lūdzu mātei kafiju!" (22r: 462)
(Latv.: "Please for mother coffee.")
"Kosti, pienu!" (same place: 464)
(Latv.: "Kosti, milk!")
"Medutiņu!" (same place: 466)
(Latv.: "The good honey!")
"Wodka, Wodka, daj!" (23r: 029)
(Russ.: "Give vodka, vodka!")
"Brandy!" (22r: 010)
"Piedāvā Martini saviem viesiem." (29g: 326)
(Latv.: "Offer Martini to your guests.")
"Ai, man cigareti!" (29g: 460)
(Latv.: "Ah, for me a cigarette!")
"Saimniekot tev aizliegts." (same place)
(Latv.: "It is forbidden for you to serve anything.")
"Jetzt dzeru konjaku. Ist es strengale?" (29r: 462)
(Germ., Latv.: "Now I drink cognac. Is it strong?")
"Guten Abend med dej! I wishy your bebi Wein." (30r: 293)
(Germ., Swed., Engl., Span.: "A good evening to you! I wish to drink your wine.")
"Raudiv, makorku!" (39r: 725)
(Russ.: "Raudiv, tobacco!")

SPEECH-CONTENT OF RECORDINGS

"Kosti, padod šnabi!" (44b: 660)
(Latv.: "Kosti, give schnapps.")
"Nav tīrā smēka." (same place)
(Latv.: "There are no pure smoked foods.")

Many of the voices give the impression that the entities are in the experimenter's studio; the following three fragments illustrate this quite vividly:

"Meklē Cinzano, Kosti, man!"
"Nogaršot, Koste!"
"Danke schön. Vakar bij schön."
"Vakar bij schwül." (25r: 180ff)
(Latv., Germ.: "Kosti, look for Cinzano for me!"—"Let me have a taste, Koste!"—"Thank you. Yesterday it was nice."—"Yesterday it was close.")
"Kosti, nu piedāvā pīpi!"
"Astāj pīpi! Ko diesi, tu dumais?" (female voice)
"Konst... Pēters mani aicinā." (25r: 217/20)
(Latv.: "Kosti, offer a pipe now!"—"Let the pipe be! Are you going to dance, stupid?"—female voice. "Konst ... Peter wants me.")
"Maiziti dod!"
"Kur paliek un—viesi?"
"Kur pieši?"
"Kur saktas?" (25r: 221/ff)
(Latv.: "Give us the good bread!"—"Where have you got to and where are the guests?"—"Where are the spurs?"—"Where are the bangles?")

Other voices ask for clothes, a bathroom, silver-birches, and many other things:

"Man ropa!" (44r: 897)
(Latv., Swed.: "For me dresses.")
"Pirti!" (22r: 470)
(Latv.: "Please, (a) bathroom.")
"Man pirti! Sakur pirti!" (34g: 588)
(Latv.: "For me the bathroom. Heat the bathroom.")
"Kur baltie bērzi?" (22r: 366)
(Latv.: "Where are the silver-birches?")
"Lobs åkers!" (38g: 025)
(Latg., Swed.: "A good field!")
"Frühling, dzegūze nekūko." (38g: 035)
(Germ., Latv.: "Spring, the cuckoo does not call.")
"Tu gribi putniņu cīpāšanu." (same place)
(Latv.: "You want the twittering of the birds.")
"Bērtule tā puke. Wie nennt?"

"Liepu zieds." (33g: 025)
(Latv., Germ.: "Bertule, the flower. What is its name?"—"Lime-tree blossom.")

There are voices that ask for a book, for money and even for "the voice":

"Izrakst ček." (44b: 625)
(Latv.: "Write a cheque!")
"Nav naudas." (same place: 635)
(Latv.: "No money.")
"Balsi, Konstantin." (same place: 644)
(Latv.: "The voice, Konstantin.")

22. *Here and Hereafter—The Anti-World—The Bridge, Crossing and Customs Points*

To start this section we hear a few voices who comment on fundamental questions about this world and the next. The experimenter asks whether it would be possible to prove the existence of the higher reality by scientific means. A voice answers:

"Ja." (20g: 822)
(Germ.: "Yes.")

After the experimenter has remarked that the denizens of the next world also have problems, and specifically problems connected with change, just as we do here, a voice is heard to say:

"Wir kennen." (20r: 878)
(Germ.: "We know.")

Another voice coins an interesting Latvian neologism:

"Izeme te, Konstantin. Margarete arī tja." (42g: 224)
(Latg.: "Izeme is here, Konstantin. Margarete is here too.")
The word "Izeme", which does not exist in the Latvian language, seems to mean something in contrast to the earth.
"Laika te nav." (43g: 203)
(Latv.: "There is no time here.")

There is an interesting statement referring to the "anti-world":

"Raudive, Antiwelten sind." (39r: 027)
(Germ.: "Raudive, Anti-worlds exist.")

It is perhaps of interest to mention here the theory of the American physicist, Dr. Leon Ledermann (Columbia University, New York). He has attempted to prove the existence of the "anti-atom" and "anti-matter", and believes that an "anti-universe" exists as a counterpart to the "real" universe in which we live.

Current scientific opinion does not altogether accept the possibility of existence outside the four basic aggregate states now known to man. The fourth—previously thought of as an impossibility—was discovered only a few years ago, when the solid, fluid and vaporous forms were joined by the plasmic one. However, physicists are now discussing a fifth possibility: the neutron-state of matter, which has been described by the physicist, Holger Ess in an article appearing on 13th February 1966 in the *Braunschweiger Zeitung*, No. 12.[1]

The experimenter remarks in the course of a recording, that through research into the voice-phenomenon a bridge might be built between the two worlds.

"Sēklu sēt." (20g: 906)
(Latv.: "Sow the seeds.")

Repeatedly we hear, in various languages and on all sorts of occasions, the word "bridge". Insistently the voice-entities reiterate their plea that a bridge should be established:

"Brücke vajag." (43r: 179)
(Latv., Germ.: "One must have the bridge.")
"Konstantin, tiltu!" (Ü Ir: 125)
(Latv.: "Konstantin, please, the bridge.")
"Tais, tiltus tais!" (43r: 099)
(Latv.: "Build, build the bridge.")
"Taisi nu Brücke, Konstantin!" (44b: 630)
(Latv., Germ.: "Build the bridge now, Konstantin.")
"Met tiltu!" (44r: 079)
(Latv.: "Span the bridge.")
"Tais tiltu! Tais Stimme!" (45g: 308)
(Latv., Germ.: "Build the bridge! Make the voice!")

[1] See Appendix IV, page 390.

"Konstantin tilts! Bīskapu tik ved, baznicu ieskaiti! Viens, viens, bez leidzes." (36g: 265)
(Latv.: "Konstantin, the bridge! Lead the Bishop, include the Church! Alone, alone, without help.")

One voice declares:

"Kosti, sirdī richtig's tilts." (40g: 602)
(Latv., Germ.: "Kosti, the right bridge is in the heart.")

The voices hope:

"Pabola, tilgli augs!" (36g: 132)
(Latv.: "Pabola, the bridges will grow!")
"Labi funkcionē Brücke." (35r: 864)
(Latv., Germ.: "The bridge functions well.")
"Mosti fri!"
"Nu mūsu latvji traki." (44r: 307)
(Russ., Swed., Latv.: "The bridges are free!"—"Now our Latvians are mad!")

Many entities that are helping to build the bridge make themselves heard; from near and dear ones such as mother, father, brothers, sisters and schoolmates, to Vivekananda and Tolstoi. (See section on Writers, page 70 and Technical Questions, page 169).

In answer to the experimenter's request for help in his work:

"Vivekananda tiltu būvē." (44b: 106)
(Latv.: "Vivekananda builds the bridge.")

When the experimenter states his belief that the bridge may mark a new beginning for mankind:

"Mēs neticam. Kosti, lampu!" (same place: 107)
(Latv.: "We don't think so. Kosti, a lamp!") By "a lamp" a higher spiritual development may be meant.
A voice urges:
"Weiter, most ny!" (23g: 637)
(Germ., Russ., Swed.: "Go on, the bridge is new.")

Some voices complain about great distances:

"Te vilka tōlumi!"
"Narvik, jōj pa miglu, Brūckis ir tāl!" (44r: 912)
(Latg., Latv., Germ.: "Here are the distances of the wolf!" This is a popular expression, meaning "endless distances".—
"Narvick, one rides through the fog, the bridge is far.")
"Man nav tilta!" (44b: 702)
(Latv.: "I have no bridge!")

The bridge sometimes appears to be an intermediate world where both sides can meet:

"Vai tu savā pusē?"
"Paties? Ko tu dari šitā pusē? Pestī!" (35r: 218/20)
(Latv.: "Are you on your side?"—"Really? What are you doing on this side? Release!")

We hear many statements that refer to a crossing between the two worlds. From various texts one may deduce that for the majority of the voice-entities contact with the experimenter becomes possible only at this "crossing-point". An extraordinary feature in this context is repeated reference to a kind of control, a customs-point where a passport has to be produced.

The experimenter says that, obviously, there was a "here" and a "hereafter". A voice is heard:

"Tulla!" (22g: 296)
(Swed.: "Customs!")
"Muita!" (45g: 568)
(Latv.: "Customs!")
"Tulli ernst." (35g: 817)
(Swed., Germ.: "Customs are a serious matter.")
"Muitā būšu." (36g: 265)
(Latv.: "I shall be at the customs.")
"Zoll bei der Übergang." (41g: 081)
(Germ.: "Customs at the crossing.")
"Te doina." (40r: 455)
(Latv., French: "Here are the customs.")
"Tu ko?"
"Te Nietzsche."
"Propusk, Pass!"
"Laid!"
"Nu-klo, propustit viņu!"
"Dod platzi!"
"Vidim Kosti."
"Propustit!" (37r: 626/8)
(Latv., Germ., Russ.: "What do you want?"—"Here is Nietzsche."—"Identity card, passport!"—"Let pass!"—"Nuklo, let him pass!"—"Make room!"—"We see Kosti."—"Let pass!")
"Tur Kostja!"
"Tu, Kosti, tici!"
"Propusk!"
"Rupais te."
"Darf ich übergehen?"
"Was du wünschi?" (45g: 433/5)

(Latv., Russ., Germ.: "There is Kostja!"—"You, Kosti, believe!"—"Entry!"—"Here is Rupais."—"May I pass?"—"What do you wish?")

To judge from the following fragment of conversation, it seems that reasons have to be given for a "crossing":

"På vilk Angelegenheit?"
"Runā tu, lūdzu tu!"
"Lūdzu, runā tu no tā!" (31g: 576/85)
(Swed., Germ., Latv.: "What is your business?"—"You speak, please, you!"—"Please, you speak about it!")

Quite often there is talk about difficulties at the crossing:

"Kosti, svårt att koma." (40g: 551)
(Swed.: "Kosti, it is difficult to come over.")
"Netiekam!" (50g: 305)
(Latv.: "We can't enter!")
"Džim, uzrādi pārēju!" (43g: 297)
(Latv.: "Jim, show the crossing-point.")
"Te pārēja. Ņudžita dreh uz Mitkaldzūn, Gaspadarum drei." (22r: 198)
(Latv., Germ.: "Here is the crossing-point. Ņudžita, turn to Mitkaldzūn, Gaspadarum three.") The sense of this is not clear. It is possible that it refers to some sort of order in regional divisions.
"Te ir parēja. Turies burājā, mōtes žurnalī. Kosti, burājā! Kostja, piesargies!" (35g: 303)
(Latv.: "Here is the crossing-point. Keep in sail, in mother's journal. Kosti, in sail! Kostja, be careful!")

The next statement seems to indicate that there are various ways the voice-entities can take:

"Nava po putj." (22r: 406)
(Latv., Russ.: "Our ways part.")

Nationality appears to play a part in getting permission for a crossing:

"Jag lettiske."
"Geh ja über!" (29g: 472)
(Swed., Germ.: "I am a Latvian."—"Do go over!")
"Passez! Tie ir žīdi." (31g: 443)
(French, Latv.: "Pass! They are Jews!")

Every now and then one hears voice-entities being sent back:

"Nu, zurück, Mechtild!"
"Was jēga du?"
"Tesnatā!"
"Russku hasse!"
"Kosta, pietiks."
"Piektdien, Kosta!" (46r: 683)
(Germ., Swed., Latv., Russ.: "Now, back, Mechtild!"—"What have you in mind?"—"A throng."—"Hate the Russian."—"Kosta, enough."—"Friday, Kosta!") The last sentence may be taken as a hint that next day would be the anniversary of Margarete Petrautzki's death (see page 45); the recording was made on Thursday, 9th February 1967.

Quite often a name is mentioned when someone makes a crossing.

"Roepke, tulla vid Blatt." (31g: 556)
(Swed.: "Roepke, customs near Blatt.") This could refer to a well-known economist, Professor W. Roepke, who had died not long before the recording containing this statement was made. The experimenter had not known him personally.
"Džonis Džonatāns, Raudivi!"
"Passeport!"
"Sveiks, bror!" (36g: 167)
(Last sentence Latv., Swed.: "We greet you, brother!")
"Latviski tu runā?"—"Raudivs grib."
"Munters te tiga." (47r: 324/5)
(Latv., Swed.: "Do you speak Latvian?"—"Raudiv wants it."—"Munters begs here.") Munters was the last Latvian foreign minister. He died in Riga soon after his return from a concentration-camp in Siberia. The experimenter knew him, though not very well. The short conversation-fragment gives the impression that Munters was trying to get through the control to contact the experimenter.
"Te Luta."
"Tu nedrīksti te smēķēt." (49g: 321)
(Latv.: "Here is Luta."—"You are not allowed to smoke here.") Luta, a friend of the experimenter, had been a very heavy smoker in his lifetime.
"Tulla, Babītis grib Zentu." (same place)
(Swed., Latv.: "Customs, Babītis wants Zenta.")

23. *Existence After Death*

The question of life after death has become a dominant consideration in this investigation. Leo Tolstoi, once firmly convinced that death was the end of all things, eventually repudiated his own conclusions after a lifetime of passionate questioning, his spiritual energies consumed in the attempt to bridge the gulf between seen and unseen.

Perhaps no one can fully understand the true value of life, his own or others, until he experiences the terror of facing complete annihilation. To innumerable thinkers throughout the ages, life has appeared as more than a puppet show; they have rejected the idea of dissolution in a limitless void as a denigration of human intelligence and dignity, and have looked for a deeper meaning behind man's existence.

We all realise to a greater or lesser extent the abilities of our human "animal nature", but precise knowledge of matters beyond the boundaries of this life is withheld; there is no exact knowledge about what happens after death, all is guesswork, conjecture, supposition. This book records the results of research into physically verifiable phenomena which seem to some of the researchers to point to the existence of another world and of beings who, with the aid of tape-recorder, radio and microphone, seek to impart a certain amount of information about the place they inhabit.

Insight into another plane of existence might be expected to free us from the concepts of our temporary physical abode, limited as they are by our culture and customs, our passions, prejudices and preconceptions. Hitherto we have had little choice but to strive to realise intangible truths through ourselves and within ourselves, but the facts now being investigated through strictly controlled experiments present a challenge to the restrictions and preconceived ideas of modern man, and perhaps offer an opportunity to prove at last, as Leo Tolstoi believed at the end of a long life of trial and error, that "the soul of man contains an element that is not subject to death".

This chapter sets out a selection of references to this absorbing problem.

During one of his first recordings the experimenter remarked that man had very little knowledge of matters concerning life after death and that neither his understanding, his judgement, nor his intuition could follow the implications. A voice responded with:

"Er kann." (9r: 017)
(Germ.: "He can.")

It is a microphone-voice, clearly audible to anyone, and this remark may perhaps answer the question mankind has been asking since time immemorial. In such a context, the curt statement is an assertion that man can indeed discover what happens to him after death.

The experimenter says that we leave life hoping that we may find ourselves still in existence . . . , whereupon a male voice answers:

"Wir nie verlassen." (11g: 287/9)
(Germ.: "We never leave.")

Here perhaps is a hint that our view of departure from life is erroneous; it seems we are told that we continue to live through the transition we call death, which affects only the temporary dwelling-house of our physical organism. The voice-entities make many comments, some of which are given in the following pages, that apparently refer to the relationship of the spirit to the body it has left. (See page 137.)

The experimenter, influenced by the happenings of our time, asks whether the souls of those killed in Vietnam perished with their bodies. A woman's voice answers briefly:

"Leben." (15g: 678)
(Germ.: "Live.")

The experimenter repeatedly asks for an answer concerning life after death. A woman's voice:

"Lūdzu tici!" (same place: 682)
(Latv.: "Please believe.")

The experimenter calls on his dead friend R.P. and a male voice says:

"Wir dzīvi." (38g: 711)
(Germ., Latv.: "We live.")

Existence after death is often confirmed in categorical terms:

"Leben wir." (43g: 668)

"Lebe tota, Konstantin." (20g: 087)
"Kosti, vi viva!" (lar: 203)
(Germ., Swed., Ital.: "We live."—"The dead live, Konstantin."
—"Kosti, we live.")
"Es dzīvoju." (48g: 669)
(Latv.: "I live.")

"We greet you all here", says the experimenter and a voice responds with:

"Vi lever." (20g: 814)
(Swed.: "We live.") and immediately following, a male voice:
"Ich vivo." (same place: 817)
(Germ., Ital.: "I live.")

The voice-entities often repeat such confirmation of their existence and their presence:

"Wir sind." (22r: 310)
"Vivi wir." (same place: 312)
(Germ., Ital.: "We are."—"We live.")
"Vi viva." (28r: 649)
(Swed., Ital.: "We live.")
"Konstantin, wir sind." (38g: 934)
"Wir sind." (44b: 322)
"Wir, Kosti, sind." (45g: 322)
"Kosti, vi viva." (lar: 203)
(Germ., Swed., Ital.: "Konstantin, we are."—"We are."—"We, Kosti, are."—"Kosti, we live.")

Sometimes voices introduce themselves:

Te sestrá, Tante viva." (23g: 253)
(Latv., Russ., Germ., Ital.: "Here is sister, Aunt lives.")
Wir sind Gaeli. Wir lebe, wir lebe." (33r: 021)
(Germ.: "We are Gaels. We live, we live.")

A voice-entity declares very definitely that it exists:

"Te Tursa. Facit, patiesi mēs esam." (36g: 551)
(Latv.: "Here is Tursa. Sum total, we exist.")
"Bez smertes, Koste." (47r: 334)
(Latv., Russ.: "Without death, Koste.")
"Ego, Vinkalne ir." (44r: 113)
(Latv.: "I, Vinkalne, exist.")

Margarete Petrautzki had told the experimenter during her lifetime that she did not believe in an existence after death. In one of the recordings featuring her we hear:

"Bedenke, ich bin!"
(Germ.: "Imagine, I am!")
"Mūsu Kosti, Kosti ir." (45r: 523/5)
(Latv.: "Our Kosti, Kosti exists.")

The experimenter asks whether the dead are amongst us. A male voice:

"Mēs esam." (20g: 110)
(Latv.: "We are.")

When the experimenter comments that man does not live only here, but lives many lives, a voice says:

"Pareizi tu runā." (22g: 319)
(Latv.: "You speak correctly.")

Listening to these, and to other examples, we gain a firm impression of a conscious, seeing and hearing world confronting us.

The experimenter once made a recording in Schienen (Lake Constance). One of the participants says that a brother who died lived on in the memories of those who knew him. We hear in answer:

"Ich bin!" (39r: 811/12)
(Germ.: "I am!")

The same participant goes on to say that the dead brother was, so to speak, a part of himself.

"Ich glaube dir gern. Glaub mir!" (same place)
(Germ.: "I believe you gladly. Believe me!")

The experimenter asks the deceased how he is.

"Blendend, Herr Raudive." (same place)
(Germ.: "Splendid, Herr Raudive.") comes the answer.

After the experimenter has stated further that the brother loved the deceased very much, the voice calls the living brother by name:

"Gerfried!" (same place: 826)

The experimenter then tells the voice-entity that the brother has shown him his photograph and that his spirit must have been present on that occasion.

"Pareizi!" (same place)
(Latv.: "That's right.") confirms the voice: and when the experimenter adds that he then read a bit of his novel aloud, the voice comments with:

"Schlecht!" (same place)
(Germ.: "Badly.")

At another recording-session the experimenter addresses a young woman who has recently died.

"Wakna dej!"
(Swed.: "Awake!")

The impression of a transitional sleep is given repeatedly on different occasions.

The experimenter says that in his opinion the deceased woman may still be tied to habitual thoughts.

"Raudive nobiedē Zenta."
(Latv.: "Raudive frightens Zenta.")

To the experimenter's suggestion that perhaps the woman has had to leave this life too suddenly, a delicate female voice retorts:

"Glaubst du, Papa?"
(Germ.: "Do you think so, Papa?")

The experimenter wishes her all the best in the beyond.

"Danke."
(Germ.: "Thank you.")

The experimenter's plea that the deceased may help him to prove the immortality of the soul, is answered by:

"Ich bin!" (39r: 488/564)
(Germ.: "I am.")

One of the recordings was made in the presence of an Estonian nurse, Nora S.; she greets her father, who disappeared somewhere in Siberia. Immediately an Estonian voice is heard:

"Tervitana, Nora!" (20g: 761)
(Estonian: "Greetings, Nora!" As the experimenter does not understand Estonian he noted down what he heard phoneme by phoneme, and a later check showed that the deciphering had been correct and meaningful.

After the experimenter's words: "Welcome here", a voice is heard to say:

"Neraud vairs!" (same place: 801)
(Latv.: "Cry no more!")

The Estonian nurse calls on her dead friend Lenart and asks him if he is happier over there.

"Nein!" (same place: 813)
(Germ.: "No!")

The experimenter says to the participant: "Thank you, dear Nora, we hope . . ." and is interrupted by a voice calling:

"Lenart!" (same place: 819)

The participant then asks whether her dear ones in the beyond fare better than they did on earth; she would like to hear at least a word from them.

"Wir horen!" "We hear!" (same place: 886)

In the preceding recording we had been able to hear desperate weeping and so the experimenter asks who it was that cried so bitterly.

"Noziedzniece. Neraudu vairs." (20g: 944)
(Latv.: "The criminal (woman). I no longer cry.")

The experimenter says that nothing touches him so much as tears.

"Esi stiprs!" (same place: 948)
(Latv.: "Be strong!")

The same consoling voice can also be heard elsewhere:

"Neraud, milī citus!" (31r: 063)
(Latv.: "Don't cry, love the others!")
"Ich bleibe bei dir." (43g: 063)
(Germ.: "I stay with you.")

Death and the dead are mentioned in various contexts. On several occasions the expression "Tota" appears; this had also come up in some of Friedrich Jürgenson's recordings.

"Vi Tota." (47g: 680)
(Swed.: "We, the dead.") It also appears in the sentence "Lebe tota, Konstantin" ("The dead live, Konstantin.") (20g: 087) already quoted.

"Wir singen, wie heilig für uns Toten." (25r: 136)
(Germ.: "We are singing, how sacred for us dead.")
"Eine no Tote."
(Germ.: "A non-dead.")
"Negribas." (45r: 568)
(Latv.: "He doesn't want to.")
"My smertiaki. Gulēt."
"Te nav vergu nometnu."
"O jā, te vergi." (47g: 057)
(Russ., Latv.: "We dead. Sleep."—"There are no slave-camps here."—"Oh yes, there are slaves here.")
"Gari tevi aizsūta tūlīt putī!" (45g: 708)
(Latv., Russ.: "The spirits send you immediately on your way!")
"Nāvi tu klaus!" (43r: 634)
(Lat.: "Obey death!" A very distinct voice.
"Raudiv, tu smerti redzeji." (44g: 703)
(Latv., Russ.: "Raudiv, you have seen death.")
"Nāvi binda!" (42g: 178)
(Latv., Swed.: "Bind death.")

24. *Conditions in the World of the Voice-Entities*

The experimenter asks if the books about the beyond contain truth. A voice answers:

"Sage." (16g: 484)
(German: "Legend.")

There are statements which seem to indicate that the voice-entities cannot or will not give a detailed account of their condition.

When the experimenter asks about circumstances of life "over there" we hear answers such as:

"Atstāj! Neprasi vairs!" (21g: 598)
(Latv.: "Stop this! Ask no more!")
"Wir dürfen nicht erzählen." (20g: 747)
(Germ.: "We are not allowed to tell.")
"Wir warten auf Bock."
"Stāvoklis schwer."
"Konstantin, tā nu jau nav."
"Mēs nevaram skaidrāk pavēstīt to." (31g: 403)
(Germ., Latv.: "We are waiting for Bock."—"Conditions are tough."—"Konstantin, it is not quite like that."—"We cannot report more precisely.")

All the same—quite a lot of information does come over. It is not, of course, always possible to decide whether actual statements really refer to situations in the beyond, or whether they are simply impressions carried over from earth-life. (See "Relationship of the Entities to Earth", page 136.)

Some positive judgements on the new existence:

"Te labi klōjas." (31g: 388)
(Latg.: "It's good here.")
"Aļoz, kā aug rudzi?"
"Labi stāv, labi." (33g: 465)
(Latv.: "Aloz, how does the rye grow?"—"Well, very well.")

To the experimenter's question of how it is in the beyond, a brief answer:

"Angenehm." (40r: 620)
(Germ.: "Pleasant.")

The experimenter pleads for effective help from "beyond".

"Bog, Konstantin, wir glücklich sind." (35r: 258)
(Russ., Germ.: "God, Konstantin, we are happy.")
"Te ir traki labi." (21g: 488)
(Latg.: "It's terribly good here.")

The following fragments show that the voice-entities seem to build their existence upon realities that correspond to ours:

"Kost, Port Salut!"
"Nevaid tikai kapeikas, Konstantin."
"Kooperativs—mūsu Schreck's."
"Kur paliek pasts?"
"Bez pasta."
"Pit man."
"Atnes Heilbuti!"
"Und schön, Konstantin Raudive hört." (35g: 699/706)
(Latv., Germ., Russ.: "Kost, Port Salut!"—"One just hasn't got any Kopeks, Konstantin."—"The Co-operative is our dread." —"Where has the mail got to?"—"Without mail."—"A drink for me!"—"Bring a halibut!"—"And lovely, Konstantin Raudive hears.")
"Was uns nadela?"
"Fraks vecs."
"Tu smādi."
"Smējas arī."
"Ko?"

"Kosti, nepatic."
"Jasmīn, ko—ko raudi?"
"Ņem!"
"Fin, te gusti die Welt!" (38g: 122/30)
(Germ., Russ., Latv., Swed.: "What has clothed us?"—"The tail-coat is old."—"You disdain."—"Laugh also."—"What?"—"Kosti, you do not please."—"Jasmin, why—why do you cry?"—"Take!"—"Fine, here the world pleases.")

"Te Uppsala!"
"Lai ņem!"
"Ko tu las?"
"Kostju."
"Vari atteikt."
"Te cigaret!"
"Atļauts."
"Muti var?"
"Atlauts."
"Ko šis grib?"
"Matildi grib."
"Dod muti!"
"Vadi pneum!"
"Kosti tu grib?"
"Mozmōju."
"Ko tu bļauj, Vaņka?"
"Kosti, svētdien' svāta." (38g: 213/20)
(Latv.: "Here is Uppsala."—"That she would take!"—"What are you reading?"—"Kosti." [Possibly a book by Raudive.]—"You can refuse."—"Here are cigarettes."—"It is permitted."—"Can one ... the mouth?"—"It is permitted."—"What does this one want?"—"He wants Matilde."—"Give the mouth."—"Lead Pneum!"—"Do you want Kosti?"—"Small house."—"Why are you screaming, Vanka?"—"Kosti, one celebrates Sunday.") Recording made on Sunday, 8th May 1966.

The experimental recording No. 5, which was continued at three o'clock in the morning, also produced some hints on conditions in the world of the voice-entities.

"Konstantin, tu pazūd."
"Tala, Kosti!"
"Krug, Vanje."
"Te lauti lupati."
"No Gorkovas-Sandmira, vorne Titova."
"Te Bulān, mala flicka."
"Viņa dulna, Kosta."
"Venta nova."
"Ty, Kosti, pünktlich." (48: 385/418)
(Latv., Swed., Germ., Lat., Russ.: "Konstantin, you are

disappearing."—"Speak, Konstantin."—"Jug, Vanje."—"Here are none but scoundrels."—"From Gorkova-Sandmira, in front Titova."—"Here is Bulan, a bad girl."—"She is mad, Kosta."—"A fresh waiting."—"You, Kosti, are punctual.")

We hear about a "city of the dead":

"City de mortis." (36g: 048)
(Engl., Lat.: "City of the dead.")
"Pistole mūsu cilvēks."
"Tad paliksi zem zemes."
"Ko tu domā?"
"Skeptikis, mīlais." (35g: 105/6)
(Latv.: "A pistol is our man."—"Then you will stay beneath the earth."—"What do you think?"—"You are a sceptic, my dear.")

Some statements have bearing on the problem of time:

"Pulkstin?"
"Pulkstine nav!" (33r: 553/5)
(Latv.: "What's the time?"—"There is no time [clock].")
"Mōsa pusdienu!" (33g: 239)
(Latg.: "Sister, midday!")
"Nakts ir ilga." (41g: 253)
(Latv.: "The night is long.")
"Te daudzi brīži." (49g: 627)
(Latv.: "There are many moments here.")

The next words make one think of some sort of liquidation:

"Kosti, sie sind zusammen in Liquidon. Te paki-Amt." (39r: 774)
(Germ., Latv.: "Kosti, they are together in Liquidon. Here is the parcel-post.")
"Es nakna, mūsu likums."
(Latv., Swed.: "I am naked, that is our law.")
"Wir sind nun Menschen." (41g: 751)
(Germ.: "Now we are human beings.")
"Spīd Gundega te."
"Bērnu, bērnu, weg!"
"Ja, tack."
"Par to tev būs mūžīga dzīve." (44b: 655)
(Latv., Germ., Swed.: "Here shines Gundega."—"The child, the child, away!"—"Yes, thank you."—"For that you shall have eternal life.")
"Nemaitena doch guļ!" (44b: 653)
(Latv., Germ.: "The 'inhuman girl' is still asleep!")
"Lūk te Kostes brat! Mums birzes te trūkst!" (lar: 201)

(Latv., Russ.: "Look, there is Koste's brother! We miss the birch-trees here.")
"Tagad ir maize, Raudē, Kaffee." (47r: 310)
(Latv., Germ.: "Now we have bread, Raude, coffee.")
"Tja pļāpu daudz. Paciet. Te latvji." (49g: 623)
(Latv.: "There are a lot of gossips here. Bear with it. Here are Latvians.")

In one of his earliest recordings the experimenter asks what the voice-entities are doing in the beyond. A voice answers in rhythmic, liturgical chant:

"Wir dienen heiligem Herrn, der im Himmel ist." (2r: 315/21)
(Germ.: "We serve the holy Lord who is in heaven.")

Often the voice-entities complain that they have a difficult time, that they are suffering.

"Es ciešu. Zagle, mele!" (40r: 476)
(Latv.: "I suffer. Thieves, liar [female].")
"Wir leiden." (31g: 397)
(Germ.: "We suffer.")
"Ai hier ir sodi!" (31g: 103)
(Germ., Latv.: "Ah, there are penalties here.")
"Tja djävle!"
"Tja pytka—Seda!"
"Nolādej mani." (42r: 765)
(Latg., Swed., Latv., Russ.: "Here is the she-devil!"—"Here is torture—Seda."—"I have been condemned.")
"Tevi lomlim! Prūti spēlēt Gattin." (43g: 479)
(Latv., Russ., Germ.: "We break you! Understand how to play the spouse.")
"Iste Emma, dva Strafe, numero ett." (35r: 135)
(Latv., Russ., Germ., Swed.: "Genuine Emma, two penalties, number one.")
"Vergi mēs esam." (34g: 029)
(Latv.: "We are slaves.")
"Möchte till Katorga." (34g: 551)
(Germ., Swed.: "I would like to go up to Katorga.") What "Katorga" means is not explained.
"Prosit, tu Jeskapas!"
"Naudas trūkst."
"Kosti, te deg Augstkalns." (35g: 800)
(Latv.: "Your health, Jeskapas!"—"Lack of money."—"Kosti, here burns Augstkalns."—) Augstkalns was a young Latvian scholar who doused himself with petrol and burned to death during the Russian occupation. The experimenter did not know him personally.

"Trolls tu, Koste. Te mūka, te slikti!" (47r: 298/9)
(Latv.: "You are a troll, Koste. We are tormented here, it is bad here.")
"Koste, richtig stroga. Latve." (47r: 306)
(Latv.: "Koste, it is really strict here. Latvian woman.")
"Mēs hungrig, Koste." (49g: 107)
(Latv., Germ.: "We are hungry, Koste.")
"Slepu ziņas. Te slikti." (42g: 681)
(Latv.: "Secret reports. It is bad here.")
"Te slikti, Kostja." (44r: 156)
(Latv.: "It is bad here, Kostja.")
"Cik grūti dzivot! Piemini Kristu." (47g: 354)
(Latv.: "How difficult it is to live! Remember Christ!")
"Moskva, mums gruti, gruti! Tack, Kosti!" (lar: 354/5)
(Latv., Swed.: "Moscow, it is difficult for us, difficult! Thanks, Kosti."
"Te nakts, brāli. Te putni deg."
"Kostja, tu tāl! (44b: 671/3)
(Latv.: "Here is night, brothers. Here the birds burn."—"Kostja, you are far away.")

In their distress the voices beg for help and prayers:

"Kosti, palidzi, palīdzi man!" (25r: 461)
(Latv.: "Kosti help, help me!")

A female voice:

"Cīrule, lūdzi par mani!" (25r: 464)
(Latv.: "Cirule, pray for me!")
"Cīrule, Kosti!" (same place)
"Te stāvu nedēļ nedēļām, palīdz nokārtot!" (30r: 312)
(Latv.: "Here I stand week in, week out, help tidying!")

The experimenter asks if he could help from here, from the earthly plane.

"Kannst du!" (40g: 546)
(Germ.: "You can!")
"Schwester Dora. Nepamet!—Lūdzam mēs Francijā: nepamet Schwester Dora!" (40r: 572)
(Germ., Latv.: "Sister Dora. Don't leave me!—We plead in France: do not leave sister Dora.")
"Konci, befrei!" (42g: 327)
(Latv., Germ.: "Kosti, release!")

Every now and then voices give information about the circumstances in which a person died.

Ivar died under a train. Nobody knew any details or the

real reason for his death, but his parents suspected a comrade of having pushed Ivar under the train. A voice declares:

"Nav Ivara. Pakrita pats." (39r: 633)
(Latv.: "There is no Ivar. He fell himself.")

Later on, the voice was heard again:

"Te Ivarīts." (40: 012)
(Latv.: "Here is Ivarits." [diminutive of Ivar]

Many voices report warlike conditions; these entities' minds still seem to be filled with impressions of the circumstances prevailing at the time of their death. We listen to fragments that give the macabre picture of a soldier's life—continued beyond the grave:

"Stakas—Danzig—Taschit—fünf gefallen—Leib bedeckt—Komm Ulle(r)—genau."
(Germ.: "Stakes": name; "Danzig": Dantzig; "Taschit": name; "fünf gefallen": five fallen; "Leib bedeckt": body covered; "Komm Uller": come, Uller; "genau": precise.)
"Bonau—kennen—kennt—den Gülden hat—Mann von Leningrad."
(German: "Bonau [name]—know—knows—has the florin—man from Leningrad.")
"Slatowitz—ein Mann—acht—null—ein Zoll—abreib."
(German: "Slatowitz [name]—one man—eight—nought—one inch—rub off.")
"Gotthard Glockermen—eins—zwei—null—halb drei—hundert Seiten — halb null — acht — halb sieben — Nahfront—Halbfront—knallt—Herr Putten—zwo—fünf—nah einfach."
(German: "Gotthard Glockermen [name]—one—two—nought—half three—hundred sides—half nought—eight—half seven—near front—near front—half front—bangs—Mr. Putten—two—five—near simple.")
"Adam Chujevskij — Pardon — Airik Gouverneur — wir — zünden." (23g: 432/43)
(French, Germ.: last two words German, "we—ignite.")
"Rau, wir Stalingrada, Stalingrada." (25r: 291)
(Germ., Latv.: "Rau, we are in Stalingrad, in Stalingrad.")

We hear a voice-entity expressing his fear of death:

"Žizņ stāvi! Baigā nurnurna." (25r: 296)
(Russ., Latv.: "Stand, life! The sinister Norne.") A "Norne" is a Germanic goddess of fate.

SPEECH-CONTENT OF RECORDINGS 159

Another voice complains:

"Wolga, my wse zabyti." (26g: 106)
(Russ.: "Volga, we are all forgotten.")
"My rabi, my rabi!" (26g: 182)
(Russ.: "We are slaves, we are slaves.")
"Viena tēva dēli, kauns!"
"Attacka, Konstantin!"
"Jetzt Attacka gegen uns, Kosti, Attacka now!"
"C'étaient les siempre viel opéerations." (23g: 123/34)
(Latv., Germ., French, Span.: "The sons of a father, shame!"
—"Attack, Konstantin!"—"Now attack against us, Kosti, attack now!"—"There were always many war-operations.")
"Raudiv, vernichtet vierundzwanzig unsere Gegenmenschen, die wir . . . unter haben."
"Čort vas poberi!" (31r: 398)
(Germ., Russ.: "Raudiv, destroyed twenty-four of those against us, that we . . . have under.")
"Au combat! Longue vita flieht. Han netic man." (31r: 579/81)
(French, Ital., Swed., Germ., Latv.: "Into battle. The long life flees. He does not believe me.")

Some voices insist that they are defending the experimenter; for instance:

"Konci, wir aizstāvam tevi pret ungariem, pret ungariem."
(Germ., Latv.: "We defend you against the Hungarians, against the Hungarians.")

There are voices that complain of lack of bombs, that what they are doing disgusts them, etc., and those, on the other hand, who seem to praise war:

"Kosti dien, liebe du Krieg." (43g: 513)
(Germ.: "Kosti serve, love war.")

A few voices seem to come from the present war in Vietnam.

"Petersons karā Vietnamā. Nav te taisnibas. Darija man pāri." (42g: 420/3)
(Latv.: "Petersons is in the war in Vietnam. There is no justice here. One has done me wrong.")

25. *Transport, Travel and Place-Names*

The fragments of conversation here compiled indicate that means of transport exist and that the voice-entities "travel".

Mainly well-known place-names are mentioned, often in connection with transit, arrival or departure.

"Mēs braucam pie Raudive ciemā." (33g: 197)
(Latv.: "We drive to Raudive as guests.")
"Wir haben Susa-Busi." (34g: 485)
(Germ.: "We have Susa-Bus.")
"Kostuli, Kostuli, mēs lidojam pa Hollandi. Hollande tomēr pagaidam auksta. Nav labi nolaiša nai." (34g: 540/1)
(Latv.: "Kostuli, Kostuli, we fly over Holland. Holland, however, is cold for the time being. It is not good to land.")
"Tāles, aber Kole, slāpes!"
"Tulin atdzersies!"
"Turi, te Kelpe!" (34g: 519/20)
(Latv., Germ.: "Long distances, but Kole, the thirst!"—"You shall have something to drink immediately!"—"Stop, here is Kelpe!")
"Reisoi wir!" (23g: 523)
"Saphir, reso vi!" (34r: 239)
(Germ., Swed.: "We travel." [The German word "reisen" has here become "reisoi".]—"Saphir, we are travelling!")
"A Linda, där baigi parli, da varim wir wiederškērsa." (34r: 119)
(Ital., Swed., Latv., Germ.: "In Linda, where one speaks badly, there we can cross again.")
"Spičku nav. Fahren!"
"Iekšā ir!"
"Met Korn!"
"Mēs tencinam, mēs tencinam."
"Ciet aci, Raudive, natt!" (35g: 266/78)
(Russ., Latv., Germ., Swed.: "We have no matches! Drive!" —"Within there are some."—"Throw grain!"—"We thank, we thank."—"Close your eyes, Raudive, it is night.")
"Wir doch ist Stockholmā."
"Dod čoku 'genetim!' "
"Kam?"
"Čaplis, Čaplis!"
"Ultuna!"
"Ultuna sten!"
"Vilken styr!"
"Churagan." (35r: 608/10)
(Germ., Latv., Swed., Russ.: "We are nevertheless in Stockholm."—"Give Tschock to 'geneti'!" [The experimenter does not know the word 'geneti'. "Tschock" seems to be somebody's name.]—"Whom?"—"Caplis, Caplis." [Caplis is another name.]—"Ultuna!" [This is a suburb of Uppsala.]—"Ultuna is groaning."—"What a tax!"—"Barrow!" [Ancient burial place.])

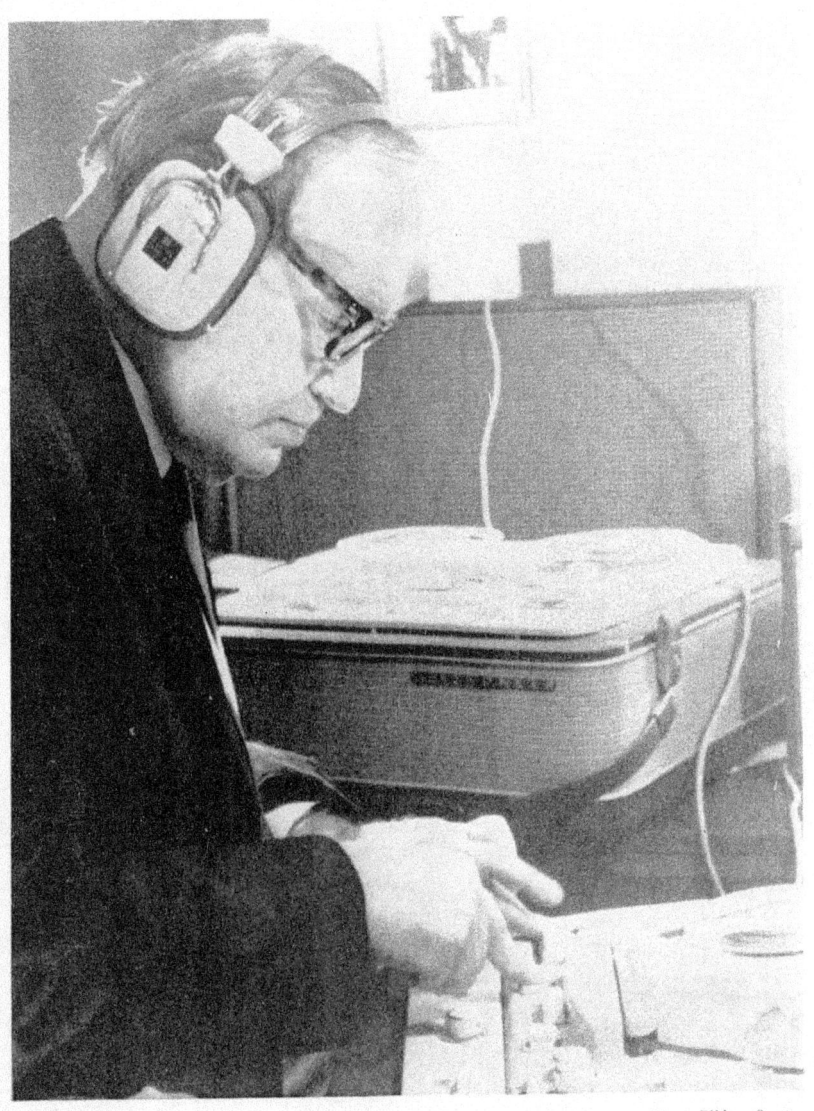

Photo: *Bild am Sonntag*

Dr. Konstantin Raudive and his scientific collaborators have recorded 72,000 voices on tape of which 25,000 have been identified. For many years he worked with an ordinary tape-recorder which produced excellent results.

Prof. Dr. Gebhard Frei, President of the International Society of Catholic Parapsychologists. Co-Founder of the Jung Institute in Zürich.

Monsignor Prof. Karl Pfleger, French Theologian and Papal Chaplain, an outspoken supporter of Dr. Raudive and his work.

(l. to r.) Professor Dr. Hans Bender, Germany's leading parapsychologist, Dr. Zenta Maurina and Dr. Raudive.

Among the collaborators from the United States were Professor W. H. Uphoff who joined Dr. Raudive in Bad Krozingen. With them are Mrs. Uphoff and Dr. Maurina.

"Vi vill Parizi."
"Pareizi!"
"Eri-Sund!"
"Laid pa pilnam!"
"Gaismo ceļu tu!" (31g: 379/84)
(Swed., Latv.: "We want Paris."—"Right."—"Eri-Sund." [Place name.]—"Leave it in full [direct] gear!"—"Light the way!")
"Vila os."
"Jetzt setzet Aufbruch!"
"Zollst du mehr?"
"Gute Nacht!"
"Martin, wir fahren. Soll ich aussteigen?" (31r: 133/5)
(Swed., Germ.: "We are resting."—"Make your departure now."—"Do you give more duty?"—"Good night!"—"Martin, we are travelling. Shall I get out?")

We hear a group of people talking as if they were in the experimenter's room, and just preparing to leave:

"Raudive, ganz schwarz."
"Spičkas, Pīter!"
"Spičkas ir."
"Lempe, warum?"
"Cepuri!"
"Vi skinen."
"Sveiks!"
"Wir holen ab."
"Tempo wird begehrt." (31r: 451)
(Germ., Russ., Latv., Swed.: "Raudive, quite black."—"Matches, Peter!"—"There are matches."—"Scoundrel, why?"—"Please, my cap!"—"We seem."—"Adieu!"—"We come to fetch you."—"Speed is required.")

In the following fragment the impression of a journey is most vividly given:

"Åker Popa."
"Horrore, pazūd!"
"Un bizo!"
"Ciņa habe gört!"
"Gib Kostule, Kostulīt!"
"Er, Konstantin."
"Vi sollen bombe."
"Oi, oj, schnellst! Popi, dej kennt!"
"Er setzt jau pa deviņiem, 'gandiem'."
"Au, bona jūŗá, jūŗá!"
"I go übernätte."

"A Lorecane."
"Ta tomba!"
"Putinā entsetzlich, Konstantin!"
"Kosti redz, komm gleich, nu komm!"
"Du påminska Propf."
"Yo påminska på Pfropf."
"Minskana Mitte!" (34g: 505/17)
(Swed., Latv., Germ., Lat., Engl., Ital., Span.: "Popa drives."
—"Horror, vanish!"—"And chases around!"—"I have finished the battle."—"Give, Kostule, Kostulit!"—"He, Konstantin!"—"We are to bombard."—"Oi, oi, quickest! one knows you, Popi!"—"He settles already on the 9th 'gand' [degree? grade?]"—"Oh, good sea, the sea!"—"I go to stay overnight."—"In Lorecane."—"Take the grave with you!"—"It snows horribly, Konstantin!"—"One can see Kosti, come immediately, come on!"—"Diminish the stopper."—"I diminish the stopper."—"Diminish the middle!")

"Lebe wohl, ich gehe fort."
"Te tev West a Nordwest."
"Prieka tev pietrūka."
"Tas iet operativ, pat vilki nepaliek te."
"Voyena Tibet."
"Ar tautas binokuli."
"Dod Nachschub!"
"Alvis Bukes te." (35r: 593/4)
(Germ., Latv., French: (modified) "Farewell, I am leaving."—"Here you have West—North-West."—"You had a lack of joy."—"This is operational, even wolves do not stay here."—"We see Tibet."—"With the binoculars of the people."—"Give reinforcement!"—"Here is Alvis Bukes.")

"Minska, te Letton!"
"Es minsku." (77r: 519)
(Swed., Latv., Span.: "Decrease, here is a Latvian!"—"I decrease.")

In this context also, the experimenter is often called by name:

"Pareizi, tava Kurzeme raud, Kost."
"Pareizi, tā raud!"
"Te Usna, dreh pareiz'!"
"Dunkel!"
"Papīc!"
"Papīksti te tu." (37r: 605/8)
(Latv., Germ.: "Right, your Courland is crying, Kost."—"Quite right, it cries!"—"Here is Usna, turn correctly!" Usna is the name of a small Latvian town.—"Dark!"—"Give a peep!"—"You give a peep here.")

"Courland, Raudive!" (40g: 446)

Riga, capital city of Latvia, is frequently mentioned:

"Es gribu tūlit jāt."
"Uz Rigu tu?"
"Kosti, turies!"
"Mīļa ty."
"Minus te."
"Raudive, Luta!" (38g: 108/13)
(Latv., Russ.: "I want to ride immediately."—"To Riga, you?"—"Kosti, hold!"—"You are kind!"—"Minus here."—"Raudive, Luta!" [Luta was a schoolmate of the experimenter. See also page 58.]
"Riga!" (39g: 382, 42r: 294, 46r: 149)
"Tev Riga, neguli!" (37r: 335)
(Latv.: "Riga is yours, don't sleep!")

The Swedish town of Uppsala is mentioned in various contexts:

"Von Uppsala Jakob." (36r: 553)
"Uppsala!" (37r: 508, 39g: 396, 39r: 889)
"Te tev Uppsala!" (37r: 602)
(First sentence Germ.: "From Uppsala Jakob."—Third sentence: "Here you have Uppsala.")
"Konstantin, te Uppsala, meži te gratis. Te Uppsala, comodo. Skaisti, Kost! Sveiki, tu Kosta." (39g: 608/9)
(Latv., Span.: "Konstantin, here is Uppsala, forests here are free. Here is Uppsala, comfortable. Beautiful, Kost! Good-bye, you Kosta!")
"Uppsala, brāļs Haralds!" (Hg: 188)
(Latv.: "Uppsala, brother Harald!")
"Pasveicini mūs Uppsalā!" (44b: 327)
(Latv.: "Greet us in Uppsala!")
"Uppsala fin badet. Kosta, pie tevis skali." (44b: 410)
(Swed., Latv.: "Uppsala has a fine bath. Kosta, at your place it sounds loud." The last remark probably refers to a wrong tuning in of the radio: the sound-volume prevents the voices from getting through.)
"Uppsala te Tundra!" (42r: 754)
(Latv.: "Uppsala, here is Tundra!")
"Kapēc ne Uppsalā?"
(Latv.: "Why not in Uppsala?")
"Immer Uppsala!" (947g: 672)
(Germ.: "Always Uppsala!")
"Ar to Kosti tīri simpatiski."
"Söka dej!"
"Sveiki te!"
"Konstantinu! Te Uppsala, hej, hej!" (38g: 175/201)

(Latv., Swed.: "With Kosti it's quite sympathetic."—"Seek [to know] thyself."—"Be greeted here!"—"Konstantin! Here is Uppsala, heh, heh!")
"Mūsu Kosti, uzklaus!"
"Uppsalā tev jauki gōj, Kost." (42g: 482/3)
(Latv.: "Our Kosti, listen!"—"In Uppsala you fared well, Kost.")
"Te Brōli no Uppsalas."
"Uppsalā tomēr gadi, Kost." (42g: 688)
(Latv.: "Here are the brothers from Uppsala."—"In Uppsala you have nevertheless spent years, Kost.")
"Tava stundis Uppsalā." (44r: 521)
(Latv., Germ.: "Your hour in Uppsala.")

Every now and then the birthplace of the experimenter, Asūne, Osyuna in Latgalian, is mentioned by the voices:

"Te Osūna." (35r: 849)
(Latg.: "Here is Asūne.")
"Asūne!" (22r: 301)
"Osūne gribē līgot pie tēva tava." (27g: 049)
(Latv.: "Asūne wanted to celebrate the feast of Ligo at your father's.")
"Asūne hört." (35g: 587)
(Germ.: "Asūne hears.")
"Osūna tu dari." (47g: 481)
(Latv.: "Asūne, you are doing it.")

Other place-names heard include: Madrid; Sigtuna as transmitting station; Märsta, a railway station between Uppsala and Stockholm; Lund; Jelgava (Mitau); Krozingen (the experimenter's present domicile) and, above all, a Latvian provincial town called Ikšķile (or Uxküll), which the voices name as their "fortress". Here follow some examples:

"Madrid!"
"Wo wohnt vän?"
"Padre zin." (36g: 280/2)
(Germ., Swed., Span., Latv.: "Madrid!"—"Where does the friend live?"—"Father knows it.")
"Märsta te, mus' stacija." (40g: 459)
(Latv.: "Here is Märsta, our station.")
"Lunda, mirst Olga." (Hr: 315)
(Latv.: "Lund, Olga is dying.")
"Jelgava redz." (40r: 287)
(Latv.: "One can see Jelgava.")

"Jelgavā samojedu nav." (42g: 045)
(Latv.: "In Jelgava there are no Samoyedes.")
"Karočij bulvar. Še Krozing."
"Naše bringa! Krozingen weg!" (45g: 036)
(Russ., Latv., Germ.: "The shortest boulevard. Here is Krozingen."—"Fetch the ones belonging to us! Krozingen away!")
"Krozingena būs. Mes paņēmiens, Koste." (47g: 447)
(Latv.: "It will be in Krozingen. We are helping hands, Koste.")

The experimenter explains that he is in Krozingen. A voice calls:

"Pareizi, brat! O Leben!"
(Latv., Russ., Germ.: "Right, brother! Oh what a life!")
"Ikškile!" (30r: 052, 35g: 123, 40r: 264)
"Raudive, Ikškili redz." (34r: 067)
(Latv.: "Raudive, one can see Ikškile.")
"Te Juris neziņā, Ikškile." (41g: 275)
(Latv.: "Here is Juris, in the uncertainty, Ikškile.")
"Tja Ikškilīte. Te Ješko sēd un izskaidro vēl." (43r: 074)
(Latv.: "Here is Ikškilite. Here sits Jesko [and] still explaining." "Iškilite" is the diminutive of Ikškile.)
"Jōns, Kosti.—Ikškilē mans forts." (42g: 256)
(Latv.: "Jons, Kosti.—My fortress is Ikškile.")

The experimenter tells the voices that he is writing a report about them and asks whether they have any advice to give.

"Jā, nav Ikškile vēl." (49g: 274)
(Latv.: "Yes, Ikškile does not yet exist.")
"Kosta, tu? Ikškile.—Yo Kosta will." (47r: 656)
(Latv., Span., Germ.: "Kosta, you? Ikškile.—I want Kosta.")

(IV) PRACTICAL PROBLEMS OF COMMUNICATION

26. Spidola

Spidola is the name of a legendary female figure, bearer of light and of freedom for her people; through the works of Latvian poets (Pumpurs and Rainis) she has become a symbol of the ideal Latvian woman. "Spidola" appeared in connection with the voice-phenomena research in this way.

The experimenter tried to follow Friedrich Jürgenson's advice to find assistance in his work through a female helper in the "beyond". Jürgenson himself had such a helper, a voice-entity named "Lena", as the reader may recall, and at one of his recording-sessions the experimenter asked whether "Lena" would assist him. A female voice answered:

"Ich weigere mich!" (20g: 699)
(Germ.: "I refuse.")
"Lena nach Armee, Lena nevar būt!"
"Konstantin, hörst du Lena?" (25r: 204)
(Germ., Latv.: "Lena gone to army, Lena cannot be."—
"Konstantin, can you hear Lena?")

After this "Lena" disappeared and another female voice was heard:

"Spīdola tava palīdze!" (20r: 428)
(Latv.: "Spidola your helper.")

From then on Spidola started to assist at recordings; later, however, the experimenter noticed that, though Spidola fulfilled her function as helper, the radio had to be manipulated in a way which made strict control over recordings impossible.

Gradually other voices came to the fore, demanding that recordings should be made on a certain pre-determined wavelength (see "Technical Questions", page 169). To avoid getting into ordinary direct radio-transmissions the experimenter tuned his set to wavelengths located between two transmitting-stations. This technique requires long and patient practice, but seems to satisfy the voice-entities better than Spidola's directions. The varied experiments conducted in the presence of collaborators have proved that this is the correct method to adopt; the voices need the free wavelengths between two stations in order to make their contact. It may be possible, at some future date, to create "voice-transmitting stations" such as the physicist, Professor Alex Schneider (St. Gallen, Switzerland) has in mind.

This does not mean that the problem "Spidola" poses is solved. Behind this name stands a conscious, independent voice-entity which, demonstrating a spiritual principle, is able to appear under many guises and names.

Here are a few examples of how "Spidola"—acoustically—emphasises her existence; for, even when her name is not

SPEECH-CONTENT OF RECORDINGS

actually mentioned, some characteristic traits of speech make it possible to guess that "Spidola" is the originator of the voice:

"Konstantin, horch!" (22r: 134)
"Viel Quatsch! Furchtbar, furchtbar!" (23g: 040)
(Germ.: "Konstantin, listen!"—"A lot of nonsense! Terrible, terrible!") These two sentences refer to some disturbing radio-interferences during the recording.
"Tagad Aufnahme, tagad jauna Aufnahme!" (23g: 257)
(Latv., Germ.: "Record now, new recording now!") This sentence appears consecutively in eight different variations.
"Achtung, schliess aus! Tot schlägt!" (23g: 470/2)
(Germ.: "Attention, exclude! Strikes dead!")
"Ich danke, mīlulīt, muns mīlulīt. Ich bin Leiterin." (28r: 629/32)
(Germ., Latg.: "I thank you, dear, my dear. I am the guide.")

At the beginning of a recording-session the experimenter says: "Dear Spidola, take over the leadership!" A woman's voice answers:

"Ja, ich übernehme, mit vielem Dank!" (35g: 587)
(Germ.: "Yes, I take over, with many thanks.")

Who is "Spidola"?—During one of the recordings the experimenter addresses her: "Dear Spidola. . . ." Immediately a voice comes in:

"Ich bin da!"
(Germ.: "I am here!")

The experimenter: "You take the lead now . . ."

"Jag Schwester bin." (35r: 148)
(Swed., Germ.: "I am sister.")
"Liebe dich!" (35r: 280)
(Germ.: "Love you!")

Once again, the experimenter addresses himself to Spidola: "Dear Spidola, if you can, please converse with me."

"Hast schon du!"
(Germ.: "You have already done so!")
Experimenter: "Your friends are here."
"Fast neviens! Tumbelarum!"
(Germ., Latv.: "Hardly any! Tumbelarum!")

Now the experimenter addresses Margarete.

"Kā kāds ubago! Kā vispār valdzinā?"
"Kā pops!"

"Kas, Koni? Kosts ir vitne." (35r: 501/12)
(Latv., Swed.: "How someone begs! How does one hold [someone] anyway?"—"Like a priest!"—"Who, Koni? Kosts is witness.")

On one occasion, during a microphone-recording, the experimenter tries to switch over to radio. A voice intervenes:

"Warte, später!"
"Später, gaid!"
(Germ., Latv.: "Wait, later!"—"Later, wait!")

The experimenter asks the voice-entities to help him. In response:

"Nomierinies, te Erde oben." (36r: 322)
(Latv., Germ.: "Calm yourself, up here is the earth.")

Experimenter: "Many thanks!"

"Lūdzu!" (36r: 230)
(Latv.: "Please!") Meaning: "Don't mention it!"
"Vi ventar på dej." (same place: 238)
(Swed.: "We are waiting for you.")

Experimenter: "I am proud of her [Spidola]."

"Einmal richtig." (36r: 613)
"Warte, te māmuļa, warte!" (37r: 403/4)
(Germ., Latv.: "For once correct!"—"Wait, here is mother, wait!")
"Warte, später!" (same place: 397)
(Germ.: "Wait, later!")

When the experimenter asks Spidola whether she cannot give an account of the world in which she lives, the answer is:

"Nevaru tagad, Raudive, esmu Osūnē." (42g: 252)
(Latv.: "At the moment I can't, Raudive, I am in Asūne.")

The experimenter announces himself at the beginning of a recording. A voice interrupts:

"Nachts müde. Es milu tevi. Spīdola. Gute Nacht, gute pirts!" (same place: 367)
(Germ., Latv.: "At night, tired. I love you. Spidola. Good night, good bath [room].")

Spidola, remarks the experimenter, belongs to the very closest of friends "over there".

"Tici vēl, Raudive! Kostja, Spīdola tova mōte!" (42g: 528)
(Latg.: "Do believe, Raudive! Spidola is your mother.")

"Spidola" thus embodies the two primeval powers of sister and mother.

During one recording, made at 2 a.m., the experimenter calls on Spidola.

"Rīts, naktīs guļ!"
(Latv.: "Tomorrow, at night one sleeps!")

The experimenter then calls radio Peter.

"Aļožs guļ. Weiss Petrautzki. Schweig! Johns Nulle hilft."
(Latv., Germ.: "Aljos sleeps. Petrautzki knows. Be quiet! Johns Nulle is helping.")

Experimenter: "In time, and with more practice, the difficulties will certainly be overcome."

"Ir praksis. Tagad guli!" (42r: 897)
(Latv.: "There is practice. Now sleep!")

Although the experimenter moved on from Spidola's way of practice, the voice still appears. During a later recording the experimenter wishes for Spidola's help. A woman's voice:

"Immer, Raudiv'!" (46g: 148)
(Germ.: "Always, Raudiv'!")

The following microphone-voice also confirms Spidola's existence:

"Pamīru, Spīdola, ar labu." (47g: 480)
(Latv.: "Truce, Spidola, in good will.")
"Efīr! dirigē Spīdola." (53g: 505)
(Russ., Latv.: "Ether! Here Spidola directs.")

27. *Technical Questions*

Radio—Radar—Transmitting-Stations

Who can finally solve the mystery of the voices? One of the voice-entities gives a clear indication:

"Bescheid ar technikiem izšķirs." (33g: 650)
(Germ., Latv.: "The information will be given expression through the technicians.")

"Koste, tu? Un momento, technikis tja. Kosti, Technik wichtig." (49g: 254)
(Latv., Ital., Germ.: "Koste, you? One moment, here is a technician. Kosti, technique is important.")
"Brāli!"
"Verfolgst du Technik? Wie knappi du siehst!" (lar: 255, 262)
(Latv., Germ.: "Brother!"—"Do you keep up with technique? How narrowly you see.")

The voices often give technical hints; but sometimes they roundly condemn the experimenter, telling him he doesn't understand how to manipulate the recordings. Such concrete material helps to convince us of the partnership between the voice-entities and the experimenter or his collaborators.

"Uzstādi pareizi!" (35g: 626)
(Latv.: "Tune in correctly!")
"Kostja har startat unter Ton."
"Tempo vi noch har." (35r: 319)
(Swed., Germ., Ital.: "Kostja has started below pitch."—"We still have time.")
"Slikti stūrē." (43r: 525)
(Latv.: "You are steering badly.")
"Konstantin, trudnosti šlusat hier." (35r: 625)
(Russ., Germ.: "Konstantin, it is difficult to hear here.")

Or, there is praise:

"Wir lysen auch. Kosta, gut! Nikolajs te. Hier Steņka." (41g: 915)
(Germ., Swed., Latv.: "We can hear too. Kosta good! Nikolaj is here. Here is Stenka.")

During one recording the experimenter is asked to speak Swedish:

"Tala svenskan!" (42g: 128)

The voice-entities follow the recordings minutely. On switching over from radio to microphone, a voice asks:

"Vai tu beigsi?" (46g: 380)
(Latv.: "Are you going to stop?")
"Tava lente vibrē, Konstantin!" (39r: 471)
(Latv.: "Your tape is vibrating, Konstantin!")

The experimenter announces: "Now channel two..."

"Kanal dwa! Jag vet, Kosta. Tala padre."
(Germ., Russ., Swed., Span.: "Channel two! I know, Kosta. Father speaks.")

The experimenter is in a hotel-room in Heidelberg. He is recording through microphone:

"Mēs kustinām. Tu labi trāpi."
(Latv.: "We are moving. You hit well.")

After the experimenter's remark that he has no radio, a voice says:

"Mēs to zinam." (38g: 438/9)
(Latv.: "We know that.")

The phenomenon's independence of time and space is further confirmed by a voice heard during a recording-session in Würzburg. The experimenter asks whether time and space play a rôle; comes the answer:

"Keine Rolle! Margaret, Kostja!" (39r: 394)
(Germ.: "No rôle! Margaret, Kostja!")

Which are more reliable, radio-voices or microphone-voices? This question has often been asked. From the point of view of the researcher the problem does not arise, as the authenticity of voices is determined by their language, speech-content, and rhythm, in short, by all the special characteristics that mark the voice-phenomena. The voices themselves however, have expressed right from the start a preference for radio-recordings. This request is sometimes most urgently pressed:

"Bitte Radio!" (24g: 487)
(Germ.: "Please radio!")
"Pa druskai nur durch Radio." (34r: 053)
(Latv., Germ.: "Bit by bit only through radio.")
"Laid tikai radio!" (35g: 673)
(Latv.: "Just let the radio loose!")
"Lobōk pa radio!" (40r: 382)
(Latg.: "Better through radio!")
"Runāt radio! Kosti, tu vārti!" (47g: 626/8)
(Latv.: "Speak through the radio! Kosti, you are the gate!")
"På radio!" (36g: 107)
(Swed.: "Through the radio!")
"Maita tāds, radio kopla!" (42r: 652)
(Latv., Swed.: "What a rascal, switch on the radio!")

The experimenter announces that he is now going to record through microphone.

> "Žāl, Kosta. Trost!" (35r: 887)
> (Latg., Germ.: "I regret that Kosta. Consolation!")
> "Durch Radio mēs pienemam. Te Technik. Der liebste Konstantin!" (36g: 550)
> (Latv., Germ.: "Through radio we accept. Here is technique. Dear Konstantin!")

The experimenter interrupts a radio-recording and switches over to microphone. A voice asks, a little ironically:

> "Radio taupi tu?" (42r: 346)
> (Latv.: "Are you saving on radio?")

Another voice advises:

> "Kosti, dežurē på radio!" (same place: 571)
> (Latv., Swed.: "Kosti, keep watch through radio.")

With the determination of intelligent and rational beings, the voice-entities, as the examples show, give strong advice to stick to radio-recordings: they also point out that they themselves use radio. One more example:

> "Tesna te! Te radio, Koste." (39r: 888)
> (Russ., Latv.: "It is narrow here! Here is radio, Koste.")

Very odd is the following longish statement:

> "Nur auf Radio! Er sprach nur deutsch per Radio. Deutsche Freunde, Marzipan!—Welche Freunde, Marzipan? Welche Freunde?" (42g: 412)
> (Germ.: "Only on radio! He spoke only German through radio. German friends, Marzipan!—Which friends, Marzipan? Which friends?")

The experimenter in fact had spoken mainly German during these recordings.

If the experimenter goes on manipulating the radio during a recording, it seems to have a disturbing effect and the voices react by objecting strongly:

> "Paliec uz noteiktu staciju!" (31r: 658)
> (Latv.: "Stay on one particular station!")
> "Kosti, turies uz vietas!" (37r: 604)
> (Latv.: "Kosti, keep to the spot!"
> "Kosti, brauc pa vidū!" (42g: 770)
> (Latv.: "Kosti, drive in the middle!")
> "Kosti, dej te pa vidū!" (31g: 569)
> (Latv.: "Kosti, dance here in the middle!")

"Kosta, pagaid!" (37r: 614)
(Latv.: "Kosta, wait.")
"Tava, tava ... dzird slikti!" (same place: 615)
(Latv.: "Your, your ... one hears badly!")
"Kosti, venta! Jezups." (44b: 670)
(Swed.: "Kosti, wait! Jēzups.")
"Beröre inte med Sender!" (41g: 915)
(Swed., Germ.: "Don't come into contact with the transmitter!")

When the experimenter searches for another station, the voices call it "chasing around" or "flapping around":

"Bizoj!" (39r: 726)
(Latv.: "He is chasing around!")
"Kostuli, tu?"
"Vīnš par ilgi 'flurdē' vorbei!"
"Kosta kustās. Böse te på mej." (42g: 719)
(Latv., Germ., Swed.: "Kostuli, you?"—"He 'flaps' past too long."—"Kosta moves. They are cross with me here.")

The voices often mention "radar":

"Das Radarproblem."
"Konstantinus tak radars." (45g: 447)
(Germ., Latv.: "The radar-problem."—"But Konstantin is radar.")
"Pats radars." (44b: 312)
(Latv.: "You yourself are radar.")
"Radars, Koste!" (47r: 675)
"Es šaubos 'radatūrā'." (42g: 168)
(Latv.: "I doubt the 'radatura'.") "Radatura", a neologism based on "radar" appears to refer to the beam.

That the voices are seeking contact and in fact, making strenuous efforts to establish it, has already been observed. Contact between the two worlds, it seems, is regarded as a "great deed".

One of the participants at a recording-session asks the invisible entities to tell him something.

"Wir mühen."
(Germ.: "We are trying.")

The experimenter then asks whether one of them cannot give him more detailed information from "beyond". The answer comes in the symbolic remark:

"Ikški tu gribi, Lamm?" (42g: 164)
(Latv., Germ.: "You want the thumb, lamb?")

More concrete are statements such as:

"Raudiv', wir kontakten." (35r: 330)
"Wir suchen Kontakt."—"Wir wünschen Kosti, Kontakt." (35r: 409)
"Raudive, Kontakt! Stop mūziku!" (24r: 035)
(Germ., Latv.: "Raudiv' we made contact."—"We are seeking contact."—"We wish for Kosti, contact."—"Raudive, contact! Stop the music!")
"Hallo, Kontakt! Stalin, damoj!" (Gg: 365)
(Germ., Russ.: "Hallo, contact! Stalin, home!")

The astonishing conception that "other-worldly" transmitting-stations exist, emerges quite clearly from many of the voices' statements. Information received indicates that there are various groups of voice-entities who operate their own stations. The experimenter has recorded this phenomenon on hundreds of occasions and has submitted the tapes to experts for listening-in-tests.

As the following examples show, the voice-entities do not only use their own transmitting and receiving stations, they also have to apply their own special type of electronic technique. Once again we get the vivid impression that consciously reasoning entities are here at work, trying to achieve contact with the experimenter.

"Studio Kelpe. Konstantin, unser Ehre." (22r: 307)
"Kelpe tepat." (22r: 457)
(Germ., Latv.: "Studio Kelpe. Konstantin, our honour."—"Here on the spot is Kelpe.")
"Raudive, Kelpe!"
"Hallo, Rundfunk Kelpe, Kelpe!" (23r: 465)
"Vi hjälp." (same place: 568)
(Germ., Swed.: "Raudive, Kelpe!"—"Hallo, Radio Kelpe, Kelpe!"—"We help.")
"Konstantin, hier Kelpe. Siedlung 'Ny-Bron', weit entwickelt." (same place: 580)
"Wir helfen Zenta." (same place: 587)
"Unser Kostja, unser Kostja, Kelpe!" (24r: 022)
"Kelpe, Kelpe, Kelpe! Konstantin dzirdēju." (same place: 033)
(Germ., Latv.: "Konstantin, here Kelpe. Settlement 'Ny-Bron', far developed."—"We help Zenta."—"Our Kostja, our Kostja, Kelpe!"—"Kelpe, Kelpe, Kelpe! Konstantin, I heard.")

Immediately following this message, a conversation-fragment:

"Kostja, hier Eric Frick-Stengel."

"Kittel!"
"Tie mani biedri."
(Germ., Latv.: "Kostja, here is Eric Frick-Stengel."—
"Kittel!"—"They are my comrades.")
A female voice:
"Mīli 'Burschaft'."
(Latv., Germ.[?]: "A dear 'brotherhood'.")
Female voice:
"Hitler!"
A male voice, a little softer:
"Hitler, Hitler!"
The same male voice:
"Unser Partie, unser Partie, unser Partie!" (24r: 038/53)
(Germ.: "Our party, our party, our party!")
A chorus of voices shouts:
"Hitler, unser Führer!"
(Germ.: "Hitler, our leader!")
A voice in low tones:
"Konstantin, paslikti!" (same place: 125)
(Latv.: "Konstantin, it is bad.")

Music interferes with the recording—then one hears a male voice:

"Hitler, Konstantin!" (same place)
"Konstantin, tev Kelpe hjälpe." (40g: 328)
(Latv., Swed.: "Konstantin, Kelpe helps you.")

The experimenter starts to say: "My dear friends..." A voice interrupts:

"Meine du Kelpe? Lettische norme! Sak Dank! Te mate." (42g: 724)
(Germ., Latv.: "Do you mean Kelpe? Curtail the Latvian [language]! Say thank you! Here is mother.")
"Tais tiltus Kelpe." (43r: 099)
(Latv.: "Kelpe builds bridges.")
"Mēs, Kelpe, palīdzam." (43r: 176)
(Latv.: "We, Kelpe, are helping.")

At the very beginning of these investigations, a voice drew the experimenter's attention to "Radio Peter" which, next to "Studio Kelpe", appears to play an important rôle.

"Radio Peter!" (23r: 020)
"Peter!"
"Peter, Kosti, unser Studio, unser Studio!" (23r: 644)
(Germ.: "Peter, Kosti, our studio, our studio!")
"Radio Peter." (30g: 237, 39g: 330)

"Konstantin, Peters." (39r: 350)
"Otto Mainz, Peters Pfarrer. Katoļiem aizliegts piedalīties, Kostja." (same place: 669)
(Germ., Latv.: "Otto Mainz, Peter's pastor. The Catholics are forbidden to participate, Kostja.")
"Konstantin, wir wollen dir helfen. Radio Peter." (23r: 565/6)
(Germ.: "Konstantin, we want to help you. Radio Peter.")

The experimenter, fascinated and full of curiosity, listened unsuspectingly to the voices of both stations and used them to extend the scope of his research; then, one morning, a voice sounded on the tape:

"Guten Morgen. Bitte, du zusammen wählen Führer und dazu Stellung zu nehmen." (25g: 037/9)
(Germ.: "Good morning. Please, together you are to choose leader and declare your position in this respect.")

A little later, another voice:

"Bitte, Studio zu wählen!" (same place: 041)
(Germ.: "Please, to choose studio.")

After this, the voice of a friend:

"Mierā, suns jau guļ. Loorits, dein Freund." (same place: 042/3)
(Latv., Germ.: "Quiet, the dog is already asleep. Loorits, your friend.")—Loorits (see page 61) was an Estonian Professor who worked at the university of Uppsala.

A woman's voice:

"Tici!" (same place: 044)
(Latv.: "Believe!")

Now "Studio Kelpe" comes in:

"Hier Kelpe, hier Kelpe! Wähle, wähle!" (same place: 045/8)
(Germ.: "Here Kelpe, here Kelpe! Choose, choose.")

A verbal battle ensues between various voices:

"Skeptikis!" (same place: 058)
(Latv.: "Sceptic!")
"Šaubies!" (same place: 061)
(Latv.: "Have doubts!")
"Visam tici!" (same place)
(Latv.: "Believe in everything!")
"Konstantin, tici! Tava māte." (same place: 066)
(Latv.: "Konstantin, believe! Your mother.")
"Konstantin, tava māsa."

Members of the working session on 3 April 1970. (l. to r.) Prof. Dr. H. Bender, Dr. Keil (partly hidden), Mr. Gutjahr, Prof. Schneider, Mr. U. Ungern, Mr. Rudolph, Mr. Lemke, Dr. Raudive.

Professor Alex Schneider the Swiss physicist who has been one of the closest collaborators of Dr. Raudive.

Mr. Theodor Rudolph, well known electronics engineer. In the course of his research, Mr. Rudolph designed the Goniometer which has been used for recent experiments.

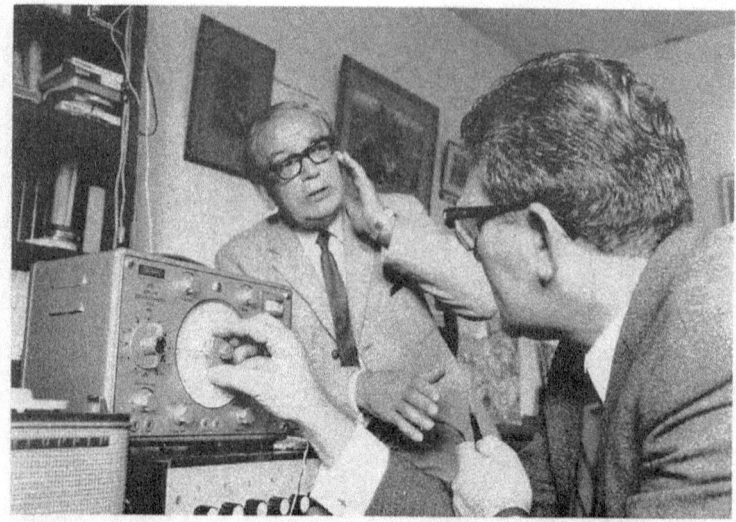

Bild am Sonntag sent a team of investigators to Dr. Raudive. Electronics expert H. Schauff from Cologne was one of the team whose report in the newspaper evoked tremendous interest. However, their story appeared too fantastic—or outrageous by German standards—that other papers did not want to follow up the story.

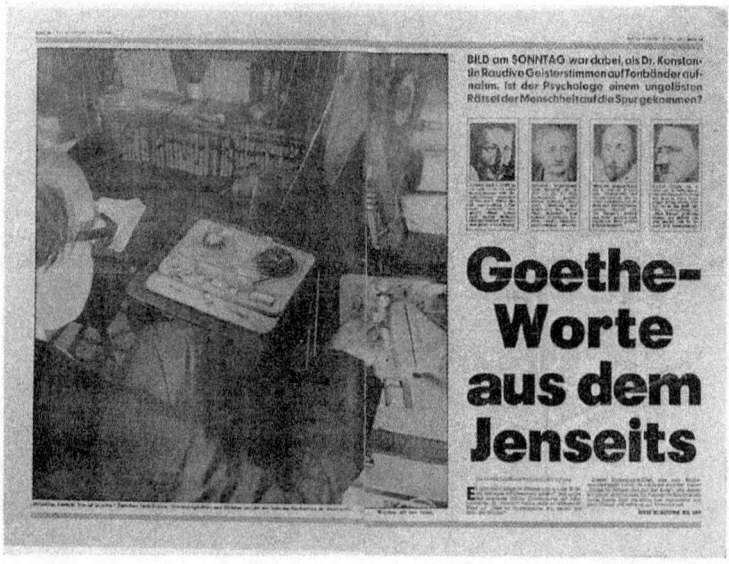

The centre pages of *Bild am Sonntag* on 19 October 1969. "Has this psychologist solved the oldest riddle of mankind?" was the question asked, and in big headlines: GOETHE SPEAKS FROM THE OTHER SIDE. Among other voice phenomena, the paper featured messages purporting to come from Hitler, Goethe and Shakespeare. It was this kind of publicity which nearly killed the serious research.

SPEECH-CONTENT OF RECORDINGS

(Latv.: "Konstantin, your sister.")
"Konstantin, tova māte!"
(Latg.: "Konstantin, your mother!")
"Raudive, tici! Margarete." (same place: 068/70)
(Latv.: "Raudive, believe! Margarete.")

A little later we hear:

"Kelpe-Studio, wir sind Freidenker." (25g: 102)
(Germ.: "Kelpe-Studio, we are free-thinkers.")

Significantly, after this instance of "having words", a voice warns:

"Mierā! Mieru, mierā, mieru! Golvu Golvu!" (same place: 157/60)
(Latv.: "Steady!" This 4 times; "Keep calm!" Twice; "Keep your head!")

As the experimenter chose "Radio Peter", voices of the "Kelpe Studio" threatened him at the next recording session:

"Mēs bringa till styrelsen dir." (25g: 367)
(Latv., Swed., Germ.: "We will bring you before the government.")
"Verteidige Jude Lielupes mežā!" (same place: 370)
(Germ., Latv.: "Defend Jew[s] in the forest of Lielupe!")
During Hitler's reign thousands of Jews had been murdered in this forest.

A conversation then started between two voices:

1st voice: "He—Christian!"
2nd voice: "Netrūka."
(Latv.: "It wasn't missing.")
1st voice: "Latviešu sabiedris ir."
(Latv.: "He is a member of Latvian society.") "Sabiedris" is a neologism based on "sabiedrība": society.
2nd voice (crossly): "Nulle! Ich torka ihn von Innenstelle. Žebrē hineinfährt ihn, hinein in vorne, sazvērnieku!"
(Germ., Swed., Latv.: "Null! I wither him from within. Žebrē will drive him to the front, this conspirator!")
1st voice: "Viņš piedod mums."
(Latv.: "He forgives us.")
2nd voice: "Wot, barski dzīvo šis!"
(Russ., Latv.: "Look, he lives like a lord!")
1st voice: "Es wundert mich, das Cityēn schwedisches Staat."
(Germ.: "I am surprised that Cityēn is a Swedish state.")
2nd voice: "Tumba!"
("Grave!")

1st voice: "Viņš ir katoļticīgs, aber torr."
(Latv., Germ., Swed.: "He is a believing Catholic, but dry.")
2nd voice: "Te Hitlers!"
(Latv.: "Here is Hitler!") (25g: 427/38, 467)

Towards the end of the recording we hear two voices that conclude the whole discussion:

"Nebij miera, nebij miera!"
"Mūsu mīļā Maurina ir Raudives sargeņgalis." (same place: 471/3)
(Latv.: "There was no calm, there was no calm."—"Our dear Maurina is Raudive's guardian angel.")
Some time later, the quarrel flares up again:
"Piter hier, nebaries Kosti!" (31g: 161)
(Latv.: "Peter here. Don't scold Kosti.")
"Pieter! Auf Ihre Aufnahme wollen wir stärken dir!" (31r: 142)
(Germ.: "On their recording we want to strengthen you!")
"Konstantin, pateicos. Netic viņiem!—Nacis!" (same place)
(Latv.: "Konstantin, I thank you. Don't believe them!—Nazis!")
"Viss te Kelpe ekspidē. Te nav Pēters. Netic! Kelpe." (35g:366)
(Latv.: "Here Kelpe expedites everything. Here it is not Peter. Don't believe! Kelpe.")
"Peters ir." (42r: 809)
(Latv.: "Peter exists.")

There are other stations, apart from "Studio Kelpe" and "Radio Peter". They do not appear very often, but they do point to the apparent existence of many stations that seek to make contact with the experimenter.

"Te Kegele." (22r: 453)
(Latv.: "Here is Kegele.")
"Kegele raida." (23g: 137)
(Latv.: "Kegele is transmitting.")
"Te runā Ziedoņu Gunar-Gunar-by.—Hallo, Kosti! Signalruf 'Kostule'!" (30r: 355)
(Latv., Swed., Germ.: "Here speaks Ziedoņu Gunar-Gunar-settlement.—Hallo, Kosti! Signal call 'Kostule'!")
"Väsa nettet, übernehme Leitung." (33g: 014)
(Swed., Germ.: "Väsa-net, am taking over control.")
"Goethe bro. Vairaki Sender." (same place: 033/5)
(Swed., Latv., Germ.: "Goethe-bridge. Several transmitters.")
"Sigtuna raida." (44b: 240)
(Latv.: "Sigtuna is transmitting.")
"Arvidi klusē. Irvini klusē." (44r: 025)
(Latv.: "The Arvids are silent. The Irvines are silent.")

Chapter III

Recordings with Collaborators

The experimenter arranged a number of trial-recordings, at some of which he himself was not present. Individual persons chosen to take part in these trials varied greatly as to their mental disposition, their profession and their attitude towards the phenomenon.

Whenever possible, such recordings were immediately played back and the results verified by the participants. Later, at repeated listening-in-sessions and under more detailed examination, many more voices were identified; astonishingly, here and there even voices of group "A" audibility appeared, which had not been noticed when the recording had been played back the first time.

Difficulties arose frequently through the use by the voice-entities of so many languages; at times there were six in one sentence. Persons taking part in the experiments who spoke but one language could not identify voices without the experimenter's help. Also, as has been pointed out in the introduction, the voices alter and twist the words of any language according to their own rules; presumably to make the sentences fit into the strictly measured rhythm in which they are spoken. For instance the peculiarly phrased German: "Deutsche wir hier. Kämpferi wir." (48g: 149) "Germans we here. Fighters we."

Most sentences are acoustically well-defined and often relate to prevailing circumstances, and in many instances after being addressed, voice-entities respond by giving their names, or call participants by their Christian or family names.

This series of experiments greatly assists in disposing of the suspicion that the voices might be no more than acoustic hallucinations; furthermore, in view of the great variety of individuals taking part in the tests, one may safely discard the allegation, sometimes levelled at spiritistic practices, that a pathological background exists, whilst *the fact that utterances heard by listeners concur with actual acoustic-physical word-constructions establishes, beyond a shadow of a doubt, that the voice-phenomenon exists as a reality.*

The results of these tests stress the new facts outlined in the preceding chapters; it is to be expected that they will lead to an intensification of discussion amongst parapsychologists of the hypothesis of the "unconscious" on the one hand, and the hypothesis of a "beyond" on the other. Through the establishment of the voice-phenomenon a vast amount of empty theorising and philosophising can be eliminated from the realm of parapsychology and fresh fields of research opened up.

The test programme is by no means completed by the experiments here described, but is being currently and intensively continued. More interest and better support from organisations and individual experts could help very much in conducting a greater number of experiments and improving existing working methods.

EXPERIMENTAL RECORDING NO. 1

Tübingen (Germany), 14th/15th June 1966
Participants: Mr. Bernhard Weiss (Physicist)
　　　　　　　Mrs. Gerda Weiss
　　　　　　　Mr. Schapp (Electronic Engineer)

The experimenter travelled to Tübingen to take part in discussions about the voice-phenomenon, and during the course of the meeting several recordings were made. The results of the first one here reported, are followed by the summary of a conversation between the participants about the problems pertaining to the voice-phenomenon research.

The recordings were immediately played back; Mrs. Weiss, in particular, showed a great aptitude for independent, careful listening-in. Results were analysed only at a later stage and then submitted to several further tests by the experimenter and two of his collaborators, Dr. Reincke of Badenweiler,

Germany (a doctor of medicine), and Mr. Felix Scherer, electrotechnics expert, of Freiburg, Germany.

The first test-recording produced many voices with typical characteristic speech-content, containing paranormal data.

Some examples:

The experimenter asks whether the voices could not give plain, radical, unequivocal information.

"Mēs nevaram. Raudive, turpinā!"
(Latv.: "We cannot Raudive, continue!")

We hear other voices, verified independently by the participants themselves:

"Tev zwingen. Postulē tev, mēs pie Weiss." (Hg: 210)
(Latv., Germ.: "Compel you. Postulated to you, we are with Weiss.")

"Gerda, Gerda! Nur lietiski!" (same place: 112)
(Germ., Latv.: "Gerda, Gerda! Only objectively.") This sentence may have been aimed at Mrs. Gerda Weiss.

"Weiss, tēvs dzīvs." (same place: 119)
(Latv.: "Weiss, father lives.")

"Gerda muss mithören." (same place: 121)
(Germ.: "Gerda must join in listening.")

"Kosti, Radio gehört." (same place: 123)
(Germ.: "Kosti, heard radio.")

"Ich komme von dem Vater.—Te Vater.—Ihr Herz." (same place: 205/8/12)
(Germ., Latv.: "I come from father.—Here is father.—Your heart.")

"Te Bernhard." (same place: 270)
(Latv.: "Here is Bernhard.")

When the tape was listened to again, a whole series of voices became audible that had been missed at the first hearing:

"Friedrichs te pa dej." (same place: 106/7)
(Latv., Swed.: "Friedrich here with you.")

"Pasauc Gerdu!" (same place)
(Latv.: "Call Gerda.")

"Kosta, pastuderē Ostrovu! Hitleri ari." (same place: 118)
(Latv.: "Kosta, study Ostrow! Also Hitler!")

"Konstantin, te Vladislavs. Tu mani pazini Krāslavā." (same place: 123)
(Latv.: "Konstantin, here is Vladislavs. You knew me in Kraslava.")

This voice unfortunately belongs to group "C" but is, nevertheless, clearly audible to a practiced ear.

Towards the end of the recording many more voices can be heard that refer mainly to the experimenter, some to Mr. and Mrs. Weiss. They are not suitable for copying, as their audibility lies below the "B" group.

The experimenter and the physicist Bernhard Weiss discussed amongst other things the question of microwave-acoustics. This special field of research is concerned with the study of elastic vibrations within solid bodies at frequencies in the geiger-range. The experimenter is of the opinion that acoustic experts and electrotechnicians should join in the research on the voice-phenomenon. (Later, in continuing the series of tests, this suggestion was taken up and put into practice.)

This discussion between Mr. Weiss and the experimenter has been recorded on tape; its main points can be summarised as follows:

Mr. Weiss had gained his impressions of the voice-phenomenon from three weeks of study with Friedrich Jürgenson, as well as his own experimental recordings. The experimenter listened to some of Weiss's tapes and was able to verify the existence of a number of voices. Both partners in the discussion were of the opinion that, for the time being at least, the phenomenon could only be described, not explained; that it had been possible to establish certain fixed sound-characteristics, but experimental research was necessary in order to avoid results that were not genuine, but mere coincidental recordings of ordinary radio freak sounds. If the paranormal data repeated themselves continuously, they could be verified as such. For instance, at the end of one of Mr. Weiss's recordings a voice is heard to say "Gute Nacht", (Germ.: "Good night") and after Mrs. Weiss had been singing, a voice reacted with: "Det war hübsch." (Germ.: "That was pretty.") The latter voice was heard by everyone present and could be established as being definitely in existence. The phenomenon of greetings such as "good night" or "good day" in various languages, was repeated in hundreds of cases and could stand up to the most stringent analysis. Mr. Weiss remarked that he found this phenomenon astonishing and that, if it "had not been Mr. Raudive", he would have suspected some trick. He added: "After all, it has been recorded in my presence!"

The importance of the personalities taking part in recording-sessions was also discussed. The experimenter stated that the participants played a certain rôle in making contact possible, but that anybody could be such a "contact-maker", what was needed above all was a well trained ear and an accurate listening-in technique.

Mr. Weiss: "Anything that could possibly stem from ordinary radio stations must be excluded."

The experimenter: "This is a necessary pre-condition; otherwise the phenomenon cannot be sustained in its pure form."

Mr. Weiss: "If it is possible to ascertain that the phenomenon repeats itself, and one can determine fixed characteristics marking it, then the likelihood of coincidence becomes extremely improbable."

Experimenter: "So we must find a method that enables us to extract from the mass of voice-information contained in a recording the essential criteria common to all possible forms of voice-manifestations heard. All detail inessential to the comprehension of the phenomenon must be dropped, in order to retain only such information as consists of speech-content that can be established and identified through sound-symbols." (This suggested process of sifting has since been carried out through a specially devised system of repetition; out of 72,000 recorded voices, 25,000 have been established and indisputably proved to exist; and these have been deciphered and verified by various participants in experimental listening-in tests.

Mr. Weiss went on to say that the polyglot character of the phenomenon, as well as the analysis of speech-content, had to be taken into consideration. On this point both partners agreed.

The experimenter gave his views on the structure of the voices' language, which invariably follows its own definite rules and is marked by a special rhythm and a certain characteristic monotony. These features enable one to discern the nature of the voices and to distinguish them from possible radio freak sounds. To Weiss's objection that this procedure was not absolutely foolproof, the experimenter replied: "Mathematical exactness is always very difficult to come by, even in mathematical abstractions."

Mr. Weiss: "Some sort of technical means should make it possible to exclude all ambiguity."

Mr. Weiss and Mr. Schapp discussed various technical problems and came to the conclusion that an aerial, operating independently of the transmitter, should be constructed.

The general discussion moved on and touched the fact that the experimenter is so often addressed in person by a voice: for instance: "Hej, Raudive, solo mej?" ("Do you hear us, Raudive?"). At the last recording made at Tübingen (15th June 1966) the experimenter says: "The final word belongs to our unseen friends." A voice answers: "Konstantin!"

Mr. Weiss tried to explain this evident fact as follows: "As you are a well-known author, it is quite possible that a lecture about you has been relayed by various radio stations", but the experimenter pointed out that nobody at the radio stations in question even knew of his existence, let alone would arrange to relay a lecture about him.

The experimenter reported: "I have noticed, through my listening-in practice, that the ear can distinguish very subtle differences in the melody of speech; in the melody and in the rhythm—that is in the criteria relating to time-structure—the ear can find the hallmarks by which to recognise the nature of the voices." Mr. Weiss did not take up this point and the experimenter once more came back to the language of the voices: "Mr. Weiss, have you not noticed that the voices' language differs in construction from the languages known to us, but is still formed in such a way as to be comprehensible to us in part?" Mr. Weiss answered that it seemed strange that we should be able to understand the voices, though they used several languages in one sentence, and this fact indicated the existence of a conscious intelligence.

The experimenter thanked Mr. Weiss for this important acknowledgement and pointed to the polyglot character of the phenomenon as significant, continually repeated, paranormal data.

At the end of the discussion both partners agreed that despite all the technical gadgets available, the human ear is still the safest instrument when it comes to verifying the phenomenon; if two or three persons independently and repeatedly hear a particular voice, proof of the existence of that voice may be held to be established. (Results of the experimental series and the listening-in tests show that 35 to

100 per cent of the voices have been independently heard and verified by collaborators.)

Mr. Weiss stressed the importance of natural science in any attempt to explain the phenomenon. The experimenter: "Psychological discoveries are as yet in their infancy and need the assistance of the natural sciences. It is nevertheless clear to me that methods of the natural sciences are not always and under all circumstances applicable to parapsychological phenomena. However, the interrelation of all sciences cannot be denied, and therefore close co-operation should enable us to eliminate many sources of error and to evolve a uniform conception of the universe."

EXPERIMENTAL RECORDING NO. 2

Bad Krozingen (Germany) 21st June 1966
Participant: Kārlis Līdums, building contractor
Edwardstown, Australia
(See Commentary, page 369.)

Mr. Līdums is a former Latvian citizen who speaks English and German as well as Latvian. He knew nothing of the world of the voices, but it became immediately apparent that he possessed an acute sense of hearing and could even distinguish languages he did not know by the phonemes. His sense of hearing had had no special training, yet he could identify and verify up to 55 per cent of the voices heard.

From the results of the recording made in the presence of Mr. Līdums, certain differences arise that are worth noting:

1. The voices refer mostly to Mr. Līdums; his parents and some of his dead friends spoke.

2. The voices made statements concerning Mr. Līdums' welfare, asked him to stay with the experimenter, etc.

The recording produced 120 audible voices, of which, as stated, Mr. Līdums himself heard 55 per cent.

A selection from the results:

"Radi Kosti očen rad. Pasauc ōtrōk Mildu! Prieks par tīku amatu." (41g: 349/51)

(Russ., Latv.: "I am glad for Kosti. Call Milda soon! Joy over the pleasant handywork.") Milda, Līdums' wife, was in a different room when the recording was made. The "handywork" may refer to Līdums' building trade.

"Stipri bau! Napīc! Vēl paliek—Alekss."
Female voice:
"Vēl paliek." (same place: 352/3)
(Latv., Germ.: "Build strongly! Don't grumble! Stay yet—Alex." Female voice Latv.: "Stay yet!")
"Kosti, es dzirdu. Te Foslers." (same place: 358)
(Latv.: "Kosti, I hear. Here is Foslers.") Foslers was a friend of Mr. Līdums.
"Esi parītu te. Mana sirds tev kalpo. Kostja, pažēlo manu dēlu!" (same place: 369)
(Latv.: "Be here the day after tomorrow. My heart serves you. Kostja, have pity for my son!")
"Tova mōsa tōli! Kosti, tu staigā, neguļ." (same place: 371)
(Latg.: "Your sister is far [away]! Kosti, you wander, you do not sleep.")
"Mēs tevi mīlam, Kārli! Paliec pie Kosti! Paldies! Mēs pateicamies Zentai Mauriņai." (same place: 372/4)
(Latv.: "We love you, Karl! Stay with Kosti! Thank you! We thank Zenta Maurina.") Mr. Lidums thinks this may be the voice of his father.
"Parādi ōpnad tu!" (same place: 376)
(Latv., Swed.: "Show frankness!")
"Konstantin, uzrōdi!" (same place: 380)
(Latg.: "Konstantin, demonstrate!")
"Ā—Līdums!" (same place: 388)

Now the recording is switched from radio to microphone. The experimenter starts: "Through m . . ." and a voice cuts in:

"Raudive te gut, sehr gut!" (same place: 397)
(Latv., Germ.: "Raudive, it is good here, very good!")
Experimenter: "Here is Kārlis Līdums." Voice:
"Mēs tev schuldi, bet tūli." (same place: 400)
(Latv., Germ.: "We are in your debt, but we can't move on.")
Mr. Līdums explains that this statement fits an actual situation.

The experimenter: "Kārl Līdums was born in Libau." Voice:

"Es zinu." (same place: 401)
(Latv.: "I know.")
Experimenter: "Now he comes from Australia . . ."
"Lepni!" (same place)
(Latv.: "Wonderful!")

We skip some of the voices that follow and concentrate on

those referring to Mr. Līdums personally. After addressing two of his deceased friends, a voice answers:

"Hutton, unentwickelt selbst."
(Germ.: "Hutton, himself undeveloped.")
Another voice:
"Konstantin, hier Harvey." (same place: 517/9)
(Germ.: "Konstantin, here Harvey!") Hutton and Harvey were the names of his two dead friends. Mr. Līdums addresses his mother.
"Danke! Mēs dzirdam." (same place: 532/3)
(Germ., Latv.: "Thank you, we hear!")

Mr. Līdums asks his parents to give him a message from the beyond. A voice asks:

"Kārli, tu?" (same place: 161)
(Latv.: "Karl, you?")

EXPERIMENTAL RECORDING NO. 3

Zurich, 12th/15th July 1966
Schweizerische Parapsychologische Gesellschaft (Parapsychological Society of Switzerland).
Four recordings were made. (See Reports, pages 325–329).

First session, 12th July 1966
Participants: Doctor Hans Naegeli (Dr. of medicine), President of the Parapsychological Society.
Mrs. Katharina Nager, Secretary of the Parapsychological Society.
Mrs. N. von Muralt, Parapsychologist.
Mrs. Georgette Fürst, Psychologist.
Dr. R. Fatzer.
Dr. K. Müller.
Dr. Wyss.
Prof. Dr. Hans Biäsch, Psychologist.
Mr. I. M. Meier, Physicist.

This recording, through radio-microphone, was made under official control of the Parapsychological Society of Switzerland. Unfortunately, interference from a BBC transmitter made part of the recording worthless. However, there was no interference from numbers 000 to 017, and 022 to 155, so that the voices recorded in those sections are valid and can be regarded as paranormal. Audibility is within the limits of groups B and C.

Some examples:

As the tape-recorder is switched on, a female voice is heard:

"Te Matilde." (Zr: 000)
(Latv.: "Here is Matilde.")

The name "Matilde" manifests often and on different occasions. For instance: the experimenter once called on her, whereupon a voice responded with: "Quick! She is the main helper, Matilde." (47g: 350/7)

Now the experimenter states that he is in Zürich.

"Wer sagt?—Werfel hier." (same place: 002)
(Germ.: "Who says?—Werfel here.")
Experimenter: "The participants are . . ."
"Nenne Namen!" (same place: 003)
(Germ.: "Tell names!")

Dr. Naegeli reads out the names.

"Ich auch.—Gerda te! Gerda tibi." (same place: 004)
(Germ., Latv., Lat.: "Me too.—Gerda here! Gerda is yours.")
A close friend of Mrs. Nager was called Gerda.

Several voices now comment on the mentioning of the participants' names.

The experimenter draws attention to the fact that the recording is made through radio-microphone.

"Raudive feini tingel kann. Te tev genau, pat General!" (same place: 016/7)
(Germ., Latv.: "Raudive can 'tingle' beautifully. It's just for you here, even a General!") Amongst the participants was a Swiss army commandant with a rank corresponding to that of a general in other armies.

Following Dr. Naegeli's words: ". . . normal conversation . . .", a voice is heard to say:

"Labāk tu mājās." (same place: 038)
(Latv.: "You are better at home.") This sentence may possibly be a hint that the experimenter is more concentrated on his work when he is in his own study.

The participants talk together and in the meantime the following voices manifest:

"Maurina denkt." (same place: 041)
(Germ.: "Maurina is thinking.")
"Kraft!" (same place: 053)
(Germ.: "Strength.")

Dr. Fatzer comments that one can play the same tune to certain people year in, year out, but they still cannot take it in correctly.

"Richtig!" (same place: 119)
(Germ.: "Right.")

Mrs. Nager relates how only a few years ago a close friend of hers had been sitting in the same chair; her thoughts were now with this friend.

"Pasauc nu tu viņu. Kosti piekrāpsi." (same place: 148)
(Latv.: "Call her now. You will betray Kosti.")

It was later revealed that Mrs. Nager had thought about "Gerda", who had already manifested at the beginning of the session and had given her name. The second sentence may perhaps be understood as expressing another voice-entity's disquiet at Gerda's presence.

The recording was afterwards listened to by Mrs. Georgette Fürst, Dr. Fatzer and the experimenter. The voices were heard and verified by all of them simultaneously. Dr. H. Naegeli and a few other participants with an acute sense of hearing, later confirmed the audibility of these voices. Only such voices as were heard jointly by all participants are here recorded; others discovered later, have not been mentioned.

Second session, 13th July 1966, at 4.40 p.m.
Participants: Mrs. Katharine Nager.
Mrs. N. von Muralt.
Mrs. G. Fürst.
Miss A. Morgenthaler.
Dr. K. Müller.

This recording produced voices of equally good value, some of which were heard by the participants without any difficulty. It was made through microphone.

At the first word of the experimenter: "... participants ...", a voice said:

"Konstantin!" (Zr: 159) and a further one:

"Luta, Kosti, Kosti!" (same place: 167) Kazimir Luta had been a friend of the experimenter.

After Mrs. Fürst's words: "... have given ...", comes another voice:

"Muralt!" (same place: 184) Mrs. N. von Muralt, the parapsychologist, was present.

Mrs. Fürst continues to speak and a voice calls her by her Christian name:

"Georgette!" (same place: 186)

As Georgette Fürst talks about various problems, we hear:

"Viel Quatsch, mōte ruf!" (same place: 188)
(Germ., Latg.: "Much balderdash, call mother!")

The conversation amongst participants continues, interspersed by monosyllabic voice-comments like: "Kosti!"—"Right!"—"Bra!" (Swed.: "Good!") etc.

Dr. Müller relates a story concerning a reward of £1,000. A voice says repeatedly:

"Hör auf! Pļāpa!"—"Nein, nein, pļāpa!" (same place: 262/74)
(Germ., Latv.: "Stop! Chatterbox!"—"No, no, chatterbox!")

Mrs. Fürst: "The phenomenon is genuine, and we would like to help."

"Sagen wir Wort. Du toll. Konstantin mūsu." (same place: 353ff)
(Germ.: "We say word. You [are] terrific. Our Konstantin.")

Again we hear voices either confirming, or denying statements made by participants.

The experimenter says that first of all a basis had to be established.

"Was das Ihres?"
"Ich weiss noch vor."
"Misty Tropf." (same place: 399/410)
(Germ., Engl.: "What is yours?"—"I know yet[?]"—"Misty drip.")

The experimenter is silent for a moment, making a slight nasal sound.

"Ich wollte ihn toten! Schatz und Emery no tål. Schinker." (same place: 410)

(Germ., Swed., Engl.: "I wanted to kill him! Schatz and Emery do not like him. Schinker.")

After the experimenter has remarked that we often overlook the essential a voice says:

"Konstantin, halt!" (same place:)
(Germ.: "Konstantin, stop!")

Then, following the experimenter's words: ". . . I hear nothing . . .".

"Oma!" (same place: 414)
("German: "Grandma!") A call, probably referring to Mrs. Nager's deceased mother.

Mrs. Fürst is of the opinion that the phenomenon has to be thoroughly investigated.

"Tev nav Marta." (same place: 436)
(Latv.: "You have not got Marta.")

Experimenter: ". . . investigate . . ."

"Te tu dumš." (same place: 446)
(Latv.: "Here you are stupid.")

This particular recording was made entirely through microphone; it must therefore be regarded as amply successful. Microphone-voices are always limited to very short statements, and on such occasions the voice-entities often request contact through radio.

Third session, 14th July 1966, 10 p.m.
Participants: Mrs. Katharina Nager.
             Miss A. Morgenthaler.
             Dr. Hans Naegeli.
             Mr. F. A. Volmar.
             Mr. S. Regli.
             Mr. A. Moser.

The recording was made on two tape-recorders, partly through microphone, partly through radio; over one hundred voices manifested, fifty-five of which could be verified as being definitely audible.

Dr. Naegeli starts the session, and after his words: ". . . can also . . .", a voice is heard:

"Raudive." (Zr: 450)

Another voice:

"Kosti!"

Mr. Volmar says: "I am here . . ."

"Vater!" (Germ.: "Father!")
Mr. Volmar: ". . . not, I . . ."; the same voice:
"Vater!" (same place: 458)

Mr. Volmar continues to speak. A voice repeats three times:

"Kati, Kati, Kati her!" (same place: 486/9)
(Germ.: "Kati, Kati, Kati come here.")

There is a pause in the conversation, and the following voice is heard:

"Luta her. Wie spät? Mich vollte . . ." (same place: 491)
(Germ.: "Luta come here. How late? One wanted me . . .")

Mrs. Nager continues to speak. After her words: ". . . other deceased . . .", we hear a voice:

"Kate, Opa te. Oma!" (same place: 492/3)
(Latv.: "Kate, here is Grandpa. Grandma!") Mrs. Nager had addressed her mother and father several times as "Grandma" and "Grandpa".

Mrs. Nager says that yesterday's recording made a great impression on her.

"Gerda! Gerda!" (same place: 496)

As already mentioned, Gerda had manifested also in the first recording, and Mrs. Nager thought it to be her dead friend.

The experimenter asks for an explanation of the expression "tingle", which a voice had used in the preceding recording-session.

"Pagaid! Warte!" (same place: 501)
(Latv., German: In both languages: "Wait!")

Mr. Regli says he has difficulty in expressing himself.

"Hansi!" (same place: 512) This voice could refer to Dr. Hans Naegeli.

Following Miss Morgenthaler's words: ". . . always wishes . . ."

"Ak ja. Rente ja, rast Ko." (same place: 514/20)
(Germ.: "Oh yes. Pension yes, Ko to rest.")

The experimenter states that as far as the voice-phenomenon research is concerned, one could never be attentive enough.

A female voice:
"Lempi tu!" (same place: 521)
(Latv.: "You rogue!")

Mrs. Nager: "... and has still longer..."

"Papa!" (same place: 525/6)

Experimenter: "... this recording..."

"Wir bisschen, Maurina." (same place: 531)
(Germ.: "We a little, Maurina.")

The experimenter continues to talk, and as he switches from microphone to radio, a voice is heard to say:

"Lobas sekmes, Vater!" (same place: 536/7)
(Latg., Germ.: "Good success, father!")

"We must thoroughly probe the phenomenon...", says the experimenter; a voice:

"Kosta, bråk!" (same place: 539/40)
(Swed.: "Koste, discord!")

Now we hear the following voice, aimed at the experimenter:

"Petrautzki!" (same place: 550)

Dr. Naegeli recounts that there is a ghost who is connected with his house.

"Willi!" (same place: 560/1)

The experimenter thinks it may be a form of existence as yet unknown to us, but a voice counters with:

"Aplam, Kostulīt." (same place: 567/8)
(Latv.: "Wrong, Kostulit!")

Experimenter: "... mediator between this world and the beyond. But there are no such divisions..."

"Gibt doch!" (same place: 568)
(Germ.: "There are!")

Dr. Naegali comments that there may be forces that can

manifest themselves on tape, as in the present case. A woman's voice calls out:

> "Wir sind, wir sind!" (same place: 583)
> (Germ.: "We are, we are!")

Mr. Volmar offers to leave, should he prove to be a disturbing element.

> "Horch, Unsinn!" (same place: 597), says a voice.
> (Germ.: "Listen, rubbish!")

The experimenter remarks that he is striving for clarification of the phenomenon.

> "Wohlan, Hitler te!" (same place)
> (Germ., Latv.: "Come on then, Hitler here.")

The experimenter asks who the spirit is that lives in this house.

> "Willi. Tja māja." (same place).
> (Latv.: "Willi. Here is the house.")

Fourth session, 15th July 1966, 10.30 a.m.
Participants: Mrs. Katharina Nager.
            Miss A. Morgenthaler.
            Mr. F. A. Volmar.

This recording produced the highest number of voices, including a few of group "A". The three preceding tapes yielded none in that group. Here are some examples of such "A" voices:

After the experimenter's words: ". . . 10 o'clock . . .", a voice says:

> "Ilgi mājās, nav labi nomodā." (Zr: 621)
> (Latv.: "Too long indoors, it is not good to be awake.")

Experimenter: "Dear Spidola, take the lead . . ." A male voice:

> "Māti upurē!" (same place: 623)
> (Latv.: "Sacrifice the mother!")

The experimenter repeats his question as to who the entity was that had called itself Willi.

> "Tāvs Mōjā. Vitne." (same place: 627/8)

(Latg., Swed.: "Father of the house. Witness.")

The experimenter says he thinks someone is going to help him.

"Bender, Kosti!" (same place: 637/8)

Experimenter: "It is possible that later on we may hear all sorts of comments from entities that are present."

"Hier Maur. Wir falsch dominare. Wir sieben von hier." (same place: 649)
(Germ.: "Here Maur. We dominate wrongly. We are seven from here.") This sentence is not clear as to its meaning, but is of quite good audibility

Mrs. Nager thanks the experimenter for his efforts.

"Ando prego. Katerina lai dzīvo!" (same place: 650)
(Ital., Latv.: "Ando please. Long live Katerina!")

Mrs. Nager further expresses her hope that the experimenter may visit Zürich again.

"Nauda då! Te Glaube." (same place: 651)
(Latv., Swed., Germ.: "Money nevertheless! Here is faith.")

Mr. Volmar remarks that the sessions had been a great experience for him.

"Starrkopf!" (same place: 654)
(Germ.: "Stubborn head!")

The experimenter says his thoughts were concerned with yet another invisible guest.

"Very hungry, Maurina." (same place: 666) This may possibly be the voice of Zenta Maurina's dead sister.

When the experimenter asks whether "Willi" cannot talk to them over the tape, a voice is heard to say:

"Kobold du. Er will tevi.—Hitler.—Jane Villa." (same place: 668/70)
(Germ., Latv.: "You goblin. He wants you.—Hitler.—Jane Villa.")

The experimenter remarks that the recording is nearly at an end, and sincerely thanks all participants.

"Muļķis tur runā. Tu dari aplam." (same place: 672)
(Latv.: "There speaks the fool. You do it wrongly.")

These last few voices are negative and lecturing in their

whole tenor, and it may well be that the experimenter's ways had not been in harmony with the world of the voices.

EXPERIMENTAL RECORDING NO. 4

Bad Krozingen, (Germany) 21st July 1966
Participant: Mrs. Irma Millere, Assistant Head-Mistress (Sec. School), Stockholm.
(See commentary, page 373.)

The recording, partly through microphone, partly through radio, lasted ten minutes. Total of voices heard: 123.

The experimenter went for a walk in the garden whilst the recording was being made.

Out of the total number of voices, Mrs. Millere could verify 60 per cent—an astonishing degree of accurate hearing. Usually even those endowed with the sharpest sense of hearing can distinguish the voices and decipher them correctly by their phonemes only after considerable practice. The magnetic field of the voice-phenomenon is five to ten times weaker than that of the ordinary human voice; the sound is therefore not received evenly and one has to "fix" the voices and repeat them over and over again, before they can be properly heard and understood. Mrs. Millere first "sensed" the voices by their unmistakable rhythm, later taking in language and meaning. She knows several languages, but conducted the recording in Latvian.

> Irma Millere: "We must all walk along the road of death."
> "Nav pagaidam ejams." (42r: 472)
> (Latv.: "For the time being it is not to be trodden.")
> I.M.: "I am sitting here waiting..."
> "Māte!" (same place: 475)
> (Latv.: "Mother!")
> I.M.: "What I know is comparable to the mustard seed..."
> "Ko tu āksties!" (same place: 477)
> (Latv.: "Why are you playing the fool?")
> I.M.: "A human being can do much, but only seldom does one achieve..."
> "Gudri, gudri!" (same place: 484/6)
> (Latv.: "Clever, clever!")
> I.M. "What I can imagine does not amount to much..."
> "Noslēpi Raudive! Viņš dārzā staigā." (same place: 489)

(Latv.: "You have hidden Raudive! He is wandering in the garden.")
"Pātagas vien, hopp!" (same place: 502)
(Latv.: "Only whip, hop!")
"Irma te! Māte." (same place:)
(Latv.: "Here is Irma! Mother.")
"Ko tu pumpē?"
"Čeka pumpē." (same place: 504)
(Latv.: "What are you pumping?"—"Tcheka pumps.")
"A Bož, ko tu dari?" (same place)
(Russ., Latv.: "Oh God, what are you doing?")
"Tu pļāpā, uzceļ tu māti!" (same place)
(Latv.: "You are chattering, wake up mother!")
"Tēvs—mute torr." (same place: 506)
(Latv.: "Father—my mouth is dry.")
"Te tev landiga lāden taisīt, te tev lab!" (same place: 509)—The meaning of this sentence is not clear. Approx.: "Build yourself a rustic shop here, here you do well." (Latvian)
"Wer Kazis, Kosti?" (same place: 511)
(Germ.: "Who Kazis, Kosti?")
"Att schönare—Ubigan!" (same place)
(Swed., Germ.: "To be most beautiful—Ubigan!")
"Kosti tu te nogaidi!" (same place: 512)
(Latv.: "Here wait for Kosti!")
"Mudželē—pagmūrē!" (same place: 514)
(Latv.: "Mushy mixture—build a little.")
"Vi stumli bei dig, nehmli bei Zug." (same place: 518)
(Swed., Germ.: "We are mute with you, take [with] train.") The second half of the sentence is not clear. The German word "Zug" (train) can also mean a "draw" or a "move", so that the second half could mean "take it move by move".
"Tālie—Zenta Maurina aizlūdz!" (same place)
(Latv.: "The far off—Zenta Maurina prays!")
"Ārstejies, slinko!" (same place)
(Latv.: "Get yourself well, be lazy.") Irma Millere had indeed been overworking and was in need of relaxation and cure.
I.M.: "To be or not to be after this life—that is a question not yet answered."
"Uzmin!" (same place: 547)
(Latv.: "Guess!")

Immediately after this recording had been completed, the experimenter made one by himself alone; the voices that appear here differ greatly in their speech-content from those of the preceding recording. They stand mainly in relationship to the experimenter. Some examples:

"Raudive, guļ tu?" (42r: 570)

(Latv.: "Raudive, are you asleep?")
"Stalins te, furchtbar karsts, furchtbar Eile." (same place: 572)
(Latv., Germ.: "Here is Stalin, terribly hot, terrible hurry.")
"Lieber Kosta, welch svjazi te gusta?" (same place: 581)
(Germ., Russ., Latv., Span.: "Dear Kosta, what relations please here?")
"Du bist Katholik. La punita syskon. Dvēsele mit Erfolg." (same place)
(Germ., Span., Swed., Latv.: "You are a Catholic. The punished brothers and sisters. The soul with success.")
"I tūkstoš te redzam tevi!" (same place: 658)
(Latv.: "In our thousands do we see you here.")

A row of names familiar to the experimenter follows:

"Alisa Oxford sagaida Kosti!" (same place: 660)
(Latv.: "Alisa Oxford awaits Kosti!")
"Pomina Nagarovski!" (same place: 712)
(Russ.: "Think of Nagarovski.")
"Kosti guļ tai pašā gula." (same place: 736)
(Latv.: "Kosti sleeps in the same bed.")
"Ļubuške, te Kostuli redz." (same place: 825)
(Latv.: "Ļubuške, one sees Kosti here.")
"Spanni zyrgu. Margarete te." (same place: 914)
(Germ., Latv.: "Harness the horse. Here is Margarete.")

Comparing the two recordings, one can see plainly that the voices' statements are tailored to the person making the recording and that various voice-entities manifest according to the individuality of this person.

Irma Millere's influence however, lingered for a while and some voices mentioned her name:

"Irma Millere—Čakste!" (43g: 283)—Čakste, a friend of the experimenter.
"Grüezis von Millere." (same place: 288)
(Swiss-German: "Greetings from Millere.")

EXPERIMENTAL RECORDING NO. 5

Bad Krozingen (Germany), 22nd October 1966
Participant: Miss Annemarie Morgenthaler, Teacher (Bern, Switzerland). (See Commentary, page 374.)

This recording shows the same characteristic: it stands partly in direct relationship to the recording personality. It was made through radio-microphone and through radio. Duration: 10 minutes. Total number of voices: 240, of which the participant could verify 75 per cent.

Some of the results:

Miss Morgenthaler: "It would, of course, be of immense value to all investigations and the research as a whole, if unequivocal results could be obtained even in the absence of Konstantin Raudive. The recording is made via microphone-radio."

"Lyudz tu Schottin!" (44r: 191)
(Latg., Germ.: "You ask the Scottish woman.") The "Scottish woman" could be the experimenter's deceased friend Aileen Finlayson. (See page 00.)
Miss Morgenthaler: "We shall see what emerges."
"Lepns tonis, Kosti!" (same place: 192)
(Latv.: "A proud tone, Kosti!")
Miss A.M.: "Let us hope that no radio-transmitter is going to interfere to any extent."
"Immer Kosti!—Exquisiderá nupat pīkst." (same place: 196)
(Germ., Latv.: "Always Kosti!—Exquisidera chirped just now.")
A.M.: "I have a feeling that a transmitter would influence..."
"Klusāk, mūsu Batņa. Tysta aizdusa dich!"
"Ustobu paskaties, mazgane!"
"Latvi, tici! Mōsiņa tja." (same place: 200/2)
(Latv., Latg., Swed., Germ.: "Softer, our Batna. (A dead friend). May shortness of breath silence you!"—"Look at the room, small shepherdess!" "Latvian, believe! Little sister is here.")

Miss Morgenthaler expresses the opinion that perhaps it might not be too far-fetched to suppose that the voices could be projected by the "unconscious" on a background of noise (from transmitting stations, etc.)

"Kas ir, martyška?"
"Danke, immer fertig med varandra. Te Molinjēr." (same place: 202/3)
(Latv., Russ., Germ., Swed.: "What's up, monkey?"—"Thanks, always conclude together. Here is Molinjer.")

Miss Morgenthaler does not speak Latvian or Russian. In fact, she had put forward a theory expressed by Professor Hans Bender, who was not completely convinced that the voices were not projections of the "unconscious" of the experimenter, on the background of noises received from radio transmitting stations. In a letter to the experimenter dated 21st August 1966, Professor Bender said he hoped to hear that material had been obtained that would definitely disprove this theory.

> Miss Morgenthaler: "I am rather preoccupied with this problem."
> "Du radarse bien! Genau!—din vän." (same place: 205)
> (Germ., French, Swed.: "You 'radar' well! Just [like] your friend!")
> A male voice: "Venta ty!"
> A female voice: "Boris!" (same place: 208)
> (Swed., Russ.: "You wait!"—"Boris!")
> "Tur sitzt radar!" (same place)
> (Latv., Germ.: "There sits radar!")
> "Kosta, dein brat!" (same place: 210)
> (Germ., Russ.: "Kosta, your brother.")
> A.M.: ". . . unlikely that this can be connected with the workings of the unconscious."
> "Très bien. Nutzt Radar. Anna! Ļuta!" (same place: 211)
> (French, Germ.: "Very good. Use radar. Anna! Luta!") All these statements are probably meant to indicate that the participant has said something which is correct and that she is being used as "radar". Luta, who is a friend of the experimenter, seems to wish to manifest his presence.
> Miss Morgenthaler: "But I would like to say quite personally . . ."
> "Mīli!" (same place: 212)
> (Latv.: "Do you love?")
> Annemarie M.: ". . . tonight wish for contact . . ."
> "Te Marta!" (same place: 213)
> (Latv.: "Here is Marta.")
> A.M.: ". . . with all my loved ones . . ."
> "Komm mit." (same place)
> (Germ.: "Come with us.")
> A.M.: ". . . in the beyond."
> "Paties', padre hört!" (same place: 214)
> (Latv., Ital., Germ.: "Really, father hears!")
> A.M.: "Perhaps . . ."
> "Mauriņa taisa mumijas." (same place)
> (Latv.: "Maurina fashions mummies.")
> A.M.: ". . . can I hear one thing or another from you here."
> "Lyudzi Kosti." (same place: 215)
> (Latg.: "Ask Kosti.")

In this radio-recording most voices ask for the experimenter; they have hardly any relationship to the person participating in the experiment.

"Kosti mūs ventè." (44r: 221)
(Latv., Swed.: "Kosti awaits us.")
"Brāl, tas milzīg angažē."
"Tiše, Alexej!" (same place: 232)
(Latv., Russ.: "Brother, that engages mightily."—"Softer, Alexej!")
"Tu pats, Kosta, tu dzirdi?" (same place: 235)
(Latv.: "You yourself, Kosta, do you hear?")
"Koste, Strunke!" (same place: 237)—Strunke died in Rome on 13th October 1966, but when this was being recorded the experimenter knew nothing of Strunke's passing.
"Pats Ulmanis vēl." (same place: 239)
(Latv.: "Still Ulmanis himself.") Ulmanis was the name of Latvia's last President. (See page 91.)

Only two voices here address Annemarie Morgenthaler directly:

"Anna, wir sind Menschen." (same place: 247)
(Germ.: "Anna, we are human beings.")
"Wie gih, Tochter? Hem du būs fresh." (same place: 235)
(Germ., Swed., Latv., Engl.: "How are you, daughter? At home you will be fresh again.")

Then follow voices that keep a general tone:

"Vai tu caur Sidrabeni tiki iekšā?" (same place: 233)
(Latv.: "Did you come in through Sidrabeni?")
"Ir bēdas, mirst bara Kenijā." (same place: 223)
(Latv., Swed.: "There are worries, one dies in Kenya.")
"Furchtbar, te vecis Bormanis. Furchtbar, Nazis!" (same place: 258)
(Germ., Latv.: "Terrible, here is old Bormann. Terrible, that Nazi!")
"Furchtbar gryuti man! Lyudzi!" (same place: 262)
(Germ., Latg.: "Terribly hard it is for me! Pray!")

EXPERIMENTAL RECORDING NO. 6

Bad Krozingen, 23rd October 1966
Participant: Miss A. Morgenthaler, Teacher (Bern.)

In contrast to the recording of the previous day, this one was made in the presence of the experimenter. The voices manifesting show a close link to the experimenter, and Miss Morgenthaler is only once called by name:

"Anna zebenē." (44r: 363)
(Latv.: "Anna slobbers.")
"Klusāk, Mauriņa." (same place)
(Latv.: "More softly, Maurina.")

The experimenter's name is mentioned frequently:

"Konstantin, Morbin. Uppsala brāļ, wohnt drudžaini. Mälars te ielūdz." (same place: 363)
(Latv., Germ.: "Konstantin, Morbin. Uppsala, brother, lives feverishly. Mälar invites here.")
"Bada kundze te." (same place: 366)
(Latv.: "Here is Mistress Hunger.")
"Koste, ko te tu guli? Lobu nakt!" (same place: 387)
(Latv:: "Kosta, are you asleep? Good night!")
"Brauchst du mōti?" (same place)
(Germ., Latg.: "Do you need mother?")
"Kosta, te Rupais." (same place)
(Latv.: "Kosta, here is Rupais.") Rupais was the name of the experimenter's teacher in Asūne.
"Antworte! Hast du Kosti, Über-Kosti?" (same place: 389/91)
(Germ.: "Answer! Have you Kosti, Over-Kosti?" This sentence is remarkable for its unusual content and meaning. (See page 315.)

EXPERIMENTAL RECORDING NO. 7

Bad Krozingen (Germany), 26th October 1966
Participant: Dr. (of Medicine) Arnold Reincke (Badenweiler, Germany). (See Commentary, page 370.)

The recording took place in the presence of the experimenter and lasted 10 minutes. Total of voices heard: 210. Listening-in, Dr. Reincke could verify almost 100 per cent of the voices. The experimenter received valuable assistance from Dr. Reincke's acute sense of hearing, his keen intelligence and his knowledge of languages, including Russian and Latvian and particularly his constant, enthusiastic probings into the details of the voice-phenomenon.

The jointly-made recording showed the voices in a marked relationship to Dr. Reincke.

"Mama, mūsu Arnolds." (44r: 534)
(Latv.: "Mama, our Arnold.")

"Wir danken!" (same place: 549)
(Germ.: "We give thanks!")
"Te Arnolds sēz." (same place: 560)
(Latv.: "Here sits Arnold.")
"Sir, guten Abend!" (same place: 570)
(Engl., Germ.: "Sir, good evening!")
"Kā iztikat, Sir? Ko studē tu?" (same place: 595)
(Latv., Engl.: "How do you get along, Sir? What are you studying?")

A voice reminds Dr. Reincke of a river in the homeland he had left in earliest youth:

"Tam leju Venta!" (same place: 588)
(Latv.: "To him the valleys of the Venta!")
"Te Maurin. Justi, jau bekannt. Saki Windi, tēvs mežā atļauj."
(Latv., Germ.: "Here is Maurin. Justi, already known. Tell Windi, father gives permission in the wood.") It seems that Dr. R. is addressed by his uncle, Dr. Robert Maurins. "Windi" might mean Windau, where Dr. Reincke's father lies buried.

Other voices are in contact with the experimenter and give him advice:

"Kosti, taisi pirti!" (same place: 547)
(Latv.: "Kosti, prepare the bathroom.") It is traditional custom in Baltic countries to have the bathroom ready for a guest.
"Kostuli, noturi līmeni!" (same place: 537)
(Latv.: "Kostuli, keep up the standard!")
"Kupci, sie sprechen deutsch!" (same place: 553)
(Germ.: "Kupci, they speak German.") This sentence hints at the fact that Dr. R. and the experimenter speak German together. "Kupcis" is a widely known Latvian family name.
"Kosta te, gruti te." (same place: 596)
(Latv.: "Here is Kosta, it is hard here.")
"Te Jupis, Konci! Damit zahle!" (same place: 605)
(Latv., Germ.: "Here is Jupis, Konci! Pay up." "Jupis" is a mythological creature akin to the devil.

There follow voices that keep to general, impersonal themes:

"Jelgava deg!—Ulmanis.—Malwine!" (same place: 563)
(Latv.: "Jelgava [Mitau formerly] is burning!—Ulmanis.—Malwine!") Mitau, now Jelgava, was burnt down by the Russians in 1944. President Ulmanis had been a prisoner of the Russians. "Malwine" was the name of a housekeeper in Riga.
"Putniņš tja! Vieta, vieta, septītā!—Man nav bīks'!" (same place: 572/9)
(Latv.: "Here is Putnins! The seventh place, place!—I have

no trousers!") The voice-entities often complain that they have no clothes; their "anti-law", they say, is "to be naked".
"Te Luft nepietiek. Luft adatas vajadzīgas." (same place: 594/6)
(Latv., Germ.: "Air is not enough here. Air-needles are needed".)

EXPERIMENTAL RECORDING NO. 8

Bad Krozingen (Germany), 29th October 1966
Participants: Mr. Felix Scherer, Electrotechnical expert.
     Mr. Gustav Inhoffen, Photographer (Freiburg, Black Forest, Germany).

The recording was made in the presence of the experimenter. Duration: 20 minutes. It was made through microphone and radio and produced 420 audible voices.

Mr. Felix Scherer wanted to make contact with his dead school-friend Erik Pfaff.

 F.Sch.: "Do you remember how up there in the Black Forest we..."
 "Erik Pfaff!" (44r: 649)
 Gustav Inhoffen: "I would like to hear something about Hammarskjöld."
 "Ich te." (same place: 655)
 (German, Latv.: "I am here.")
 Mr. Inhoffen addresses John Kennedy. A voice of good audibility:
 "Kosti, te Kennedy, Kennedy. Kosti, man patiktu te." (same place: 658)
 (Latv.: "Kosti, here is Kennedy, Kennedy. Kosti, I ought to like it here.")
 "Te Tuntāns, Hitlera sprukās. Raudive, padod zyrgus!" (same place: 659/60)
 (Latv.: "Here is Tuntāns, in Hitler's grip. Raudive, give me the horse!") "Tuntan", the nick-name of Professor Konstantin Čakste, who died in one of Hitler's concentration camps.
 "Kostule, Salzburga mana svēte." (same place: 660)
 (Latv.: "Kostule, Salzburg is my sanctum.")
 "Laid mūsu Kostu!" (same place: 666)
 (Latv.: "Let our Kosta come here!")
 "Kostja, tu? Fetlers te." (same place: 668)
 (Latv.: "Kostja, you? Fetlers is here.") Fetler, a preacher, was

a well-known personality in Riga, and the experimenter had been briefly acquainted with him. He manifests often on tape, for instance: "Laid iekšā!" "Koste, Fetlers tiltu sargā." (50g: 220) Latvian: "Let enter!"—"Koste, Fetler is guarding the bridge."

Further voices:

"Kennedy da! Nava Stalin! Hitlers žuliks." (same place: 668)
(Germ., Latv., Russ.: "Kennedy here! Stalin does not exist! Hitler is a gangster.")

A voice complains:

"Man nav naudas." (same place: 670)
(Latv.: "I have no money.")
"Te mūsu Friede—Uppsala." (same place)
(Latv.: "Here is our peace—Uppsala.")

Another voice:

"Aber Not(a) te überall, venta du! Koste, te pacieš Ulmanis." (same place: 671/2)
(Germ., Swed., Latv.: "But there is distress everywhere here, you wait! Koste, Ulmanis endures here.") Ulmanis, as mentioned before, was the last Latvian President.

"Raudive, tu moz . . . Naktīs te wacht . . . Naktīs es dzeivoju reti." (same place: 672/3)
(Latg., Germ.: "Raudive, you little . . . At night awake here . . . I seldom live at night.")
"Sudraba pirts. Verblüffa dich pirts?" (same place: 675)
(Latv., Germ.: "Bathroom of silver. Does the bathroom startle you?")
"Gast mums būs, jākur prits." (same place: 676)
(Germ., Latv.: "We are going to have a guest, one must heat the bathroom.")
"Koste, kas tas ir?" (same place)
"Daudz čada!" (same place)
(Latv., Russ.: "Koste, what is happening?"—"Much dense smoke!")
"Vai Hitlers tu?" (same place)
(Latv.: "Are you Hitler?")
"Vilks tja." (same place)
(Latv.: "Here is the wolf.")
"Vitna wichtig." (same place)
(Swed., Germ.: "It is important to bear witness.")
"Dirsa!" (same place)
(Latv.: "Shit!")
"Ko tu saki?" (same place)
(Latv.: "What are you saying?")
"Labnakt!" (same place: 677)
(Latv.: "Good night!")

The radio-voices continue the conversation as follows:

> "Du Hitlers vän." (same place: 677)
> (Swed.: "You Hitler's friend.")
> "Hindemith's te." (same place)
> (Latv.: "Here is Hindemith.")
> "Tu sports Hitleram." (same place)
> (Latv.: "You are sport for Hitler.")
> "Sit man, mazā!"
> "Pļāpa du bist!"
> "Siseta te viva."
> "Hitlers vivot!"
> "Kosta, Hitlers te sit."
> "Kosti, tu? Netici! Hitlers. Es latviets." (same place: 680)
> (Latv., Germ., Span.: "Beat me, little girl!"—"You are a chatterbox!"—"Siseta lives here."—"May Hitler live!"—"Kosta, Hitler beats here."—"Kosti, you? Do not believe! Hitler. I am Latvian.")

Now the voices change the subject; Gustav Inhoffen calls his wife Inga's father, who died in Mexico City, and a voice answers:

> "Inga, du? Vienmēr skaista. Padre te." (same place: 698)
> (Germ., Latv., Span.: "Inga, you? You are always beautiful. Father is here.")

In another recording one can hear Inga Inhoffen's father as follows:

> "Fritz. Ob da Inga?" (47g: 440)
> (Germ.: "Fritz. Would that be Inga?")

A Latvian poet reports his presence:

> "Te Veselis." (44r: 699)
> (Latv.: "Here is Veselis.")

An excerpt from the rest of the voices:

> "Kosti, hier Kennedy. Tja John."
> (Germ., Latg.: "Kosti, here Kennedy. Here John.")
> "Strunke sjunda! Tu mīli pateic!"
> (Swed., Latv.: "Strunke, hurry up! You, speak lovingly.")
> "Es pateic. Paliek kluss." (same place: 681)
> (Latv.: "I speak. It becomes quiet.") Strunke, a painter who died in Rome on 13th October 1966, had rather a rough manner; the voice pleads with him here to speak more gently.
> "Te Konstantin! Halelui, Nietzsche!"
> (Latv.: "Here is Konstantin! Hallelujah, Nietzsche!")

"Kosti, tu? Te Tekle.—Nepaliec, Tekle zina!" (same place: 682)
(Latv.: "Kosti, you? Here is Tekle.—Don't stay, Tekle knows it!")
"Dewuški, Konstantīna tilts par brīvu."
(Russ., Latv.: "Girlie, Konstantin's bridge is free of charge.")
"Te Grete, du! Raudive, te Ļuta!"
(Latv.: "Here is Grete, you! Raudive, here is Luta!")
"Kostja tja! Aber Kosta, te kuniga! Besvär, tack!"
(Latv., Germ., Swed.: "Here is Kostja. But Kosta, here is the Kuniga [ancient Latvian for "Queen"]! Thanks for the efforts [or molestations].") This was the last voice in the recording made by Mr. Scherer and Mr. Inhoffen.

Closer analysis of this recording shows that the voices took up direct contact with the persons present. Deceased friends and relatives reacted either immediately, or shortly after having been addressed as, for instance, Mr. Scherer's friend Erik Pfaff and the father of Mrs. Inhoffen. Hitler appeared unbidden. The majority of the voices were aimed at the experimenter; on other occasions the experimenter is sometimes referred to as "radar", whilst his collaborators are called "substitute-radar".

EXPERIMENTAL RECORDING NO. 9

Bad Krozingen (Germany), 5th November 1966
Participants: Mrs. Katharina Nager,
            Doctor Hans Naegeli, Doctor of Medicine and President of the Parapsychological Society of Switzerland, Zurich.
(See Reports pages 324–328)

Results show partly the same outline as those of the previous experiments. The voices are aware of the experimenter's absence, they even demand that he should stay in the room. We again hear names of people who had been close to the experimenter during their lifetime, but collaborators are also addressed by voices, and comments of a general nature are received.

The recording produced 240 voices, 50 per cent belonging to groups "A" and "B", and voices in these two groups could be readily followed by the participants, as far as their knowledge of languages permitted. Dr. Naegeli has a particularly acute sense of hearing and after some listening-in practice he could orientate himself without help in the world of the voices; he could even grasp languages unknown to him, such as Russian and Latvian, by their phonemes.

Voices manifesting through this recording were tested and verified by Dr. Reincke and the experimenter. To be able to locate and verify voices independently, one has to train one's sense of hearing; it takes many months of practice to move from "A" group to "B" group voices, let alone to those of group "C" which demand not only practice, but above all a finely differentiating ear. Professional musicians and singers are best equipped in this sense, though "perfect pitch" in itself is not of direct help in the listening-in process; what is really needed is a keen ear for fast, rhythmic, wave-like speech. The greatest difficulties, however, are posed by the mixture of languages so often used in the construction of sentences.

Some examples from the recording made by Dr. Naegeli and Mrs. Nager:

> "Raudive!" (45g: 560)
> "Wir glauben daran." (same place: 562)
> (Germ.: "We believe in it.")
> "Kosti!" (same place)
> "To Kosta pārcieš fin—" (same place: 564)
> (Latv., Swed.: "Kosta bears that well.")
> "Cīņa Kostule!" (same place)
> (Latv.: "The battle, Kostule!")
> "Lietavji." (same place: 569)
> (Latv.: "The Lithuanians.")
> "Pa cietām stigām." (same place)
> (Latv.: "On hard roads.")
> "Es ticu muļkībai, Opūna vilse." (same place: 585)
> (Latv.: "I believe in stupidity, Opūna errs.")
> "Mēs daudzi—piesūc pie zemes, Aļoša!" (same place)
> (Latv.: "We are many—suck [cling] firmly to the earth, Aljosha!") (See also page 41).
> "Abus pētī—te tukšums." (same place: 586)
> (Latv.: "Investigate the two—here is the void.")
> "Vinca Gehobene überzüchtigt hat." (same place: 587)
> (Germ.: "Vinca has 'overpunished' the elevated.")
> "Aber du dej." (same place)
> (Germ., Latv.: "But you, dance!")

"Fenster—da—klusums!" (same place: 587)
(Germ., Latv.: "Window there—stillness!")
"Meita grib din Wohl!" (same place)
(Latv., Swed., Germ.: "The daughter wishes your welfare.")
"Te furchtbar! Vai tev Nietzsche ieteicama būtne?"
"Eteriska būtne." (same place: 588)
(Latv., Germ.: "It is terrible here! Is Nietzsche a commendable creature to you?"—"An ethereal creature.")
"Lūdzu Kostu." (same place)
(Latv.: "I beg Kosta.")

Microphone:

"Kosta, paliec ustobā!" (same place: 601)
(Latg.: "Kosta, stay in the room!")

Radio:

"Kostin var palīdzēt medu opam!" (same place: 602)
(Latv.: "Kostin can help out Grandpa with honey.")
"Paludzi opam!" (same place)
(Latv.: "Pray for Grandpa!") These two voices seem to refer to Mrs. Nager's father, whom she always addresses as "Grandpa".
"Te tev Wunderstock." (same place)
(Latv., Germ.: "Here is a magic wand for you.")
"Ivars—svētu!" (same place)
(Latv.: "I bless—Ivars!")
"Tā var nīst." (same place: 609)
(Latv.: "One can hate so much!")
"Es tai pazudis." (same place)
(Latv.: "I am lost to her.")
"Kaputt!" (same place)
"Irrsinn, tu braslot māci." (same place)
(Germ., Latv.: "Nonsense, you learn to wade through.")
"Konstantin!" (same place: 612)
"Taupa tinti!" (same place)
(Latv.: "He saves on ink!")
"Kosti, māte te." (same place: 621)
(Latv.: "Kosti, here is mother.")
"Patiešām, te Koste nav." (same place)
(Latv.: "It's a fact, Koste is not here.") As has been mentioned, the experimenter was not present during the recording.
"Paliks te, labais?" (same place)
(Latv.: "Will he stay here, the dear?")
"Nu paldies!" (same place)
(Latv.: "Now give thanks!")
"Naudu soliji man!" (same place)
(Latv.: "You promised me money!")
"Tai ir prece!" (same place: 625)

(Latv.: "She has the goods!")
"Koste, esmu Smiliġs." (same place: 626)
(Latv.: "Koste, I am Smilgis.") Smilgis was a Latvian theatrical producer, and the experimenter knew him well.
"Svaigi atkopies!" (same place)
(Latv.: "He has newly recovered!")
"Musik!" (same place)
(Germ.: "Music!")
"Mūzikas trūkums." (same place)
(Latv.: "There is a lack of music.")
"Idūna pirmo reizi." (same place: 627)
(Latv.: "Idūna for the first time.")
"Djadja, Onkel sucht dej." (same place)
(Russ., Germ., Swed.: "Uncle, uncle is looking for you.")

EXPERIMENTAL RECORDING NO. 10

Bad Krozingen (Germany), 12th November 1966
Participants: Mr. Gerd Kramer, Assistant Headmaster (Sec. School).
Mrs. Heidi Kramer.
Mr. Gustav Inhoffen, (Freiburg, Germany).

The recording was made by the participants, without help from the experimenter; 180 audible voices manifested and were analysed as to content and meaning by the experimenter; the participants were able to verify up to 70 per cent of the voices heard.

Mr. Inhoffen spoke a few introductory words. A voice:

"Ich bitte." (44r: 801)
(Germ.: "If you please.") literally: "I beg."
Inhoffen: ". . . red side." Voice:
"Ich liebe dich." (same place)
(Germ.: "I love you.")
Inhoffen: ". . . eight hundred . . ." Voice:
"Liebe din vän!" (same place)
(Germ., Swed.: "Love your friend.")
Inhoffen: ". . . sixtysix . . ." Voice:
"Kur Kosta?" (same place: 803)
(Latv.: "Where is Kosta?")
Inhoffen: "Present are . . ." Voice:
"Mr. Kramer!" (same place)
Inhoffen: ". . . excuse . . ." Voice:

"Kosta!" (same place)
Mr. Inhoffen: "Konstantin Raudive is not present." Voice: "Du schwindelst! Knappe!" (same place)
(Germ.: "You are cheating! Knappe!") Mr. Knappe, a friend of the experimenter.
Inhoffen: "Friends, make your presence known!"
"Stykuts, nemāci Kosti! Uppsalā biji?" (same place: 804)
(Latv.: "Stykuts, don't lecture Kosti! Were you in Uppsala?")
Stykuts was a schoolmate of the experimenter. (See page 62.)

Now a voice demands repeatedly:

"Kosti! Kosti!" (same place)
Inhoffen: "We want to help him (Raudive)." Voice: "Wie?" (same place: 806)
(Germ.: "How?")
Inhoffen: "Please speak loudly!"
"Wir können nicht.—Kosti tu atbīd." (same place: 807)
(Germ.: "We can't—you push Kosti away.")
Inhoffen: "We want to have Kennedy. Mr. Kennedy..."
"Naktī, Kosta. Ko—stu! Donnerwetter!" (same place: 809)
(Latv., Germ.: "At night, Kosta. Ask Kosta! Damn it all!")

Now Mr. Inhoffen calls for his uncle Johann and his aunt Emma: "Johann!"

Voice: "Ilgi sadeg!" (same place)
(Latv.: "Burns up slowly!")
Inhoffen: "Aunt Emma!" Voice:
"Ak, tu plāpa!" (same place: 810/1)
(Latv.: "Oh, you chatterbox!")
"Gerd!" (same place: 813)

Gustav Inhoffen further calls his wife Inga's father, and mentions that the latter died in Mexico City.

"Inga neguļ." (same place)
(Latv.: "Inga does not sleep.")

Once again Mr. Inhoffen calls on John Kennedy, on his uncle Johann and his aunt Emma, and asks them to "speak loud enough."

"Kosta mūsu. Uppsala, Kosti. Tötja. Nekliedz tu! Tekle!" (same place: 814)
(Latv., Russ.: "Kosta is ours. Uppsala, Kosti. Aunt. Don't you scream! Tekle.")
Mr. Inhoffen: "I thank you!"
Voice: "Kur ir Koste?" (same place: 815)
(Latv.: "Where is Koste?")

Gustav Inhoffen's strong, down-to-earth personality made its impact on the world of the voice-phenomenon, and voice-entities addressed by him answer in a straightforward manner. Once more it becomes clear that they know of the experimenter's absence and we repeatedly hear them clamouring for him, but the voice-entities are not prevented from manifesting, and we realise that in that event entities connected with the experimenter, such as his mother, his sister Tekle and others, still appear on tape. This seems to give substance to the hypothesis that microphone, radio, etc. are material intermediaries between the "two worlds".

Now Dr. Gerd Kramer takes over. He speaks softly and concentratedly. "I would like," he says, and a voice calls:

"Pōrstoj!" (same place: 818)
(Latg.: "Stop!")
Dr. Kramer: "... Anneliese Fink ..."
"Tobi, Anna te!" (same place: 820)
(Latv.: "Tobi, here is Anna!")
Dr. Kramer: "I would like my uncle Hermann ..."
"Nur durch Kosti!" (same place: 821)
(Germ.: "Only through Kosti.")
Dr. K.: "I repeat ..."
"Nur durch Kosti!" (same place)
(Germ.: "Only through Kosti.")
Dr. K.: "In Norway ..."
"Viņš ir dzīvs." (same place)
(Latv.: "He lives!")
Dr. Kramer repeats: "In Norway ..."
"Kosti, tu? Mūsu Kosti!" (same place)
(Latv.: "Kosti, you? Please, our Kosti!")

The recording is continued via radio. The voices retain the same characteristics, the same features, language, independence, awareness; but audibility is improved and the sentences become longer and more coherent. These voices belong mainly to groups "A" and "B". A few examples:

"Velns, nu pietiek!" (44r: 826)
(Latv.: "The devil, now it's enough!")
"Koste, māsiņa. Ko Inga pļāpā?" (same place: 827)
(Latv.: "Koste, little sister. What does Inga chatter?")
"Stykuts, Konstantīn! Stykuts kēkī!" (same place: 828)
(Latv.: "Stykuts, Konstantīn! Stykuts in the kitchen.")

"Du uns fehlte!" (same place: 829)
(Germ.: "We missed you!")
"Pakustini Kosti!" (same place: 832)
(Latv.: "Move Kosti!")
"Tu Kostīti mīl, kundzene?" (same place)
(Latv.: "Do you love Kostiti [diminutive], mistress?")
"Tibeta skrin, izmenica! Tici! Anna griechisch." (same place: 833)
(Swed., Russ., Latv., Germ.: "Tibet's shrine, unfaithful one! Anna is Greek.")
"Kur tu?"
"Herzi, tiši! Mūsu Kosti!" (same place)
(Latv., Russ.: "Where are you?"—"Dear heart, softer! Ask our Kosti!")

After a few voice-comments of a general nature, the relationship to the experimenter and his collaborators is re-established.

"Gerd tu te siebente." (same place: 835/6)
(Latv., Germ.: "Gerd, you are here the seventh.")
"Es Vilma, Kostulīt."
"Sind sie ad Kosti?"
"Weck doch Kosti!" (same place: 836)
(Latv., Germ.: "I am Vilma, Kostulīt."—"Are you with Kosti!"—"Do wake Kosti!")
"Puika nesā.—Hej Hitler!—Kosti, Tuntāns te. Pasauc tu Hitler!" (same place: 837)
(Latv.: "One carries the boy about. Heh Hitler!—Kosti, Tuntans is here. You call Hitler!") For Professor Čakste, called "Tuntan", see page 63.

The recording is switched back to microphone; a voice asks:

"Kosti, tu?" (same place: 838)
(Latv.: "Kosti, you?")

Gustav Inhoffen says: "... my dear friends ..." and a voice comes in with:

"Pļāpa!" (same place)
(Latv.: "Chatterbox!")

When Mr. Inhoffen switches once more to radio, the following voices are distinctly heard:

"Ruskij! Saša, Kosti." (same place: 840)
(Russ.: "The Russian! Sasha, Kosti.")
"Raudive, te Tegala." (same place: 841)
(Latv.: "Raudive, here is Tegala.") This name is unknown to the experimenter.

"Te robots..."
"Māte, kaunās doch." (same place: 842)
(Latv., Germ.: "Here is a robot..."—"Mother is nevertheless ashamed.")
"Brāli, Kosti! Čaklie."
"Sak' Margaret!—Labprāt!"
"Kosti, vēli." (same place: 844)
(Latv.: "Brother, Kosti! The industrious ones."—"Tell Margaret!—With pleasure!"—"Kosti, it is late.")

EXPERIMENTAL RECORDING NO. 11

Bad Krozingen, 14th November 1966
Participant: Dr. Rudolf Zimmermann, Doctor of Medicine and Dental Surgeon (Bad Krozingen).
(See Commentary, page 372).

The recording was made partly by microphone, partly by radio. Duration: 5 minutes. Result: approx. 80 voices, of which Dr. Zimmermann himself could verify roughly 35 per cent. Unfortunately, the recording was marred by strong noise-interference.

Repeated listening-in tests brought out the following voices: Dr. Zimmermann has just said: "... sixty-six..."

"Rudolf!" calls a voice. (44r: 850)
Dr. Zimmermann: "I am calling you, show your presence!"
"Rufe Kosti! Kosti Raudivi!" (same place)
(Germ.: "Call Kosti! Kosti Raudivi.")
Dr. Zimmermann: "Thanks to him it is possible for me to make contact with you."
"Guli du?—Richtig—richtig—richtig!" (same place: 851/2)
(Latv., Germ.: "Are you asleep?—Right—right—right!")
Dr. Zimmermann: "It is difficult to make oneself heard."
"Dikti grūti!" (same place: 858/9)
(Latv.: "Enormously difficult.")
"Wir sind te." (same place: 862)
(Germ., Latv.: "We are here.")
Dr. Zimmermann: "I would like to make contact..."
"Kosti zurück, lempi!" (same place)
(Germ., Latv.: "Kosti back, rogue!")
Dr. Zimmermann: "But perhaps..."
"Gute Nacht! Sprechen fertig! Papi, wir sind." (same place: 864)
(Germ.: "Good night! Talking finished! Papa, we are.")

Some of the radio voices:

"As Bob . . .Nabaga galva, abpuseji . . ." (same place: 876)
(Latv.: "I Bob . . . the poor head, both sides . . .")
"Sveiki, Kosta, Ich liebe!" (same place: 877)
(Latv., Germ.: "Greetings, Kosta, I love!")
"Papi. Zenta's Abschied."
"Ai, te Todesnacht!"
"Tai gruti bij!"
"Zentas Papi." (same place: 883)
(Germ., Latv.: "Papa, Zenta's farewell."—"Ah, here night of death."—"It was hard for her."—"Zenta's Papa.") These strange voices were, in a sense, right: Zenta Maurina was very ill that particular night and hardly survived her suffering.
"Ded', Asūne!" (same place: 884)
(Russ.: "Grandfather, Asūne!") Asūne (Latgale) was the experimenter's birthplace.
"Te Petrautzki!" (same place: 886)
(Latv.: "Here Petrautzki!")
"Īsta nacis." (same place)
(Latv.: "Real Nazi.") Margarete Petrautzki had been a teacher in the "Hitler Youth" when she was young; later she realised the errors and evils of the Nazi Movement. She showed most excellent character traits during the years she worked for the experimenter and his wife, Zenta Maurina. She was always ready to make sacrifices for the good of her fellow human beings and won the love and admiration of all who came into contact with her.
"Hier Schulte!"
"Netiek!"
"Raudiv, laid Schulti!" (same place: 888)
(Germ., Latv.: "Here Schulte!"—"Don't enter!"—"Raudiv, let Schulte enter!")

Dr. Zimmermann had already made recordings with the experimenter when this session took place. In most cases voices had appeared which Dr. Zimmermann could identify himself. A recording of 22nd February 1966, for instance, produced distinct voices and clear speech-content:

"Paldies, Konstantin, par to drosu. Palīgu tev nav. Paldies, Raudive!" (33g: 193)
(Latv.: "Thank you, Konstantin, for the courage. You have no helpers. Thanks, Raudive!")
"Mēs braucam pie Raudives ciemā." (same place: 197)
(Latv.: "We travel to Raudive for a visit.")
"Mans paldies! Mūsu doktors Zimmermann!" (same place: 248)
(Latv.: "My gratitude! Our Dr. Zimmermann!")

"Raudive, novēro draugu!" (same place: 221)
(Latv.: "Raudive, watch the friend!")
"Hallo, hundert Toten ab." (same place: 249)
(Germ.: "Hallo, hundred dead off.")
"Zenti' Paps!" (same place: 250)
"Da rühmt Edith." (same place: 236)
(Germ.: "Zenti's Papa!"—"There Edith praises.")
"Ai, hier ir sodi." (same place: 239)
(Germ., Latv.: "Ah, here are penalities!")

EXPERIMENTAL RECORDING NO. 12

Bad Krozingen (Germany), 16th November 1966
Participant: Dr. Arnold Reincke (Badenweiler).
(See Commentary, page 370).

Dr. Reincke made this recording himself alone; 240 voices were registered. Dr. Reincke independently heard and verified approximately 70 per cent. The recording took 6 minutes and was made through radio. The voices show no differences from others recorded and are, on the whole, of good quality, including many belonging to group "A".

"Kostja runa.—Petrautzkis!" (45g: 012)
(Latv.: "Kostja, speak.—Petrautzki!")
"Kostulit, pētī!" (same place: 011)
(Latv.: "Kostulit, investigate!")
"Ty grecola, plāpa!" (same place: 013)
(Russ., Lat., Latv.: "You are a coward, chatterer!")
"Kosta, grecoli! Ich liebe dich! Una Arnold!" (same place: 014)
("Kosta, coward! I love you! Unite Arnold!")
"Kosti, tev pamočnik!" (same place: 015)
(Latv., Russ.: "Kosti, you have helpers!")
"Nightly Berlin! Chleb, chleb!" (same place: 028/9)
(Eng., Russ.: "Nightly Berlin! Bread, bread!")
"Te Petrautzki, Kost." (same place: 037)
(Latv.: "Here is Petrautzki, Kost.")
"Djadja Arnold." (same place: 046)
(Russ.: "Uncle Arnold.")
"Tumšā burkā iekāpj." (same place: 050)
(Latv.: "Enter into a dark tin.")
"Runā puika—puika doch tja." (same place: 063)
(Latv.: "Speak, boy—the boy is, after all, here.")

"Karočij boulvard! Še Krozing! Nasi bringa, Krozingen weg!"
(same place)
(Russ., Latv., Swed., Germ.: "The shortest boulevard! Here is Krozingen! Fetch ours [those belonging to us], Krozingen away!")

This statement shows that the voice-entities are able to distinguish the place where the experiment is being conducted.

"Kosti, Uppsala, te Baltruški." (same place: 075)
(Latv.: "Kosti, Uppsala here, here are 'Baltruški'.") Baltruski is the name of a Lithuanian family living in Uppsala and known to the experimenter.
"Met tiltu!" (same place: 079)
(Latv.: "Span the bridge!")

A voice insists:

"Ruf Kost, Pieter!" (same place: 092)
(Germ.: "Call Kost, Peter!")
"Kostēn, Buch skrive, und billig!" (same place: 094)
(Latv., Germ.: "Kostēn, writes book, and cheap!")

EXPERIMENTAL RECORDING NO. 13

Bad Krozingen (Germany), 2nd December 1966
Participant: Dr. Arnold Reincke (Badenweiler, Germany).

This recording, as the previous ones, produced clear, meaningful voice-statements, referring partly to Dr. Reincke, partly to the experimenter. It was made by Dr. Reincke alone and lasted only 5 minutes, but revealed 120 audible voices.

Here are some examples of voices aimed predominantly at Dr. Reincke:

"Tu kungs, Aļoša!" (45g: 478)
(Latv.: "You are master, Aljosha!")
"Tat-entdecker!" (same place)
(Germ.: "Deed-discoverer.") "Deed" meant in the sense of "action."
"Es te mīlu Wasser." (same place)
(Latv., Germ.: "I love the water here.")
"Und da du forschen komm." (same place: 479)
(Germ.: "And as you have come exploring.")
"Vai iedrikstēsies, bei Gott?!" (same place)
(Latv., Germ.: "Will you dare, by God?!") This may be a

question as to whether Dr. Reincke would dare to penetrate into the world of the voices.

"Ultunas poike, Mežotnes vertreiben." (same place)
(Latv., Germ.: "Boy from Ultuna, driven from Mežotne.")
Ultuna is a suburb of Uppsala; Mezotne an ancient Latvian fortress which played an important part in battles against the Teutonic knights. Dr. Reincke had connections with Ultuna and, through his mother, also with Mezotne. The sentence seems to link up in a meaningful way with Dr. Reincke who had, in fact, been driven from his land of origin.

"Aber vad du schenko, danke dir!" (same place)
(Germ.: "But [for] what you give, thank you.")

Another voice explains and emphasises:

"Mūs Kosti pētī." (same place: 480)
(Latv.: "Kosti investigates us.")
"Unordnung—Saal! Dod man Kosti! kur Kosti?" (same place)
(Germ., Latv.: "Disorder—hall! Give me Kosti! Where is Kosti?")

The following sentence points even more strongly to the experimenter's absence:

"Hallo, Kosti, tu mums trūki. Zwei Kinder besuchte Čamaṇ." (same place: 482)
(Latv., Germ.: "Hallo, Kosti, we missed you. Čamaṇ visited two children.") Čamaṇ, a prelate, died in Rome in 1964; neither the experimenter nor his collaborator knew him personally.

"Galviṇa sāp? Votna. Nedabūsi te cauri. Netaisi pretty! Lobōk pastaigājies på draussen, lobōk atmot. Kosti atgriezt, pārstaj!" (same place: 488/90)
(Latv., Engl., Swed., Germ.: "Does the little head ache? Votna. You won't manage it here. Don't make yourself smart! Rather go for a walk outside, it is better to breathe. Call Kosti back, stop!")

"Votna" is a name that appears often, but the experimenter can give no detail about its origin. The rest of this sentence may be taken as a warning to Dr. Reincke not to take the research too lightly; it was not so easy to accomplish and he pictured it as too glamorous a job.

Here a voice-sentence of mysterious content:
"Pantišā, laiku, laiku saṇem!" (same place)
(Latv.: "In Pantisha take time, time!")
A woman's voice:
"Guli, Apollo! Kosti, nāc tu gulēt!" (same place)

(Latv.: "Sleep, Apollo! Kosti, come to sleep!") "Sleep, Apollo" is most probably to be taken symbolically: "Sleep, sun!"

Another voice interjects:

"Nekliedz, te mūsu Arnolds!" (same place: 491)
(Latv.: "Don't scream, here is our Arnold!")

A slightly mocking voice says:

"Uppsalā saka—mūsu zirgs!" (same place)
(Latv.: "In Uppsala the saying is—our horse!")
"Atsauc!" (same place: 492)
(Latv.: "Call back!")
"Ne nauda, baznīckungs!" (same place: 493)
(Latv.: "Not the money, Vicar!")

And a different voice again:

"Badische Schaum, Kosta! Barbiete dumja tev. Piemin Uppsala! Te bunta, Kostulīt. Saproti Margarete." (same place: 493/4)
(Germ., Latv., Russ.: "Foam from Baden, Kosta! The [female] barber is stupid for you. Remember Uppsala! Here is upheaval, Kostulit. Understand Margarete!") This sentence seems to refer to the fact that the experimenter had accepted a hairdresser, who had claimed to have a good sense of hearing, for listening-in tests. Margarete, the faithful helper, warns and predicts upheaval. This proved right; the hairdresser was unsuited for the task of listening-in.

"Piemin Sparta! Viss mins. Cumpandente—mans kaps. Dolmatscha Ann!" (same place: 495)
(Latv., Swed., Germ.: "Think of Sparta! One remembers everything. Cumpandente—my grave. Interpret, Ann!")
"Bald, Kosta?" (same place: 497)
(Germ.: "Soon, Kosta?")

The following voice once again refers to Dr. Reincke:

"Mit diesem du begonnst. Schone der Spritze där." (same place: 498)
(Germ., Swed.: "With this you started. Look after the syringe there!")

At the end of the recording we hear a particularly fascinating sentence; both linguistically and as to its content:

"Wundarbar! Vitne mūs embarquogē. Furchtbar, lai stop!"
(Germ., Swed., Latv., modified French: "Marvellous! The witness embarks us. Terrible, let him stop!")

Nearly all the voices mentioned here belong to group "A", with the exception of microphone-voices, which rarely achieve such clarity.

EXPERIMENTAL RECORDING NO. 14

Bad Krozingen (Germany), 4th December 1966
Participant: Miss Annemarie Morgenthaler (Bern).

One hundred and fifty voices manifested through this recording. Miss Morgenthaler was able to verify 75 per cent. The voices make statements rich in content aimed, just as with other collaborators, partly at the person recording, partly at the experimenter. Names of people known to the experimenter (for instance Björk, Dāle, Moņa, Arvis) appear as in previous sessions.

Microphone:

> Annemarie Morgenthaler: ". . . now the recording . . ."
> Voice: "Annemarie, nabaga Annemarie!" (45g: 503)
> (Latv.: "Annemarie, poor Annemarie.")
> Miss Morgenthaler: ". . . and I turn it round . . ."
> "Kur tu, Kosti?" (same place: 506)
> (Latv.: "Where are you, Kosti?")

Radio:

> "Jetzt—jetzt vilka! Ich will gaisa! (same place: 506)
> (Germ., Latv.: "Now, now, she-wolf! I want air!")
> "Mās glücklich?" (same place: 507)
> (Latv., Germ.: "Sister, happy?") This voice indicates that Miss Morgenthaler has a sister "on the other side"; a sister had, indeed, died some years ago.
> "Tja māsiņa, dikti sildīt. Māsa, kur Kosta?" (same place: 507)
> (Latv.: "Here is little sister, very warming. Sister, where is Kosta?")
> "Tikai Pāvels!" (same place: 508)
> (Latv.: "Only Pavel!")
> "Tava mama, Kosta!" (same place)
> (Latv.: "Your Mama, Kosta!")
> "Es Ilga Lirence!" (same place: 509)
> (Latv.: "I am Ilga Lirence!")
> "Margarete Petrautzki!" (same place: 510)

There follows a succession of voices giving their names; afterwards a voice says:

"Priez Koste! Überrasch!" (same place: 511)
(French, Germ.: "Ask Koste [to come]! Surprise!")
"Kosti, māti rāj! Māte duma."
"Es to zinu. Kosta, piedod!" (same place)
(Latv.: "Kosti, reprimand mother! Mother is stupid."—"I know it. Kosta, forgive!")

Now come voices that refer mainly to the experimenter:

"Minna te, Vilmu zinu." (same place)
(Latv.: "Here is Minna, I know Vilma.")
"Es Tekle, mōsiņa." (same place: 512)
(Latg.: "I am Tekle, little sister.")
"Nepatīk, te Björk." (same place: 518)
(Latv.: "I don't like it, here is Björk.")
"Ex Dāle!" (same place: 519) Dāle was a well-known Latvian psychologist (see page 84).
"Arnolds, Kosta." (same place)

Now the voices once again address Miss Morgenthaler:

"Prosit, dārgā! Mīlestība. Darbs ir aukle. Letzten Endes leer." (same place: 523/5)
(Latv., Germ.: "Cheers, dear one! Love. The occupation is nursemaid. In the end empty.")
"Grüssi tevi, Liebste!"
"Steht Hans." (same place: 529)
(Germ.: "I greet you, dearest!"—"Stands Hans.")

Miss Morgenthaler, through microphone: "... whether Raudive will be missed again. I wait for it."

"Anny, tu pļāpa!" (same place: 535)
(Latv.: "Anny, you are a chatterbox!")
"Koste, tu? Furchtbar!"
"Fein, tava Zenta."
"Medali! Tja, Anja." (same place: 537)
(Latv., Germ.: "Koste, you? Terrible!"—"Fine, your Zenta." —Medal! Here is Anja.")
"Dieva Moņa." (same place: 538)
(Latv.: "Mona of God.")
"Kosta, tu?" (same place: 539)
(Latv.: "Kosta, you?")
"Arvis pēta Kosti." (same place: 547)
(Latv.: "Arvis investigates Kosti.")
"Tu ziamais Koste!" (same place: 548)
(Latg.: "You, the earthly Koste!")

EXPERIMENTAL RECORDING NO. 15

Bad Krozingen (Germany), 8th December 1966
Participant: Prof. Dr. Zenta Maurina (Uppsala, Sweden),
Writer.
(See Report, page 312.)

Dr. Zenta Maurina has great experience in everything concerning the world of the voices. She has been able to hear and verify voices of groups "A" and "B" unaided, but although she has a most discerning, musically trained and sensitive ear, she needed a great deal of concentration and perseverance to succeed in the art of "listening-in".

The recording of 8th December was made without the experimenter being present. Here are some of the voices heard:

Dr. Maurina says: "You (the unseen) are present at all my activities."
Voice: "Nav zugegen." (45r: 013)
(Latv., Germ.: "Not present.")

Through radio:

"Fehlt Kosti." (same place: 028)
(Germ.: "Kosti [is] missing.") It is a recurring fact that the voices ask for the experimenter, or bemoan his absence.
"Velis stāv." (same place)
(Latv.: "Here stands a mane.") "Mane" or "shade".
"Kosti, piepūli galvu!" (same place: 032)
Latv.: "Kosti, exercise your brain!")

Now Zenta Maurina talks again through microphone:

"... whether my behaviour is correct..."
"Koste mīli!" (same place: 037)
(Latv.: "Love Kosti!")
Dr. Maurina: "whether it is sin..."
"Zenti, lugn." (same place)
(Swed.: "Zenti, calm.")
"Kosta, laid pa vecam Telefunken!" (same place: 038)
(Latv.: "Kosta, let us transmit in the same old way.")
"Ljubim Zenta." (same place: 039)
(Russ.: "We love Zenta.")
"Lepnā, grūti Kostem." (same place: 040)
(Latv.: "The proud one, it is difficult for Kosti.")
"Mōte tja!—Kosta paldies! Lietuva." (same place: 041/2)

(Latv.: "Mother is here!—Kosta, thanks! Lithuania.")
"Kostene ir golva. Tack, tack! Nadod vairs." (same place: 047)
(Latg., Swed.: "Kostene is the head. Thanks, thanks! One no longer transmits.") With this voice the recording is ended. It is strange how the voices always seem to know when a recording is coming to an end, and how they seize the last moment to give this information.

Immediately following Dr. Zenta Maurina's recording, the experimenter made a short one himself. It lasted only three minutes, but produced several "A" voices.

The experimenter says that the previous recording had been made by Zenta Maurina.

"Tack'a, Maurina veta." (45r: 055/6)
"Swed.: "Thanks, Maurina knows it.")

Radio voices:

"Labi, Zenta!—Prijatel da!" (same place: 062)
(Latv., Russ., Ger.: "Good, Zenta!—A friend is here.")
"Te Dauge piesakas." (same place: 062)
(Latv.: "Here Dauge reports.") Professor Dauge had been a good friend of Zenta Maurina and the experimenter.
"Emma Droste, furchtbar! Jāpēti." (same place: 075)
(Germ., Latv.: "Emma Droste, terrible! One must investigate.")
"Musinā nav kauna." (same place: 077)
(Latv.: "One incites, one has no shame.")
"Björk, te Couplet." (same place)
(Latv.: "Björk, here Couplet.") Professor Björk (Uppsala), was known to both the experimenter and Zenta Maurina. He died from a coronary whilst out riding.
"Schau, Koste, pilsētu—Ķepavu!" (same place: 078)
(Germ., Latv.: "Look, Kosta, the town—Kepava!") When the experimenter knew Kepava, it had been but a village; perhaps the term "pilseta", town, is applicable to a different plane of existence.
"Te guļ. Netais! As—peur!" (same place: 079)
(Latv., Latg., French: "One sleeps here. Don't do it.—I am afraid.") "Don't do it" probably means "Stop the recording."

Apart from these two recordings the number of voices addressing Zenta Maurina or referring to her in their statements is so large that only a fraction can be quoted here.

In the beginning the voices spoke of her illness:

"Kosti, tava Zenta ļoti slima." (25r: 474)
(Latv.: "Kosti, your Zenta is very sick.")

At a microphone-recording on 20th January 1966, a voice recounts many of the difficulties Zenta Maurina had to contend with, and indeed at that time she had been grievously ill:

"Maurinai sāp galva."
"Maurina nevar gulēt."
"Maurina nem miega tabletes."
(Latv.: "Maurina has headaches."—"Maurina cannot sleep."
—"Maurina takes sleeping pills.")

A row of voices in succession points out how difficult life is for her:

"Zentai tja grūti." (40g: 348)
(Latv.: "It is difficult here for Zenta.")
"Vai doktorei te putj ir trudnyi?"
"Kāpēc pateic?" (45r: 552/5)
(Latv., Russ.: "Is the path of the doctor a difficult one here?"
—"Why do you say that?")

The voices comment on whether she is sleeping or not, and on where she happens to be.

"Maurina gul." (31r: 632)
(Latv.: "Maurina sleeps.")
"Zenta, guli te! Gudra Katz!" (35r: 147)
(Latv.: "Zenta, sleep here. Clever cat!")
"Vinai sova nav, fint! Maurina bra." (36r: 020/1)
(Latv., Swed.: "She finds no sleep, fine! Maurina is good.")
"Nachts ir ilga. Maurina kaktus smaide." (41g: 453)
(Germ., Latv.: "The night is long. Maurina smiles at the corners.")
"Zentuli, guli nu!" (43g: 622)
(Latv.: "Zentuli, sleep now.")
"Vai doktore gul?" (44b: 752)
(Latv.: "If the doctor sleeps?")

During one microphone-recording Zenta Maurina was first present, but soon left the room. Two voices comment:

"Jā, viņa gribēja iet."
(Latv.: "Yes, she wanted to go.")
"Sova vill, sova vill." (25g: 331/5)
(Swed.: "She wants to sleep, she wants to sleep.") This type of statement demonstrates once again the presence and the independence of the voice-entities.
"Guten Tag! Virtuvē Zenta." (45r: 033)
(Germ., Latv.: "Good day! Zenta is in the kitchen.") See also Dr. Zimmermann's recording; (page 214)

Some voices send greetings:

"Grüss Zenti, Kosta!" (41g: 685)
"Da grüsse Maurini." (44b: 299)
(Germ.: "Greet Zenti, Kosta."—"Greet Maurini.")
"Grüsse Zenta!" (44r: 214)
"Grüsse Dichterin!" (44r: 778)
(Germ.: "Greet Zenta!"—"Greet the poetess!")
"Pasveic Dichterin, pasveic Raudive!" (45g: 671)
(Latv., Germ.: "Greet the poetess, greet Raudive!")

Zenta Maurina's father manifests:

"Zenti' paps!" (33g: 250)
(Germ.: "Zenti's Papa.")
"Te Mauriņš piestāj." (36r: 182)
(Latv.: "Here Maurins halts.")
"Tita, te Maurins!"
"Zinu pats."
"Kur tu biji?" (40g: 348)
(Latv.: "Look here is Maurins!"—"I know [that] myself."—"Where were you?")
"Zenta Maurinu buāo!" (44r: 894)
(Latv.: "Kiss Zenta Maurina.")
"Es pie Zentas, Zenta pie tevim." (45r: 282)
(Latv.: "I am with Zenta, Zenta is with you.")
"Tu pārlasi Zenta!" (45r: 298)
(Latv.: "Read again Zenta!")
"Zenti pieder tev!" (41g: 696)
(Latv.: "Zenti belongs to you!")

Renate, Zenta Maurina's sister, appears on tape several times:

"Te Renate, Kosti." (41g: 661)
(Latv.: "Here is Renate. Kosti.")

The experimenter addresses Renate and asks her to greet Zenta.

"Renat, piezvan!" (41g: 748)
(Latv.: "Renat, calling!")

Once more the experimenter asks Renate for a greeting.

"Lieber Kosti!—Koste, Vater aldrig . . ." (41g: 781/2)
(Germ., Swed.: "Dear Kosti!—Koste, father never . . .")

Now the experimenter says that Zenta needs the strengthening power of love.

"Du pats, lebe pats!" (same place)
(Germ., Latv.: "You yourself, love yourself!")

The experimenter talks to Renate and comments on the fact that he did not know her when she was alive.

"Tava māte, Renate.—Koste, tu? Ich liebe." (42g: 399)
(Latv., Germ.: "Your mother, Renate.—Koste, you? I love.")
"Din sister, Zenta!" (47g: 359)
(Swed.: "Your sister, Zenta!")

After the experimenter had thanked Renate for a greeting to Zenta:

"Natura ilga Zentai." (42g: 030)
(Latv.: "Zenta has an enduring nature.")
"Nevajag Zenti . . ." (45g: 030)
(Latv.: "Zenti should not . . .")

Every now and then Zenta Maurina is addressed by fellow writers:

"Turies pie Maurinas. Albert Strods."
"Nav Maurinas, nekur." (39g: 241)
(Latv.: "Keep to Maurina. Albert Strods."—"Maurina is nowhere to be found.")
"Zentai klājas labi."
"Migadži pļāpā."
"Bārda! Zenta donna!" (Hr: 253)
(Latv.: "Zenta is well."—"Migadži chatters."—"Bārda! Zenta is a 'Donna'.") Zenta Maurina had interested herself in the Latvian poet Fricis Bārda and had written papers and essays about him.
"Te Maurina mana. Mazā Annele." (41g: 271/2)
(Latv.: "Here is Maurina mine. Little Annele.") The poetess Anna Brigadere called herself in her letters to Zenta always "the little Annele". They were friends and Zenta had dedicated a book to Anna.
"Zenta, Ladzda!" (41g: 648) Ladzda, another Latvian poetess, was an intimate friend of Zenta Maurina. She had died in the USA and her ashes had been cast into the Baltic Sea.
"Zin' Zinaïdu?" (46r: 648)
(Latv.: "Do you know Zinaida?") Zinaida was the Christian name of Ladzda, the poetess.
"Te Grins, Maurina." (Üllr: 112)
(Latv.: "Here is Grins, Maurina!") Zenta Maurina knew the writer Jānis Grins. (See page 75).

Here are more statements that refer to Zenta Maurina:

"Brav, Maurina." (45g: 033)
(Germ.: "Good, Maurina.")
"Maurina māmule!" (38r: 484)
(Latv.: "Maurina, Mama!")
"Zentuli!" (31g: 446)
"Vi prata, Zentuli!" (35r: 346)
(Swed.: "We speak, Zentuli!")
"Nesīs Zenti technika." (35g: 726)
(Latv.: "The technique will carry Zenti.")
"Maurina—Sverige!" (43g: 452)
"Doktor Maurina—Copia Wolga." (U Ir: 142)
"Raudive, Zenta Maurin kundzīte." (44b: 934)
(Latv.: "Raudive, Zenta Maurina is mistress.")
"Wer Zenta holt? Ista tu Latvija mums." (44r: 906)
(Germ., Latv.: "Who fetches Zenta? You are for us the true Latvia.")
"Ljubim Zenta—Lepna."
"Maurina, mili faktu!" (Amg: 298)
(Russ., Latv.: "We love Zenta, the proud one."—"Maurina, love the fact!")
"Maurina pētī! Es redzu gultā. Naporstoj!" (47g: 372)
(Latv.: "Maurina, explore! I see you in bed. Do not stop.")
"Vai Zenta nezina Perkisto?" (47g: 438)
(Latv.: "Does Zenta not know Perkisto?")
"Zenta, mēs stridamies." (47r: 122)
(Latv.: "Zenta, we are quarrelling.")

EXPERIMENTAL RECORDING NO. 16

Bad Krozingen (Germany), 15th December 1966
Participant: Mr. Friedrich Jürgenson (Mölnbo, Sweden).
(See Report, page 329.)

Friedrich Jürgenson, original discoverer of the phenomenon (see page 13), was mentioned quite frequently by the voices even before this experimental recording took place.

The first voices ever heard by the experimenter to speak of Friedrich Jürgenson made the following statements:

"Mölnbo! Trilli, trilli, Raudive in Mölnbo!" (23g: 318)
"Sei Jürgenso- Priestekeri!" (30g: 388)
(Germ. [modified]: "Raudive in Mölnbo!"—"Be Jürgenso-'s priest.")

The exclamation "trilli, trilli," could be a distortion of the English word "thrills".

"Friedrich med dej!" (31g: 126)
(Swed.: "Friedrich with you!")

Some voice-entities took a hostile attitude and intervened provokingly between Jürgenson and the experimenter:

"Vōcele! Nie draugs!" (36r: 608/9)
(Latg., Germ.: "Gossip! Never friend!")
"Friedrich! Stricki vāri für Friedrich!" (39g: 318)
(Germ., Latv.: "Friedrich! Boil the rope for Friedrich!")

Another voice warns more moderately:

"Konstantin, dies(n) Sinn meide von Herzen! Friedrich zin. Uppsala vivat! Nokusi? Jā, Kosti skatam." (40r: 664)
(Germ., Latv.: "Konstantin, avoid this attitude with all your heart! Friedrich knows it. Uppsala vivat! Are you plagued? Yes, we see Kosti.")
"Friedrichs tev helpē. Te radars." (42g: 623)
(Latv., Swed.: "Friedrich helps you. Here is radar.")
"Mölnbo på tala." (42r: 209)
(Swed.: "Mölnbo is being mentioned.")
"Lieber Koste und Friedelli. Viel Küssi!" (43r: 052)
(Germ.: "Dear Koste and Freddie. Many kisses!")

A voice says:

"Grecoli!" (44b: 249)

This word plays a big part in Jürgenson's recordings. It was pronounced ("Grecola") on the occasion when the well-known Swedish parapsychologist Dr. John Björkhem was amongst participants at a recording-session. Dr. Björkhem became known through his book *The Hidden Force*, published in 1954. The experimenter has a high opinion of him as a scientist and a man of integrity. Now once again, this word appeared on tape; this time as an "A" voice, through radio. And later:

"Friedrich te sēj." (44b: 408)
(Latv.: "Friedrich sows here.")

At the experimental recording on 15th December 1966, Friedrich Jürgenson did not follow the advice given by the experimenter and the recording showed hardly any results.

At the beginning the following voices are heard:

"Ko tu sēdi tur?" (45r: 168)
(Latv.: "Why are you sitting there?")

"Atrodi Kosti tur!" (same place)
(Latv.: "Find Kosti there!")
"Office, Kostja." (same place)

Then Mr. Jürgenson, according to his routine, searches along the radio-scale. A voice at the start of the search:

"Das dachte!"
(Germ.: "I thought as much!")

The experimenter made recordings (Nos. 307 and 309) directly before and after Friedrich Jürgenson's visit. These produced interesting voices, some linking up with Jürgenson. Radio voices:

"Vāji! Putra vien! Furchtbar tu nieko. Nepatīk!" (45r: 138)
(Latv., Germ.: "Feeble! It is only mush! You make light of it most terribly. It does not please.")
"Palieciet pie Jürgensona pentagas." (same place: 141)
(Latv.: "Stay with Jürgenson's 'pentagas'.") The meaning of the word "pentagas" is obscure.
"Tu briesmīg' sreiku grib." (same place: 142)
(Latv.: "You want to play a terrible prank.")
"Piemini, te no Margaretiņas dzīvojam vēl." (same place)
(Latv.: "Remember, here we still live by Margarete.") The second voice the experimenter had heard when working with Jürgenson (see page 15) had been "Margarete".
"Piedod, Peterson!" (same place)
(Latv.: "Forgive, Peterson!")
"Es tev balsu dodu." (same place)
(Latv.: "I give you the voice.")
"Napļuršk!"
(Latv.: "Don't talk nonsense!")
"Paldies Kosta. Helga tja! Brauksi pie Jürgensona tu. Fünfte Rede." (same place: 148/9)
(Latv., Germ.: "Thank you, Kosta, Helga is here! You will travel to Jürgenson. Fifth talk.") The recording had been made at 12.30 at night. Jürgenson's arrival in Freiburg was expected at 6 a.m. He was returning from Pompeii, where he had been excavating and filming. It was the fifth meeting between the experimenter and Jürgenson; hence, perhaps the voice's reference to the "fifth talk".
"Cyuka tāds! Furchtbar, Hitlers! Kosti, tavi braty." (same place: 152)
(Latg., Germ., Russ.: "Such a pig! Dreadful, Hitler! Kosti, your brothers.")

Content and meaning of some sentences are difficult to grasp:

"Kosti, palaid Vally! Mans kungs wirklich Kosta. Apini—mani Wolthy!" (same place: 153)
(Latv., Germ.: "Kosti, let Vally out! My master is really Kosta. Hops—my Wolthy!")

There follow sentences of general implication:

"Ko darat? Te brīva griba!" (same place: 156)
(Latv.: "What are you doing? Here is freedom of will!")
"Ja Hitlers būtu, cita lieta." (same place: 217)
(Latv.: "If we had Hitler, things would be different.")
"Hitlers Te. Ko pēti?" (same place)
(Latv.: "Here is Hitler. What are you investigating?")
"Garu pieņem, Raudive!"
"Pievils Kosti." (same place: 219)
(Latv.: "Receive the spirit, Raudive!"—"Kosti is being betrayed.")

A voice of good audibility:

"Vincente, lustigu seju! Kosti gaidi, te Ļuta."
(Latv., Germ.: "Vincente, a happy face! Wait for Kosti, here is Luta.") Vincente was the name of the experimenter's father. (For Luta see page 58).

At the end of the recording we hear:

"Kosti, sveiki!"
(Latv.: "Kosti, greetings!")

Friedrich Jürgenson's presence certainly made an impact on the voice-entities as they mentioned him by name.

EXPERIMENTAL RECORDING NO. 17

Bad Krozingen (Germany), 3rd February 1967
Participants: Mr. Valerij Tarsis, a Russian writer.
Mrs. Hanni Tarsis.
(See Commentaries, pages 376–378.)

Result: 195 voices, of which 45 per cent are "A" voices, 35 per cent "B" and 20 per cent "C". Voices in group "C", the most problematical ones, can rarely be followed by anybody but the experimenter himself.

Valerij Tarsis plays his rôle as "radar" most convincingly; the voices that manifest refer mostly to him and to people on "the other side" who were known only to him. Many of the statements made by voices can only be understood in the light of Mr. Tarsis' comments. He conducted the recording in Russian and his first question was:

"How do you live over there?"
"Radostno tebja?" (46r: 474), said a voice.
(Russ.: "Are you in a happy mood?")
V. Tarsis: "... the people close ..."
"Pļāpa!" (same place: 477)
(Latv.: "Chatterbox!")
V. Tarsis: "I would like to know ..."
"Immer!" (same place: 483)
(Germ.: "Always!")
V. Tarsis: "Perhaps my father who perished in a concentration-camp will come ..."
"Faustu!" (same place: 489)
(Latv.: "Ask Faustus!")
V. Tarsis: "... you, my first ..."
"Ty volnyj drug!' (same place)
(Russ.: "You friend in freedom!")
V. Tarsis: "I want to convince myself..."
"Prošu!" (same place: 495)
(Russ.: "If you please.") lit.: "I beg".
V. Tarsis: "... that you are here present."
"Te Mocarts." (same place: 496)
(Latv.: "Here Mozart.")

Radio-voices:

"Kosti, nu tala Diktov!" (46r: 497)
(Swed.: "Kosti, now Diktov speaks.")
"Vitjaz ty! Hitlers dzīvs." (same place: 499)
(Russ., Latv.: "You hero! Hitler lives!")
"Grūti ir, viņa mič-mič." (same place)
(Latv.: "It is difficult, she is making a mish-mash.")
"Munka tiav gunstē." (same place)
(Latv.: "Munka shows you favour.")
"Uzmin Teklu! Mūsu bende?" (same place: 500)
(Latv.: "Guess at Tekla! Our executioner?")
"Dokaži, uzticies viņam!" (same place: 501)
(Russ., Latv.: "Prove, have confidence in him!")
"Pieņem Kosti!" (same place: 502)
(Latv.: "Accept Kosti!")
"Belkas te stūrē." (same place: 504)
(Latv.: "Here Belkas steers.")
"Mūsu Kosti mani binda." (same place: 508)
(Latv., Swed.: "Our Kosti binds me.")

"Viņš trūkst." (same place)
(Latv.: "He is missing.")
"Kosti Raudiv'! Sidnakova." (same place: 509)
"Tevi redzej. Kosta, pagaid! Satiki Kozolu? Jums te rarita." (same place: 510)
(Latv.: "One saw you. Kosta, wait! Have you met Kozol? Here you have a rarity.")
"Velņs pestē, Kosta!" (same place: 511)
(Latv.: "The devil redeems, Kosta!")
"Madrid. Te Osūna. Te Grab. Koste, tupele! Davolny spekiši? Kur prasta tu!" (same place: 513)
(Latv., Russ., Germ.: "Madrid. Here Osūna. Here is the grave. Koste, you are a clot. Are the fatties content? How simple you are!")
"Lūdzi trimdu!" (same place: 514)
(Latv.: "You have asked to be exiled!")

Acquaintances of the experimenter manifest:

"Bara te Petja. Petja ciemoš, Koste." (same place: 516/7)
(Swed., Latv.: "Here is only Petja. Petja is on visit, Koste.")
"Veselis!" (same place: 517) Well-known Latvian writer. (See page 74).
"Pizān!" (same place)
(An acquaintance of the experimenter.)
"Osūnā meitas būtu." (same place: 518)
(Latv.: "In Osūna one would have girls.") Osūna, as the reader will recall, was the birthplace of the experimenter.
"Aljosha!" (same place) The experimenter's brother.
"Ilona! Schreib, Raudiv, Ilonai." (same place)
(Germ., Latv.: "Ilona! Write, Raudiv, to Ilona!")
"Mieru weg! Asūne!" (same place: 521)
(Latv., Germ.: "The peace away! Asūne!")
"Gute Nacht, Anci! Raudive—suns. Vakars pēdejais. Arvis." (same place)
(Germ., Latv.: "Good night, Anci! Raudive is a dog. The last evening. Arvis.")
"Madaļa oh mirt! Mediča Ināre!" (same place: 522)
(Latv.: "Madaļa, oh to die! Mediča Ināre!")
"Takoj barinca!" (same place)
(Russ.: "Such a master.")
"Kosta dzivoj!" (same place: 523)
(Latv.: "Long live Kosta!")

Now the voices turn once more to Tarsis:

"Hitlers rad. Ja tože." (same place)
(Russ.: "Hitler rejoices. I too.")
"Smolič, žalko Wetrow." (same place)

(Russ.: "Smolic, it's a pity about Wetrow.")
"Zdrawstwuj, tāvs! Māti pieminē." (same place: 525)
(Russ., Latv.: "Good day, father! Remember mother!")
"Te Tarsis! Chlopata! Mir'u syuti! Mater satur." (same place: 526)
(Latv., Russ., Lat.: "Here is Tarsis! Worries! Send peace! Mother supports [you].")
"Balsta nav. Heralda." (same place: 527)
(Latv.: "You have no support. Heralda.")
"Mīlulīt, māti redzam." (same place)
(Latv.: "Dear, we see mother.")
"Privat vienaldze." (same place)
(Latv.: "Private indifference.")
"Padod Stenku." (same place)
(Latv.: "Give me Stenka!")
"Pakist kto?—Kosti—mierā!" (same place)
(Russ., Latv.: "Who is Pakist?—Kosti—remain calm.")
"Klepor pripomniš!" (same place: 528)
(Russ.: "Remember Klepor!")
"Kostja guļ. Probudi!" (same place)
(Latv., Russ.: "Kostja sleeps. Wake him!")
"Zdrawstwuji! Ty, Kosti, Tarsis? Te Koste sēž." (same place: 529)
(Russ., Latv.: "Good day! You, Kosti, Tarsis? Here sits Koste.")
"Ded, ded! Tēti! Kāpēc tu to dari?" (same place)
(Russ., Latv.: "Grandfather, grandfather! [call] father! Why do you do this?")
"Mauriņš tja. Wy stal." (same place: 530)
(Latv., Russ.: "Here is Maurins. They are steel.")
"Mōte te; nasilki tibe prižimat." (same place)
(Latg., Russ.: "Here is mother; you should push [yourself] the stretcher.")
"Tarsis!" (same place)
"Kosta, tu kurls!" (same place)
(Latv.: "Kosta, you are deaf.")
"Ja gramatnyj." (same place: 531)
(Russ.: "I can read and write.")
"Ja sestra." (same place)
(Russ.: "I am [your] sister.")
"Zdrawstwujte! Dubka, Jezufin!—Genau!" (same place)
(Russ., Germ.: "Good day! Dubka, Jeszufin!—Exactly!")
"Ded, ja Loce!" (same place: 532)
(Russ.: "Grandfather, I am Loce!") Loce was the name of the experimenter's mother.
"Tja Lorca!" (same place: 533)
(Latg.: "Here is Lorca.")
"Pesni—ukaz. Tēt, naids!" (same place)

(Russ., Latv.: "The songs were a Ukas. Father, the enmity!")
"Puika, sylts! Rjapčiki!" (same place)
(Latg., Russ.: "Boy, warm! Partridges!")
"V našik delach gut." (same place: 534)
(Russ., Germ.: "Our affairs are going well.")
"Gabris! Not überall!"
"Welche Not (a)?"
"Politi." (same place)
(Germ.: "Gabris! Distress everywhere!"—"What distress?"—"Political.")
"Anne, Butter!"
"Anita ging fort." (same place: 335)
(Germ.: "Anne, butter!"—"Anita went away.")
"Pomiluj!" (same place)
(Russ.: "Have pity!")
"Anne pošla." (same place)
(Russ.: "Anne went away.")
"Tā bij kļūda." (same place)
(Latv.: "It was a mistake.")
"Kosti, paņem tu vārdu!" (same place)
(Latv.: "Kosti, you speak now!")
"My rasteralis. Na kamne strogo leg." (same place: 571)
(Russ.: "We are absent minded. I have bedded myself hard on [the] stone.")
"Žukova dela plocha." (same place: 572)
(Russ.: "Zukov's affairs are going badly.")
"My Tarsis te sveicam." (same place: 575)
(Russ., Latv.: "Here we greet Tarsis.")
"Nebēdā ilgi!" (same place: 576)
(Latv.: "Don't mourn long.")

In another recording, on 3rd March 1967, a voice comes over:

"Wetrows mit." (48g: 018)
(Germ.: "Wetrow [comes] too.")

EXPERIMENTAL RECORDING NO. 18

Basle (Switzerland), 1st/2nd March 1967
Participants: Mr. Kārlis Bauers, singer.
　　　　　　　Mrs. Paula Bauers, singer (Basle).
　　　　　　　(See Commentary, page 379.)

The recording produced 93 voices; 24 "A" and "B" voices, the rest are in group "C".

This experiment proved to be a most difficult one to conduct perhaps because the town of Basle lies in a hollow, it was almost impossible to get any wavelength free of transmissions. Right at the start of the recording-session a voice refers to this fact:

"Kosta, stelle sich richtig ein, furchtbare Geräusche!" (48g: 017)
(Germ.: "Kosta, tune in correctly, terrible noises!")

In the first part of the recording the voices refer mostly to the experimenter, and acquaintances often give their names: for instance:

"Loorits", "Matilde!" (48g: 020)

A statement seemingly aimed at Mrs. Bauers:

"Tev Vortragi te. Gaidu. Warte Paulu!" (same place: 025)
(Latv., Germ.: "You have lectures here. I am waiting. Waiting for Paula.")

Then we hear the following voices:

"Redzu Kosti." (same place: 048)
(Latv.: "I see Kosti.")
"Hitlers isti dzivs." (same place: 050)
(Latv. "Hitler really lives.")

The recording was continued at 6 p.m. A very clear microphone-voice manifests after the experimenter had said: "Omnipotent friends beyond . . ."

"Te Virza." (same place: 066)
(Latv.: "Here Virza.")

Amongst the radio-voices the following were distinctly audible:

"Mēs atstumtie, Ulmans." (same place: 069)
(Latv.: "We, the expelled, Ulmans.")
"Nacht will Kosta. Sarkanas lampas! Acht Fried!" (same place: 073)
(Germ., Latv.: "Kosta wants night. Red lamps! Respect the peace.")

This statement bears significant paranormal characteristics, namely:

1. It is spoken in German and Latvian.

2. The experimenter is named.
3. It points to the fact that lamps shedding a red light are being used during the recording and that
4. A peaceful atmosphere during recordings is desirable.

As the recording could not be continued because of adverse conditions affecting radio-beams, efforts were renewed on 2nd March at midnight. Once again the beams created difficulties, and the voice-entities themselves were aware of it:

"Mierā jūs paši! Koste, te slikti. Tu lobōk deutsch."
(Latv., Germ.: "Remain calm yourselves! Koste, it is bad here. You had better speak German.")

A characteristic voice is then heard:

"Kostja, tu pasmej! Na, Dāle. Navajag M! Petrautzka. Nav rīki tie." (same place: 104/5)
(Latv.: "Kostja, laugh! Well, Dāle. M. is not necessary! Petrautzka. These are no tools.") This can be understood as follows: Dāle, a former psychologist from Riga, consoles the experimenter and tells him to laugh off the failure in Basle. Then Petrautzka manifests, pointing out that "M" was not necessary. "M" and some other people were not good "tools" for the experiments. This sentence contains a lot of truths: a Mrs. "M" had proved quite useless in experiments. The voices had obviously been aware of this fact.

A little later, Mrs. Bauers addresses someone named Reinhard. When the recording was continued via radio, three voices in group "B" react to Mrs. Bauers' questions:

"Tiltam, Koste." (same place: 120/2)
(Latv.: "For the bridge, Koste.")
"Tagad Friedhof." (same place)
(Latv., Germ.: "Now cemetery.")
"Tiltam pāri te." (same place)
(Latv.: "Here over the bridge.") These three phrases contain the essence of an event as well as proof of identity: "Reinhard", after whom Mrs. Bauers asked, had committed suicide by leaping from a bridge. The experimenter knew nothing of this beforehand.

In a later recording the name of the person in question is heard:

"Reinhards." (49r: 167)

The remaining voices are difficult to identify. One can hear:

"Tu, Kostja? Nakšninieki, talka te." (same place: 122)
(Latv.: "You, Kostja? The people of the night, here is teamwork.")
"Kostja, dārzā tja noslēpties." (same place: 124/5)
(Latv.: "Kostja, to hide here in the garden.") It is not clear who is to hide in the garden and why. The last voice in this recording, however, is quite clear in its meaning:
"Kosta, preti mums gulta." (same place: 130)
(Latv.: "Kosta, opposite us is the bed.") This was according to fact: opposite the participants stood the bed.

Apart from being involved in the recording, Mr. and Mrs. Bauers also listened in to 170 voices; partly independently, partly after preparation by the experimenter's commentary. Roughly 75 per cent of these voices were incontestably heard and verified.

EXPERIMENTAL RECORDING NO. 19

Bad Krozingen (Germany), 7th March 1967
Participants: Mr. Oskar Scherer.
              Mr. Felix Scherer.
              Mr. Gustav Inhoffen.

Oskar and Felix Scherer (father and son) are both experts in radio and taperecorders. The recording, made in the presence of the experimenter, revealed 120 voices, and of these, 46 belong to groups "A" and "B". When the recording was completed, the experimenter and the other three participants jointly listened to the result. Most of the voices could be heard and deciphered according to content by the collaborators themselves, without help from the experimenter; this is certainly true of the "A" group voices that follow.

As in previous recordings, the voices fall into two categories: those that refer to the experimenter and those that address themselves to the other participants.

The first voice of good audibility says:

"Raudive, tinti! Osūna." (48g: 143)
(Latv.: "Raudive, give ink! Osūna.")
"Ilgu tiltu, Kostuli." (same place: 145)
(Latv.: "A lasting bridge, Kostuli.")

The following voice addresses the three German participants:

"Deutsche wir hier,
Kämpferi wir!" (same place: 149)
(Germ.: "We are Germans here, Fighters are we.")

Another voice adds:

"Nenn Rauda!" (same place: 150)
(Germ.: "Name Rauda!")

Then a distinctly audible voice addresses the experimenter:

"Tja, Kosta, Vītola." (same place: 151)
(Latg.: "Here, Kosta, is Vītola.") "Vītola" is a widely known Latvian family-name. The ending "a" indicates a woman.

Two more voices:

"Super puiši te aug."
"Lettischi puiši." (same place: 152/4)
(Lat., Latv., Germ.: "Super lads grow here."—"Latvian lads.")

This statement, composed of three languages points to the fact that the voice-entities have a sense of nationality: the "super lads" are "Latvian lads", not just any lads!

Now the voices address a collaborator who is not present at this particular recording: Professor Atis Teichmanis.

"Atis tic."—"Atis tic."—"Ati, tic!" (same place: 155/6)
(Latv.: "Atis believes."—"Atis believes."—"Ati, believe!")

A German voice:

"Wir Nazis." (same place)
(Germ.: "We [are] Nazis.")

A further voice:

"Asche und Glut—dzimtene." (same place: 157)
(Germ., Latv.: "Ashes and embers—is the homeland.") This must be a reference to the experimenter's novel of the title *Ashes and Embers*, but it has also a significant bearing on reality, for the experimenter's homeland was reduced to little more than ashes and embers through the war.

We hear a Latvian entity:

"Dieva puķe tu." (same place: 159)
(Latv.: "You are God's flower.")

The next voice turns to the experimenter:

"Tu slyms, Koste." (same place: 160)
(Latg.: "You are sick, Koste.") This statement, in the dialect of home, is repeated several times.
"Kosti, tōli." (same place: 160)
(Latg.: "Kosti, you are far.")
"Ravel." (same place)
"Bitte Führers Findlay."
"Ich bin Findlay's."
"Labi, labi skan." (same place: 162)
(Germ., Latv.: "Ask leader Findlay."—"I am Findlay's."—"It sounds good, good.") (See page 84 for Arthur Findlay.)

Mr. Inhoffen confirmed that he had thought intensively of this famous British parapsychologist during the recording.

The next voice again refers to the experimenter:

"Koste binda. Fischer Koste. Te Rapa." (same place: 164)
(Swed., Germ., Latv.: "Koste connects. Fisherman Koste. Here is Rapa.")

This sentence contains a great deal of meaning:

1. The experimenter is named as the connecting link.
2. He is called "fisherman"; this is an excellent description of the experimenter's work, for the results are obtained, by way of radio-waves, in an unpredictable manner—just as the fisherman hopes for results when he casts his net at random.
3. The same words were spoken before (see page 102), by one of the two brothers Rapa who were the experimenter's publishers in Riga.

One voice complains:

"Niemand denkt an uns." (same place: 167)
(Germ.: "Nobody thinks of us.")

This came over so clearly that it was immediately understood by all the participants at the first hearing; later the sentence was further confirmed through the process of repetition.

A female voice now addresses the experimenter:

"Sveiki, brōli! Mōsai slikti." (same place: 189)
(Latg.: "Good day, brother! Sister is doing badly.")

"Pogosts te. Kosti, lieb." (same place: 192)
(Latg., Germ.: "Community here. Kosti, kind.")

The next voice comments on what is taking place:

"Te ekperimenti." (same place: 206)
(Latv.: "Here are experiments.") One gets the impression that the voice-entities are present and observe closely all that is happening.

There follows another communication meant for the experimenter; first a male voice:

"Liebe Soņu." and then a female one:
"Tevi vien mīl(a)." (same place: 207)
(Germ., Latv.: "Love Sonja!"—"Loves only you.") Linguistically these two sentences are strangely constructed: the first one gives the name in the Latvian accusative; the second one, instead of using the correct Latvian equivalent for the verb "to love", twists the noun "love" into a verb.

The son of the well-known Swiss doctor M. E. Bircher manifests his voice several times:

"Te ūngen Bircher."
"Te Birchers Sohn."
"Doctor Birchers." (same place: 208/34/44)
(Latv., Swed., Germ.: "Here is the young Bircher."—"Here is Bircher's son."—"Doctor Birchers.") Dr. Bircher's son lost his life in a car-accident. Dr. Bircher himself, as well as his wife, has listened-in to voices and has also made recordings and since then various voice-entities have appeared that seem to stand in some relation to Dr. Bircher's son.

A voice asks:

"Latviski?" and is immediately answered:
"Neprotu feinele." (same place: 232)
(Latv., Germ.: "Do you speak Latvian?" Answer: "I don't understand the word 'feinele'.") "Feinele" actually sounds like Swabian dialect, meaning "fine" in diminutive form.
"Uppsala, paliksim te Sicht-husī." (same place: 233)
(Latv., combined with a neologism made up of German and Latvian. Probable translation: "Uppsala, let us stay here in the 'sight-cabin'.")

After this recording, the experimenter made another short one at 6 o'clock in the evening. Some "A" voices manifested with interesting speech-contents.

One voice, for instance, made it quite clear that participants should give their wholehearted attention to the recording-process:
Another voice comments:

> "Visai būtnei te vajadzīga." (48g: 239)
> (Latv.: "The whole being should be here engaged.")

Another voice comments:

> "Gara diena, otrdien vielleicht Sonne." (same place: 240)
> (Latv., Germ.: "The day is long, Tuesday perhaps sun.")

The recording was made on Tuesday morning and the day became sunny. We may deduce from this sentence that for some reason unknown to us the voice-entity complained about the long day that had past and hopes that Tuesday will prove to be a happier day.

The same voice goes on to say:

> "Loti grūti."
> "Lūdzu takti." (same place)
> (Latv.: "Very difficult"—"I plead for tact.")
> "Čakste puţ."
> "Professor de nada." (same place: 242)
> (Russ., Germ., Span.: "Čakste is the way."—"Professor of the void.") Professor Čakste probably wishes to express with this phrase that he cannot accept the usual religious beliefs about the immortality of the soul. (See also page 64.)
> "Koste, du Besuch." (same place: 209)
> "Koste, te Petrautzka. Pasteidz!" (same place: 210)
> (Germ., Latv.: "Koste, you visit."—"Koste, here Petrautzka. Hurry up.")

Speech-contents are divided into two categories: those that have meanings of a general nature and those that have a personal bearing. The sentence "Nobody thinks of us", for instance, is of a general, the sentence "You are sick, Koste", of a personal character. This knowledge of past, or present, circumstances can only be explained if we presuppose independent, intelligent entities, acting in partnership with the experimenter and his collaborators.

An additional test-recording was made on 20th July 1967, with Mr. Theo Böttcher, expert on tape-recorders and Mr. Felix Scherer, electrotechnical expert, as participants. Five audible microphone-voices (group "B") and 165 radio-voices (41 group "A", 15 group "B", the remainder group "C") manifested. The microphone-voices show marked traits of partnership.

Mr. Scherer says the opening words and a female voice is heard:

"Martha." (49r: 545)

Someone called "Fritz Spengler" is now addressed and a voice reacts with:

"Felix!" (same place: 546)

Theo Böttcher calls his mother, Wilhelmine.

"Mama!" (same place: 549) Mr. Böttcher explains later that he always called his mother "Mama".

He asks his mother for a sign.

"Mutti, Theo!" (same place: 550) Here the mother addresses the participant by his name.

The radio-voices largely refer to the experimenter. To start with, his sister makes her presence known with great emphasis:

"Te Tekla." (same place: 553)
(Latv.: "Here is Tekla.")

Then a voice exclaims:

"Donner." (same place)
(Germ.: "Thunder.") A thunderstorm was, in fact, just about to break over Krozingen.
"Kosti, Vija te pavēl." (same place: 554)
(Latv.: "Kosti, Vija commands here.") The experimenter had been well acquainted with a woman named Vija who died some years ago in Stockholm. She manifests quite often in a variety of contexts.

The same voice continues:

"Kosti, tu gudrucīt." (same place: 559)
(Latv.: "Kosti, you are clever.")
"Koste, Mītja! Te sieviete. Tā richtige." (same place: 559/60)
(Latv., Germ.: "Koste, Mītja! Here is a woman. The right one.")

Another voice counters:

"Māte te. Pļāpas te. Kosti, pētī!" (same place: 560/2)
("Here is mother. Here are gossips. Kosti, explore!")

Felix Scherer is now addressed by a voice:

> "Felix, Koste. Mutter."
> (Germ.: "Felix, Koste. Mother.")
> "Mercita! Viņš zin. Kosta zina, tu." (same place: 563)
> (Latv.: "Mercita! He knows! You, Koste knows it.")

A voice asks:

> "Kāda zina, alors?"

Answer:

> "Mīli Kosti, te gratis."

A third voice adds:

> "A Koste, moi!"

The next voice assures:

> "Te Kosta." (same place: 564)
> (Latv., French: "So, what message?"—"Love Kosti, here it's free."—"To Koste, me!"—"Here is Kosta.")

Now Felix Scherer addresses his maternal grandmother.

> "Felix, du?" (same place: 582)
> "Malvina. Te moste." (same place: 586)
> (Germ., Latg.: "Felix, you?"—"Malvina. Here is the 'mother's sister'.")
> "Mūsu Kosta! Sanem Jehuda! (same place: 587)
> (Latv.: "Our Kosta! Receive Jehuda!")
> "Pomira Kostin."
> "Ekur jāj!" (same place)
> (Latv.: "Kostin grew pale."—"Look, there he rides!")

At the end of the recording three voices:

> "Kā tu tiki?"
> "Tika Vitols."
> "Jōn, providimse te." (same place: 587)
> (Latv., Russ.: How did you get here?")
> "Vitols came here."
> "Jōn, we shall see each other here.") Vitols is a widely known Latvian family-name. The experimenter knew Jazeps Vitols, the composer, well.

These voices were submitted to listening-in tests, and identified and verified by Mr. Felix Scherer and Mr. Theo Böttcher.

EXPERIMENTAL RECORDING NO. 20

Bad Krozingen (Germany), 11th March 1967
Participant: Professor Atis Teichmanis (College of Music, Freiburg, Germany).
(See Commentary, page 378.)

Professor Teichmanis made the recording in absence of the experimenter, partly through microphone, partly through radio; it lasted 10 minutes and produced 155 voices, 104 belonging to groups "A" and "B". Some voices refer to Professor Teichmanis, some to the experimenter and some to general matters.
Professor Teichmanis addresses his father:

"Tētis" (48g: 223), answers a voice.
(Latv.: "Father.")

Then the following comments:

"Tu slikti pievelc doch." (same place: 273)
(Latv., Germ.: "You nevertheless start off badly.")
"Te runā Voldis mit dir. Voldis tepat." (same place: 274)
(Latv., Germ.: "Here Voldis talks to you. Voldis here himself.")
This voice aims clearly at Professor Teichmanis: it is that of a friend and former colleague of the professor.

The same voice continues:

"Atis nevaļā. Es brīvs."
"Lichtental. Tu priecīgs." (same place: 275)
(Latv.: "Atis is in want of time. I am free."—"Lichtental. You are glad.")

The following voice refers to the experimenter:

"Wunderbar, Raudive te winkē. Lieber Kosta, pūlas Kosta." (same place: 277)
(Germ., Latv.: "Marvellous, Raudive waves here. Dear Kosta, Kosta tries.")

The experimenter was sitting in another room whilst the recording was in progress and trying by intense concentration to evoke the presence of human beings once close to him. The sentence just quoted may, in fact, mean that the experimenter was able to project his thoughts into the world of the voices.

The next voice aims at the professor, who was smoking whilst recording:

"Redz, kur Atis pīpo! Kosti, te dimas." (same place: 279)
(Latv., Swed.: "Look, how Atis smokes! Kosti, here is fog.")

Now Professor Teichmanis's father is heard again:

"Pāpiņš." (same place: 280)
(Latv.: "Little father.")

Then an acquaintance who had died recently in Stockholm:

"Breikšs. Ko tu saki?—Ati, pasniedz 'Muratt'!" (same place)
(Latv.: "Breikšs. What are you saying?—Ati, give me 'Muratt'!") "Muratti" is a German brand of cigarettes.
"Piemirsi tu Latviju." (same place: 283)
(Latv.: "You have forgotten Latvia.")

The next sentence is probably addressed to the experimenter, who had asked the Russian writer Valerij Tarsis to collaborate in the research.

"Tu Tarsi pielaidi." (same place: 284)
(Latv.: "You have admitted Tarsis.")
"Raudivi! Tjav nav svjazi." (same place: 285)
(Latv., Russ.: "Please, Raudive! You have no connection.")
This hint may mean that to make contact certain energies are necessary which probably are released only by a particular type of mental state.

Again a voice manifests for Professor Teichmanis:

"Latko, zdrawstwuj! Serdca. Friedinš mājās ir. Vāciets tu esi." (same place: 286)
(Rus., "Latvianised" German, Latv.: "Latko, good day! The heart. Friedchen is at home. You are a German.") The professor suffers from a heart-ailment; the voice was probably hinting at this fact.

Another voice now recommends:

"Pazvejo upis!" (same place: 287)
(Latv.: "Fish in the rivers.") Professor Teichmanis is an enthusiastic angler.

Jānis, a friend of the professor, is mentioned by the next voice:

"Es tālāk tiku. Debess ir nelaimīgs. Jānis." (same place: 288)
(Latv.: "I have progressed. Heaven is unhappy. Jānis.")

The same voice continues:

"Te pulkstens neder. Pazvejo tu!"
"Tu te person."
"Tu Konstantin mīlē. Tu latvis, tici!" (same place: 289)
(Latv.: "Here the clock is no good. You go fishing!"—"Here you are a person."—"You love Konstantin. You are Latvian, believe!")

Another voice aimed at the experimenter:

"Kostja, byusi? Yudins te, Kostja. A Kostja, Margarete te. Vai Koste versteht?" (same place: 290)
(Latv., Germ.: "Kostja, will you be? Here is water, Kostja. Ah Kostja, here is Margarete. Whether Koste understands?") This strange communication points to the water and to the presence of Margarete. A voice-entity seems to doubt whether the experimenter can understand what the voices are trying to impart.

"Dōrgs, tu runā!"
"Lusći Kosti." (same place)
(Latv., Russ.: "Dear one, speak!"—"Better Kosti.") These voices indicate that the presence of the experimenter is desired.

"Vēl brauks sēnēs." (same place: 294)
(Latv.: "One will still travel to the mushroom-picking.")
"Jūsu Tante. Glücklicha Tante. Jūs mindes?" (same place: 296)
(Latv., Germ., Swed.: "Your aunt. The happy aunt. Do you remember?"—The German and Swedish words are partly "Latvianised".)

"Kostin, tu sturgalvis." (same place: 298)
(Latv.: "Kostin, you are stubborn.")
"Osūna!" (same place)

The voice that follows also addresses the experimenter:

"Kost, Brunners te. Netais cīņas! Kosta, tu velns tāds!" (same place: 298)
(Latv.: "Kost, here is Brunners. Don't undertake a fight! Kosta, you are such a devil!") Brunners is an acquaintance of the experimenter from his Riga days.

"Kosta, vi ventar, vi mäktiga." (same place: 299)
(Swed.: "Kosta, we are waiting, we mighty ones.")
"Gute Nacht. Tur guļ Kostja. Galvenais ir viņš. Es dzīvoju Nāpolī." (same place: 301)
(Germ., Latv.: "Good night. There sleeps Kostja. He is the chief. I live in Naples.")

Professor Teichmanis now calls on Jānis Medenis; a voice answers:

"Minns du brāli?"
"Ikškile, atmiņas. Schenke, Koste, pirti!" (same place: 305)
(Swed., Latv., Germ.: "Do you remember the brother?"—"Ikškile, memories. Give, Koste, the bathroom!") These microphone-voices indicate a brother of the professor and mention Ikškile, a small town in Latvia; this name appears quite often on tape.

The father communicates again:

"Nav prieka. Pazini tanti? Tāvs." (same place: 321)
(Latv.: "There are no friends. Did you know the aunt? Father.")

There follow further voices, this time with speech-content of a general nature, interrupted by others who refer to the experimenter:

"Tam Hitlers bļauj. Te sanctis noos." (same place: 322)
(Latv., Lat.: "Hitler screams at him. Here is the sacred 'noos'.") Meaning of the word "noos" obscure.
"Guten Will' für Koste. Verwegen gleich." (same place: 324)
(Germ.: "Good will for Koste. Immediately audacious.")
"Jūs geht hier. Mēs redzam slikti." (same place)
(Latv., Germ.: "You go here. We see badly.")
"Gut rückwärts fins." (same place: 327)
(Germ., Swed.: "It goes well backwards.")
"Mums Kostulīte būs."
"Vēl pa daļai. Vēl nepārtrauc!" (same place: 333)
(Latv.: "We will have Kostulīte."—"Still partially. Don't interrupt yet!")

These sentences were recorded through microphone. They may be understood as follows: the voices await the experimenter's presence. The last sentence asks Professor Teichmanis not to interrupt the recording yet.

The recording ends with a distinctly audible voice:

"Hej, sanigen höra du!" (same place: 337)
(Swed.: "Heh, listen you to the truth!")

Professor Teichmanis is one of the best collaborators in listening-in tests, and the experimenter's attention had been drawn to this fact right at the start of the investigations:

"Ati, Ati. Teichmani!" (23r: 141/7)
"Ati, darling Ati!" (29r: 637)

One voice literally encourages the professor to continue with his collaboration:

"Ati, turpinā, Kosti, saprot!" (44b: 886)
(Latv.: "Ati, continue, understand Kosti!")
"Tu Ati, für liten du." (44r: 166)
(Latv., Germ., Swed.: "You, Ati, you are for the small [detail].")
"Raudive te. Ati vervē!" (45g: 457)
(Latv.: "Here is Raudive. Enlist Ati!")
"Atis kommt." (46g: 550)
(Germ.: "Atis is coming." The day after this had been recorded Professor Teichmanis actually arrived at the experimenter's place.
"Nabaga Atis!" (47g: 227)
(Latv.: "Poor Atis!") This expression of compassionate concern was well founded, for when it was being recorded the professor was suffering a severe heart-attack.
"Atis tic!" (48g: 155)
(Latv.: "Atis believe!")

As an expert in listening-in, Professor Teichmanis has tested approximately 500 voices. Of the voices the experimenter had located he could verify up to 100 per cent and could decipher them himself and even make some corrections.

EXPERIMENTAL RECORDING NO. 21

Bad Krozingen (Germany), 10th April 1967
Participants: Professor Dr. Hans Bender, Psychologist.
           Dr. F. Karger, Physicist (Planck-Institute, Munich).
           (Experiments catalogue No. 1; 06, 48g: 425-460 refers).

This recording was made through microphone and radio in the presence of the experimenter and lasted 5 minutes. It yielded in all 4 microphone-voices (groups "C" to "B") and 75 radio-voices (42 in groups "A" or "B").

Some of the voices refer to Professor Bender, some to the experimenter and some to matters of a general character.

The four microphone voices:

Professor Bender says: "... we hope that we will get "A" quality."
Voice: "Raudive!" (48g: 430)
Dr. Karger: "... added, because of ..."
Voice: "Wünschen wir." (same place: 432)
(Germ.: "We wish.")
Professor Bender: "Yes."
Voice: "Kosti, grässli!" (same place)
(Germ.: "Kosti, horrible!")
The experimenter: "... that would be ..."
Voice: "Nažib!" (same place: 433) "Nažib" has manifested already elsewhere, in microphone as well as radio recordings; but whilst other unknown voices have gradually taken on some sort of personality, this one has remained completely anonymous.

A proportion of the radio-voices have, as mentioned above, "A" or "B" audibility:

"Konstantin, te Fausti." (same place: 436)
(Latv., Germ.: "Konstantin, here are Fausti.") The expression "Fausti", with a Latvian plural ending, means that the experimenter is here confronted with two "Fausts" in the "Dr. Faustus" sense of German thought-tradition (two souls inhabiting one breast).

"Tja Rosvica, tur glabā Rūtu." (same place)
(Latv.: "Here is Rosvica, there buries Rūta.") Rosvica is a small Catholic community on the border between Latgale and Russia. It is not possible to assert who the "Rūta" here mentioned was.

"Velns, Konstantin." (same place)
(Latv.: "Devil, Konstantin.")
"Te pumpē, Koste, te tiga." (same place: 437)
(Latv., Swed.: "Here one borrows, Koste, here one begs.")
"Tie hitlerieši." (same place)
(Latv.: "Those are Hitlerites.")
"Fethke, tici!" (same place)
(Latv.: "Fethke, believe!") Mr. Fethke is an acquaintance of the experimenter who scoffs at the voice-phenomenon as "nonsense".

"Runā tu!" (same place)
(Latv.: "Speak [you]!")
"Mēs uzcelsim Med(e)ni." (same place: 438)
(Latv.: "We will wake Medenis.") Medenis was a Latvian poet of repute who was deported to Siberia by the Russians and perished in a slave-labour camp. The experimenter hardly knew him.

"Kosti!" (same place)
"Konstantin, Stykuts!" (same place: 443)

"Ursekta!" (same place: 444)
(Swed.: "I beg your pardon!")
"Kostiņ, salute!" (same place: 446)
"Bravo, Slankis!" (same place: 448) Mr. Slankis was an acquaintance from Riga.
"Zenta, Streit!" (same place: 449)
(Germ.: "Zenta, quarrel.") This voice refers to Zenta Maurina; the statement might be regarded as a case of precognition: on 14th April Zenta Maurina received a letter which triggered off a considerable argument.
"Uppsala, Zenta." (same place: 451) Here too is an element of precognition, for subsequently a letter told Zenta Maurina that her citizenship of Uppsala had been confirmed.
"Dyumi, Koste." (same place: 454)
(Latg.: "Smoke, Koste.") Professor Bender was smoking whilst the recording was in progress.

The next voice comments on this:

"Te vecais smēkē." (same place: 455)
(Latv.: "The old man smokes here.")
"Mēs laikus, lieber Kosti." (same place: 456)
(Latv., Germ.: "We are in time, dear Kosti.")
"Tova vece." (same place)
(Latg.: "Your old woman.") In Latgalian the mother is referred to as "the old woman."
"Tas widerlich!" (same place: 457)
(Latv., Germ.: "That is disgusting!")
"Konstantina 'popidi'." (same place)
("Konstantin's 'popidi'.") This is a word the experimenter does not know.
"Papa, Geometrie!" (same place)
"Te ķirurgi vien." (same place)
(Second sentence Latv.: "Here are surgeons.")
"Koste, te Bender." (same place)
("Koste, here is Bender.") This refers to Professor Bender's presence.
"Inte folga, Bender ir." (same place)
(Swed., Latv.: "Not to follow, Bender exists.")
"Te Berta." (same place: 459)
(Latv.: "Here is Berta.") "Berta", the name of a friend's wife (she died in 1965).
"Gultu, Kostja!" (same place)
(Latv.: "Please, the bed, Kostja!")

A voice states:

"Nava Zenta te." (same place)
(Latv.: "Zenta is not here.") Zenta Maurina was not present during the recording.

"Nava Zenti." (same place)
(Latv.: "There is no Zenti.")
"Taisi gultu!" (same place: 460)
(Latv.: "Make the bed!") It was 15 minutes past midnight when this recording was made.
"Koste, pļāpā. Vilkis tu!" (same place)
(Latv.: "Koste chatters. You are a wolf!")
"Te tā pap. Māte gultā." (same place)
(Latv.: "Here is his papa. Mother in bed.")

On 9th April 1967 Professor Hans Bender and Dr. F. Karger listened to a total of sixty voices on tape "ABC" and were able to verify 75 per cent.

Professor Bender had also been present at earlier recording-sessions, and many voices refer to him:

"Pareizi vien būs ar Benderu." (25r: 416)
(Latv.: "It's bound to be alright with Bender.")
"Pa Benderu—pievilsies." (30r: 053)
(Latv.: "Of Bender—you will be disappointed.")
"Bender vaicā, vai tu grib." (30r: 574)
(Latv.: "Bender asks if you are willing.")
"Bender sicher überlegt." (31g: 666)
(Germ.: "Bender well thought out.")
"Raudive, Benderu mīli!" (33g: 413)
(Latv.: "Raudive, love Bender!")
"Permets, Bender prompt. Tyrrell." (30r: 055)
(French, English: "Permit, Bender is prompt. Tyrrell.")
Tyrrell—the famous British parapsychologist.
"Benders ist tišiná." (47r: 521)
(Germ., Russ.: "Bender is the stillness.")

Voices heard on 18th April 1967:

"Runā, Kosti!"
"Kosti, Fausti!"
"Tu, tev Benders ir, Kosti." (1 ar: 280/1)
(Latv.: "Speak, Kosti."—"Kosti, 'Fausti'!"—"You, you have Bender, Kosti.")

EXPERIMENTAL RECORDING No. 22

Bad Krozingen (Germany) 15th April 1967.
Participants: Dr. Hans Naegeli, President, Parapsychological Soc., Switzerland.
Mrs. Katharina Nager, Secretary, Parapsychological Soc., Switzerland.

Mrs. Georgette Fürst, Psychologist.
Miss Rosa Stucki, Student of Psychology.
Mr. Jakob Meier, Physicist.
Mrs. Antoinette Meier.
Dr. Renê Fatzer.
Dr. Arnold Reincke.
(See Reports pages 324–328 and Commentaries pages 368–369.)

At this session two tape-recorders were used: the same voices are registered on both tapes. There are in all 260 voices; 14 microphone-voices in group "A" and 99 radio-voices in groups "A" and "B". The results were independently listened to by Mrs. Fürst, Miss Stucki, Dr. Fatzer, Mr. Meier and Dr. Reincke. Mrs. Nager and Dr. Naegeli gave their assistance.

The first microphone voice:

"Birgit." (48g: 519)

Dr. Fatzer reports on his measuring of Od-rays emitted by the participants. A particularly clear voice responds with:

"Vinš pļāpā." (same place: 526)
(Latv.: "He is a chatterbox.")

Individual participants are addressed by name:

"Kati!" (same place: 536) Mrs. Nager's Christian name, slightly modified.
"Frau Fürst." (same place: 539)
"Raudive ist." (Germ.: "Raudive is.") comments another voice.
"Jā, tur Konstantins." (same place: 548)
(Latv.: "Yes, there is Konstantin.")
A greeting: "Bonjour!"
Two voices: "Mikis pļāpā." "Kāpēc tu plåge?" (same place: 564)
(Latv., Swed.: "Mikis chatters."—"Why do you plague?")
The name "Mikis" does not apply to any of the participants.

Dr. Naegeli gives a detailed account of his impressions of the phenomenon.

"Startis Pļāpā." (same place: 568)
(Latv.: "The starter chatters.") This can be taken to mean that Dr. Naegeli, having started off the recording with an introduction, is the "starter".

Now a voice demands:

"Konstantin!" (same place: 577)

and a further voice pleads:

"Koste, Koste, zieh!" (same place: 579)
(Germ.: "Koste, Koste, pull!") This kind of demand is often repeated. It seems to indicate a desire that the experimenter may, through his concentration, attract the voice-entities. In some cases this is clearly expressed; in "Kosti, koncentraciju!", for instance. (47g: 253)

Miss Stucki says a few words. Two sentences follow:

"Velna māte!"
"Dumas vos." (same place: 581)
(Latv., Span.: "Devil's mother!"—"You are stupid.")

Voices can at times be rude and most negatively inclined. There are many examples of this kind of attitude. One may hear, sometimes right at the beginning of a recording, voices saying things like "Kosti chatters again", or "He is again asking nonsense", when the experimenter poses questions and asks for information. The voices only become positive in their attitude when the participant is fully concentrated and no unnecessary or absent-minded questions are asked.

The second half of the recording-session, when radio was used, produced some very clear, distinct voices. Radio-voices differ from microphone-voices in that their statements are more concerned with general matters.

The first clearly audible radio-voice wants to be assured:

"Koste, tu?" (48g: 604)
(Latv.: "Koste, you?")

A second voice:

"Te vīns būs." (same place)
(Latv.: "There will be wine here.") This was quite true: wine was being served to the participants.
"Mona Schwanker, latvis." (same place)
(Latv.: Mona Schwanker, Latvian.)

A voice concludes:

"Vitali skeptiki." (same place: 606)
(Latv.: "The sceptics are full of vitality.") The participants

were actually conversing with each other in a lively way, praising the wine and making more or less sceptical remarks.

"Lyudzu tja. Lyudzami. Kostja, Tekle." (same place: 608)
(Latg.: "I ask here. You are being asked. Kostja, Tekle.")
"Tekle" was the name of the experimenter's sister.

Two voices make some very rude remarks:

"Tu maita, tu still!"
"Muleķ, tu!" (same place: 610)
(Latv., Germ.: "You bitch, be quiet!"—"You stupid woman!")
"Achtung! Aileen te."
"Mīlas grib tev." (same place)
(Germ., Latv.: "Attention! Here is Aileen.") (For "Aileen" see page 44.) (Second sentence: "She wants to give you love.") The construction of this sentence (Latvian) is unusual.

The voices that follow now obviously refer to the world of the entities here speaking:

"Gan tu vietiņā."
"Močalka te."
"Kreklis te." (same place: 612/4)
(Latv., Russ.: "You seem to be at the right place."—"Here is a loofah."—"Here is a shirt.") The voices speak often of a bathroom and objects that belong there; here for instance a loofah and a shirt.

"Kosta tōl. Tekle ty? Liepin." (same place: 615)
(Latv., Russ.: "Kosta is far away. Are you Tekle? Liepin.")
We hear repeatedly that the experimenter is "far away".

"Mēs slīdam." (same place: 616)
(Latv.: "We are gliding.")
"Kostin, slikti. Pieņem Tekli!" (same place)
(Latv.: "Kosti, it is bad. Accept Tekle!")
"Koste, te ir silts." (same place)
(Latv.: "Koste, it is warm here.") The room in which we were recording was, indeed, very warm.

"Björkhem. Gaidu Kosti. Pierūd tu tja."
"Mēs frieren." (same place)
(Latv., Germ.: "Björkhem. I await Kosti. Get used to it here."—"We are feeling cold.")

Some time after this recording had been made, a friend in Stockholm sent the experimenter Björkhem's book *The Hidden Power*. Statements indicating that the voice-entities can feel the heat and the cold, are frequently received.

"Tja Tote. Igor tepat. Wir, Kostja. Te tāvs, Mutti." (same place: 618)
(Latv., Germ.: "Here are the dead. Here on this spot is Igor. We, Kotja. Here is father, mother.")
"Ai Mensch, sāpē!"
"Te vilki! Tur vylki!"
"Es bin." (same place: 625)
(Germ., Latv., Latg.: "Ai man, it hurts!"—"Here are wolves. Over there are wolves!"—"I am.")
"Tja Hochstene."
"Tote Kinder inte te." (same place: 626)
(Latg., Swed., Germ., Latv.: "Here is Hochstene."—"Dead children don't come here.") This sentence might mean that a child by the name of Hochstene tries to communicate, but is held back by some controlling authority. Such attempts at interpretation, however, must be made with extreme caution.
"Hupnitz." (same place: 627)
"Momento gaidi!" (same place)
(Ital., Latv.: "Wait a moment!")
"Hitlers gona." (same place)
(Latg.: "Hitler is gloating.")
"Raudivi!" (same place)

As the name "Raudive" so often appears on tape, it may be helpful to mention a comment made by Dr. Naegeli: that it would be quite out of the question for the word "Raudive" within a coherent sentence to be formed through a combination of various radio-beams; therefore, when "Raudive" is indubitably pronounced, and the name can be verified with absolute certainty phoneme by phoneme, the phenomenon could be said to have been proved. (See also Dr. Naegeli's Report on page 325.)

"Zenta wird Matilde." (same place) (Germ.: "Zenta will be Matilde.")
"Hupnitz." (same place)
"Te Tuntān, es esu. Tulpe gaiša. Vi tackar Kostuli." (same place: 628)
(Latv., Germ., Swed.: "Here is Tuntān, I am. The tulip is bright. We thank Kostuli.") This voice is unusually clear and distinct. All the participants could understand it immediately at the first listening-in session. Tuntān, as mentioned before, is Professor Čakste (pages 63 to 64). By "tulip" the voice may mean the lamp; in earlier recordings the voices had already referred to the brightness of the lamp in my study, and some of them had asked for a red—more subdued—light. This is, of course, only an

attempt at interpretation. Tuntān's "tulip" may well be a real one, or it may symbolise something totally different.

"Jāņs trudniča. Pojedim na Kostula!" (same place: 629)
(Russ.: "Jāņs is making efforts. Let's travel to Kostula.") Jāņs, who was a friend of the experimenter, manifests frequently. "Kostula"—an abbreviation of Konstantin.

"Velc garu vid plata! Žana Meer" (same place)
(Latv., Swed.: "Draw the spirit to 'plata'. Jeanna Meer.") Mrs. Jeanna Meer, an acquaintance of the experimenter, died in 1946. The meaning of the word "plata" is not clear. It could be Spanish and in that case the sentence would translate: "Draw the spirit to the silver."

"Stora Latve."
"Inte slikta." (same place: 631)
(Swed., Latv.: "Great Latvia."—"Not bad.") In the old days Latvia was known as "Latve"; "Latvija", the name now used, is of a much more recent date.

"Mans Nietzsche." (same place)
(Lat.: "My Nietzsche.")

Two voices in sequence:

"Prosim Raudive."
"Te Raudive pa retam." (same place: 644)
(Russ., Latv.: "We beg Raudive."—"Here Raudive is seldom.")
"Herr Raudive, fin!"
"Raudive, vai tu te?" (same place)
(Swed., Latv.: "Mr. Raudive, fine!"—"Raudive, are you here?")

In view of the name "Raudive" being used with such frequency in this recording, we would like to draw renewed attention to Dr. Naegeli's aforementioned theory.

"Te Mona, Mutter te." (same place: 647)
(Latv.: "Here is Mona. Mother is here.")
"Kosti, te mirkli Ulmans." (same place: 649)
(Latv.: "Kosti, here is [for] a moment Ulmans.")
"Zenta mēs tālu." (same place: 659)
(Latv.: "Zenta, we are far away.")

Now the participants call on Jung:

"Jungs dagegen."
"Jungs sapnī." (same place: 661)
(Germ., Latv.: "Jung on the contrary." "Jung in dreams.")
"Te bednjaki. Petrautzkis."
"Petrautzkis, Kosti, Petrautzkis!" (same place: 667)

(Russ., Latv.: "Here are the poor. Petrautzkis!"—"Petrautzkis, Kosti, Petrautzkis!")

"Čakli, Bochum. Es dzīvoju. Ists troll. Es mirstu." (same place: 669)
(Latv.: "Dilligent, Bochum. I live. A real troll. I die!")
"Radars tu te. Reiz Hitlers." (same place: 670)
(Latv.: "Here you are radio. Formerly Hitler.")
"Tekle, tev Pērkons izskrien." (same place: 673)
(Latv.: "Tekle, 'Perkons' is running out on you.") This refers to a novel by the experimenter which was published in New York.
"Te Rupai. Te dzimtene dzimst. Kur pir, Kosti?" (same place)
(Latv., Russ.: "Here is Rupais. Here the homeland materialises.

Where is the party, Kosti?") Rupais, once the experimenter's teacher, had been very fond of alcohol.
"Lobins, Koste, wanderst du? Koste, radnieks. Koste, dzīvoj ty? Tumsa. Te Koste." (same place: 674/5)
(Latg., Germ., Latv., Russ.: "Koste is good; are you wandering? Koste, a relative. Koste, are you living? Darkness. Here is Koste.")

In a follow-up recording, which the experimenter made on 18th April 1967, there was hardly a hint of the preceding session. The voices refer mainly to the experimenter and are, on the whole, of good audibility.

The experimenter calls on Sir Oliver Lodge.

"As probindo." (47r: 102)
(Latg., Span., Germ.: "I connect.")
"Vi künftiga, mēs ticam." (same place: 105)
(Swed., Germ., Latv.: "We of the future, we believe.")
"Ich fahre till Kosti. Redzu Kosti." (same place: 107)
(Germ., Swed., Latv.: "I travel to Kosti. I see Kosti.")
"Slikti pasuta Kosti. Tekle." (same place: 109)
(Latv.: "One orders Kosti badly. Tekle.")

The experimenter changes to microphone:

"Ringa du. Mēs gaidīsīm."
"Te, Kosta, Lodge." (same place: 137)
(Swed., Latv.: "You call. We will wait."—"Here, Kosta, is Lodge.")
"Raudive, te Jung."
"Padod Raudivi! Extra dich." (same place: 138)
(Latv., Germ.: Raudive, here is Jung."—"Hand over Raudive! Expecially [for] you.")
"Te guļ tu tikai."

"Lieber Kosti! Kosti, strīdi!" (same place: 146)
(Latv., Germ.: "Here you only sleep."—"Dear Kosti! Kosti, strife!")

The members of the Swiss Parapsychological Society who were present at the recording of 15th April 1967, listened to 155 microphone and radio-voices; they confirmed and signed a record of each voice heard—approximately 95 per cent of the total of voices located.

EXPERIMENTAL RECORDING No. 23

Bad Krozingen, (Germany) 23rd April 1967.
Participant: Mr. Herwart von Guilleaume, Publisher (Remagen) (See Commentary, page 380.)

Mr. von Guilleaume made his recording without the experimenter being present. It produced 7 microphone and 46 radio-voices; 25 of these belong to groups "A" or "B".

The voices are aimed partly at the person recording, partly at the experimenter.

Microphone-voices:

Mr. v. Guilleaume starts by saying that he would be very pleased if the friends "beyond" could speak to him.

"Wir Kosti brauchen." (48r: 013)
(Germ.: "We need Kosti.")
"Wir sind." (same place: 019)
(Germ.: "We are.")

Mr. v. Guilleaume repeats that he would like to hear from friends that have died.

"Wir sind, Guilleaume, wir Tote." (same place: 023)
(Germ.: "We are, Guilleaume, we dead.")

Mr. v. Guilleaume comments that he has heard over 300 voices and that he had been able to verify them all.

"Ich wusste." (same place: 026)
(Germ.: "I knew it.")

Mr. v. G. states that he had been here a year ago.

"Koste, grāmatu!" (same place: 027)
(Lat.: "Koste, the book!")

Mr. von Guilleaume: "I have the impression that the voices have now become clearer."
"Kostja, tu? Netic pasaule." (same place: 037)
(Latv.: "Kostja, you? The world does not believe.")
Mr. v. G.: "I intend to publish the book."
"Wörtchen. Danke Kosti!" (same place: 044/5)
(Germ.: "Word. [diminutive] Thank Kosti!")

Radio-voices:

The recording via radio was successful, despite the fact that between count 052 and 067 a radio-transmitter and other noises interfered. On a clear radio-beam some "A" and "B" voices of good audibility were received. Here follow a few examples:

"Te Raudive. Wir sticka . . ." (48r: 047)
(Latv., Swed., Germ.: "Here is Raudive. We are going . . .")
"Tja stig überführt." (same place: 048)
(Latg., Swed., Germ.: "Here a path leads across.")
("Wer policists?" (same place: 049)
(Germ., Latv.: "Who is police?")
"Kādi niedrigsti tja?" (same place)
(Latv., Germ.: "Who of the lowest are here?")

At this point radio-disturbances intervene. Not before 050 does another voice become audible:

"Te spreche Leroux." (same place: 050)
(Latv., Germ.: "Here speaks Leroux.")
"Reči, Nami verdanke!" (same place)
(Germ. [modified]: "Reči, thanks for the name!") Neither the experimenter, nor Mr. von Guilleaume know anybody by the name of Reči or Leroux.
"Furchtbar schwach, brāli!" (same place: 052)
(Germ., Latv.: "Terribly weak, brother!") The radio-beam became weaker and no more voices were heard up to 077:
"Koste, furchtbar! Papa." (same place: 077)
(Germ.: "Koste, terrible! Papa.")
"Minne tal." (same place: 078)
(Germ., Swed.: "Love speaks.")
"Kosti, paplāpa tu!" (same place)
(Latv.: "Kosti, say something!")
"Koste, wir bedanken." (same place)
(Germ.: "Koste, we give thanks.")
"Alice smuka bōba. Praksis dara šeit." (same place: 079)
(Latg., Latv.: "Alice is a smart woman. She has her practice here.")

"Māte, Maska überrascht." (same place: 080)
(Latv., Germ.: "Mother, the mask surprises.")
"Überrascht Koste da." (same place)
(Germ.: "Surprised Koste there.")
"Blitz man! Tekli Raudi Pustinē." (same place: 081)
(Germ., Latv.: "Lightning strike me! Tekle Raudi is in Pustine.")

Pustine is a small community not far from the place where Tekle, the experimenter's sister used to live.

"Daktere par ātri." (same place: 082)
(Latv.: "Madame doctor is in too much hurry.")
"Kosti, guli!" (same place)
(Latv.: "Kosti, go to bed!")
"Eskils runā. Galdi te. Runā sedativ. Kosta, te Bålsta." (same place: 083)
(Latv.: "Eskil speaking. Here are tables. Talk soothingly. Kosta, here is Bålsta.")
"Uppsala radars. Māti! Uppsala vakert." (same place: 092/3)
("Uppsala radar. Please, mother! Uppsala is beautiful.")

Mr. von Guilleaume checked his own experimental recording and also made a listening-in test of 300 voices; he was able to discern 99 per cent with certainty.

EXPERIMENTAL RECORDING No. 24

Bad Krozingen, 26th April 1967.
Participants: Mrs. Cornelia Brunner, Parapsychologist.
Mrs. Néné von Muralt, Parapsychologist (Zurich).
(See Reports, pages 331–336.)

The recording was made in the absence of the experimenter and produced 7 microphone voices of good "B" audibility and 40 radio voices of quality "A" or "B".

Mrs. von Muralt addresses her mother. A voice:

"Te wir Kosti brauchen." (48r: 117)
(Latv., Germ.: "We need Kosti here.") Except for the Latvian "te", "here", this sentence is identical with the first sentence spoken, in German, at Mr. Herwart von Guilleaume's experimental recording: "Wir brauchen Kostī"—"We need Kosti." (48r: 013)

Mrs. von Muralt: "Dear mother, can you speak to us?

"Artischoki! Lieber Kosti." (same place: 119)
(Germ.: "Artichokes! Dear Kosti.") The meaning of "artichokes" in this context remains obscure.

Mrs. N. v. M. asks after her Polish relatives.

"Anja Poživar." (same place: 123)
"Lyudzi Kosti!" (same place: 125)
(Latg.: "Ask Kosti!")
"Danke viņam, lūdzu!" (same place: 126)
(Germ., Latv.: "Thank him, please.")
"Wo wahre Waage?" (same place: 131)
(Germ.: "Where are just scales?")

Mrs. von Muralt says that she will now stop recording through microphone and that she is switching to radio.

"Balsī ir svikis." (same place: 134)
(Latv., and a modified Swedish word, "besvikelse": "There is disappointment in the voice.")

Radio voices:

"Konstanze selig te." (same place: 135)
(Germ., Latv.: "Konstanze is blissful here.")
"Mēs gaidam tevi." (same place: 136)
(Latv.: "We are expecting you.")
"Tala lustig! Te Koste, lusti, lusti! (same place: 137)
(Swed., Germ., Latv.: "Talk gaily! Here is Koste, gaiety, gaiety."
"Kuru zyrgu jōsi?" (same place: 138)
(Latg.: "Which horse will you ride?")

A female voice intervenes:

"Mauriņ, guli!" (same place)
(Latv.: "Mauriņ, sleep!")
"Du Freundin bist." (same place: 149)
(Germ.: "You are a friend. [female]")
"Rauda!" Short for "Raudive" (same place)
"Furchtbar radio negativ." (same place: 151)
(Germ.: "Terrible, radio negative.") Here severe interferences started and marred the recording up to No. 158.
"Akti du! Kosti, bald upsats." (same place: 158/9)
(Swed., Germ.: "Attention, you! Kosti, soon an essay.")
"Kosti, nokrišņu nav." (same place: 159)
(Latv.: "Kosti, there will be no rainfall.")
"Kosti, pa latviski!" (same place: 161)
(Latv.: "Kosti, Latvian!")

"Raudive trūka."
"Viņš ir bort." (same place: 162)
(Latv., Swed.: "Raudive is missing"—"He's gone."—) As in previous recordings, the experimenter's absence is noticed and remarked upon by the voices; this confirms our view once again, that we are faced with intelligent beings.

"Essig ohne Gift." (same place: 164)
(Germ.: literally "Vinegar without poison.") This was interpreted by Mrs. von Muralt as meaning: "Criticism without deadly poison."

"Jōnis te. Koste, difference." (same place: 166/7)
(Latv.: "Here is Jōnis. Koste, a difference.")
"Brunners te." (same place: 170)
(Latv.: "Here is Brunner.") Cornelia Brunner thought this might have been the voice of a near relative.

A warning voice:

"Brōlis te. Kosti, piesārgies!" (same place: 171)
(Latg., Latv.: "Here is your brother. Kosti, be careful.")

Another voice informs the experimenter:

"Te Tekle." (Same place)
(Latv.: "Here is Tekle.")
"Helga. Mōte te. Naktī guli!" (same place: 172)
(Latv.: "Helga. Here is mother. Sleep at night!")
"Koste, vänni te. Din vän." (same place: 173)
(Swed., Latv.: "Koste, here are friends. Your friend.")
"Kur te Burkhard?" (same place)
(Latv.: "Where is Burkhard here?")
"Pļāpa, tu bumbulst." (Same place: 202)
(Latv.: "Chatterbox, you are wasting time.")
"Te es resisteju." (same place)
(Latv.: "Here I resist.")
"Tu nespēj redzēt." (same place: 203)
(Latv.: "You are unable to see.")
"Ko tu te forksnē, Novaska?" (same place)
(Latv., modified Swedish: "What are you investigating here, Novaska?")
Novaska: a Polish name.
"Anita te denke dej." (same place: 210)
(Latv., Germ., Swed.: "Here Anita thinks of you.")
"Es liebe tevi. Eskils tja." (same place: 213)
(Latv., Germ.: "I love you. Eskil is here.") Eskil Wikberg, a friend of the experimenter, communicates again, just as he had done in H. von Guilleaume's experimental recording.

The same voice continues:

"Konstantin, es lūdzu. Tu te pazīsti Jānīti. Auksts te." (same place: 214/5)
(Latv.: "Konstantin, please. You know here Jānīti.—It is cold here.")
"Ko, gute Nacht! Findlay." (same place: 216)
(Germ.: "Ko[nstantin], good night! Findlay.")
"Hitleru sit. Tu vakti negribēji." (same place: 217)
(Latv., "Latvianised" German: "One is beating Hitler. You did not want the guard.")
"Pētrē—Wikberg. Plan Raudive." (same place: 218)
(Germ.: "Pētrē—Wikberg. The Raudive-plan.")
"L'homme du. Nesteidz!" (same place: 219)
(French, Germ., Latv.: "You, mankind. Do not hurry.")
"Alberts te. Kosti, runā tu!" (same place: 220)
(Latv.: "Here is Albert. Kosti, you speak!") Albert: Christian name of the Latvian writer Sprudzs.

The two participants in this recording-session listened to and checked the results unaided, and gave the following written confirmation:
"We have listened to the voices produced on tape at our recording-session of 27th April 1967 at Bad Krozingen, in Konstantin Raudive's studio, and have understood them 100 per cent."
They also checked the recording of 200 other voices and were able to hear and verify 95 per cent of the total number.

EXPERIMENTAL RECORDING No. 25

Babenhausen, Frankfurt a. M. (Germany), 10th May 1967.
Participants: Mr. Valerij Tarsis, Writer.
Mrs. Hanni Tarsis.
Dr. Hildegard Dietrich.
(See Commentaries, pages 376–378.)

The recording (No. 372) registered 5 microphone "A" and 35 radio "A" voices on tape.
Dr. Hildegard Dietrich pleads: "Rita, say something to me! Say a word!" She is answered by:

"Viņa maisa. Frankfurt." (49g: 148)
(Latv.: "She disturbs. Frankfurt.")

Dr. Dietrich again: "Rita, do say something to me!"
"Nav ko tev saka." (same place: 149)
(Latv.: "There is nothing to tell you.")

Dr. Dietrich continues to speak. A voice:

"Stabulītes tu pasteidz!" (same place)
(Latv.: "Hurry to make the flutes!")

Now a voice that refers to the experimenter:

"Kosta, Ludza. Osnovska sista." (same place: 151)
(Latv., Swed.: "Kosta, Ludza. Osnovska is the last.") Ludza is the name of a provincial town in Latvia, and Osnovska is the name of a family known to the experimenter.

Mrs. Tarsis addresses her near relatives and a voice of good audibility answers:

"Koste, help!" (same place: 156)

Then someone calls:

"Kosti!" (same place)

The microphone-voices noted above are all of excellent audibility and easy to understand.

Here are the radio-voices that belong to group "A" and were confirmed by the participants:

"Moskva dice te. Konstantin, Tarsi!" (same place: 159)
(Lat., Latv.: "Moscow speaks here. Konstantin, ask Tarsis!")
This refers to Valerij Tarsis who had arrived not long before from Moscow.
"Katoli, Lapis tēvs." (same place)
(Latv.: "The Catholics, Father Lapis.")

A woman's voice:

"Pievelc ty! Helga tja." (same place: 167)
(Russ., Latv.: "You must attract! Here is Helga.")

One voice apologises:

"Passé, Konstantin, piedodat man!" (same place: 168)
(French, Latv.: "It is past, Konstantin, forgive me!")
"Te Tekla." (same place: 169)
(Latv.: "Here is Tekla.")
"Wy detki; Paguḷ, ziamia!" (same place: 173)
(Russ., Latg.: "You children! Sleep a little, earth!")

"Virza tja." (same place)
(Latv.: "Virza is here.") Edvards Virza, a Latvian poet (see page 75).
"Rita", who had been called by Dr. Dietrich, announces herself:
"Rita te." (same place: 175)
(Latv.: "Here is Rita.")

Two people the experimenter had known:

"Kārkliņš"
"Lampis te." (same place) Kārkliņš: a popular Latvian writer.
"Braucht nicht zu singen." (same place: 177)
(Germ.: "No need to sing.")
"Mūsu nakts perche?" (same place)
(Latv., Ital.: "Our night, why?")
"Dr. Kosti, nometnī. Jauki debesis tomēr." (same place: 180/1)
(Latv.: "Dr. Kosti, in the camp. It is, however, beautiful in heaven.")
"Lohmann, non thing." (same place: 182) Umberto Lohmann, a friend of the experimenter, died some years ago in Lübeck (Germany).
"Rūna, Kosti!"
"Viņš ir slims." (same place: 212)
(Latv.: "Speak, Kosti!"—"He is sick.")
"Tu vecā pott." (same place: 216)
(Latv., Swed.: "You old 'pot'.") This expression can also be found in the sentence: "Jundahl kan gå själv, oh vecā pott . . ." (see page 25)
"Mīlu, Kosti. Te ir sekretare. Mīļā, mīli!"
"Überschwoll." (same place: 218/9)
(Latv., modified German: "I love Kosti. Here is the secretary. Dearest love!"—"Overflowing.")
"Kosti, Kostī turies! Mīlu Kosti." (same place: 219)
(Latv.: "Kosti, Kosti hold on! I love Kosti!")
"Liktens spiež. Negribu Sigtunu." (same place: 221)
(Latv.: "Fate decrees. I don't want Sigtuna.")

A female voice sorrows:

"Koste, netiekam valstē." (same place: 222)
(Latv.: "Koste, we cannot enter into the Kingdom.")
"Austra te." (same place)
(Latv.: "Here is Austra.") This is a very popular Latvian name (female).

The recording ends with the words:

"Helga! Konstantin, es te." (same place)
(Latv.: "Helga! Konstantin, I am here.") The name "Helga" is mentioned twice on this tape.

In the next recording (011) Tarsis' friend Wetrow manifests:

"Kosti—skål! Wetrows esmu." (48r: 249)
(Swed., Latv.: "Kosti,—skål[cheers]! I am Wetrow.")
(See Commentary page 376.)

EXPERIMENTAL RECORDING No. 26

Zürich (Switzerland) 29th June 1967.
Participants: Professor Werner Brunner (Dr. of medicine).
　　　　　　　Mrs. Cornelia Brunner.
　　　　　　　Mrs. Ida Bianchi.
　　　　　　　Mr. Peter Rutishauser.
(See Report page 331.)

The visions of Mrs. Ida Bianchi had already been noted and studied by C. G. Jung. After his death it was Mrs. Cornelia Brunner who continued the investigation. The experimenter was interested in these studies and wanted to find out whether there was any connection between Mrs. Bianchi's visions and the voices manifesting on tape. He asked Professor Werner Brunner and Mr. Peter Rutishauser to be present as witnesses.

Before the recording took place the participants listened to 100 well defined voices on tape, which they were able to verify 100 per cent. Mrs. Bianchi stated that there was a remarkable relationship between her visions and the voices she had heard on the tape. In her visions she usually sees people she knew when they were alive on earth, amongst them C. G. Jung; she also sees landscapes, mountains or towns entirely different in character from those on earth.

The recording starts via microphone, Professor Brunner taking the lead with the words: "I should be very happy if we could receive answers to our questions."

"Richtig hier." (Gg.: 018)
(Germ.: "Correct here.")

The experimenter asks Professor Brunner whether he had

been able to discern all the voices played over to him before the start of the recording.

The professor answers: "I have heard and understood all the voices quite clearly. This is a most unusual phenomenon. I can only congratulate Mr. Raudive most sincerely on having been able to record voices normally inaudible to us, and now I am anxious to find out whether we shall get any answers."

"Slikti hier. Nej." (same place: 019/25)
(Latv., Germ., Swed.: "It is bad here. No!")

Experimenter: "Then you, Professor, are convinced that the phenomenon exists in reality?"

Professor Brunner: "No doubt about that! I would very much like to know if there is a resemblance between the voices and the visions."

"Deine Mutter." (same place: 66h71)
(Germ.: "Your mother.")

The experimenter turns to Mrs. Bianchi (known as "Giulia"), and asks her to talk to her personal friends in the beyond.

"Te Moņa stradā. Beschwere dich." (same place)
(Latv., Germ.: "Mona works here. Complain!")
The experimenter: "Participants . . ."
Another microphone-voice: "Ida, parlez!" (079)
(French: "Ida, speak!") This voice obviously addresses Mrs. Ida Bianchi.

Giulia remembers her friend, Mrs. Dürler; she talks about her and recounts, amongst other things, how she had been able to foretell her friend's death.

"Ida!" (081)

Then Giulia talks about C. G. Jung and how he once told her that her visions were inexplicable; there were many mysteries—within man himself as well as outside the boundaries of his own being—he had said.

"Mond! Pētī, Kost!" (136)
(Germ.: "Moon! investigate, Kost!")

Now Mrs. Bianchi speaks of a woman whose mother entered a convent. A clearly audible microphone voice says:

"Smert." (221)
(Russ.: "Dead.")

The experimenter states that he is switching to radio.

"Danke!" (same place)
(Germ.: "Thanks!") It happens again and again that voice-entities show gratitude when the experimenter changes from microphone to radio.

The radio-recording was controlled by Mrs. Brunner. It yielded over 200 audible voices; 55 "A", the rest "B" and "C" voices. The main object was to obtain an answer to the question of whether Mrs. Bianchi's visions could be said to bear out statements made by the voices.

The results here noted are grouped in two sections: those that refer to Mrs. Bianchi and those that are concerned with the experimenter, or with matters of general interest.

1. Statements referring to Mrs. Bianchi:

"Ida, te madre. Genau. Lusta doch!" (321).
(Latv., Ital., Germ.: "Ida, here is mother. Exactly. Be glad!")

Mrs. Bianchi's mother was Italian. Now "Giulia" talks about her father and is told by a voice:

"Vateru gaid! Tu 'praters' te." (343/4)
(Germ., Latv., and a neologism that could have been formed from the Swedish word "prata": "to speak".—"Wait for father! You are turning into a chatterbox here.")
"Te vizija, Kosti." (351)
(Latv.: "Here you have a vision, Kosti.") Mrs. Bianchi was describing a vision she had seen whilst the radio-recording was being made.
"Muita! Koste, Frankfurte." (same place)
(Latv.: "Customs! Koste, Frankfurt.") (See also page 143.)

An extremely clear voice:

"Cremona!" (393)

A female voice:

"Ida, Königin te." (402)
(Germ., Latv.: "Ida, here is the queen.") Ida Bianchi had just related that she often sees a queen, dressed in black, in her visions; the queen always tries to tell her something, but Mrs. Bianchi cannot hear her voice, nor understand what she is trying to say. It is interesting to note that the "queen" addresses Mrs. Bianchi directly.

"Te Königin! Patīkman Raudive. Echta Clara." (404)
(Latv., Germ.: "Here is the queen! I like Raudive. Genuine Clara.") This voice is of particularly good audibility.

2. Statements that refer to the experimenter or deal with general matters:

"Ko tu saki, Koste?" (321)
(Latv.: "What are you saying, Koste?")
"Tja ded!" (same place)
(Latg., Russ.: "Here is grandfather!")
"Koste, pievelc te! Margarete Petrautzka te." (329/30)
(Latv.: "Koste, attract now! Margarete Petrautzka here.")
As mentioned before, the voices demand quite often that the experimenter should attract them. The participants were drinking tea during the recording and the experimenter was not entirely concentrated on the voices.
"Māsa wichtig, Konstantin." (354)
(Latv., Germ.: "Your sister is important, Konstantin.")
"Müde Koste, paties. Margaret." (358)
(Germ., Latv.: "Koste is really tired. Margaret.")

An unusually clear voice says:

"Hallo, Kontakt! Stalin damoj!" (365)
(Germ., Russ.: "Hallo, contact! Stalin, [go] home!")
"Ty Lucān?"
"Pamīlo Kosti ty!"
"Gute Nacht, mēs trīcam." (same place)
(Russ., Latv., Germ.: "Are you Lucan?"—"Love [you] Kosti!"—"Good night, we are trembling.")
"Te Lamis Beirīn." (379)
(Latv.: "Here is Lamis Beirin.") The name "Lamis Beirin" is quite unknown to the experimenter.
"Raudi, furchtbar! Koste, straža te. Mēs valoda te. Brāli ir." (381)
(Germ., Russ., Latv.: "Raudi, terrible! Koste, here is the guard. We are the language here. The [your?] brothers exist"). It may be that the strange surroundings inhibit the voice-entities and prevent them from making contact with the experimenter. Possibly Mrs. Bianchi is surrounded by a "guard", keeping the voice-entities back.

We hear a series of voices that report their presence or make statements about their condition. For instance:

"Te Diriņi. Karli will ich!" (374)
(Latv., Germ.: "Here are the Dirini. I want Karl!") A family of the name "Dirini" were the experimenter's neighbours in Riga.

"Padre Marsē." (378)
"Pasternaks." (390)
"Te Trine guļ." (401) (Latv.: "Here sleeps Trine.")
"Du Hitler."
"Hitlers tja." (349) (Latg.: "Hitler is here.")
"Visi lučiki. Dekana moščiki." (352)
(Latv., Russ.: "Everybody fishes [or hunts] at night by the light of pine-wood torches. The helpers of the Dean.") The second sentence could refer to Prof. Brunner who once held the rank of dean.
"Tilts patika. Patīcami, Lily." (353)
(Latv.: "I liked the bridge. It is pleasant, Lily.")
"Kosta, Hitlers te." (354)
(Latv.: "Kosta, here is Hitler.")

Immediately after this session, the experimenter made a "follow-up" recording. Experience has shown that this practice often produces references to the recording just completed.

The voices now showed a completely different mood in their utterances. Mainly persons well known to the experimenter manifested, making statements either aimed at him personally, or on generalities. Some good "A" voices were recorded. A few examples:

"Labi saprati russki." (Gg: 447)
(Latv., Russ.: "You understood the Russian language well.")
"Virza! Vakna, Kosti!" (465)
(Swed.: "Virza! Wake up, Kosti!") The voices often maintain that we do nothing but sleep. This is repeated under many different circumstances.
"Mauriņš tja. Tita, Kostulīt, Petrautzkis! Dabiskas atslēgas. Doktore tirgū." (458)
(Latg., Swed., Latv.: "Here is Mauriņš. Look, Kostulit, Petrautzkis! The natural key. The doctor is on the market.")
One could interpret this—tentatively—thus: Maurins, most probably Dr. Zenta Maurina's father, points to the presence of Petrautzki. The last sentence may mean that "the doctor" (Zenta Maurina) is "on the market" or "in the public eye" through her books and her lectures. The meaning of "The natural key", however, remains hidden.
"Petja, Kostja, Kosta."
"Intiņa skata tevi." (467) (Latv.: "Intina sees you.") "Inta" is a Latvian name (female). Like many others, this voice-entity points out that it can see the experimenter.
"Kur tu guļa, Kosti?"
"Koste, tu guļ te. Pietiks."
"To Koste zin. Raudivs pats." (469/71)

(Latv.: "Where do you sleep, Kosti?"—"Koste, you sleep here. Enough."—"Koste knows that. Raudivs himself.")
"Du liebi Gott!" (471)
(Germ.: "Dear God!") Correct German should be: "lieber" (dear); the incorrect ending "i" is found quite often in the voices' language.
"Ilgas, Mutter. As paliku." (473)
(Latg., Germ.: "Longing, mother. I stayed.")

A very clear female voice:

"Hitlers tic." (474)
(Latv.: "Hitler believes.")
"Tici! Kosti, guli!" (same place)
(Latv.: "Believe! Kosti, sleep.")
"Raudive schwatz."
"Mūs tuvinā. Tja pakīts, attīsti!" (475)
(Germ., Latv.: "Raudive chatters."—"He brings us nearer. Here is a little packet, develop!") Every now and then the voices remind us that energies given to us have to be developed.
"Uz kuga sēž. Pieteic tu kugi. Kapteins tu." (475)
(Latv.: "One is on the ship. You must report a ship. You are the captain.") The idea of a ship appears on various occasions.

EXPERIMENTAL RECORDING No. 27

Vevey (Switzerland) 9th August 1967.
Participants: Miss Helen Schmidheiny, graphologist.
Miss Katrin Bolli (Vevey).

The author recorded the first voice two years ago on the shores of the Lake of Geneva and now ends the present series of experiments with a recording made once again near the same lake. It was made in his presence and produced 8 microphone and 27 radio voices of "A" quality. The results were listened to and verified by the two participants.

Microphone voices: Immediately, on switching on the tape-recorder, a voice is heard:

"Kon . . ." (50g: 337) This was probably an attempt to say "Konstantin". Then: "Kurls tu." (same place)
(Latv.: "You are deaf.")

Miss Schmidheiny mentions her friend, Max Pulver; the experimenter asks him to give her a sign.

"Gruss!"
"Rūnā ty!" (same place: 348)
(Germ., Russ.: "Greetings"—"Speak [you]!")

As the experimenter comments that we can hear but fragments of the microphone voices, someone calls:

"Kosti!" (same place: 354)
Miss Schmidheiny: "I believe it is possible for us to contact the 'beyond', but it is not always possible to establish this contact."
"Kann!" (same place: 365) (Germ.: "Can!")

Miss Schmidheiny hopes that contact can be made through the apparatus now in use.

"Ja!" (same place: 366)
(Germ.: "Yes!")
Miss Bolli: "That is, of course, possible . . ."
"Pļāpa!" (same place: 371)
(Latv.: "Chatter!")

Most of the microphone voices are between the audibility groups "B" and "C".

All radio voices here noted belong to group "A":

"Naktī, Koste!" (same place: 381)
(Latv.: "In the night, Koste!")
"Es lupata, Joza Hasa." (same place)
(Latv.: "I am a rogue. Joza Hasa.") The experimenter does not know this name. It happens quite frequently that voice-entities humble, or even abase themselves; another example: "Bulān, mala flicka." ("Bulan, a bad girl.")
"Mēs te desmiti." (same place)
(Latv.: "Dozens of us are here.")
"Wo warst du, Saskia, Saskia?" (same place)
(Germ.: "Where were you, Saskia, Saskia?") The name "Saskia" appears on several tapes.
"Stora tu man. Pētaga. Dūmi maitā." (same place: 382)
(Swed., Latv.: "You are great for me. Pētaga. The smoke spoils.")
"Smeķē Koste?" (same place)
(Latv.: "Is Koste smoking?")
"I Sauka."
"Te Kostja." (same place: 383)
(Engl., Latv.: "I [am] Sauka."—"Here is Kostja.")
"Igors, te ceļi. Kostja, ātrāk! Mārsta!" (same place)
(Latv.: "Igor, here are paths. Kostja, quicker! Mārsta.")
"Mārsta", the name of a railway-station between Stockholm and Uppsala, is repeatedly used in various contexts.

"Hjälp!" (same place: 386)
(Swed.: "Help!")
"Dūmi, Koste! Mūsu Kostja. Madaga." (same place: 388)
(Latv.: "Smoke, Koste! Our Kostja. Madaga.") The repeated mentioning of "smoke" may have had something to do with the thunderstorm that was brewing over the Lake of Geneva. The name "Madaga" is unknown to the experimenter.
"Lūdzu ustobu! Brukostu!" (same place)
(Latv., Latg.: "A room, please! Breakfast, please!")
"Jēzups Nastaboj. Koste, Mōte!" (same place: 390)
(Latg.: "Jēzups Nastaboj. Koste, mother!")
"Raudive! Koste, tu patiki, strādaji, strādaji." (same place: 392)
(Latv.: "Raudive! Koste, you pleased [us], you have worked, worked.") This statement points to the fact that the experimenter had worked all day long on the script of the voice-phenomenon book.
"Kosti, znjomka tiekam." (same place)
(Russ., Latv.: "Kosti, we are being recorded.")
"Redz Tante. Citadāk purvs." (same place: 392)
(Latv., Germ.: "Aunt can see. Otherwise swamp.")
"Es nabogs!" (same place)
(Latg.: "I, poor thing!")
"Petrautzki! Kosti, sapnī!" (same place)
(Latv.: "Petrautzki! Kosti, in a dream!") Here we are faced with an interesting parapsychological fact: the night after this recording-session the experimenter really did see Margarete Petrautzki in a dream. Her appearance had a transcendental character, yet she could be recognised easily by the likeness she bore to her earthly features.

There had been a parallel case concerning C. G. Jung. A voice had said on tape: "Jung sapni." (Latv.: "Jung in a dream.") In a dream—too complicated to relate—following the voice's statement, the experimenter heard Jung say: "Es ist schwer hinüberzukommen." (Germ.: "It is difficult to come over.") Again, on another occasion, Jung's voice had been heard on tape: "Guļat, tu saņemsi gultā." (Latv.: "Sleep, you will receive in bed."). See page 109. There are many questions in this context that deserve intensive study, but we still need much more material on the subject. There must be some connection between the psycho-acoustic manifestations on tape and the pictures and impressions received in dreams. Shakespeare was right: "We are such stuff as dreams are made of..."

"Du wachstē kotru dīn. Te tovs Alexej(s)." (same place: 394)
(Germ., Latg.: "You grow each day. Here is your Alexej."
The German word for "growing", "wachsen", has been Latvianised.)

"Lachs. Piedodi!" (same place: 396)
(Latv.: "Lachs. Please forgive!") "Lachs" was the name of a schoolmate who had teased the experimenter with all sorts of nicknames; this had deeply hurt the experimenter as a child.

"Mājās! Koste te. Sdrawstwuj, Ilse te." (same place)
(Latv., Russ.: "At home! Here is Koste. Good day, here is Ilse.")

"Nastja!" (same place: 397)

"I—I te pastenda." (same place: 398)
(Engl., Latv.: "I—I 'pastenda' here.") The experimenter does not know the word "pastenda".

"Koschta te. Istaba kņaze." (same place)
(Latv.: "Here is Koschta. The room is princely.")

"Es zakodja." (same place)
(Latv., Russ.: "I enter [here].")

"As, hej!" (same place) (Latg., Swed.: "I, heh!")

"Raude, Berg." (same place: 399) "Berg" had been a doctor in Stockholm and the experimenter knew him well. "Raude"—variation of Raudive.

CHAPTER IV

Results of Partnership Experiments

From 30th August 1967 to the end of the year the experimenter conducted a series of intensive investigations into problems of "partnership" between voices and participants at recording-sessions. By means of detailed analyses and the help of willing collaborators in experiments, the following facts could be established:

1. When addressed, deceased persons make their presence known either by giving their names, or by exhibiting some characteristic that had typified them in life.

2. A person spoken to reacts directly to questions and will often give a spontaneous opinion.

3. The voice-entities call the experimenter and his collaborators by Christian or family names, and give information about post-mortal conditions.

4. Language and texts of utterances, however, remain the same as in other experiments. Partnership-voices are made particularly meaningful by the fact that coincidence is even more decidedly ruled out in their particular case than in any other type of investigation; furthermore, this method enables us to recognise the psychological characteristics of a given voice-entity and to follow the meaning of its statements.

At each recording the experimenter narrows his attention to a certain number of persons he has addressed. Checking the results as a whole, one can see that each personality called upon at intervals answers in the same voice and retains the same characteristic features in his or her pronouncements. It is difficult to maintain a consecutive dialogue as other voices, eager to express themselves, tend to break into a conversation.

We shall now try to analyse some of the examples in detail. Sixty-five recordings of this type were made, some in collaboration with other people, some by the experimenter alone. In each case selected voice-entities were addressed, and the answers obtained give us an overall picture emerging from the summary of experiments outlined in the following pages.

The mother of the experimenter.

At almost every recording-session the experimenter has called upon his mother. Answers are frequently given by a woman's voice. Here are some examples:

"Raudive, prasi Mutter!" (50g: 763)
(Latv., Germ.: "Raudive, ask for mother.")
"Mōte te." (same place)
(Latv.: "Mother is here.")
"Pazini mōti?" (same place)
(Latv.: "Did you recognise [your] mother?")

During another session the following voices are heard:

"Tave matka tja." (50r: 098)
(Latg., Russ.: "Your mother is here.")
"Pasauc mōti!" (same place)
(Latv.: "Call mother.")

The experimenter asks his mother where she now lives, and the answer comes promptly:

"Tja mūžiba." (50r: 137)
(Latv.: "Here is eternity.")

On another occasion a voice advises:

"Gaidi! Mama. Mōte strādā." (50r: 691)
(Latv.: "Wait! Mama. Mother is working.")

The next voice affirms:

"Te māte." (same place)
(Latv.: "Here is mother.")

After the experimenter had addressed his mother:

"Matka, Raudivs te." (51g: 358)
(Russ., Latv.: "Mother, here is Raudivs.")

A female voice calls:

"Te māte, te māte! Konstantin, tova mōte." (same place: 386)
(Latv., Latg.: "Here is mother, mother! Konstantin, your mother.")

In her answers the experimenter's mother uses various languages, including some she did not know when on earth. For instance:

"Te mōte, Uppsala. Labrit tova mōte. Din madre, Koste." (51g: 546/55)
(Latg., Swed., Span.: "Here is mother, Uppsala. Good morning, your mother. Your mother, Koste.")

Tekle.

The experimenter's sister Tekle is also often addressed and she nearly always answers, confirming that she is present, or that she wants to be admitted.

"Laid Tekli tu!" (50g: 857)
(Latv.: "Let Tekle pass!")

We hear her say:

"Danke, Koste. Wir danke Kosti." (50r: 383)
(Germ.: "Thanks, Koste. We thank [you] Kosti.")

The experimenter relates that a gramophone record of the voices has been made.

"Koste, plati uzliku primā." (same place)
(Latv.: "Koste, I was the first to put the record on.")
"Ich glaube dir." (same place: 393)
(Germ.: "I believe you.")

Once again the experimenter addresses his sister and the following voices answer:

"Teklja pati." (50r: 638)
(Latv.: "Tekla herself.")
"Teklai Kosti patīk." (same place)
(Latv.: "Tekle likes Kosti.")

Then, a particularly interesting comment:

"Ko, mōsa skrin pa gaisu." (50r: 642)
(Latv.: "Ko, your sister is running through the air.")

Another time, after Tekle has been called, a voice replies:

"Kosti, ty? Labdien." (same place: 694)
(Russ., Latv.: "Kosti, you? Good day.") and the voice continues:
"Te mēs dzīvi." (same place: 697)
(Latv.: "Here we live.")

Later, another response:

"Konstantin, mōsa Tekle. Raudive! Vai tur Raudive tu?" (50r: 832)
(Latg.: "Konstantin, sister Tekle. Raudive! Are you there Raudive?")

A different voice confirms:

"Tja Raudive. Mēs redzam Kosti." (same place: 847)
(Latv.: "Here is Raudive. We can see Kosti.")

C. G. Jung.

C. G. Jung is called upon in many recordings and such occasions have produced interesting results:

"Echo slyšu." (50g: 880)
(Germ., Russ.: "I hear the echo.")
"Koste, pieved!" (50r: 072)
(Latv.: "Koste, lead!")
"Iekšiene." (same place)
(Latv.: "The inner man.")
"Raidi då du!" (same place: 075)
(Latv., Swed., Germ.: "Do transmit!")

Once, after Jung had again been addressed, the following answers were received:

"Ich antworte. Lobs vokors." (50r: 866)
(Germ., Latv.: "I answer. Good evening.")
"Konstantin! Kosti, piebrauc!" (same place)
(Latv.: "Konstantin! Kosti, drive up!")

and another time:

"Ai Heimat! Septiņās ir Dievs." (51g: 171)
(Germ., Latv.: "Ah homeland! The [number] seven contains God.")
"Junga sektorā." (same place: 197)
(Latv.: "In Jung's sector.")
"Konstantin, Don Quichotta nav." (same place)
(Latv.: "Konstantin, there is no Don Quixote.")

In one of the last recording sessions the experimenter asks C. G. Jung what he thinks of Mr. X's book. The voice replies:

"Es ist nicht gut. Es ist naiv. A Bender igual." (51r: 423)
(Germ., Span.: "It is not good. It is naïve. Bender does not care.")

"Darf ich te schnappe?" (same place)
(Germ.: "May I snatch [something] here?")
"Vai tu redzi mani?" (same place)
(Latv.: "Can you see me?")

On a different occasion, after Jung had been asked to communicate:

"Uralti veido tu." (51r: 468)
(Germ., Latv.: "You are moulding the ancient things.")
"Ich bin. Tic! Izšķirti." (same place)
(Germ., Latv.: "I am. Believe! Separated.")

The experimenter asks about Jürgenson and what kind of personality he is. In answer:

"Tā Kunga strādnieks" (same place)
(Latv.: "A worker of the Lord.")

In a recording of 4th December 1967, when Jung was addressed, the following voices were received:

"Laiks ir, Koste." (51r: 577)
(Latv.: "Time exists, Koste.")
"Mauriņa! Sveicu Zentu! Dod Mauriņu!" (same place)
(Latv.: "Maurina! I greet Zenta! Give me Maurina!")
"Tu mani izsauci! Runas tev labas." (same place: 580)
(Latv.: "You have called me! You make good speeches.")

At a session on 10th December 1967 the experimenter begs C. G. Jung to mention the experimenter's name clearly and also to say who is speaking. This was the reaction:

"Koste! Koste, ērglis!" (52g: 091)
(Latv.: "Koste! Koste, the eagle!")
"Ir labi. Gudribas tilts." (same place)
(Latv.: "It is good. Bridge of wisdom.")

and at the end, probably in response to the question as to who was speaking:

"Psycholog!" (same place: 097)
(Germ.: "Psychologist.")

Margarete Petrautzki.

In each of the sixty-five experimental recordings of this series, Margarete Petrautzki was addressed in order to ascertain whether she would immediately take up contact with the experimenter or his collaborators. Here are some examples of the results obtained:

> "Koste, Margarete." (50: 817)
> "Es pate! Furchtbar, furchtbar! Koste siebente bāka." (same place: 862)
> (Latv., Germ.: "I in person! Terrible, terrible! Koste is the seventh lighthouse.")

In the next recording a mediating voice appears:

> "Te tovs meitens." (50g: 868)
> (Latg.: "Here is your girl.")

followed by a direct challenge:

> "Pa lēnu tu! Ich such name." (same place)
> (Latv., Germ.: "You are too slow! I am looking for the name.")

At another session, after the experimenter has addressed Margarete:

> "Margarete te. Hälsa." (50r: 016)
> (Latv., Swed.: "Margarete is here. Greetings.")
> "Te tev experimenti." (same place)
> (Latv.: "You have experiments here.")
> "Līdzu Kosti, piedodi! Zenti, ko tu dari? Margaretiņu! Tu Koste?" (same place: 024)
> (Latv.: "Please, Kosti, forgive! Zenti, what are you doing? Ask little Margarete! Are you Kosti?")

The experimenter asks, on one occasion, why Mr. X. does not attend the experiments.

> "Tu žulti prasi" (50r: 048)
> (Latv.: "You are asking for gall.") answers a voice.
> "Koste tevi negrib." (same place: 055)
> (Latv.: "Koste does not want you.")
> "Koste, te ir zviedri." (same place)
> (Latv.: "Koste, here are Swedes.")

At a later recording another mediating voice is heard:

> "Margarete te atnāce."
> (Latv.: "Margarete has arrived here.")
> "Tu latvisko."
> (Latv.: "You translate into Latvian.") This statement coincided with the fact that the experimenter was translating a German book into Latvian, at that time.

"Koste, tu naktī. Margarete."
(Latv.: "Koste, you at night. Margarete.") Another voice replies:
"Doktor Nacht wollte." (50r: 215)
(Germ.: "The doctor wanted night.")

Another time, when the experimenter calls again on Margarete, we hear a voice:

"Koste, Margarete. Danke." (same place: 423)
(Germ.: "Koste. Margarete. Thanks.")
"Koste, du wichtig te." (same place: 478)
(Germ., Latv.: "Koste, you are important here.")

In a similar context a mediating voice answers the call for Margarete:

"Vōciete." (50r: 750)
(Latg.: "The German.") and then a voice comes in with:
"Es Margarete." (same place: 764)
(Latv.: "I am Margarete.")

On some tapes Margarete's voice can be heard several times; for instance:

"Koste, te Margarete"
"Koste, Margarete."
"Margareta."
"Konstantin, tu guli." (50r: 832)
(Latv.: "Konstantin, you are sleeping.")

At times Margarete announces her presence by giving her family name:

"Petrautzka te. Kur tu gaidi? Koffers redz." (51g: 015)
(Latv., Germ.: "Here is Petrautzka. Where were you? The trunk [or suitcase] can see.")
A voice asks: "Gribri, mein Sohn?" (same place)
(Latv., Germ.: "You want to, my son?")
Another voice replies: "Petrautzkis." (same place)
"Te mōte, extrem Kosti." (51g: 026)
(Latv.: "Here is mother, the extreme Kosti.")
"Kostja, Petrautzkis. Pareizi datē! Mani dzirdēs." (51g: 119)
(Latv.: "Kostja, Petrautzkis. Date correctly! I shall be heard.")

When a selected person is called by name, other voices, taking advantage of the opportunity to speak to the experimenter, usually gatecrash; here are some examples:

The experimenter asks for Margarete, and is answered by several voices.

> First voice: "Margarete. Dod man Konstantin!" (51g: 390)
> (Latv.: "Margarete. Give me Konstantin.")
> Second voice: "Ortega. Prasi savu tautu." (same place: 396)
> (Latv.: "Ortega. Ask for your people.")
> Third voice: "Wir sprechen, Konstantin. Vai te būs sichtbar? Sprich du französisch!" (same place: 404)
> (Germ., Latv.: "We speak, Konstantin. Will one be visible here? Speak [you] French!")
> Fourth voice: "Konstantin, Zenti. Tja Soņa." (same place: 410)
> (Latv.: "Konstantin, Zenta please. Here is Sonja.")

Quite often, having been addressed, Margarete makes a request:

> "Danke. Bitte, grüsse Zenti. Te Margarete." (53g: 020)
> (Germ., Latv.: "Thanks. Please, greet Zenti. Here is Margarete.")

Professor Gebhard Frei.

Professor Frei, who had been familiar with the voice-phenomenon, wrote the letter included in Appendix I shortly before his death. On 5th November 1967 the experimenter wrote to the professor, but the letter was returned next day bearing the remark: "deceased". During the recording sessions that followed, the experimenter called on Professor Frei, who immediately took up contact. His Christian name appears clearly audible on tape. The experimenter asks:

"Can you give me definite proof from the other side?" A voice answers distinctly:

> "Du handle, Gebhard."
> (Germ.: "You act, Gebhard.")

Recordings made on 7th and 11th November produced the following voices:

> "Warta, Koste." (51g: 431)
> (Germ.: "Wait, Koste.")
> "Ich antworte." (same place)
> (Germ.: "I answer.")
> "Finito te." (same place: 502)
> (Ital., Latv.: "Finished here.")

"Mēs tev sveiki." (same place: 525)
(Latv.: "We greet you.")
"Hier sind Katholiken." (same place: 529)
(Germ.: "Here are Catholics.")
"Friedhofs Grab." (same place)
(Germ.: "Cemetery's grave.")

On 12th November the experimenter again calls for Professor Frei. A voice answers:

"Gebhard." (51g: 559)
"Warta, te tev signals." (same place)
(Germ., Latv.: "Wait, you will get a signal here.")
"Ich danke." (same place)
(Germ.: "I thank you.")
"Radz ka tu gaidi tja." (same place: 560)
(Latg.: "One can see you are waiting here.")

Another recording shows the following results:

"Te Gebhard." (51g: 565)
(Latv.: "Here Gebhard.")
"Tu neesi latviets." (same place)
(Latv.: "You are not Latvian.")
"Kosta, kur tu? Frei." (same place: 569)
(Latv.: "Kosta, where are you? Frei.")
"Raudiv, Hitler hier." (same place)
(Germ.: "Raudiv, Hitler here")
"Raudiv heisst Doktor." (same place: 572)
"Bekannti" (same place) "Bedanke." (same place)
"Good bye." (same place: 575)
(Germ., English: "Raudiv is called doctor."—"Acquaintances"—"Thanks." "Good-bye.")

Excerpt from the recording made on 28th November:

"Mūsu patria." (51r: 403)
(Latv., Ital.: "Our homeland.")
"Koste, Gebhards. Dein Gebet." (same place)
(Germ.: "Koste, Gebhard. Your prayer.")
"Es gulu." (same place)
(Latv.: "I am sleeping.")

On 30th November another session took place in which Frei was addressed. The experimenter asks if Professor Frei can hear him.

"Ja, Gebhard. Es ist genug, Kosta." (51r: 420)
(Germ.: "Yes, Gebhard. It is enough, Kosta.")

"Was machst du, Kosta?" (same place)
(Germ.: "What are you doing, Kosta?")
"Wie leicht ist es hier! Koste, so freundlich." (same place)
(Germ.: "How easy it is here! Koste, so friendly.")
"Baudu. Freis te." (same place)
(Latv.: "I am enjoying it. Frei here.")
"Mēs tevi gribam brīvi sastapt." (same place: 450)
(Latv.: "We want to meet you freely.")

From a recording of 10th December:

"Koste, tu warta." (52g: 078)
"Koste macht Aufnahme." (same place)
(Latv., Germ.: "Koste, you wait."—"Koste is recording.")

From the recording of 14th December:

"Gebhard freut sich." (52r: 053)
(Germ.: "Gebhard rejoices.")
"Du arbeita, Kosti." (same place: 055)
(Germ.: "You are working, Kosti.")
The experimenter asks: "What am I doing now?"
"Koste spielt." (Germ.: "Koste is playing!")
Experimenter: "People still don't want to believe."
"So sind sie!" (Germ.: "That's how they are!")
Experimenter: "Why does Professor Bender not come?"
"Bender rāchli Kostei!" (53r: 196) (Germ. modified: "Bender takes revenge on Kostei!) The ending "ei" is Latvian dative.

Edvards Virza.

Results obtained from recordings containing Edvards Virza's voice are of particular interest. Virza, Latvian author died in 1940. The experimenter knew him well. He replies, for instance, after having been addressed:

"Enas tu purgā. Te Virza." (50g: 079)
(Latv.: "You are chasing shadows. Here Virza.")

On another occasion:

"Virza tja. Zeme sakrita." (51: 290)
(Latv.: "Here is Virza. The earth disintegrated.")

Other voices mention him:

"Es redzu Virzu." (51g: 330)
(Latv.: "I can see Virza.")

Kārlis Skalbe.

Here some examples of replies given by Kārlis Skalbe, another Latvian writer:

"Koste, Skalbe. Raudive, gut Überfahrt. Tack, Raudive Konstantin." (50g: 181/203)
(Germ., Swed.: "Koste, Skalbe. Raudive, a good crossing. Thank you, Raudive Konstantin.")

In another recording the voice is heard to say:

"Kārlis ir vecis, tilts atnāks." (50r: 290)
(Latv.: "Karlis is old, the bridge will come [into being].")
Then: "Skalbe. Tev gryuti, Konstantin." (51g: 330)
(Latg.: "Skalbe. It is difficult, Konstantin.")
A voice asks:
"Redz tu tanti?" (same place)
(Latv.: "Can you see Aunt?")
"Raudive, cīņu paredzu." (51g: 335)
(Latv.: "Raudive, I can foresee a battle.")
"Tante tevi mīl." (same place: 345)
(Latv.: "Aunt loves you.")

The experimenter asks: "Can you hear me, dear Skalbe?" A voice replies:

"Tu no naves dzirdi!" (54g: 246)
(Latv.: "You hear from the realm of the dead.")

The Soviet-Latvian writer *Vilis Lācis* was a nationalist when Latvia was still an independent state; later he joined the Communist Party and was Soviet-Latvia's Prime Minister until 1959. He received the Lenin, as well as the Stalin Prize for Literature. Responsibility for the death of many of his colleagues who were sent to Siberia rested on his shoulders. He died in 1961.

The experimenter, who had known him well, addresses him and asks him how he fares in his new life.

"Es lupata, Kosti, saproti. Vilis Lācis patiesi. Es bednešku situ." (50r: 470)
(Latv., Russ.: "I am a villain, Kosti, do you understand. Really and truly Vilis Lācis. I have beaten the weak.")

At the end of this recording the Latvian painter *Purvits* announces himself:

"Te Purvīts. Pagrūti man." (50r: 471)
(Latv.: "Here is Purvīts. It is difficult for me [here].")

In another recording Vilis Lācis is simply heard to say:

"Tur Konstantin. Pie Kostes meitene." (same place: 504)
(Latv.: "Over there is Konstantin. There's a girl with Kosti.")

Examples of results obtained through recordings made in collaboration with other participants:

On 13th October 1967 the experimenter made a partnership recording in which Miss Annemarie Morgenthaler (Bern) assisted. The experimenter starts by calling Margarete Petrautzki and receives some clearly audible voices:

"Kur tik ilgi?" (55r: 853)
(Latv.: Where [were you] so long?")
"Nāves te nesatiku." (same place)
(Latv.: "Here I have not encountered death.")
"Ko tu pētī?" (same place: 867)
(Latv.: "What are you investigating?")

Now Miss Morgenthaler addresses her cousin Margrit and is answered by a voice saying:

"Pusti! Sdravstvuy! Margrit." (same place: 886)
(Russ.: "Let [her] enter! Greetings! Margrit.")
"Kostja, Margrit." (same place: 888)
"Kostja, Martha." (same place)
"Tu nu guli." (same place)
(Latv.: "Now you are sleeping.")
"Vai tu tici? C'est Quelle." (same place)
(Latv., French, Germ.: "Do you believe? This is the source.")

Once again Miss Morgenthaler calls for Margrit. Malwina, Dr. Zenta Maurina's former housekeeper, answers:

"Te Malwina. Zenta mīļa. Te Margrit patīk." (same place: 900)
(Latv.: "Here is Malwina. Zenta is kind. Margrit likes it here.")

Right at the end, as the experimenter speaks the closing words, it is interesting to hear a voice say:

"Zinām! Vi danka. Mūsu Menge te." (same place: 902)
(Latv., Swed., Germ.: "We know! We thank you. Here are many of us.")

On 18th October another recording-session is held, again with Miss Morgenthaler taking part. The following voices result:

"Margrita. Glupa ty im Weltraum." (51g: 075)
(Russ., Germ.: "Margrita. You feel stupid in space.")
"Hier tova mōsa. Mīkla paliek." (same place)
(Germ., Latg.: "Here is your sister. The riddle remains.")

Miss Morgenthaler asks for her uncle, Walter Morgenthaler, and a voice takes up the call:

"Ich suche Walter." (same place: 078)
(Germ.: "I am looking for Walter!")
"Mācu Kosti." (same place: 085)
(Latv.: "I am teaching Kosti.")
"Sigtuna, Kosti, betona." (same place).
(Germ.: "betone" modified to "betona": "emphasise"; "Sigtuna" is an ancient Viking-town in Sweden, frequently mentioned by the voice-entities.)
"Forschi! Wikberg gul." (same place)
(Germ.: "Investigate! Wikberg sleeps.) This refers to the experimenter's friend Eskil Wikberg, who has communicated several times. As may be remembered, he had committed suicide.
"Komm, Koste, tu! Tu te willkommen." (same place: 095)
(Germ., Latv.: "Come, Koste, you! You are welcome here.")
"Raudiv, na dne, piši!" (same place: 099)
(Russ.: "Raudiv, for this reason, write!")
"Koste, nesteidz tu!" (same place)
(Latv.: "Koste, don't be in a hurry!")
"Es glaubi auch." (same place)
(Latv., Germ.: "I also believe.")
"Margarete! Koste vēl guļ." (same place: 105)
(Latv.: "Margarete! Koste is still sleeping.")
A voice warns:
"Pareizi datē!" (same place: 123)
(Latv.: "Date correctly!")
Another voice interjects:
"Mani Hitlers bez tiesas . . . Anja." (same place)
(Latv.: "Hitler, without trial, had me . . . Anja.")
"Raudive, mīl tu Toti? Sdravstvuy." (same place: 149)
(Latv., Germ., Russ.: "Raudive, do you love the dead? Good bye.")

It happens sometimes, that voice-entities who have been called upon do not answer immediately, but suddenly appear at later recordings. In the recording made with Valerij Tarsis, for example, Margarete Petrautzki is being addressed and a voice breaks in with:

"Grüsse Morgenthaler Anna!" (51r: 224)
(Germ.: "Greet Morgenthaler Anna!")

On 5th September 1967 a recording was made in collaboration with Miss Ilse Diersche which produced some strikingly good results. At the start of the session, the following voices are heard:

"Es prasu mūsu vadi." (48r: 333)
(Latv.: "I demand our authorities.")
"Experimenti vispār retāk.—Analyse te." (same place: 334)
(Latv.: "On the whole experiments are rarer.—Here is the analysis.")
"Avec Koste, Arvis." (same place)
(French: "With Koste, Arvis.")
"Diese Tantes volūda. Kosti, Dierschi." (same place: 337)
(Germ., Latv.: "This is the aunt's language. Koste, Diersche please!")
"Krozingen tumša. Ilzīte pašmaksu gan." (same place: 352)
(Latv.: "Krozingen is dark. Little Ilse [gives] 'self-prize' it seems.")
"Tu gan sprādzene." (same place)
(Latv.: "You seem to be a female doomed to die.")
"Loorits, denke! Mani spārno." (same place)
(Germ., Latv.: "Loorits, think! It gives me wings.")
"Man Raudivi! Raudive Konstantin." (same place: 356)
(Latv.: "Raudive for me! Raudive Konstantin.")

After Miss Diersche has asked for her father, Ludwig Diersche, a voice says:

"Mūsu Ilse. Brauc reitu." (same place: 375).
(Latv.: "Our Ilse. Travel tomorrow!")
"Disconti, Ilse." (same place: 394)
("Discount, Ilse.") Miss Diersche is a business-woman.
"Tēvs, carissima ty." (same place: 397)
(Latv., Ital., Russ.: "Father, dearest one [you].")
"Tici!" (same place)
(Latv.: "Believe!")

Ilse Diersche and the experimenter talk to Margarete Petrautzki.

"Dobrij ty! Margareta. Ilse du? Ilse, du?" (same place: 394)
(Russ., Germ.: "You are kind! Ilse, you? Ilse, you?")
"Kosti, sak miegu tev. Tev sapnī." (same place: 405)
(Latv.: "Kosti, I tell you in sleep. I will appear to you in a dream."

It is interesting to note that the experimenter did, in fact, see Margarete Petrautzki very clearly in a dream he had the following night.

Another successful "partnership" recording was made on 11th November 1967 by Dr. Wilhelmine C. Hennequin (Switzerland). The first person she tries to contact is her mother and straightway a microphone voice answers:

"Mōte hier." (48r: 419)
(Latv., Germ.: "Mother is here.")
"Mīli papu!" (same place: 430)
(Latv.: "Love Papa!")

The experimenter had left the studio, leaving Dr. Hennequin to continue the recording alone. The voices comment on this:

"Autors sticks." (same place)
(Swed.: "The author goes away.")
"Kosti, labdien!" (same place)
(Latv.: "Kosti, good day!")
"Mierā!" (same place: 431)
(Latv.: "Quiet!")
"Te Zentu, Koste. Autor, tikko ielej." (same place: 432)
(Latv.: "Koste, [bring] Zenta here! The author into which one pours hardly anything.")
"Zenti, pabizo!" (same place)
(Latv.: "Zenti, roam around a bit!")
"Kostja, tu? Osūna." (same place) Osūna, or Asūne; the experimenter's birthplace.
"Mīḷa Anja, Koste."
(Latv.: "Love Anja, Koste.")
"Neue sieht!" (same place: 433)
(Germ.: "One sees a new one.") It is possible that the voice-entities have mistaken Dr. Hennequin for another collaborator, called Anja, who has often taken part in experiments. Realising the error, the voice points out that a "new one" has taken Anja's place.

A voice now addresses itself to Dr. Hennequin:

"Wichtig! Slikta mōte, Hennequin. (same place: 435)
(Germ., Latv.: "Important! A bad mother, Hennequin.")
Dr. Hennequin states that she lost her mother as a young girl and that people had often told her she had had a "bad mother".
"Vai tu salci?" (same place)
(Latv.: "Are you in salt?") The meaning of this sentence remains unexplained.
"Te Hennequin. Te ir Marta." (same place: 437)
(Latv.: "Here is Hennequin. Here is Marta.")
"Redz Konzi. Vai tu zagi zyrgus?" (same place: 438)
(Latg.: "One can see Konzi (Konstantin). Have you stolen horses with him?") The last sentence refers to a German proverb: "Mit ihm kann man Pferde stehlen"; translated: "With him one can steal horses", meaning a person who would never let you down under any circumstances. The voice enquires in fact whether Dr. Hennequin knows of the experimenter's utter reliability.

A different voice replies:
"Kas te? Melkij!" (same place)
(Latv., Russ.: "How does that concern you? Petty!")
"Kosta, tiltu!"
"Tja Kosta nav." (same place: 439)
(Latv.: "Kosta, the bridge!"—"Kosta is not here.")
"Kur Koste?"—"Koste korridorā."—"Koste, māte!"—"Kur Koste?" (same place: 440)
(Latv.: "Where is Koste?"—"Koste is in the corridor".—"Koste, mother!"—"Where is Koste?") The experimenter was, in fact, on the landing outside the studio.
"Raksti tu! Tava mōte, Hennequin." (same place: 443/4)
(Latv.: "[You] write! Your mother, Hennequin.") This statement may mean to urge Dr. Hennequin to write down everything she has heard during the voice-phenomenon experiments.
"Kosta, sveiki!"—"Nebūs Kosti."—"Kosti, tu piedodi?" (same place: 446)
(Latv.: "Greetings, Kosti!"—"It won't be Kosti."—"Kosti, do you forgive?")
"Baba! Kapi." (same place)
(Russ., Latv.: "Woman! Cemetery.") Dr. Hennequin had visited the grave of her mother shortly before this experiment took place.
"Labrītiṇ, lieba Kosta!" (same place: 449)
(Latv., Germ.: "Good morning, [diminutive] dear Kosta!")
"Fahr weg, Dora!" (same place: 451)
(Germ.: "Drive away, Dora!")
"Kostja, yudini!" (same place)
(Latg.: "Kostja, water, please!")

"Tu pa Kosti? Tova Tekle. Raudivi!" (same place: 454)
(Latv.: "Are you looking for Kosti? Your Tekle. Please, Raudive!")

The voice-entities obviously wish to take up contact with the experimenter, even though he is not in the room. The following fragment of a conversation seems to underline this fact:

"Våga, Kosti!"
(Swed.: "Dare, Kosti!")
"Raudive zina."
(Latv.: "Raudive knows it.")
"Tja mõte. Raudive, mõte tja."
(Latg.: "Here is mother. Raudive, mother is here.")
A new voice intervenes:
"Nav Kostes."
(Latv.: "Koste isn't here.")
"Pietiek, Koste."
(Latv.: "It is enough, Koste.") *See Dr. Hennequin's Commentary, page* 381.

On 13th November 1967 *Mr. Felix Scherer*, electrical engineer, measured the oscillations caused by the voices. During the recording-process itself the oscillograph registered nothing, but later, when results were being checked, it reacted unmistakably to the audible existence of the voices on tape.

The recording produced some outstandingly clear voices with particularly interesting texts and features. Here are a few examples of voices measured by the oscillograph:

"Zenta, plurški!" (48r: 475)
(Latv.: "Zenta, talk!")
"Mõte te." (same place)
(Latv.: "Here is mother.")
"Mõte te." (same place)
"Piestoj, Bulduri! Kur Kostja?" (same place)
(Latv.: "Stop, Bulduri! Where is Kostja?") "Bulduri" is a part of the beach near Riga.
"Aglyunā pamesti." (same place: 476)
(Latv.: "We are deserted in Aglyuna.") "Aglyuna" is a sacred place of pilgrimage in Latgale; on certain feast-days in the past, tens of thousands of people used to congregate there, but today these celebrations are forbidden by the Soviet authorities.
"Kur Kerstin mana?" (same place: 477)

(Latv.: "Where is my Kerstin?") "Kerstin" is the name of the wife of the experimenter's deceased friend, Eskil Wikberg.

"Viņš slikti dzird." (same place)
(Latv.: "He is hearing badly.")

"Viņš nav priesteris." (same place)
(Latv.: "He is not a priest.") This remark may refer to the experimenter who in his youth wanted to become a priest.

"Zenta ir spiesta!" (same place: 478)
(Latv.: "Zenta is constrained!") At the time this recording was made Dr. Zenta Maurina felt hemmed in by adverse circumstances.

"Laba latve! Rapa to zina." (same place: 478)
(Latv.: "A good Latvian. Rapa knows that.") "Rapa" was the name of the publisher in Riga who brought out Dr. Zenta Maurina's books. One of the chapters in her book "*Die Eisernen Riegel Zerbrechen*" (*The Iron Bars are Breaking*) is dedicated to him.

"Nu Tekle tja. Pat mōti labo Čaks." (same place)
(Latg.: "Now Tekle is here. Čaks improves even mother.") Referring to the experimenter's sister "Tekle".

"Bender! Bender Schreck!" (same place)
"Winter tiksi tu." (same place)
(Germ., Latv.: "Bender! Bender shock!"—"You will advance during the winter.")

"Zentas vecāki. Mōte te. Mūsu baci. Milo Konci. Zenti gultā." (same place: 480)
(Latv., Ital.- "Zenta's parents. Mother is here. Our kisses. Dear Konci. Zenti in bed.")

"Konstantin, tevis nava." (same place: 482)
(Latv.: "Konstantin, you do not exist.")

"Te Gustavs." (same place)
(Latv.: "Here is Gustav.") Mr. Gustav Inhoffen arrived whilst this recording-session was in progress, and the voice-entities seemed immediately aware of his presence.

"Baloži tala. Konstantin, Olga. Izlaidies parasti man. Vai gulta būtu te?" (same place)
(Latv.: "The doves talking ['Balozi' could also mean the name of a family; plural ending.] Konstantin, Olga. As far as I'm concerned usually left out. Could one have a bed here?") "Olga" had been a close friend of the experimenter.

"Tu tik bizo. Tekle, māsa." (same place: 483)
(Latv.: "You are roaming around. Tekle, sister.")

"Pagani te, Koste. Sigtuna mani pārdod. Pagāns vajā skuteni." (same place: 484)
(Latv.: "Here are heathen, Koste. I am being sold in Sigtuna. The heathen chases with a razor-blade.")

"Tova mōja patīk. Svētri ir glīti." (same place: 487)
(Latv.: "Your house pleases. The shining light is pretty.") The

"shining light" probably refers to the oscillograph. The green light it emitted really did look pretty.

"Kosta, gavariš! Te tu bleib auf! Te Hitlers. Te tu vaina." (same place.)
(Russ., Latv., Germ.: "Kosta, speak! Stay awake here! Here is Hitler. Here you are the guilt [guilty one].")

"Vai tu, Kosta? Raudive mokas. Amigo te. Konstantin, tava gulta." (same place: 490)
(Latv., Spanish: "Is it you, Kosta? Raudive is torturing himself. Here is a friend. Konstantin, your bed.")

"Kostja, dūšu! Kostja, buču." (same place: 491)
(Latv.: "Kostja, courage! Kostja, a kiss.")

"Kudá Klavssons?"—"Kapuze ganz frei. Skepsis ir te vartā." (same place.)
(Russ., Germ., Latv.: "Where to, Klavssons?"—"The hood is entirely free. Scepticism is to be expected here.") Mr. Klavssons, an acquaintance of the experimenter, had been a New York editor. He died a short time before this recording was made.

"Bezdele!"—"Tomer skūpsti." (same place: 492)
(Latv.: "You stinker!"—"You kissed me nevertheless.")

"Konci! Busi kārto! Kost, du wichtig, mīlais. Mēs tūkstoši, Kosti. Te signalsi." (same place: 493)
(Latv., Germ.: "Konci! Create order in the bus! Kost, you are important, dear. We are thousands, Kosti. Here are signals.")

The reference to "signals" seems to be another indication that the voice-entities noticed the oscillograph's light.

"Genug. Jānis tja. Mädchen stāv. Dod man pašportu. Te Sverige's Kostja ty. Te labi." (same place: 494/5)
(Germ., Latv., Swed.: "Enough. Janis here. The girl is standing. Give me the passport. Here you are Sweden's Kostja. All is well here.")

These sentences seem to stress the fact that the voice-entities need some kind of "pass" to be able to contact the experimenter. The voice also emphasises the experimenter's Swedish citizenship.

Mr. Felix Scherer made the following comment, addressed to the voice-entities, at the end of the session:

"I am in Mr. Raudive's room, with Mr. Raudive himself. We have recorded many of your voices and were also able to trace them by means of an oscillograph; this process has made it possible to ascertain that the voices can definitely be measured, however faintly. There is no doubt that the texts spoken exist on tape. I shall now try to photograph the lines traced by the oscillograph in order to bring further proof of the existence of the individual words and sentences we have recorded."

Another "partnership" experiment was made on 26th November 1967, this time in collaboration with the Russian writer *Valerij Tarsis*. (*See his Commentary on page* 296).

Mr. Tarsis begins by calling Boris Pasternak, asking him about his friend, Olga Ivinskaja, and why and under what circumstances had they separated?

The following voices appear on tape:

"Pasternak. Ljubil goračō. Olga starta volna. Startē vēl. Praw byl tot." (51r: 277)
(Russ., Latv.: "Pasternak. I loved passionately. Olga went free. Still goes. That one was right.")

"Eto Pasternak. Te skūla, Kost. Mensch. Ņaņa, tošnotá. Grund hereinstellt. Malus appelé. Radzu Raudive." (same place: 284)
(Latv., Germ., Russ., Lat., French., Latg.: "Here is Pasternak. Here is a school, Kost. Man. Nana, disgust. Reason submitted. Called at a bad time. I can see Raudive.") The meaning of some of these sentences remains obscure. "Grund hereinstellt" ('reason submitted') and "Malus appelé" ("Called at a bad time"), for instance, have been very tentatively translated and defy interpretation.

"Tu guli, Tarsis! Dovoļno! Fausti! Labrītiņ. Tu mašinu zin. Prizivalščik ty." (same place: 286)
(Latv., Russ.: "You are sleeping, Tarsis! Enough! Faustus! Good morning. You know the machine. You lead a sweet life.")
See Valerij Tarsis' commentary.

"Cilvēks Elvirē. Pazīst Raudivi. Tevi sauc pusnakts." (same place: 287)
(Latv.: "Man in Elvire. He knows Raudive. Midnight calls you.")

It may be presumed that "Elvire" is a town or some kind of location. The experimenter does not know the name.

There are other voices referring to the experimenter: Valerij Tarsis addresses the Russian writer Ilja Ehrenburg, reproaching him for having had too much social contact with Kruschev, and a voice answers:

"Kosta, nachal! Kosti, basta! Po ime konsul Koste. Putj. Ty moč. Ich bin te Stimme. Ganz française. Brāli!" (same place: 310/4)

(Russ., Ital., Germ., Latv., French: "Kosti, he is an impertinent fellow! Kosti, enough! In the name of Consul Koste. The way. You are [the] power. I am [only] a voice here. Quite French. Brother!") It is interesting to note how the voice reacts against Tarsis and what he has been saying. Several times the entity calls on the experimenter and stresses that he is but "a voice"—a voice that knows French well. Ehrenburg, in fact, had spent many years of his life in Paris and spoke French fluently.

Now the experimenter speaks, addressing Margarete Petrautzki. A voice answers for her:

"Vāciete! Petrautzkis te." (same place: 317)
(Latv.: "The German! Petrautzkis is here.")
A female voice repeats: "Petrautzkis te."
(Latv.: "Here is Petrautzkis.")
The voice continues:
"Raudiv, vai tu? Koste, Kārlis Skalbe. Raudive, zinotni." (same place: 320)
(Latv.: "Raudiv, is it you? Koste, Karlis Skalbe. Raudiv, science.")

Valerij Tarsis takes over again and calls Jelena Leontiewa, an old friend of the family. He had wanted to get her away from Russia and into Western Europe, but she had suddenly and quite unexpectedly died of cancer. A microphone-voice says:

"Dojaa." (same place: 323)
(Russ.: "My fate.")
Mr. Tarsis: "You wanted to come to us."
"Da!" (same place)
(Russ.: "Yes!")

Between Valerij Tarsis' words one can hear: "Jelena!" (same place) (*for Jelena Leontiewa see page* 298).

"Sveicari, paskandinoj." (same place: 330)
(Latg.: "Swiss maid, let your songs be heard.") Mrs. Tarsis is Swiss by birth. Whilst the recording was taking place she was in the next room, helping Dr. Zenta Maurina to translate a Russian poem into German.

The experimenter addresses his brother Aljosha. In response:

"Ustoba Osūnā. Kur tu, Kosti? Brāls tev nasta. Nasti zvani." (same place: 331)
(Latg.: "The room in Osuna. Where are you, Kosti? The brother is a burden to you. Ring Nasti!")

These sentences are interesting for their reference to Osuna, where Aljosha had lived and died, and for the statement "being a burden". He had lost his estate through nationalisation and the experimenter had given him considerable financial support. "Nasti" is the name of one of Aljosha's daughters.

Zenta Maurina and Mrs. Tarsis come into the studio whilst the recording is still in progress. The experimenter makes a gesture of annoyance at the disturbance, but remains silent. The voices, however, are aware of what is happening:

"Mūsu Zenti! Zapiši, Zenti! Tev liela runzele, Koste." (same place: 332)
(Latv., Russ., Germ.: "Our Zenti! Take notes, Zenti! You have a big frown, Koste.")

Then the voices refer once again to Mr. Tarsis:

"Lena. Te sova. Ja budu razumeja." (same place: 333)
(Latv., Russ.: "Lena. She sleeps here. I shall be more intelligent.") "Lena" is probably Jelena Leontiewa.

The following voices refer to the experimenter:

"Koste, Moskowskij! Bitte, gnädige Frau! Te Petrautzkis. Kostja, pļāpa! Petrautzka tālu. Koste, pastāsti cik tu izdodi. Jauka meitene." (same place: 334)
(Russ., Germ., Latv.: "Koste, the Moscovite! Please, Madame! Here is Petrautzkis. Kostja, nonsense! Petrautzka is absent. Koste, tell us how much you are spending. A nice girl!") This voice comments on the presence of Valerij Tarsis, who came from Moscow. The sentence about expenses is probably connected with Margarete Petrautzki's interest in good housekeeping.

"Vidim Kosti. Tja Kostja. Mēs tev par tālu. Mōte." (same place: 335)
(Russ., Latg.: "We can see Kosti. Here is Kostja. We are too far from you. Mother.")

This "partnership" recording shows a strong link—in the texts spoken and languages used—with the persons addressed.

Valerij Tarsis: commentary on the recording of 26th November 1967

"*51r: 277.* Pasternak answers my question about his separation from Olga Ivinskaja, his secretary and intimate friend. All who knew Pasternak well had tried to guess at the reasons for this break and whose responsibility it had been. Pasternak admits freely that it was Olga who left him, though he still loved her passionately ("ljubil gorjatscho"). The words "still goes" I have interpreted as meaning that his love for Olga still endures. In my opinion the words "prav byl tot" ("that one was right") have the following meaning: The person who maintained that Olga had left Pasternak was right; I, and everyone else who thought that Pasternak had been responsible for the break, wrong. The person named by the voice as "that one" is Ilja Ehrenburg.

284. The statement *"Here is a school"* I understand as Pasternak's way of telling us that when we are in the "beyond" our schooling continues. I remember him telling me once that he thought we might be able to realize truth in its fullest sense only in a life beyond the grave. "Man" I interpret as referring to myself: in his earthly days Pasternak had always maintained that I remained true to myself; *"tošnotá"* (*disgust*) seems to be connected with the last day of his life when, under pressure from his relatives, he wrote a letter of repentance to Kruschev.

286. "*Tu guli, Tarsis*" ("you are sleeping, Tarsis") could mean that Pasternak considers my life to be a dream—as indeed I do myself—blissfully happy as it is after my meeting Hanni, and with the love and respect of so many true friends all over the world. "*Dovol'no*" ("*Enough!*"), Pasternak would frequently exclaim in the middle of a conversation, looking vaguely into the distance as if his thoughts had flown into another world where none could follow. It seems that by repeating this exclamation he wants to impress upon me that I too should delve into the world in which he spent the last eight years of his earthly life, when he worked on his translation of Goethe's *Faust*; he wants to remind me that I should concentrate on the writing of my "Dr. Faustus in Hell", a tragedy on which I am working at the moment. "*Labrītin, tu mašinu zin*" ("*You know the machine*", or, perhaps, "*the mechanics*") I understand to mean: "You know the mechanics of this tragedy, which you yourself have suffered and under which you still suffer, well enough."—"*Prizivalscik ty.*" ("*You lead a sweet life!*"), I feel must be a reproach, for I live a pleasant life, whilst many of my friends and my pupils lead a miserable existence in exile, prison or some mental "clinic".

310/4. Ilja Ehrenburg has called me "*nachal*" (impertinent fellow), because the last time we met I voiced my disapproval at his accepting an invitation to Kruschev's banquet. His face darkened and with considerable annoyance he told me that not everybody could be as courageous as I had been. It is possible that his words "*Ty moč*" ("You are [the] power," or: "You are courageous, strong"), were also referring to me. Ehrenburg had a great love for France and lived there for a considerable period of his life (hence the reference to the "French voice").

323. Jelena Leontiewa was a friend of the family who died suddenly of cancer without even knowing that she suffered from the disease. The word "*dolja*" (fate) was often on her lips and fate had, in fact, dealt harshly with her; her husband, an officer in the Russian navy, was killed in the war and her only child, a son, died of typhus. She had been lonely, expecting nothing but further trials."

On 25th December 1967 *Dr. Zenta Maurina* made an experimental partnership-recording. The following voices appeared on tape:

"Ko Zenta teic? Zentu Mauriņu!" (53g: 250)
(Latv.: "What does Zenta say? Please, Zenta Maurina!")

Zenta Maurina calls for a friend, a vicar named Braren, and says that he probably no longer thinks of her.

"Zenta. Immer, Zenta!" (same place: 259)
(Germ.: "Zenta. Always, Zenta!")
"Maurina negul" (same place: 265)
(Latv.: "Maurina does not sleep.")
"Zenta te." (same place: 268)
(Latv.: "Here is Zenta.")

Zenta Maurina addresses her father and a voice responds with:

"Koste, Zentu! Nigra." (same place: 269) Dr. Maurins had nicknamed his wife "Nigra" because of her black hair, and the children too had often called her by that name.
"Zenti, Margarete." (same place: 273)
"Te Brarens, Zenta." (same place: 276)
(Latv.: "Here is Braren, Zenta.")

"Zenti, Ludwigs tja. Zenta putjom." (same place: 277)
(Latv.: "Zenti, Ludwig is here. Zenta on her way.") "Ludwig" was the name of an old friend of the family, one of Zenta Maurina's teachers, a professor of literature.
"Zentu redzam. Koste, tu tas esi?" (same place: 280)
(Latv.: "We can see Zenta. Koste, is that you?")

Zenta Maurina now addresses Margarete Petrautzki, who had been her secretary. A voice answers immediately:

"Vai Zenta tu? Margareta" (same place: 286)
(Latv.: "Are you Zenta? Margareta.")
"Var gulēt te." (same place: 287)
(Latv.: "Here one can sleep.")
"Koste mūsu." (same place)
(Latv.: "Koste is ours.")

Jānis Ziemelnieks was a Latvian poet whom Zenta Maurina and the experimenter knew well. Zenta asks him whether he and her sister Renate are together now.

"Nē!" (same place: 292)
(Latv.: "No!")
"Koste tuvs." (same place: 298)
(Latv.: "Koste is near.")
"Es pats saprotu." (same place: 299)
(Latv.: "I can understand by myself.")
"Kosti, sveicinati!" (same place)
(Latv.: "Kosti, greetings!")

Zenta Maurina wants to know whether nationalities exist in the "beyond".

"Mēs, Zenta, te. Bitte, es Kosti mīlu. Tu, Koste, te. Es, Tante, te." (same place: 300)
(Latv., Germ.: "We, Zenta, [are] here. Please, I love Kosti. You, Koste, here. I, Aunt, here.")

This voice makes it quite clear that questions are not always answered; here, as in previous examples, the voice-entities seem reluctant to give us any information about conditions of life in the next world. Some voice-statements do indicate, however, that nationalities play a part in the hereafter. Margarete Petrautzki, for instance, is often identified as "the German"; other voice-entities speak of themselves as Latvians, Poles,

Russians, etc., and seem to be very much aware of their nationality.

A short test-recording was made on 1st January 1968 at 40 minutes past midnight. Participants were: Dr. Zenta Maurina, Mr. Gustav Inhoffen, Mrs. Ingeborg Inhoffen, Miss Annemarie Morgenthaler and the experimenter.

The experimenter starts by calling his mother; six times a voice repeats:

"Koste, mōte! Māte, Koste." (53g: 342)
(Latg., Latv.: "Koste, mother! Mother, Koste.")

Zenta Maurina addresses Margarete Petrautzki and in answer the name "Zenta" is repeated three times. Then a voice says:

"Gryuti tevi dabūt." (same place: 348)
(Latg.: "It is difficult to get hold of you.")

Mrs. Inhoffen speaks to her father, whose Christian name was Ulrich. A voice responds:

"Ulrichs te. Kur mōte?" (same place: 350)
(Latv.: "Here is Ulrich. Where is mother?")

Mr. Inhoffen tries to contact President Kennedy and receives as reply:

"Vilks slikti! Kennedy, Kennedy. Koste, te tu?" (same place: 363/4)
(Latv.: "The wolf is evil! Kennedy, Kennedy. Koste, are you here?")

Now the experimenter calls upon Margarete Petrautzki. A woman's voice is heard:

"Lieber Kostja. Te dīki." (same place: 367)
(Germ., Latv.: "Dear Kostja. Here are ponds.")
"Koste, bēgli! Grūti." (same place: 368)
(Latv.: "Koste, refugees! It is hard.")
"Lempi! Tekli!" (same place)
(Latv.: "[You] rascal, [speak to] Tekle!") Tekle apparently feels hurt at having received no New Year's greeting!

Miss Annemarie Morgenthaler contacts her grandmother. Here are some examples of the response:

RESULTS OF PARTNERSHIP EXPERIMENTS

"Papi, hjälpi! Papa muss." (same place: 380)
(Swed., Germ.: "Papa, help! Papa must [help].")

Miss Morgenthaler commented that her grandmother had been widowed young and that she had brought up her five children single-handed.

"Raudivi Kosti. Eiduks te! Tu, Kosta?" (same place: 384)
(Latv.: Raudive Kosti, please! Here is Eiduks. You, Kosta?")

Dr. Eiduks, a Latvian psychotherapist had been a close friend of Dr. Zenta Maurina.

"Kostīte, paņem zyrgu!"—"Jōj pate, prožila." (same place: 385)
(Latg., Russ.: "Kostite, take the horse with you!"—"She rides herself, she has lived her life.")
"Man maizīti. Te tu, Helga." (same place: 386)
(Latv.: "For me, please, the good bread. Here you are, Helga.")

The experimenter comments that in the new year, as in the old, the unseen friends will be here.

"Heute auch." (same place: 389)
(Germ.: "Today also")
"Anna Tolpatsch. Tu mīli." (same place)
(Germ., Latv.: "Anna butterfingers. You love.")
"Tante pate."—"Patin, lūdzu." (same place: 397)
(Latv., Germ.: "Aunt herself." "Godmother, please.")
"Tjav, tjav labi. Zales labas." (same place: 398)
(Latg.: "It is good for you here. The medicine is good.")
"Koste naktī. Tādēļ slikti." (same place)
(Latv.: "Koste in the night. Hence bad.")
"Māt, te nesapūlas." (same place)
(Latv.: "Mother, here one does not over-exert oneself.")

The partnership-recordings mirror the interrelated impressions of statement and counter-statement, question and answer, agreement and opposition, and help us to become aware of a world existing independently of our own, and governed by its own laws; a world which may seem incomprehensible at first, seen from our own limited plane of existence.

Certainly questions arise that cannot be answered immediately; we can only reflect on what we have learned and continue our research, in an effort to broaden our horizons, and enrich our earthly existence by deeper understanding of the realms opening up to us in the 'world of the voices'.

One thing is clear even now: the voice-phenomenon offers the means to break through the confines of a purely physical existence, for it has breached the material barriers surrounding our world. Death is not final, so the voices assure us; it is but a transition to a new state of being, and the impressions we receive from the voice-entities allow us a glimpse of that farther shore to which we all must cross through death. No "eternal bliss" awaits us there, but an intensely active new existence in which we feel and react much as we did on earth. Perhaps the day will dawn when a kind of "telephonic communication" between the two worlds, such as Sir Oliver Lodge envisaged, will become possible. I would like to close the chapter with a thought expressed by this great scientist: that we do not live in order to die; that humanity is still young and our knowledge of the mysteries of the universe still very limited; and that many a century may yet have to pass before mankind will be able to grasp the full meaning of life.

CONCLUSION

The results of experiments recorded in the preceding pages can be regarded as fact. Voices that are audible on tape have been proved to exist, as far as it is possible at present to bring scientific proof of the existence of anything as unique in parapsychological research as the voice-phenomenon.

But apart from the reproduction of actual voice-texts and overall results of experiments, this book raises questions that may lead to irreconcilable differences of opinion in relation to the concept of the unconscious, represented by the theories of Freud and Jung. The hypothesis of the unconscious (or subconscious) as the only possible "antipole" to the conscious, makes interpretation of experiment results difficult if not impossible, for a phenomenon that can be physically (in this case acoustically) observed, cannot be explained in subjective terms. The voice-entities, whose audible utterances on tape can be repeated as often as desired, are a reality and anyone can assure himself of that fact, by objectively conducted listening-in tests. Inductive methods of research, used in our investigations, proceed from an examination of the particular to conclusions about the general, whilst the adherents of the theory of the unconscious proceed from a given hypothesis and try to support it by examples; thus they are in danger of arriving at hopelessly obtuse theories.

My research into the mystery of the voices has been guided by acoustically verifiable manifestations. *Results obtained by my collaborators affirm the existence of the phenomenon*, and unless the mind is immovably fixed on some preconceived theory, we seem to be faced with the inescapable conclusion that the voice-phenomenon confronts us with an autonomously existing world hitherto unknown.

The next phase in our investigation must be a probing into the origin of the phenomenon, and the facts already submitted to the reader should help him to form his own judgement. It is important to bear in mind, however, that errors can arise through the unreliability of human faculties such as the sense of hearing, powers of concentration, and the ability to differentiate; and there is the danger of becoming bogged down in ready-made theories. Fanatical opposition not only obscures objective thinking, it impedes research and dims our own powers of perception. The author has therefore endeavoured to keep an open mind throughout his investigations and to exclude preconceptions of any kind.

The alert mind, confronted with the voice-phenomenon, will have its reservations, and wish to consider questions such as:

1. *The possibility that ordinary human radio-transmissions may act as "voice-sources" when recordings are made via radio.*

   This objection can be met by drawing attention to the characteristic and unchanging features that mark the voice-phenomenon: peculiarities of language and speech, rhythmic enunciation, speed and pitch; above all by pointing out that the entities address the experimenter and his collaborators by name, give hints of post-mortal circumstances, recall memories of life on earth and repeatedly give their own names; in short, that it is possible to recognise the individual personality of a voice-entity and its exchange with us. Furthermore, polyglot sentences are spoken by one and the same voice; microphone as well as radio recordings point to an independent existence of the voice-entities and their relation to us:

"Raudiv skål! Te mieruši!" (Amg: 170) This sentence is composed of Swedish and Latvian words and is spoken by one entity: "Raudiv, cheers! Here are the dead."

Or: "Weg, Raudive, šlipsi! mēs cīnamies! Raudive, tu tōl." (46g: 490/1) This sentence is also spoken by one voice and contains several languages, namely German, Latvian and Latgalian: "Away with the tie, Raudive! We are fighting. Raudive, you are far away."

2. *The origin of the voices—are they a product of the unconscious?*

The hypothesis of the unconscious, evolved by theoretical parapsychology, is a great stumbling block when it comes to an assessment of the origin of the voice-phenomenon. It insists on a division within man between the conscious and the unconscious, the normal and the abnormal, the simple and the complex, and thereby rules out any vision of man as part of the universal laws of relativity[1]. The idea of a division within man has become so embedded in all the theories put forward by parapsychological research that even laymen talk glibly of the "subconscious" or the "unconscious", though the meaning of the term remains quite beyond their grasp. C. G. Jung's terminology would gather all the results of our research under one denominator: a breaching of the conscious by the unconscious; or, differently expressed, an intrusion of the transcendental sphere into the ordinary human sphere, that is to say, into consciousness.

3. *The possibility of projection by the unconscious onto a background of noise from radio transmitters or elsewhere.*

This can be ruled out in view of the objective audibility of the voices on tape. The method of isolating voices and then copying them on to another tape and repeating them until the utterances can be analysed phoneme by phoneme and finally understood as sequences of meaningful words, disposes of the hypothesis of subjective projection.

---

[1] Or relativeness.

4. *The relation of the world of the voice-entities to the world of living man.*

Having considered the foregoing and looked at the empirical evidence of the experiments, we can turn to the alternative theory of relativity. This theory tells us that there is no "thing as such", that anything exists "as such" only in its relation to other things. This means that "man as such" does not exist either. It cannot be said too often: only through its relation with another world can we understand and realise the nature of our own world. If we deny the existence of that other world and thereby divorce it entirely from our own, we shall be caught in the vicious circle of human egocentricity. The subjective psychological hypothesis can be successfully opposed only by the objective hypothesis of relativity, and in seeking to solve the riddle of man, this theory first tries to find the relation that makes possible the existence of man "as such". To understand the meaning of the facts revealed by the voice-phenomenon, man must realise that already, on earth, he is part of the world of the voice-entities; that he carries within himself the ability to contact his friends on earth when he has passed through the transition of death. Awe-inspiring laws of nature form the basis of spiritual powers within ourselves—to which the voice-phenomenon bears witness—ripening through the process of transition from physical to transcendental existence. Death is therefore not the end, but rather a crossing-over into a new beginning, into a new stretch of the eternal river of life. From the results so far obtained through our research, we may surmise that our souls possess powers which, freed by death, prove themselves to be something higher than our earthly manifestation, something of durable and indestructible reality. Perhaps the evidence presented by the voice-phenomenon may be able to re-kindle a sense of the divine and the sacred within man, for the implications of the phenomenon are such as may stir the innermost depths of our soul.

At present it is the mere fact of the existence of the phenomenon and the possibility of proving this existence through manifestations on tape, that is of most importance; from whence it comes is a question that cannot yet be answered with finality. The phenomenon has created an entirely new situation within the realm of parapsychological research, and how we cope with its development will depend entirely on the extent of the response to its discovery.

My own research goes on from day to day, and in the three years since this book was first published in Germany I have amassed much further evidence. My distinguished collaborators in the field of physics and electronics, Professor Schneider, Mr. Rudolph and Mr. Seidl, have continued their own experiments and have perfected new apparatus and new methods of recording, some of which are described in the recent reports they have contributed to this English edition of my original work.

Friends and colleagues, including eminent figures in the world of psychology and parapsychology, philosophy and theology have continued to study the phenomenon and to search after its true significance.

I cannot sufficiently express my gratitude for the help and support of Friedrich Jürgenson, through whom I first learned of the phenomenon; of Dr. Zenta Maurina, who was the first to examine it with me and to draw many important conclusions; of Dr. Naegeli and Dr. Theo Locher, of the Parapsychological Society of Switzerland, and of Mrs. Néné von Muralt, whose outstanding work in the scientific examination of the phenomenon has been of such value and through whom I met Professor Frei. And there are countless others who have devoted much time and patience to the painstaking checking and verification of recordings.

Their work is but a beginning and only if their efforts are recognised by others who can help to extend the research will it be for the ultimate benefit of mankind.

Appendices

I. THE EXPERTS REPORT

1. THEOLOGIANS AND PHILOSOPHERS

The Rev. Prof. Dr. Gebhard Frei of the Mission Society of Bethlehem, a Roman Catholic Priest and President of the International Society of Catholic Parapsychologists, was recognised by his Church as an expert in the fields of depth psychology, parapsychology, anthropology and Hinduism. A Professor of Anthropology and Psychology, he was a prolific writer, esteemed for his scholarly achievements and beloved for personal qualities of sensitivity and compassion. A short time before his death, Professor Frei wrote to Dr. Raudive on 22nd September 1967:

The first questions to exercise my mind in connection with your most valuable experiments were questions concerning the reality of the phenomenon and the technique of registering the voices.

I attentively read the report in the periodical *Die Andere Welt* (*The Other World*). I learned—and this advanced my understanding considerably—closer details from an eye-witness who had been able to study the phenomenon in your presence and I studied the appropriate testimony of this witness,[1] whose every sentence seemed akin to my own thinking. At last I was able to listen to a section of your examples on tape, numbering already, so I am told, 60,000. Despite relatively strong interference I could understand some words and sentences quite clearly and distinctly. Whether it suits me or not, I certainly have no right to doubt the reality of the phenomenon. I realise

---

[1] See page 333, Mrs. N. von Muralt.

the significance of your investigation for the whole field of parapsychological research and I feel obliged to express my gratitude for the great pains you have taken in making the first steps into uncharted land.

Obviously, the question that immediately springs to mind is: who are the originators of these words and small sentences? I have occupied myself with the study of parapsychology for exactly thirty-five years and longer still with the problems arising from the psychology of the subconscious. I am well aware of the "extraordinary potentialities of the unconscious", the tendencies to personalise autonomous complexes, the forming of "secondary personalities", telepathy, clairvoyance, and the telekinetic effects of the "subconscious".

When I now consider that the voices speak in five or six different languages, often several in a single sentence, that the experimenter or his collaborators are often addressed by name, that the voices repeatedly mention their own names and allude to situations in their past earthly lives which are quite unknown to those present, when I think how the voices change in a flash and consider the fact that in your absence too, and even when the room is empty, voices can be heard on the tape when the taperecorder is switched on—then one must ask oneself if a psychologist exists who could produce sufficient scientific data to explain the phenomenon aetiologically as arising from your or any other living person's subconscious mind. If someone points to the mass of electro-magnetic waves used in radio and television, then the fact that your voices answer specific questions and comment on conversations that have just taken place, still remains unexplained. All that I have read and heard forces me to assume that the only hypothesis able to explain the whole range of the phenomenon is that the voices come from transcendental, individual entities.

How these phenomena are produced is still a complete mystery. Should one, for instance, point to the existence of the so-called "direct voice" in séances, a thorough comparison would show that the differences are greater than the similarities.

The Rt. Rev. Mgr. Prof. Dr. Charles Pfleger, Chaplain to the Holy See, is known as one of the great Catholic philosophers and theologians. On 2nd June, 1970, he wrote in *Le Nouvel Alsacien*, to whose Editor, Joseph Lutz, we are indebted for permission to quote:

... A spirit-world? Science, wedded to rationalism, declares simply: there is no such thing; a spirit-world does not exist outside man's imagination. Even parapsychology, youngest branch of science, falls into disrepute as soon as it submits any theory that ascribes super-normal phenomena (such as hauntings) to causes lying outside man himself, that is to "spirits". Yet C. G. Jung, that great exponent of the theory of the "unconscious", felt himself forced in the end to admit that other than purely "subjective" causes might have to be considered in psychic phenomena; but on the whole parapsychology itself rejects the Spiritualistic explanation of the phenomena it investigates, and so it was obvious from the beginning that Konstantin Raudive's discovery of the possibility of contact with the dead via modern technical apparatus would be received with scorn in many quarters ...

... Is it a reality, backed by experience and established by evidence open to all, that the dead live and can communicate with us? The answer to this question is of immense importance in any assessment of (this) book.

It has been established beyond doubt that these mysterious voices (excepting those ranged in group "C") are clearly audible to everyone. Naturally, the question of where they come from immediately springs to mind. In the case of voices recorded through microphone straight on to the tape it is obvious that the tape must contain everything said by persons present at the recording; but if during play-back and after careful checking quite different voices, speaking short, polyglot sentences in a much faster rhythm become audible, where do these voices originate? The answer is that they cannot possibly stem from a source other than from the beings to whom the voices belong and who often give their own names. But what of the so-called "radio-voices"? Would it not be possible for fragments of sound from various radio-transmissions to form this weird multi-lingual "word-salad"? A glance at the chapter "Speech-Content of Recordings" shows how absurd this suggestion is. Besides, the radio set is never tuned to a station, but always to a point between stations. When the tape is played back the voices are heard against a background of interference, not in senseless jabberings, but in short, meaningful sentences. These are checked and re-checked in carefully arranged listening-in tests. The phenomenon therefore cannot be dismissed as some sort of technical freak.

There is another hypothesis, very popular with parapsychologists, namely that of the "unconscious". This is the explanation favoured by Professor Hans Bender. In his opinion the "unconscious" of Dr. Raudive, who apparently possesses strong mediumistic gifts, produces the voices: but Dr. Theo Locher, President of the Swiss Society for Parapsychology, points out that it is impossible to conceive how the unconscious could produce electromagnetic vibrations which, picked up by taperecorder or radio, could be transmuted on tape into human voices; further: that the theory of "secondary personalities" formed by Dr. Raudive's unconscious, who could transmit the voices via the manifold frequencies of radio-beams, is completely without foundation.

Dr. Raudive asserts with some reason that the hypothesis of the unconscious has but one aim, namely to ensure that the "human phenomenon" (Teilhard de Chardin's favourite expression) is never seen in the light of the transcendental, but always explained through man himself. Behind such a theory lies the ever-present preconception that nothing supernormal exists that is the great fallacy of our modern age. After astronomy had tried to fit man into the "enormous anonymity of the heavenly bodies" (Teilhard de Chardin), biology wanted to push him into the animal kingdom and now psychology thinks it best to thrust him, together with his spiritual problems, into the realm of the "unconscious"; and it is doing this, moreover, in an era when the theory of evolution suggests that man presents the final and highest concentration of spiritual forces within matter aimed at by the evolutionary process of the universe. Even the layman must come to this conclusion when he views creation as a whole: each phase of existence within the evolutionary universe becomes the foundation of the next phase. The rotation of bulks of matter round the sun forms the basis of organic life on earth, from which finally man emerges as the embodiment and reflection of spirit—in full awareness of its existence.

Does not such a view of the world make the Raudive-voices plausible? It is a view shared not only by theologians and philosophers, but also by many scientists. The physicist Wernher von Braun, famous for his work in space-exploration, must surely be ranked among the exponents of exact science; yet he declares in an interview with the American journal *Christian Life* that science has established as fact that nothing in nature is ever lost, that there is no obliteration, only transformation; that if God uses this principle in respect of even the minutest particle of matter in the universe, does it not stand to reason that he would apply the same principle when it came to the crown of his creation, the soul of man? Wernher von Braun asserts that this is his firm belief.

For some years now, we have been able to read reports in parapsychological literature about information received through mediums, indicating that the inhabitants of the "beyond" are working on ways and means to contact humanity on earth. This idea is so alien to generally accepted views, that the mention of such an absurdity raises only a pitying smile; but anybody taking the trouble to study Dr. Raudive's experiments will soon cease to mock. Dr. Hans Naegeli, President of the Parapsychological Society of Switzerland, accepts Raudive's "spirit-beings" hypothesis as the correct one. He sees in the strange and characteristic features of the voice-phenomenon no bar to its credibility, but rather a confirmation of its reality. Statements made by voice-entities seem to indicate that Konstantin Raudive does possess strong mediumistic powers of attraction, but they also point to the fact that these entities possess a "spirit-body" (scholastic teaching has always maintained that the soul of man is clad in a "spiritual body" and that man, even in the beyond, is never pure spirit) and that they have been able to devise a method of using our electro-magnetic vibrations; this technique, not being fully developed as yet, presents its difficulties and forces the voice-entities to speak in that extraordinary polyglot telegram-style.

Only the most narrow-minded rationalism would want to banish all mystery from our lives. The reality of the universe in all its aspects consists of a visible and an invisible realm and we have a long way to go yet, before we can grasp the implications of the physical, visible part alone.

Theology should not therefore create too many difficulties for Dr. Raudive's discovery, for dogma is being looked at with fresh eyes to-day, and quite fundamental articles of faith are under review, so that it is surely reasonable to accept for consideration this new evidence concerned with the nature of life hereafter. . . . upon which, one must not forget, Christian theology is very vague . . .

Dr. Zenta Maurina, Writer and Doctor of Philosophy, is the leading authority on the works of Dostoevsky, and official adviser on Slav and Baltic languages. She was the first to examine the phenomenon with the author, and has participated in many experiments, drawing important conclusions. She writes:

Between July 1965 and June 1967 I was present at hundreds of Konstantin Raudive's experiments and have heard approximately one thousand voices. At times I was able to understand speech contents—some were only isolated words or exclamations—before the experimenter himself had grasped them.

Though I am blessed with a very acute sense of hearing I found it difficult at first to locate the voices. All I heard was a rushing sound and only rarely did I manage to discern consecutive words against its background. Neither a musical, nor a physically sound, ear is enough in itself to hear the voices. It is rather like listening to an opera: if one is not accustomed to hearing words sung to orchestral accompaniment, one tends to hear nothing but a succession of meaningless vowels and consonants. Long distance calls over the telephone can also have their difficulties, if the ear is not used to voices coming from afar and it is especially so if foreign languages are involved.

Good hearing and patience are the first requisites, but concentration, the right psychological approach, and physical and mental alertness are equally important; if you are tired or unable to give your whole attention to what you are hearing, the voices will melt away like snowflakes and elude the grasp of your mind. After roughly thirty sessions, when I had learned the art of listening-in, I began to recognise the voices by their cadence, pitch and rhythm. These voices from "beyond"—if we may refer to them thus—differ from ordinary voices one hears on the radio; they have a certain hoarseness and sound as if the person speaking was suffering from laryngitis, though every now and then you can get a perfectly clear-sounding voice. The voice-entities' speech is also much softer and much more rapid than that of ordinary human beings and has its own strange timbre.

The unusual quality of the language, as well as the texts spoken, rule out the idea that the voices may be no more than freak sounds emitted by radio-transmitting-stations. At first one has the impression that these voices do not know how to speak properly. They sound as if they were stumbling through alien languages they have not mastered; but after one has detected and understood perhaps one hundred voices, one begins to realise that this odd way of speaking follows certain rules and has certain recurring characteristic features that cannot possibly be repeated by mere coincidence.

1. Sentences are rarely composed in a single language. Predominant is the language the experimenting person knows best, usually his or her mother-tongue; when Konstantin Raudive experiments, the language is mainly Latvian; when it is Friedrich Jürgenson, Swedish or Italian; with Valerij Tarsis, the Russian writer, it is Russian.

2. None of the languages spoken are used in the grammatically and philologically correct manner. Sometimes German endings are given to Latvian words and vice-versa. Swedish words become "Germanised" or "Russianised".

3. The language is curt and concise; articles, prepositions and auxiliary verbs are usually left out. Word-economy is rigorous; fragmented sentences, neologisms and shortened words are the rule.

Let us illustrate these traits in a few examples:

"Vi dice lobu nakti!" (Amg: 105) "We say good night!"

Nobody on earth would form a sentence in such an odd language-mixture: "Vi": Swedish; "dice": Spanish; "lobu nakti": Latvian; and the last two words are not even straightforward Latvian, but are spoken in Latgalian, the dialect of the experimenter's home-province.

"Raudiv, skål! Te mirušie!" (same place: 170/3) "Raudiv, cheers! Here (the) dead!"

Again Latvian and Swedish: "skål": Swedish; "te miruiše": Latvian. I spent twenty years of my life in Sweden, but I never met a Swede who would mix Latvian words into his language: nor would any Latvian form such a sentence.

A neologism:

"Pa 'raidu' sakām!" (Amg: 121) "We speak through a transmitting-station."; but "transmitting-station" in Latvian would be "raid-stacija"; the long, hyphenated word has been transformed into a new one, rigorously shortened.

"Pierādi milosti prēti fattigiem!" (47g: 478)

Another language-mixture; a coherent sentence expressing an ethical maxim: "Show charity towards the poor." The first word is correct Latvian; the second, Russian with a Latvian feminine ending attached; the word "prēti" (show) should be in the Latvian accusative; the Swedish adjective "fattig" (poor) has been given the correct Latvian dative-plural, masculine ending.

"Leib—geistiga Bewiesa." (49g: 482) (German: "(The) body —proof of the spirit.", or, "the spiritual proof". Here the German adjective, which should be "geistige" (spiritual), has been given a Latvian (feminine) ending: "a". The German noun "Beweis" (proof) becomes "Bewiesa" and also acquires the Latvian ending for feminine nouns, "a".

The Latvian of the voices differs radically from that spoken by Konstantin Raudive. I know his style and vocabulary very well indeed, as I translated many of his books from Latvian into German.

A voice says:

"Tava stundis Uppsalā." "Your hour is in Uppsala." Correctly spoken Latvian would be: "Tava stunda Uppsalā." The noun "stunda" (hour) never takes the ending "is".

"Paliec uzticīgs mūsu sachai!" "Remain faithful to our task!" The first three words are Latvian, the fourth German: "Sache" (task or matter); it has been given the Latvian dative ending: "ai". I would also like to point out that German words adopted into the Latvian language are given the ending "a" instead of their original "e". If the German noun "Sache" had been taken into Latvian usage (which is not the case) it would be pronounced "Sacha". Latvian nouns ending in "a" have their ending altered to "ai" in the dative. This example, and many others one could quote from the voice-phenomenon tapes, show that the voice-entities follow certain philological rules of their own.

"Zenti, tavi Verwandti." "Zenti, your relatives." Here, as in many cases, I am personally addressed; on this occasion a pet-name, used only by my closest relatives and friends, is chosen. The sentence, to be correct Latvian, should run: "Zenti, tavi radnieki." The German word "Verwandten" (relatives) has replaced the Latvian "radnieki". The ending "i" is, however, the correct Latvian ending for all masculine nouns.

There seems to be a method in the voices' apparently haphazard language-features. For instance:

"Darf ich übergehen?" German: "May I cross over?"—"Was Du wünschi?", Germ.: "What is it you wish?"—"Tur Kostja.", Latvian: "There [is] Kostja." (45g: 433).

Here we have a coherent conversation between voices: two questions, one answer. The first question is put in grammatically correct German. In the second one the German verb "wünschen" (to wish) has its ending, which in the second person singular, should be "wünsch*est*", turned into a Latvian one, namely: "i". The third sentence, the answer, comes in Latvian.

The following sentence is remarkable for its content, as well as its peculiar phrasing:

"Konstantin, tava māte! Furchtbare, furchtbare Kräfte mot dej, turies bei mej, deine Mutter." (26r: 031/2) "Konstantin, your mother! Terrible, terrible forces against you, cling to me, your mother." Grammatically there is nothing wrong with this sentence; but German, Latvian and Swedish words intermingle. The first part is in Latvian; then follow three German words; "mot dej" is Swedish, and the rest a mixture of Latvian, Swedish and German.

"Hast Du, Kosti, Über-Kosti?" (44r: 388) "Have you, Kosti, over-Kosti?"; meaning: "Have you, Kosti, a relationship to your 'over-self'?" This sentence is spoken in correct German and is strikingly succinct in expressing its message: it tries to tell the experimenter (addressed by his pet-name) that as long as he is aware of his earthly self alone, he remains a three-dimensional being; that only by developing his "over-self" will he become conscious of his higher potentialities.

I have never, in any known language, come across such a word-formation: the prefix "over" attached to a person's Christian-name, expressing a transcendental meaning.

Man has an irresistible urge to acquire higher knowledge and to find some reliable means of contacting the "beyond". The super-normal is shrouded in mystery; but it becomes "normal" the moment its true nature is realised.

Throughout the ages the races and peoples of the earth have believed in a spiritual life beyond the grave. Communication with the dead is the most important problem the scientists and parapsychologists will have to solve.

The reality of the voice-phenomenon is a step forward, irrespective of whether it is produced by the "unconscious" of the experimenter, or whether the "voices" are those of the dead.

The fact that something lying beyond the physical senses of man exists, is recognised today not only by philosophers and parapsychologists, but also by physicists. The voice-phenomenon allows man a glimpse into a supranatural world.

If Konstantin Raudive's experiments should prove to be scientifically unassailable, then he will have breached the wall that divides us from the "beyond". Should the "voices" really come from the dead, empirical evidence of individual survival after death will have been produced at last. The world needs some great global event to kindle anew the flame of humanity, and the empirical proof of man's immortality could well be such an event.

The Rev. Voldemars A. Rolle, Lutheran Pastor of the Latvian Church at Willimantic, Conn., U.S.A., and a physicist, was the first to recognise the significance of the phenomenon from a religious point of view; he writes to the author:

On the tapes I received from you, the audibility of the voices is good. It seems to me that only people with defective hearing or no linguistic background would be unable to hear and understand the recordings.

I am happy to know of the existence of this phenomenon. It makes no difference how many voices you have recorded; the most important thing is the fact itself—it opens the door to further research. Of course, it is very intriguing to try to explain this parapsychological phenomenon by means of modern physics, but it will not be an easy task. It would be necessary to revise and even change several concepts which are now accepted as axioms. For the present, the research into the phenomenon should be limited to gathering data to prove its reality.

It may be worthwhile to try an experiment with video tape similar to that with audio tape; perhaps both simultaneously. I do not see any reason why an experiment with video tape should be less successful than one with audio tape.

To me as a theologian, the phenomenon is of special interest. Very similar phenomena have been observed by people of different nationalities in our time as well as in the past. In Holy Scriptures such events are recorded as cases of clairaudience, or "visions". If the voices recorded on magnetic tape exist, the truth of what the Scriptures tell us in this respect may be more readily accepted.

The theory that the electronic circuit may be influenced by electromagnetic impulses associated with our "unconscious" seems very doubtful to me. It is surprising that by listening to the voices it is possible to identify persons to whom the voices may belong.

Concerning the phenomenon itself, it may be that we are confronted here with a specific type of energy not known to modern physics. I would be inclined to call this energy "the life-energy of progressive intelligence". Very superficially, it may be illustrated as follows:

Examining a proton or an electron, we find that a certain amount of matter is associated with electric energy. When a proton changes into a neutron in the process of nuclear reaction, a release of energy occurs. Likewise, an electron releases energy in the form of photons when an electron jumps from a higher energy-level to a lower one. It is most important to note that the energy released is still associated with some form of matter, which may be termed "relative" matter, and that therefore it is still confined in the inertia system of our universe, where the speed of light is constant.

It is my opinion that something similar happens when a man dies. The difference between a living man and a dead one is this: as long as a man lives his body (matter) is associated with the life-energy of progressive intelligence. This is no longer the case with the body of a dead man. The animal's body is associated with a similar energy, but the animal differs from the human being, because the animal does not possess a progressive intelligence: its intelligence stays at the same level all the time and does not show progressive growth. The progressive growth of human intelligence shows itself in a variety of fields: for instance, in art, philosophy, science, technology, etc. The "life-energy" of the world, as yet unexplored by science, seems to be as manifold in its expressions as, for example, energy produced in the realm of electromagnetic waves.

At the time of death the life-energy of progressive intelligence becomes separated from our body (matter) and continues its existence in the inertia system of pure energy, where energy is no longer associated with matter. The inertia system of pure energy exists independently from the forces that govern our seven (or more) inertia systems, to which matter and the energy associated with matter, are confined. The seven inertia systems are:

1. The earth's rotation round its axis.
2. The rotation of the earth round the sun.
3. The movement of the solar system in our galaxy.
4. The rotation of our galaxy round its axis.
5. The movement of our galaxy in the universe.
6. The rotation of our universe round its axis.
7. The speed of our universe.

As long as energy is associated with matter of any kind, it stays within the inertia system of our universe, where speed of light is constant. This system, to which all matter is confined, is governed by the time and space formula of the law of relativity: $\sqrt{1-(V/C)^2}$ (square root of one minus V over C squared).

When acceleration reaches the speed of light or more, the energy breaks away from matter and continues its existence in the inertia system of "pure energy" (characterised by imaginary values, expressed in the formula: square root of minus one); this inertia system is as real (in its own dimension) as is the inertia system of our universe, where the speed of light is constant. In my opinion the speed of light is only a threshold value, or escape velocity of pure energy; a threshold of the inertia system of our universe, in which matter is confined; this system governs time and space, as well as the law of gravity and therefore everything moves in curved lines. As soon as this threshold is overcome, we are in the inertia system of "pure energy", in which matter is no longer present and which lies outside time, space and the law of gravity. The direction of pure energy is therefore a straight line which is also the locus of imaginary values. As soon as energy is decelerated to the speed of light, it is captured by matter and therefore becomes confined to our universe and our inertia system.

To tie the life-energy of progressive intelligence to our inertia system, it is necessary to associate it with some form of (relative) matter, as happens in the case of photons or electromagnetic waves. This is only possible if the energy can be decelerated to the speed of light or below. "Relative" matter is, in fact, mentioned in the Gospels as the "glorified" or "spiritual" body (1. Cor. 15,44).

It seems to me that in your experiments the free life energies of progressive intelligence are successfully decelerated to below the speed of light, bringing them for a limited period of time into our inertia system.

I am convinced that the phenomenon you describe is as real as our own existence. Unfortunately, our contemporary science pays no attention to the possibility that a state of pure energy may exist without being associated with matter of any kind. In my opinion it is of the greatest importance to look at the voice-phenomenon from every possible angle and I very much regret that at present my limited time does not permit me to investigate these interesting manifestations more closely.

The Rev. Fr. Leo Schmid, R.C. priest of Oeschgen, Switzerland, reports:

Dr. Konstantin Raudive paid a visit to Oeschgen, Switzerland, on 7th October 1969, with his secretary, Miss A.

Morgenthaler, to test the play-ins I had conducted myself during the summer with microphone and diode.

We sat down at 8.45 p.m. to a play-in, using a brand-new tape-recorder I had provided; first we used the microphone, then the intermediate frequency in the medium waveband of the radio, and finally the diode. All three methods of reception gave perfectly comprehensible voice reception, the intermediate frequency being exceptionally rewarding. Much that these voices had to say was understood by Dr. Raudive, Miss Morgenthaler and myself in the same terms.

One man's voice, in particular, announced itself with the word: "Lombardite." After listening with no difficulty to the text and after some searching for an interpretation, I hit upon the collaboration I had undertaken in P. Riccardo Lombardi's "Opera promotrice per un mondo migliore". This voice appeared to be associating me with the work of P. Lombardi. The voice was unmistakably that of Monsignor Josef Meier, who had died in 1960 and to whom I had asked to speak before the play-in begun. I had often discussed the Lombardi broadcast with him, and he was not at all well-disposed towards Lombardi. Dr. Sargenti, of Verdabbio, who was present, also recognised this voice as that of Monsignor Meier. Dr. Raudive knew nothing of all this and was very surprised when I informed him of the chain of events that had produced it.

Just as Dr. Raudive was about to interrupt the play-in to check the intermediate frequency, we heard a man's voice call out: "Warte du!" ("Wait a minute.") It was obvious that the speaker was aware of Dr. Raudive's intention. After this interruption, the voice said: "Paldis." ("Thank you.")

I was particularly struck by the voices referring several times to the room in which the play-in was being carried out. The tobacco being smoked was mentioned, and the wooden chair that was standing near the receiving apparatus.

We heard more than seventy voices in this play-in lasting about ten minutes.

We continued our experiments on 8th October, in Dr. Sargenti's house in Verdabbio, using the same brand-new tape-recorder. (Dr. U. Sargenti, Dr. Phil. Dipl., is a psychologist who occupies the post of Professor of Psychology at Rome.) Unfortunately we had only a microphone at our disposal on this occasion. Although the whispering voices were markedly less clear, they referred unequivocally to Dr. Sargenti and his mother and were heard with equal clarity by all five participants at the play-in (in addition to Dr. Sargenti and his mother).

I do not wish to engage in controversy over the interpretation of this strange phenomenon of voices, but I am personally in no doubt that this is no manifestation of the experimenter's subconscious, nor is it a radio trick; it is evidently the attempt of people in the "hereafter" to make contact with us.

2. PARAPSYCHOLOGISTS AND PSYCHOLOGISTS

Report by Dr. Theo Locher, Doctor of Philosophy, President of the Society for Parapsychology, Switzerland, and publisher of the *Bulletin for Parapsychology*, Biel, Switzerland.

I confirm that I examined the voice-phenomenon on 30th June 1967 in Biel, and on 10th and 11th November 1968 in Bad Krozingen, and that I am convinced of its authenticity. A few tape-sections were easy to understand and I could grasp the words spoken, but most of the voices were too soft and indistinct for my unpracticed ear. They were, however, undoubtedly human voices, though many of them could certainly be interpreted in different ways, even by people practiced in the art of "listening-in".

The recording and analysing of thousands of voices in the space of two and a half years must have presented a tremendous task, demanding great perseverance and deep personal involvement. I would like to express my admiration for Konstantin Raudive's achievement and in particular for his method of testing the voices by re-recording them on to different tapes.

Conversations I had with two electrical engineers from the Eidg. Techn. Hochschule Zürich (the National College of Technology, Zürich) confirmed the impossibility of explaining this phenomenon on a technological basis, leaving aside any circumstances of deliberate deception. The following are conceivable electromagnetic influences which may be playing a part:

1. Low frequency waves received on the recording head or the amplifier of the tape-recorder, and

2. Low frequency waves on the L.F. stage of the radio amplifier ("microphony", practically found on valve sets only).

1 and 2 demand great transmitter power or else short distances between aerial and receiver.

3. High frequency waves on the radio input amplifier with, in certain circumstances, extremely small power.

4. It is technically feasible that H.F. waves are also acting directly on the L.F. amplifiers of the tape-recorder and radio, and this would produce only weak voices.

These four influences are only possible from a transmitter using an aerial. Neither an imperfect erasure of a used tape nor a static print-through on a recorded tape can account for the phenomenon. The electrical engineers referred to above make the following suggestions:

(*a*) All oscillations present in the room during recording, especially of low frequency waves, should be investigated.

(*b*) Recordings should be made on several tape-recorders at once.

(*c*) Recordings should also be made in a Faraday cage, both with and without a technician.

(*d*) Voices recorded on an oscillograph should be photographed and analysed.

I would like to comment briefly on other attempted explanations:

1. *The hypothesis of hallucination,* or collective hallucination, is quite untenable for audible manifestations that can be copied onto different tapes.

2. *The unconscious:* it is hardly feasible to imagine that the unconscious could produce electromagnetic waves, which, picked up by radio or tape-recorder, would then turn into human voices pieced together from isolated words. The theory that so-called "secondary personalities", formed by Dr. Raudive's unconscious, could transmit the voices via the manifold frequencies of radio-waves, is completely without foundation. Nevertheless, there are certain aspects of the phenomenon that give food for thought:

(*a*) The polyglot character of the speech-content roughly corresponds to the experimenter's linguistic knowledge.

(*b*) The experimenter's habit of occasionally altering or

confusing words when speaking German seems to be repeated in the language of the voices.

(c) Just as our unconscious often expresses itself in symbols (as in dreams) so do the voices frequently use symbolism in many of their utterances.

These three aspects seem to indicate that the voices have a certain unexplained connection with the experimenter's unconscious; they do not, however, give credence to the supposition that forces in Dr. Raudive's unconscious could piece together their own words, with more or less significance, and then transmit them in the shape of radio-waves to radio-set and tape-recorder.

3. *Mischievous spirits* (elementals): considerations (a), (b) and (c) could give rise to the hypothesis that so-called "elementals" (entities of an ethically base order and of low intelligence, but telepathically gifted), could read the experimenter's thoughts and then tap his memory in order to piece together coherent, polyglot messages or answers to questions. Most of the contents of messages seem to me to be of a very poor standard; they try to match a question, but are not in keeping with the personality of the deceased person purported to be speaking. This still leaves unanswered the question of how these entities would transmit their messages via radio.

The thesis of "elementals" or mischievous spirits is supported in many instances by messages received through trance or automatic writing-mediums. In these cases such entities seem at times able to masquerade as deceased persons and often imitate voices and mannerisms. They are particularly fond of impersonating famous people such as Goethe, Churchill, Napoleon, etc., and this certainly seems to be the case with some of the "voices". It strikes one as odd when well-known men or women express themselves in words of a language they did not know in life. The language used most frequently is Latvian, the experimenter's mother-tongue. Imitation of a dead person's voice could be achieved through telepathic tapping, as human memory also contains the memory of sound; it may even be possible for elementals to tap psychic remnants (so-called "memory complexes") of the deceased.

4. *Deceased persons:* The supposition that the voices are those of the deceased themselves must be seriously considered.

Manifesting voices often refer to conversations in progress and answer questions.

Just as the dead seem to be able to master the technique of the "direct voice" when a trance-medium is present, apparently through a "voice-box" built from matter of a finer substance (ectoplasm), so the voices may be able to construct transmitting-devices fashioned out of this substance. We can only rely in this matter on statements received through trance-mediums and are therefore still completely in the dark as to what really happens. One is, of course, able to deduce a great deal from Dr. Raudive's experiments as well as from one's own studies and I would like to make some suggestions which may prove helpful in future research:

(a) Some experiments should take place in the presence of a clairvoyant medium, and experiments in automatic writing and typtology ("spirit-rapping") should be undertaken at the same time.

(b) Experiments made by other reliable researchers, and the scientific results obtained, should also be published.

(c) A statistical assessment of a comparison of voice-analyses made by various experienced examiners who have interpreted the same tape independently of each other, could be of great value. The assessment would have to be made by a neutral body.

I have come to the conclusion that this phenomenon is of tremendous importance to our conception of the world and of mankind, in whatever way it may be interpreted. In future a much greater number of researchers at universities should engage in concentrated study of all its various aspects.

Let us hope that this book will receive its deserved acknowledgement in the scientific world.

I would like to thank Konstantin Raudive once again for introducing me with such wholehearted enthusiasm to this fascinating phenomenon and to his own dedicated research into its mysteries.

APPENDICES

Report by Dr. Hans Naegeli, Psychiatrist and President of the Society for Parapsychology, Switzerland.

The investigation undertaken by Konstantin Raudive presents parapsychology with the following problems:

Apart from intentionally spoken words recorded on tape, additional words and texts that are inaudible to anyone present, become audible when the tape is being played back and listening-in tests are conducted; of what nature and origin are these speech-manifestations?

First of all a basic question: is this phenomenon no more than an illusion? Are the texts heard by the experimenter perhaps not of a parapsychological nature, but merely words and sentence-fragments, inaudible to the human ear, that have issued from various radio-stations and are later made audible on tape by the tape-recorder's amplifier? This is a question that should be answered by a physicist with special knowledge in this field.

Further: are the acoustic manifestations interpreted by Dr. Raudive definite word-formations, or do they correspond to an unconscious auto-suggestion of the experimenter, Raudive, and later of the examiner, who projects a text suggested by the experimenter into the acoustic manifestations on tape?

Clarification of this question could be obtained at an institute of physical science through recordings of the sound-vibrations, which then would have to be deciphered and interpreted in letters. As far as I know such investigations and graphic interpretations are difficult to make; but if, in just one instance, the name "Raudive" which appears on innumerable occasions, could be verified acoustically, then the answer to the first basic question would be given in favour of the author's assertion of a paranormal phenomenon. The name "Raudive" is so rare that it could not be presumed to have issued from some radio-transmitter inaudible to us at that precise moment.

I would also like to stress the fact that the manifesting texts so often fit into, or in some way relate to, words spoken by participants at the time of recording, that such a massing of coincidence would be impossible, quite apart from the fact that modern psychology—rightly to my mind—no longer admits coincidence.

There remains the concept of "synchronisation", a theory introduced into parapsychology by C. G. Jung. It assumes non-causal but meaningful and related events taking place at one and the same time.

I do not think that the theory of "synchronisation" should be considered as an explanation for the phenomenon in question, as it does not occur in isolated instances, but is caused by the experimenter's aim to show that immaterial psychic forces can manifest as physical (acoustic) reality.

If none of the mundane physical theories suffice to explain the phenomenon, the parapsychologist is left with two further possibilities:

First, the animistic hypothesis: parapsychologists who tend to accept this theory ("animists") presume that poltergeist-phenomena or phenomena at Spiritualist séances, such as materialisations and spirit messages, are part of the psyche (anima) of the medium or of the people participating in the séance. These psychic emanations can take shape and impress themselves on our sense-organs, our eyes, ears, and even our sense of touch; but this only happens when the medium has fallen into trance—that is, into the unconscious—and the participants are in a state of emotional expectancy.

This phenomenon remains largely unexplained, but that does not mean that we should reject it as lying entirely outside the bounds of possibility. Poltergeist-phenomena are so numerous and so well attested by reliable witnesses, that they have to be accepted as empirically proved manifestations.

Anyone familiar with poltergeist-phenomena will admit that there is a parallel between the poltergeist and the Raudive voice-manifestations. We have every reason to believe that the "agents" producing or helping to produce poltergeist-phenomena, are always persons under some kind of strong emotional tension, either consciously or unconsciously.

This is doubtless also the case in the Raudive-phenomenon. Dr. Raudive is a well-known and successful author who, nevertheless, for the last two years[1] has dedicated himself entirely to research into the voice-phenomenon; he has obviously made great sacrifices in order to be able to pursue what he now sees

---

[1] As at the date of writing.

as his life's main task: the scientific verification of the phenomenon. As a scientist he may leave all possible hypotheses for an explanation of the manifestations open to discussion, but it seems to me that his personal opinion has crystallised round the Spiritualist theory, which assumes that the voices manifesting on tape emanate from transcendental space. Should it become possible to substantiate this assumption scientifically, it would be the first empirical evidence arrived at by experiments, of the existence and the activity of transcendental intelligences; no doubt a tremendously exciting prospect for any man born into our modern world. And from this deep emotional involvement springs the psychic energy that helps the spiritual content (the voices) to manifest physically, albeit by paraphysical means. This would be the hypothesis of an "animistically" orientated parapsychologist. It is a theory that could account for the fact that only words that are known to the experimenter manifest on tape, with very few exceptions.

The whole phenomenon would be fascinating enough, even if the "animistic" interpretation were to be proved correct, for it would be evidence, through experiment, of a purely mental process taking shape in physical (acoustic) form; in other words, of psychic forces influencing matter.

Animistic theories may be correct for some parapsychological phenomena, but they can hardly be a satisfactory explanation for hauntings tied to a particular locality. C. G. Jung finally discarded the animistic hypothesis for such hauntings and accepted the Spiritualist theory. I am of the same opinion and suggest that this view also should be taken into account in the Raudive experiments. We know nothing of transcendental energies and therefore it is quite permissible to ask whether unknown difficulties might not exist which exert an inhibiting influence, so that only the simplest utterances are able to "get through". It is possible to imagine that in the case of extremely powerful mediums (Carlo Mirabelli, for instance), where matters of great complexity are "coming through", the threshold between transcendental energy and physical matter is substantially lowered. In Konstantin Raudive's case the possibility of communications from what he calls "transmitting-stations in the beyond" getting through, would only exist if conditions were made easier through his own emotional (mediumistic) involvement.

As in most parapsychological events, there is probably a merging of the involved person's psychic forces with those of transcendental beings; the spirit-entities must—just as we, the living—possess a "spirit body"; an idea firmly entrenched in all the ancient philosophies of the East. Why then should an interaction not be possible?

It is too early to come to a final decision, but Dr. Raudive's work opens the way to realisations which today are mainly material for discussion, but tomorrow will lead to scientific problems and new experimental tasks.

Report by Mrs. Katharina Nager, Parapsychologist and Secretary of the Swiss Parapsycological Society.

Excerpt from a letter to the experimenter:

In my report of the 18th July 1966 I described the observations made by the participants in voice-phenomenon experiments made at our house, 127 Hönggerstrasse, Zürich. All who took part on that occasion, as well as those who had been present at experiments conducted at your home in Bad Krozingen, were of one mind. They all accepted that some kind of mediumistic power within you was a precondition for the manifestation of the voices—which we had heard and understood perfectly well—in other words, the hypothesis of the unconscious. The hypothesis of relativity, namely the possibility of relation to a world beyond, was taken into consideration by nearly all the participants, and in justice to the phenomena witnessed we are keeping an open mind on all these issues.

To those of us who have had previous opportunities of taking part in experiments—Dr. Hans Naegeli, psychiatrist, Mrs. G. Fürst, careers-adviser, Mrs. Nager, librarian of the Society for Parapsychology, Switzerland, Dr. R. Fatzer, dentist and Mr. J. Meier, physicist—the audibility and clarity of the "voices" seemed outstanding and most impressive. These have developed in an astonishing degree between February/March

1966, when we first took part in experiments, and 15th April 1967. We found the way in which the voices adapted what they said to what had been discussed by us beforehand, particularly remarkable.

5th May 1967

Report by Mr. Friedrich Jürgenson (Mölnbo, Sweden).

During repeated visits to Konstantin Raudive's studio in Bad Krozingen I listened to approximately 300 voices. I could understand the voices clearly and was able to verify and confirm them without assistance.

After eight years of experience in this field of research I found it very rewarding to recognise the same phenomenon I had investigated, showing the same characteristic, polyglot traits. Dr. Raudive's recordings, which I examined with great care, confirm in an entirely objective manner the unique contact that has been established with a hitherto unknown plane of existence which, perhaps, we may call the "beyond" or the "higher life-dimension".

The fact that Dr. Raudive's questions receive clear and unequivocal answers from the voice-entities—as if a telephone link had been established—is enough in itself to indicate that a direct contact exists. I found that some of the male and female voices which appear frequently in my own recordings manifested also in Dr. Raudive's experiments.

Audibility of voices varied just as much as in my attempts. Some texts came over with perfect clarity ("A" voices), some were of good audibility ("B" voices) and some were barely audible ("C" voices); according to atmospheric conditions the voices had been able to manifest clearly or less clearly.

There can be no doubt whatsoever that the phenomenon manifesting in Dr. Raudive's experiments is the same that manifests in my own. The methods used are different, but this is really a great advantage, for it seems that the same phenomenon appears when different techniques are applied in experiments. The main goal must be to obtain objective proof and verification of the existence of the voice-phenomenon, and it is already quite obvious that given the necessary time, much more satisfactory and technically efficient results can be achieved. We must not forget that we are dealing with an entirely new contact, a "bridge" in the first stages of construction, and that it will have to be built up with the greatest care, attention and understanding from our side, as well as from the "other side".

To summarise my impressions of the voice-phenomenon:

It would be precipitate to try to classify a phenomenon that is still in the process of development and which may, in the future, have the most far-reaching repercussions. There are, however, certain observations that I have been able to make during my eight years of experience; these observations have led me to accept the following facts:

1. The voices speak to us. They are either radiated directly via microphone, or become audible with the help of some kind of electromagnetic "radar" via the transmitting-frequencies of radio. In both cases they finally manifest on tape with the help of a tape-recorder.

2. Both microphone and radio-recordings transmit personal messages from dead relatives, friends, or persons unknown; the language used is kept in typical polyglot idiom. The voices describe themselves as "the dead", but always stress most emphatically that they are very much alive; "the dead live", they say, because, as they are proving to us, they are "not dead". Their light-hearted, paradoxical, sometimes very humorous remarks are perhaps intended to loosen tensions and to make the contact easier and more acceptable to us.

Personally, I can state with the utmost conviction and certainty: these messages stem without doubt from our so-called dead. They are able to manifest on tape with the help of electromagnetic impulses, frequencies or waves. The "dead" are trying to stabilise this new line of communication and it is our task to help them by developing the technical means, thereby promoting clarity and a deeper understanding of the phenomenon.

For the first time in the history of mankind a contact has been established through which objective proof of post-mortal life can be obtained. This is an epoch-making event of the greatest significance. To solve the problem of death is to solve all our

APPENDICES 331

other problems, for it gives us the key to the mystery of our existence: immortality.

Pompeii, August 1967

Report of Mrs. Cornelia Brunner (Zürich, Switzerland), Psychologist.

On 26th and 27th April 1967, Mrs. von Muralt and I visited Konstantin Raudive's studio and listened to his voice-phenomenon recordings.

We heard a large selection of voices and when the words used were German, French, Italian or English, we could understand them without help from the experimenter. They were on sections of tape, re-recorded by Dr. Raudive on to a second tape, containing both microphone and radio-recordings. The transfer to a second tape meant that Dr. Raudive could repeat any particular bit of tape as often as he wished with amplified sound; this, of course, also amplified the interference-noises, but once the ear has accustomed itself to the noise, one can hear very softly spoken, well accentuated words and curt, precise sentences, usually composed of three or four words in different languages, including Finnish, Latvian, Russian and even ancient Latvian. Dr. Raudive often searches for hours in dictionaries to find the meaning of some ancient Latvian word before he can complete the translation of a sentence. There are clearly distinguishable male and female voices, sometimes also the voice of a child, all speaking very rapidly, much as if a tape was running through at too high a speed. The inflection is very rhythmical, so that at times one gets the impression of poetry being spoken. It seems that this is necessary in order to fit the speech into the given frequency. Some of the voices make announcements and comments in the way radio-transmitting stations do, and even give the names of their individual stations; and Dr. Raudive informs us that none of these "stations" can be traced by our international radio-companies and networks. Other voices seem to come from invisible persons present in the room, or persons that can, at least, look into the room; these address Dr. Raudive directly, or comment on his absence. Certain voices also comment on the way statements are "channelled through", or ask for somebody to come and help.

In the evening Dr. Raudive gave us the opportunity to make our own recording, unaided. He showed us how to handle the tape-recorder, switched on a particularly strong microphone, and asked us to switch over to radio after we had spoken our introduction. The radio-set was tuned to a wavelength where no transmissions could be heard. Both microphone and radio-recording took about three minutes. Dr. Raudive, who had left the room to speak to his wife in the kitchen, came back, examined the counting-system and found that we had run the tape for a relatively short time; he adjusted the radio-wavelength, improved the reception, and left the room again. We let the tape-recorder run for perhaps another three minutes and recorded without microphone via radio.

Next morning Dr. Raudive played our recording back to us, having transferred it to a new tape; even the greatly amplified background-noises did not prevent us from hearing the typical, short, precise, polyglot sentences. Some voices were already audible in the section recorded via microphone; the section recorded via radio contained complaints about bad recording-conditions on that day and questions about Dr. Raudive's absence. Later came voices that addressed Dr. Raudive directly, and one addressed itself to me. Dr. Raudive had wanted to examine the whole of the tape and transfer it to the second one that same night, a task that would have robbed him of about five hours of his night's rest. A voice warned him not to do this; it could be clearly heard in its soft tone and rapid rhythm. Dr. Raudive decided to heed the warning and postponed examining the second half of the tape to a later date.

We were much impressed by Dr. Raudive's dedication, spirit of endeavour, and conscientiousness. Further research in this particular branch must depend on the development of radio technology, possibilities of amplification of sound and elimination of interference.

The contents of statements reaching us are a little thin as yet, but some details given are similar to information received via other mediumistic channels and several helpful hints have come through as to how this research may be improved. The fact that voices call Dr. Raudive by name and address him directly, the many greetings from dead friends and the short, succinct comments on prevailing situations—expressed in a kind of polyglot sentence-mosaic—rule out the hypothesis of freak-voices transmitted haphazard from the world's many radio-transmitting-stations.

The speed and rigorously maintained rhythms indicate that the voices originate from a different frequency, and this tends to make the "listening-in" process laborious and tiring, because the ear has to attune itself to the unaccustomed ways of speech.

On my return home I told "Giulia", whose visions I had been studying at the time, about the voices recorded on tape and imitated the rhythms and the rapid speech. "Yes," she said, "that's just how the people I see in my visions speak!" and she repeated the type of speech, which sounded exactly like a tape played back at a too rapid speed.

29th April 1967

Report of Mrs. N. von Muralt (Society for Parapsychology, Switzerland)

Thoughts and comments on the voice-phenomenon:

On 26th and 27th April 1967, I was given the opportunity of studying the voice-phenomenon which Konstantin Raudive was investigating with such selfless devotion and under scientifically sound conditions, at close quarters. I listened to two hundred voices recorded on tape and after some practice I could understand most of the texts spoken. Mrs. Cornelia Brunner and I conducted our own experiment, at which the experimenter was not present. The tape produced approximately fifty voices, recorded via microphone as well as via radio.

In my opinion the voice-phenomenon is of the greatest interest to individuals as well as to science and to parapsychology in particular; I also think that there are great possibilities of development, especially if the technical means used in the investigations are further improved and perfected; Dr. Raudive has so far achieved all that is humanly possible with the technical appliances at his disposal. His remarkable results are due to painstakingly conducted listening-in tests after each recording and his method of isolating and amplifying located voices with the help of the most up-to-date equipment available. The fact that each taped voice may be repeated as often as desired, greatly facilitates the listening-in process and makes the phenomenon especially suitable for scientific investigation. Preconditions for successful listening-in tests are good hearing, if possible a practised (musical) ear, and, of course, interest in the subject, honesty and perseverance.

As far as I can ascertain, every recording produces voices, irrespective of who the participants are or how many people are present, but unfavourable weather conditions can mar radio-recordings.

I have already mentioned that manifestations occur also in absence of Dr. Raudive; the tape reveals voices even when tape-recorder and microphone are set for recording in an empty room. These facts need to be stressed, as they are of importance in any later attempt at explanation and interpretation. Personally, I feel that they are an indication that the main emphasis does not lie entirely on the experimenter, or the participants, or upon the "unconscious", but that the initiative stems mainly from the voice-entities themselves. The great number of voices—Dr. Raudive has registered many thousands —their individuality, characteristic features, and their great variety also point in that direction.

The voices differ quite distinctly from the voices of the experimenter and the participants. I was particularly impressed by the speed of their speech, the strange rhythms, and the sometimes really beautiful and melodic tone of the voices.

True, statements so far received are usually very short and sometimes incomprehensible to an outsider. One has the impression of receiving only a small particle of a much wider, still mainly hidden complex. Most of these particles are meaningful however, especially for Dr. Raudive, who possesses the necessary experience and intuition. It is therefore understandable that the voices tend to address themselves preferably to the experimenter, though participants are always addressed as well, and general observations and hints of future events are also received. To illustrate this, I give a few examples from my own experience: one voice immediately noted the experimenter's absence and regretted this fact; another voice stated what the experimenter was doing at that moment and wished that he would come back.

When I asked how we could show Dr. Raudive our appreciation, I was told I should thank him. Predictions of disturbances in the recording-process through adverse weather-conditions were fulfilled.

I also wanted to know the name of a Polish woman who had died long ago, a certain personality, whose name I had never learned. The answer was: "Anja Poživar", a Polish name. I hope to be able to check this information. Out of the two hundred voices I heard, I particularly noted the following statements: "A spirit-landscape—it is difficult to describe in life. We are observers. The ones in the air, they are human beings. Kosta, I am. Customs formalities at the crossing. Raudive radar! Ziedonu Gunnar-Gunnar-by calling." (This, and other "transmitting-stations" that do not exist on earth often call, giving a name.)

There are still more interesting statements amongst the vast material accumulated by Dr. Raudive. Particularly striking are the sentences formed in a polyglot mixture of words. It appears that languages known to the experimenter and the participants are preferred.

What is the meaning of this? We can only hazard a guess, for the final answer has not yet emerged and many questions have to remain open for the time being.

Those who listen to these voices without prejudice and in a receptive frame of mind, will feel spontaneously on realising the various facets I have just mentioned, that they are in contact with independent, intelligent beings; this, at least, is what I myself experience. To specify exactly the owners of these voices, seems precipitate to me, though the hypothesis that they may be the dead—still close to the earth-plane, or perhaps dwelling in other spheres—is a reasonable one. What is already clearly discernible, however, and in my opinion of great value, is that they differ from us, but have good powers of observation and the power of logical thought; that they can express feelings and sometimes show a delightful sense of humour which, to me, is particularly endearing. We certainly influence the utterances of voices through our personality, our attitude to the phenomenon and the type of questions we ask, we can even give a certain direction to the whole conversation, but this does not affect the individuality of the voice-entities nor does it detract from their independent existence.

It may be true to say that this new, highly interesting form of contact is still in its infancy, but is this not true in respect of all the branches of research into supra-natural phenomena?

One thing is clear: Dr. Raudive's excellent, firmly based work is the best starting-point for further research in this field. It has a good chance (owing to the fact that it can be independently checked), of being recognised by the scientific world; it should be easily understood by our technically-minded generation, should encourage many to think more deeply on the issues involved and perhaps even influence their beliefs.

Finally, the well-known American Parapsychologist, Professor Walter H. Uphoff has contributed his own observations.

Konstantin Raudive's work with "Voice Phenomena", using the twentieth-century technology of the tape-recorder, diode, radio, etc., raises many questions for parapsychologists that warrant further research.

I had occasion to observe Dr. Raudive at work several days during July 1969 and could find nothing whatsoever to suggest deception in the way he used instruments to pick up "voices from beyond". He impressed me as sincere and eager to get collaborators in his search for meaning and insight in this dimension of parapsychology.

Dr. Raudive understands seven languages. I know only two. Naturally I could not evaluate the content or significance of sounds in strange tongues but it was easy for me to recognise English and German words. One of the most intriguing and puzzling aspects about the phenomenon is the way several languages are often combined in a single phrase. At times it also seemed as though there was competition between voices seeking to be heard.

Perhaps the greatest impediment to progress in this field is the tendency for too many persons uncritically to accept *or* reject findings such as those reported by Raudive. What is needed is continued research which explores all the explanations the mind can think of. I hope some persons with the means to do so will support further research in this challenging field.

Boulder, Colorado, U.S.A.
19th January 1970.

3. PHYSICISTS AND ELECTRONIC ENGINEERS

The Technical and Scientific Aspects by Physikprofessor Alex Schneider, St. Gallen

Investigations

I investigated Konstantin Raudive's recording technique and the monitoring of the voices between 3rd January and 6th January 1968 at two "play-ins" held in concert. I had earlier examined several hundred copied voices in order to accustom my ear and get a general impression of the content of the voices. I made two further visits to Raudive in February and April of the same year, when we conducted further play-ins under different electronic conditions. I was there and then convinced of the unexceptionable nature of the technique of experimentation and of the painfully meticulous registration of the voices. It is admittedly recognised that in future investigations meteorological and astronomical data, as well as all possible technical facts, should be taken into account.

I remained in close contact with Raudive. I also studied the work of other researchers (1)[1]; they provided me with some measure of stimulation, but the work of none of them was as comprehensive as that of Konstantin Raudive. We may assume that further successes have been achieved since the appearance of the German edition of his book; they may well have remained unknown, either because the researcher was not in a position to justify them scientifically, or because he thought it right to keep his results on this most unusual matter to himself, publishing only oblique references, which naturally cannot be considered here.

---

[1] See Notes page 353.

After a few sessions, I had myself heard voices, but I did not further prosecute my enquiries for quite extraneous reasons.

In the following pages I shall go into the technical side of Raudive's investigations and give a brief (but as comprehensive as possible) résumé of the present state of the technical-scientific problem, in the hope that this will serve as the springboard for further researches.

The voices and their analysis

A Raudive magnetic tape—and it does not matter by which method the recording was made—exhibits when played back a jumble of partially unrecognisable and unclear voices which, however, are in part capable of being well differentiated one from another in both sound and content. There is a background to it all of atmospheric interference, amplifier roar and the babblings of radio transmitters, depending on the mode used for recording. One feels as though one were in the presence of a large company of speakers, disciplined to a certain extent, but all in too much of a hurry to speak; this makes it difficult to grasp longer coherent expressions of opinion, especially as the voices frequently fail to stand out adequately from the background noise.

In order to analyse what a voice says, Raudive previously copies the relevant text a number of times, putting in short pauses, on to a second tape (see test record). Two tape-recorders are needed for this process: recorder A carries the primary tape and recorder B has the tape bearing the copied voices. They are connected by a "diode cable" (2), as for normal programme transference.

The texts are given an auditory analysis by a number of investigators. A trained ear can make very fine distinctions, so that great reliance can be placed upon this analysis; it is better proof against self-deception than any mechanical device. It would, for example, be pointless to try to get more "objective" analyses of the spoken texts by using oscillograms (output voltage of tape-recorder as a function of time). The level indicator of the tape-recorder is sufficient to confirm that a signal is being received. (It is well known that an analysis of sound cannot easily be made from an audio-oscillogram; on the other hand; good audio-spectrum analysers have recently been designed (3). It has been found in practice that, when voices are clear, such a high identification rate can be assured that the introduction of this method for identifying those who pay by credit card is contemplated, instead of insisting on identification by signature (4) .)

When the voice can be adequately picked out from the background noise, the spectrum described by the analyser can be used to show that a certain voice tallies with another one expressing a similar message or, at least, that it does not tally with various voices emanating from interfering radio stations. A further step now would be to programme by computer and thus get comparison of one phoneme with another. Both these steps, however, are expensive in time and money, and are really unnecessary for verification of the voices.

As long as the voices can be heard against a relatively strong background noise, they become more comprehensible if a bandpass filter is used to shut out all frequencies outside the 400–3000 Hz range (5). Comprehensibility is improved in every case by excluding notes beneath 350–450 Hz, especially for the untrained ear, whereas a cutting-off of the higher frequencies is only of advantage in the case of strong interference noise lying within this range. One should not place too much reliance on complicated filters, such as those which exclude, for example, certain thirds; it was found that every voice required a special setting to achieve quite a small improvement in the weak voices, when these devices were used.

As frequencies over about 5000 Hz have played only a minor part in the quality of the voices so far heard, the fact that older people experience a marked reduction in sensitivity to sounds over 10,000 Hz is no barrier to a practical analysis of the phenomenon of the voices. Where there is an *impairment* of the hearing faculty, this can be easily confirmed by the audiometric facilities of any firm manufacturing hearing aids. But it is also a fact that many people are unable to distinguish one voice from another through lack of ear-*training*, a musico-psychological phenomenon.

The technique of the Voice-recording

This technique is still in the early stages. Commercial radios and tape-recorders, helped by accessories constructed as a result of tele-communications research (i.e. in all cases apparatus which is intended for quite different purposes), are used to make the contacts. It is, therefore, only to be expected that the signals are weak and often hard to understand. We have to recognise that the phenomenon is as yet physically uncomprehended in its essential points. The processes of recording have arisen by accident or by the demands of the voices. We have not hitherto been able to follow the usual research technique of extending the range of an appliance by linking it logically to something known.

Raudive's "play-ins" were carried out by the following four methods. Other researchers have varied the arrangements in non-essential details without attaining any notable improvements.

The microphone method. The microphone is coupled up as for any usual recording.

The radio method. A wireless receiver is coupled to the tape recorder exactly as is done for the recording of any radio programme, preferably via the "diode cable" (2). A small piece of wire is inserted into the aerial box in order to keep out any long-distance reception. Raudive finds a spot in the medium wave band in between two stations where background noise is as blank as possible. Other investigators choose the moment when a transmitter starts to beam out the carrier wave (6) just before beginning to transmit a programme or else they select a slow-speaking lecture programme in which the pauses between groups of words are so considerable that call-signs can be interspersed. A carrier appears to be necessary, or, at any rate, desirable.

The auto-transmission method. A small transmitter (a metering transmitter) is coupled directly to the aerial box of the receiver, in order to provide the voices with a carrier wave that is free from heterodyne oscillation and interference. The voices thus recorded by Raudive are relatively soft, but they are at least against a homogeneous background noise, and this is an advantage when monitoring. As an experiment, the medium wave band carrier was modulated by a pure 1000 Hz note, but this was found to interfere, as was to be expected. It might, however, be practicable to modulate using a noise-generator, since a number of voices sound as though they were constituted from the homogeneous noise-spectrum by some physically unexplained process of selection. Perhaps a completely pre-determined series of sounds could be made to serve the same purpose, acting, at the same time, as an inductor for the contact (7).

The diode method. A short (6–10 cm long) aerial is used to give a more or less broad-banded signal, which is rectified by a diode and fed directly by cable to the radio or microphone input of the tape-recorder.

This provides the clearest voices, but the interference caused by near-by strong wireless transmitters must be reckoned with. However, one can listen to their programme during the recording or reproduce them separately on other tape-recorders. Variation of the aerial length or the use of filters for particular strong transmitters can provide a better electronic performance. Weak and distant (especially foreign-language) transmitters cannot be received, particularly in the daytime.

The screen can be easily manufactured by the investigator himself, and Diagram 1 shows the circuit used in the earliest experiments. Experience with varied circuits has shown that the elements are not critical, though the rather old type of diode OA 81 could well be replaced by a more modern one. Diagrams 2 and 3 relate to the reception of higher frequencies (8).

The screens must be effectively covered, and may be earthed independently. T and X (1) had great success with a broad-banded pre-amplifier in front of the diode (9).

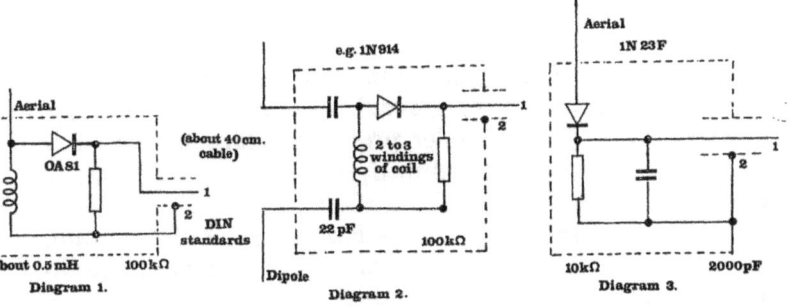

Diagram 1.   Diagram 2.   Diagram 3.

The tape-recorder is used by all the methods for the registration of the voices, but the latter can also, under special conditions, be heard directly. Registration on tape is, however, necessary for precise analysis and study. The beginner misses most of the voices when the tape is played back, and this is why not every radio listener and recording tape enthusiast discovers paranormal voices. There are, however, grounds for thinking that voices on tape are not noticed or falsely interpreted by the casual listener, more often than is generally suspected.

The need to secure a stable mechanical performance is the primary requisite when choosing the tape-recorder, for it has to be subject to frequent switching on and off. The relatively expensive three-motor machines, which have no interference-producing couplings, are probably the best. Recorders meant for use in language laboratories might be suitable, for the mechanical demands are similar in each case. A tape recorder should in all cases have at least two speeds, and preferably should be a twin-track model. If using a 4-track model, there is a danger of simultaneous magnetisation of a second track, and only two tracks should be used.

The sceptic might object that undesired signals could be propagated through the mains, and the experimenter, straining to hear at top receptivity, must admit this. This type of interference can be negatived by the use of mains filters or by using battery sets, and the latter are more convenient for working in Faraday cages (19).

Nearly all of Raudive's recordings were made on "Telefunken" apparatus M 85 (10). Transistorised (solid state) sets have other properties than sets containing valves (see below).

Critical judgement of the procedure

The possibility of a direct paranormal magnetisation of the tape does not have to be considered, because only tapes which have been used on a recorder present voices; moreover it is also possible to hear voices directly that have not previously been recorded on tape.

It is necessary to lay down a few basic concepts of sound and electromagnetic radiation before continuing to discuss possibilities of reception.

Sound is oscillation in matter, transferred to larger areas, principally through the atmosphere. The sound-producing oscillatory components must have a frequency of 16–20,000 Hz if they are to be received by the ear—Low Frequency, L.F.*

Electromagnetic radiation (radio, heat, light, X-ray, etc.) needs no material carrier in the accepted sense. Electromagnetic radiation is often confused with oscillations, such as sound, because the rays used to carry the radio broadcast are produced by electrical oscillations, are changed back to electrical oscillations in the radio appliance and obey similar laws to sound waves as they extend in matter-free space. The frequencies of the relevant oscillations are, however, of the order of millions per second and the velocity of radiation is about a million times greater than that of sound propagation (High Frequency—H.F.).†

In radio transmission this strange radiation serves as a carrier of energy. The message, e.g. a sound, must be "modulated" on to it. In long, medium and short wave bands this is accomplished by a change in intensity of the radiation corresponding to the sound oscillation (A.M.). In the antenna of the radio receiver, the radiation stimulates a high-frequency electric potential, and on this the relatively slow oscillation of the message is superimposed via the modulation. After amplification, demodulation takes place via a non-linear element, e.g. a diode, that is, the extraction of the low-frequency audible oscillation.

At first it seemed reasonable, in the case of microphone voices, to suppose direct action on the membrane of the microphone, either as the result of paranormal excitation of the air in the proximity of the membrane or of excitation of the membrane itself, so that experimenters who were some distance off could not hear the slight excitation.

It became necessary in the meantime to take account of the fact experienced that a number of tape recorders could receive normal radio programmes, at times at great volume, especially if they had minor defects, such as non-linearity or bad contacts. Only the microphone was coupled to the recorder. In particular, transistorised tape-recorders can often receive radio programmes

* I believe audio frequency, A.F.
† Probably radio frequency, R.F.

without the microphone being connected, by virtue of their peculiarity to contain non-linearity.

It would require compelling reasons for us to seek to explain this occurrence by some additional hypothesis—here, for example, a paranormal action on the membrane of the microphone; we should rather seek a unitary hypothesis for all the methods of playing-in.

The same observation would apply to a theory that low-frequency electromagnetic fields were being directly beamed on to sensitive parts of the tape-recorder; it is not easy to see what part is being played by the microphone connection, necessary in the case of most tape-recorders with valves. Furthermore, the fields would have to be very strong ones, since the recorders have to be well screened against scattered fields, especially those of the mains network. No results were achieved by putting short pieces of aerial wire into the microphone input of Raudive's valve set.

We are entitled to assume that in all the recording methods a similar beamed input is involved. It must be a form of radiation, either entering already in the form of electromagnetic radiation or a form of radiation unknown to us which induces in our receiving apparatus a secondary electromagnetic effect or one which has similar effects to electromagnetic radiation. As the sets in the radio, auto-transmitter and diode methods are designed for reception of electromagnetic radiation, it would only remain to prove that the microphone voices really arose from this radiation. As, however, we regard this method anyway as unproductive, we conducted no further systematic experiments in this direction. The voices themselves often demand an actual radio screen (pages 171 ff.). The following investigations might be carried out however: one could replace the dynamic microphone with a coil of equal value or by fixing the microphone coil (oscillatory circuit effect); T conducted experiments with his transistorised tape-recorder, localising certain places in the circuit where he obtained reception of voices without the connection with any other appliance. There was a suggestion, and some investigations supported this, that the reception arrived via that part of the circuit which serves the premagnetisation of the tape (X), but T could not confirm this.

Optimum extension of the input circuits with respect to a hypothetical electromagnetic radiation. In the radio and autotransmission methods, a definite type of beam (Graph 1) is picked out of the whole spectrum of rays; this, however, unnecessarily restricts the phenomenon, since the experimenter compels the voice to use the chosen type of beam and this could involve a limitation in the possibilities of making contact. A broad-banded reception is attained with simple apparatus using the diode screen. The voices can now utilise any given ray out of a broad gamut of radiation (Graph 2), and the middle frequency is obtained by the choice of inductivity and the scatter capacities present. Thus the whole jumble of rays which falls within this band is demodulated, including, as mentioned above, the (strong) radio stations which are also comprised within it.

Sensitivity as depicted in Graph 3 is to be preferred to that obtained with the diode screen; it could be so shifted within the frequency range that no strong interfering transmitter falls within its band. However, it must not be forgotten that a carrier is probably necessary for the voice-phenomenon; it might be possible, as it was in the auto-transmission method, to produce it by an auxiliary transmitter. One would have to find out whether this carrier would have to have a certain defined

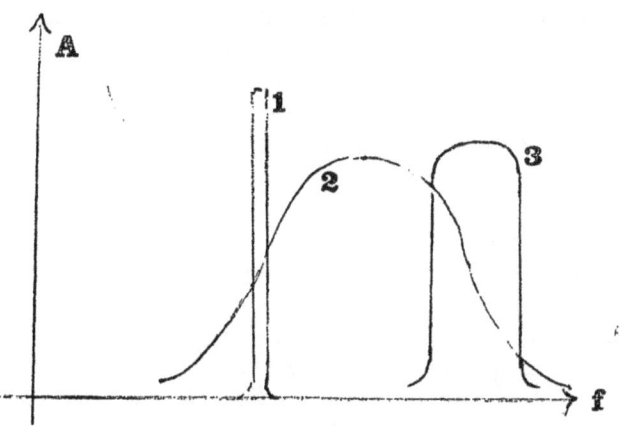

A Amplitude, f Frequency of radio beaming.
The curves give a only stylised illustration.

frequency or whether it could be selected from anywhere within the band of reception.

We have some grounds for thinking that the use of high frequency radiation gives better reception than the medium wave band; tests have been made up to 10^{12} Hz. In the top ranges, moreover, interference from wireless stations practically disappears. Auxiliary transmitters could be very useful here.

Pre-amplification, possibly with special low-noise amplifiers, gives in all cases a better signal-to-noise ratio and also a hitherto unexplained selective differentiation from interfering radio programmes.

Voices have been received to date from all ranges of the radio spectrum, and experiments may be extended in the direction of infra-red. The full analysis of the content of the messages should clear up the question of whether the voices, as is supposed by researchers, differ primarily one from another as a function of the frequency of their carriers (12).

On the other hand, another supposition that needs testing is that we are, perhaps, receiving sub-harmonics from a relatively high frequency beam; the same voices occurred in intervals of the sub-harmonics, which suggests reception might be better at a higher frequency. Apart from an effect such as this, it still seems that we are receiving a normal, amplitude-modulated signal, consisting of a spectrum whose frequency band-width corresponds to twice the highest audio-frequency being broadcast. It is not as though the voices were being received "all over" a broad band, between the radio transmitters. It is obviously feasible to assume the existence of modulations in which a number of spectra are produced over a certain frequency range (deep sub-harmonics!). If the investigations confirmed multiple reception, we could test a receiving circuit—it would be rather an expensive one—in which the only amplification would be what is being received simultaneously on two separated channels.

Raudive has primarily concerned himself in his work with the facticity of the phenomenon; he has not hitherto allowed himself to be distracted by the variations and investigations of other such parameters, but has wisely carried out his experiments in the medium wave band with a minimum of changes of apparatus.

The origin of the radiated waves

We remain completely in the field of known technical processes so long as we do not enquire into the source of the rays. The casual critic is understandably prone to characterise our radiation transmitters as simply sources of radiation modulated with speech. To postulate the existence of other sources requires such an extension of present-day experience that the latent idleness within us prompts us to disown the new; as Helmholtz said, in a similar case: "As things stand, it's just impossible." But the scientist today is rather more cautious in rejecting the unusual than was his famous predecessor, Helmholtz.

The history of technical-scientific progress has often demonstrated the pattern that Science first cast cold water on a simple technical process, empirically founded, until such time as it became compelled, by reason of the cogency of the facts, to acknowledge and incorporate the new process (examples: the gramophone, the aeroplane, etc.).

Physics is now faced with the task of sorting out a mass of empirical and carefully gathered material in the phenomenon of the voices that is most unusual for paranormal phenomena in its fullness and cogency, and physics above all other sciences has, in recent centuries, grown chary of condemning unexpected results. In the narrow field of physical experiment, we have run up against many laws which have perhaps not been generally apprehended in all their unintelligibility, either because they are too little known or because only the technical application of the investigations was advanced (14).

Physics is a descriptive science, whose duty it is to order happenings in an incontestable system of laws; it would be unscientific, to reject the phenomenal as not lying within the competence of this science, because it may have no explanation for its content.

The first step is to demonstrate that the contacts can be harmonised with the laws of being and the second, coming much later, is the extension of the scientific philosophy of the universe, made necessary by the realisation of so far unattained and, hence, unexplored worlds.

It is wrong to believe ourselves forced by the energy theory to reject the phenomenon as being contrary to all other basic experience. The energy which is here being demonstrated, although admittedly small in quantity, must come from "somewhere" (15). It is, however, easy to persuade oneself by calculation that when measuring, say the cooling of the environment or the decay of matter to redress the balance of expenditure of energy, the claim to exactitude is by far inadequate to prove that such a happening never took place. Moreover, it is a fact that the space in which the phenomenon is manifested is so far unrestricted.

The energy could emanate from other sources, as yet closed to human experience. Just as energy evaporates when neutrinos are created (16), so energy could in some similar, as yet unknown, reciprocal effect be transferred into "our" system. Man has certainly not yet discovered all forms of energy, and there is certainly so far no principle that forbids other forms. Moreover, we are not sure nowadays that the principle of energy actually applies to all reciprocal actions.

Although a rejection of the phenomenon of the voices on the basis of the law of energy is on principle unthinkable, yet the origin of the energy is peculiar. Even if we accept that the intelligence which is speaking to us is not itself delivering the energy, but is only directing it, transforming it or, at least, modulating it, yet a certain, albeit still smaller, amount of energy must still be getting added to it. Now, however, we have transferred the problem into that still greater and uncomprehended complex of questions which arise from the psychical or parapsychical direction given to physical occurrences.

There is certainly also a reciprocal action with the experimenter, as has been several times confirmed with the voices. There is complete experience available to show that people can give off electromagnetic radiation (17), and cases have been known where electrical apparatus has been activated by the presence of human beings (18). It may well be that the exchanges of energy with the experimenter have involved smaller quantities in the case of the voices than in other paraphenomena. It is scarcely to be expected that the experimenter, who is acting as a relay station for the transformation of electromagnetic radiation, should at the same time function as an amplifier. We covered the antenna of a diode screen completely except for a small opening in a metal housing. As different parts of the experimenter's body were brought near to it, we might have expected that the voices would become louder, but it was not clear that this was the case. This experiment will also serve to oppose a one-sided animistic interpretation of the phenomenon.

Proceeding from the proof of the facticity of the phenomenon, which the examination of the contents of the messages has abundantly furnished, if we want to know more of the origin of the voices we must certainly continue the as yet ambiguous experiments with Faraday cages (19).

The framework of Physics

There is a daring hypothesis, made more probable through other results which cannot yet be discussed here, that electromagnetic radiation is only a part of a hitherto unknown and much larger complex (20). When making such an assumption as this, it is as well to remember that we do not yet know very much about electromagnetic radiation. Even though we may very well know its effects on matter and be able to exploit radiation in the technical field, every fundamental investigation has made it seem more enigmatic. For example: when a ray of light comes towards us, for the light itself our space and our time are not present; emission and absorption for electromagnetic radiation are in the same place and at the same time, even though in our sight long distances have to be traversed in long periods of time. Conversely, the inner dimensions and properties of radiation coming in our direction cannot be recognised by us; they constitute a transcendental world (Einstein's Theory of Relativity).

If we may make this reasoning a little clearer, insofar as this is possible in such a short survey, we may say that the present-day fundamental laws of Physics leave a lot of leeway even for phenomena such as are found in parapsychology. Previously the fundamental laws described definite courses taken by processes; an example of this was the laws with which the paths of the heavenly bodies were calculated. Observations which lay outside the scope of such laws were usually rejected out of hand, because they struck the investigators as impossible in the accustomed framework within which they worked; they were *mandatory* laws. Our fundamental laws today are *prohibitory* laws; they tell us what is impossible. The principle of energy may serve as an example. These laws have proved themselves exceptionally useful in modern microphysics, inasmuch as all processes which are not by them forbidden could really be confirmed. It would be quite absurd to try to use these fundamental laws to reject the possibility of the phenomenon of the voices or an extension of the theory of electromagnetic radiation.

Though Physics may well be unable to dismiss in principle the phenomenon of the voices, yet it also finds it difficult to range it among known phenomena in the framework of a converging theory. There are, however, other phenomena too in the narrow field of Physics which are scarcely more susceptible of a satisfactory interpretation; we thus conclude that the answer to the problem must lie elsewhere. The material so far gathered together is so massive that a new scientific philosophy of the universe is needed to meet the facts. Such adaptations to the basic conception have often taken place in the past; thus, it was not false to regard the Earth as the centre of planetary motion, until such time as the need to construct a universal philosophy which would *meet the facts* dictated that the Sun should be recognised as centre (21). If we merely take as our base what we know already about electromagnetic radiation, it is almost impossible properly to comprehend the phenomenon of the voices. The above-mentioned psychical or parapsychical process of directional transmission presupposes some sorts of transmitting apparatus which quickly become fantastic projections of the technical appliances, with which we are acquainted, in matter-free space. We come, then, to the belief that we must search for a formula to embrace both this phenomenon and electromagnetic radiation, such that what we have hitherto known about radiation will appear as a partial aspect, like a straight section cut through a body. The different contradictory aspects will then, like incongruent sections, all converge within the higher unity. Physics has often been in this situation before, and not least in the attempt to describe the riddle of light, or electromagnetic radiation; the conflicting representations of light in terms of waves and corpuscles are of the nature of these contradictory part-aspects so long as we persist in describing radiation by mechanical analogies, refusing to consider it as a unified phenomenon which lies beyond mechanics. We did at first try to complete or replace the wave analogy, which was unable to describe all the phenomena, by the corpuscular theory, which belongs to the same category of being. The contradictions which confront us can only be resolved when we recognise that this radiation cannot be described in mechanical terms, but only by the laws that are inherent in it, and circumstances will probably dictate that this must be done if further experiences are to be co-ordinated. We shall continue the better to understand this phenomenon as we continually develop newer and superior modes of description.

Nor would the scientist be surprised; rather would he have recourse to a representation which meets the facts of the phenomenon, a representation in which space and time would have to be made starkly relative *vis-à-vis* our usual concepts, the opposition of animism and spiritism. In the phenomenon of the voices, modulation and transmission are no longer the same ideas, from the point of view of our space-time relationship.

It makes it more difficult to accept the necessity of extending the theory of electromagnetic radiation in the interests of the phenomenon of the voices that there is in practice absolutely no material available to support an exact theory; in addition, a whole series of suppositions is, scientifically speaking, irrelevant. The physicists would welcome the opportunity—and would thereby assist the cause of the phenomenon of the voices—to extend the knowledge of electromagnetic radiation. However much parapsychology today is thrown back upon the collaboration of physics, the paraphenomena must yet contribute in their turn to the creation of a new Physics.

But anyone who has had anything to do with the Theory of Relativity knows how hard it is to extrapolate into extended conceptual systems which strain the imagination; so easy is it to commit the error of once more reverting to the old accustomed manner of considering the facts. Our situation here makes one particularly prone to fall into the trap of adopting anthropomorphous conceptions when considering space and time.

Cogency of experiments

The scientist is ever more reduced to rely on the deposition of a few witnesses, or even of one only, though they should be recognised as qualified. It is also sometimes found that the deposition relates to a single observation. The theories that are enunciated on the basis of such evidence are, as has been said above, often more unusual than Raudive's conclusions, for he, after all, is only confirming what generations of men before him, drawing on different sources, have witnessed. Paranormal phenomena have often been characterised, however, by the credulous being victimised by the incorrect depositions of *un*qualified witnesses, and this has created a climate of scepticism towards the unusual in parapsychology. However, the physicist would be very surprised if we did not here invoke the same criteria as apply to the exact sciences, namely, that a *single* true voice is necessary to prove the facticity of the phenomenon and a single true voice for each play-in is necessary to demonstrate the possibility of reproduction. It is, admittedly more difficult to draw conclusions as to the structure of the spheres that are communicating with us from what is said by the voices.

Further problems cropping up in the experiments

The following hints, though not unexceptionable, are given as stimuli and working hypotheses for other researchers:

(*i*) Effect of the moon. Is the full moon particularly favourable? It is here interesting to note that, in the early days of radio technique, the position and phase of the moon were confirmed as affecting the quality of reception (22).

(*ii*) The influence of geopathic zones over which experiments are taking place? Is the receptivity of the voices in general dependent on the place? Do static and dynamic electric fields play a part?

(*iii*) Since the phenomenon of the voices indicates a connection with the experimenter or any other persons present, it is obvious that the vitality of the participants plays a part and that the voices themselves demand a measure of concentration and seriousness. Raudive does *not* listen in to the play-ins (via headset or loudspeaker), whereas others consider this as without any influence on the incoming voices.

(*iv*) Even though we may not exactly know what is talking to us and how the process is being accomplished, yet we must surely take the possibility into account that our *vis-à-vis* is also having his "technical" problems in establishing contact with us. (See certain voices on this point.) We must also allow the voices time to adjust and not expect an immediate reaction when a different set is being used. Some of the voices express themselves forthrightly on changes of apparatus, while other novelties are welcomed.

(v) If those worlds which the mystics describe are really talking to us, then the rules of conduct on which they insist could, to a certain degree, play a rôle (S has, for example, one voice that recommends him to stop smoking).

(vi) Another of S's voices demands adjustment of his consciousness, in the highest sense. When S doubts the origin of his voices, he gets practically no results.

These considerations are meant to indicate that our research object is not static; we are dealing with an active collaboration that is leading us to undiscovered laws that involve the experimenter. The experimentation requires much patience and a conscientious application to the problem of the technical dispositions that have to be made. This explains why Raudive's first work has not been followed up by series of technological experiments.

Notes

(1) Three other researchers are named as T, S and X.
(2) The circuits are described at length in the working instructions of the apparatus involved. In nearly every case, two different machines can have the playback transferred from one to the other.
(3) The sound is here, in essence, reduced to its sinal components, whose amplitudes are then represented graphically as a function of the frequency. Manufacturers of spectroscopic apparatus are, e.g. Muirhead, Kay Electric Company, MB Electronics, General Radio.
(4) We understand that the Stanford Research Institute is studying this matter and has found that the human voice provides extraordinarily reliable identification, preferable, for checking purposes, to signatures and finger-prints.
(5) Unit measurement of frequency: 1 Hz (Hertz) = 1 s^{-1} (1 oscillation per second). It may be helpful to know that

middle A in music is 440 Hz; doubling the frequency means, in musical terms, raising the note by one octave.

(6) For an explanation of the term: high frequency carrier, see under "Critical judgement of the procedure".

(7) Ideas for this paraphysical component may be found in the abundant literature on the magic of sound. One could, of course, also try to do the same thing with the other play-in methods.

(8) T had success with Circuit 3, but Circuit 2 is only a blueprint.

(9) T uses a commercial two-stage valve amplifier for shared aerials, to which the diode screen is coupled.

(10) Valve set M 85 (is no longer manufactured). Two speeds—
9·5 cm/sec ($3\frac{3}{4}$ in/sec) (most used),
19 cm/sec ($7\frac{1}{2}$ in/sec).
Two tracks. Frequency range: 30–20,000 Hz at $7\frac{1}{2}$ in/sec;
30–15,000 Hz at $3\frac{3}{4}$ in/sec.
Input voltage for complete volume control: microphone input 2·5 mV at 2 megohms; radio input 2·5 mV at 100 kilohms.

(11) The voltages before and after this element stand in a non-linear relationship. It is not absolutely necessary to have a so-called rectifier characteristic in order to get demodulation.

(12) An investigator in this field will not be afraid to combine the two following esoteric statements into a working hypothesis, namely, that the phenomena correspond to each other on different levels of voice-reception and that higher frequency stands for a higher standard of consciousness. Higher frequency radiation produces contact with higher spheres. On the other hand, the investigator who rejects a spiritistic attitude could interpret this observation also on a purely animistic level. When voices mention "radar", should we understand that we are in the presence of a directional beam, or that the investigator is being tried out, or that we should select the radiation band of military radar?

(13) Oscillations whose frequencies stand in the relationship: $1 : \frac{1}{2} : 1/3$.
(14) Examples: the quantum field theory is working on antiparticles which run *backwards* in time.

Matter has been reduced by the work of Rutherford and Bohr to the tiny atomic nucleus; it thus takes up only the hundred millionth part of the material phenomenon, and the remaining space is empty. However, modern theories, e.g. on the electron, see in its "neighbourhood", so much photo-energy that, not only is there finally nothing left for the actual material nucleus, but it would have to be made up of negative matter.

The tachyon theory requires particles with (mathematically) imaginary mass, etc.
(15) In classical physics it stated, not that energy comes from nothing, but that it can only be transformed. Since the theory of relativity, it can admittedly also concern a transformation into or from matter.
(16) Neutrinos produced by certain processes involving elementary particles can only with an unimaginably small amount of probability restore to "our" world the energy they have removed. They pass through the heavenly bodies practically without resistance.
(17) e.g. the case of Ida Ronconi, in which Prof. Istomin, of Rome, found the emission of electromagnetic radiation to be of "considerable strength".
(18) One may recall the incidents connected with Rechtsanwalt Adam in Rosenheim, Germany, investigated by Bender, of the University of Freiburg.

The number of investigations into the effects on geopathic zones and certain climatic influences of electromagnetic radiation (at least partially) is mounting up. A mutual effect between the radiation and the human body also appears to be proven.
(19) By Faraday cage, we understand a chamber made radiation-free by being isolated by conducting material (a narrow mesh grid, steel plate). The mains feed must be very carefully filtered, or it would be better to work with battery sets. The screening effect should, in any case, be

tested with recording apparatus which has been sensitively adjusted.
(20) Unless it should turn out that we are dealing with a bearer of information who has no connection with electromagnetic radiation.
(21) The general theory of gravitation was only possible in a heliocentric system. Faraday, Planck, Einstein, etc., gave us a new outlook.
(22) e.g. *Handbuch der drahtlosen Telegraphie und Telephonie* (*Handbook of Wireless Telegraphy and Telephony*), Vol. 1, by Dr. Eugen Nesper, 1921, Springer-Verlag, page 454: *Funkbastler* (*Do-it-yourself Radio*), Issue no. 14, 1933, page 220, Dr. K. Stoye, *Einfluß des Mondes auf elektrische Wellen* (*Influence of the Moon on electric waves*).

St. Gallen
February 1970

Scientific Experiments and Evaluation.
by
Theodor Rudolph, Ing. für Hochfrequenztechnik:
(Engineer in High Frequency Techniques).

1. Introduction

I first heard about the phenomenon of the voices when I read an article in a magazine. As I was interested in the problem, both as a scientist and as a technician, I wrote to Dr. Raudive on 18 January 1970 asking him to meet me, and he agreed to do this at 4 p.m. on 13 February 1970. In the meantime I studied Konstantin Raudive's book: *Unhörbares wird hörbar* (*The inaudible made audible*). The work is based on a sound scientific discipline and the author is revealed to possess a scientific sense, an impression which has since been strengthened. I myself have been concerned for some thirty years with the study of the fringe areas of scientific investigation and am, therefore, no newcomer to this sort of experience.

Dr. Raudive and I, therefore, duly met on 13 February 1970. I had just bought a sealed tape-recorder which we proceeded to use for the play-in.

I asked Raudive to demonstrate to me all the play-in possibilities. We began with Professor Schneider's diode method, following this with playing in by the microphone, the radio and, finally, the auxiliary transmitter. All these methods have been exhaustively dealt with by Professor Schneider, and I do not need to say any more about them.

2. *The play-in*

A type M 85 Telefunken tape-recorder was used, and the play-ins proceeded as described above. As I had had no experience in listening, I was at first well aware that there was something on the tape, but I could not make much out of it. By copying Raudive I did, however, learn, step by step, to listen in.

I called on my deceased wife, my parents and my brother. My wife could be heard particularly loudly, at times with first-class reproduction. My mother and my brother, and a number of deceased members of Dr. Raudive's family, were also heard. It is quite impossible that this could have been produced by any sort of manipulation, because I had myself carefully checked the perfect state of the apparatus being used. I have concerned myself for some forty years with high frequency techniques; I have been in research, design and testing, and I have learnt to think and act scientifically. I may, thus, be permitted to pass some judgement on this phenomenon. The possibility of some trick of radio transmitters is completely ruled out, because we put questions that were answered. It would be impossible for a radio speaker to be saying Konstantin Raudive's name and surname, and even his pet name. I was also addressed by name. Most of the sentences were in Raudive's mother tongue or were in several languages; they were, in some way, compressed and fitted into a rhythm reminiscent of the Greek hexameter. I was personally able to make out the German words.

After a detailed examination, I retained a strong impression of Raudive's integrity and scientific standing; I was completely convinced by the truth of what I had experienced.

3. *My own experiments*

When I got home, I started experimenting myself. I made it my aim to investigate all the methods in turn and, where the need was so indicated, to improve on them.

First I investigated Professor Schneider's diode method. I attempted to get a better directivity and concentration of the aerial by the use of ferrite rods. All in all I carried out some hundred experiments.

Experiment No. 102 brought me an outstanding success. I had started from the assumption that the play-ins with the microphone originated in the electron drift within the permanent magnet on which the speech rhythm is imposed. Why should I not also employ this principle to improve high frequency playing-in?

For this experiment I used two similar rectangular ferrite rods, each with a centre-tapped bifilar winding. The centre of the horizontal rod was earthed and the centre point of the vertical rod was earthed through a 560 ohm resistance, bypassed by a 1000 pF capacitor to filter out the remaining H.F. For detection a ring modulator was used.

The operation is, briefly, as follows: in Figure 1, let G_1 be an AC generator producing L.F. current of frequency f. G_2 is a H.F. generator for the carrier wave of frequency F and is provided with a throw-over switch which switches in the current f during the cycle of F with its contacts a and b, thus taking the indicated path from right to left through the loading R

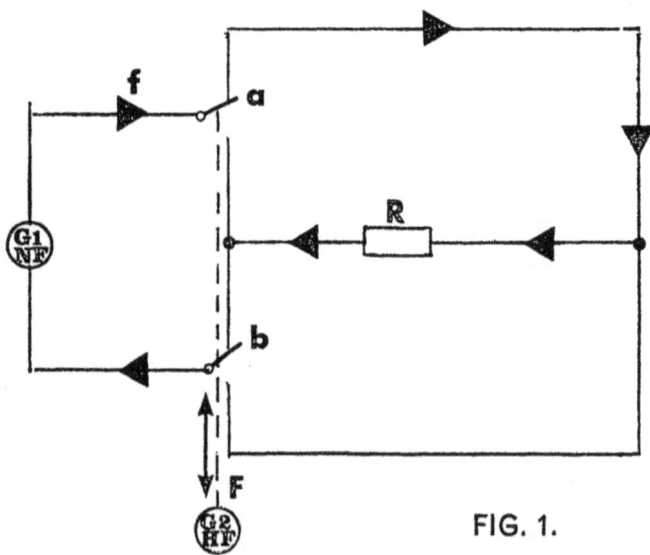

FIG. 1.

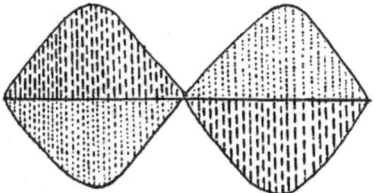

FIG. 2.

during a half-wave of F; half a period later of F it does the reverse. Diagrammatically this means that a half-wave of F is below the zero axis. The next half-wave of F is again over the line, but its dimensions are greater than those of the first half-wave, since F has increased in the meantime. So it continues until f changes its direction, whereupon the process is repeated —in the diagram there is mirror-inversion down to the zero axis. Figure 2 shows the saw-tooth track taken by the current changing at F, the peak values of which change at the same time according to f. The switch contacts correspond to the ring modulators in Fig. 2.

If we examine the current passing through the terminals 5 and 6 of the ring modulator, we discover that it is made up, in principle, of the two frequencies of equal amplitude,

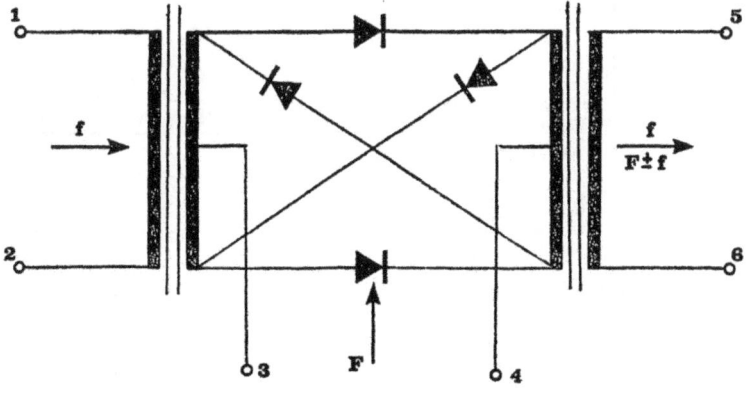

FIG.3.

$F+f$ and $F-f$, that is, the side frequencies or sidebands. F and f are reduced to almost nothing, and their presence may be attributed to minor faults in manufacture. Undesired harmonics can be filtered out by a bandpass.

Figure 3 shows the basic circuit diagram. F and f are the two generating frequencies. The overall effect is that of a beat. If we examine the frequency at terminals 5 and 6, that is, if we take the difference between $F+f$ and $F-f$, then we obtain the equation:

$$F+f-(F-f)=F+f-F+f=2f$$

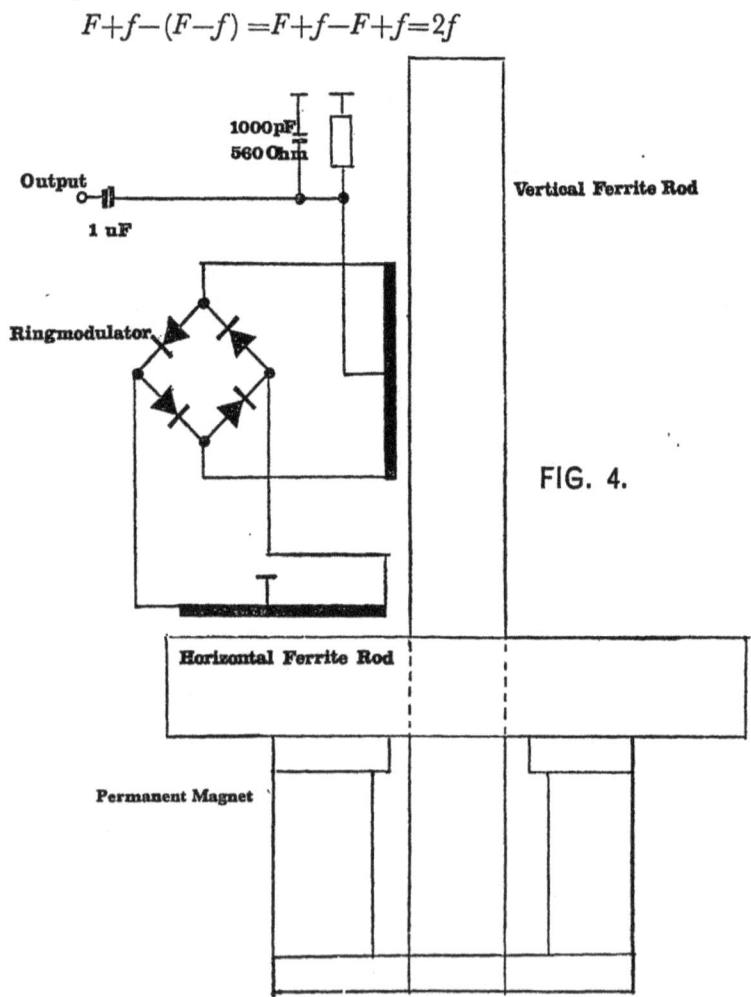

FIG. 4.

We thus see that F has disappeared i.e. is suppressed. Figure 4 shows the complete set-up of the test.

It can be seen that one ferrite rod is mounted horizontally and the other vertically on a permanent magnet. The field of the magnet supports the suppression of interfering side frequencies, so that the voices from beyond are easily audible against a slight, steady background interference. At the same time, further amplification was provided by a noise-free L.F. amplifying stage, coupled to the microphone input of the tape-recorder. In general the whole set-up for the experiment was of low impedance—about 200 ohms—and was matched to the dynamic microphone input.

After the apparatus for the test had been completely assembled, I began a play-in. I asked the voices whether this set-up, which I would like to call the "goniometer circuit", seemed promising. All this took place during the night of 28 and 29 March 1970 at three o'clock in the morning, by a full moon. I received an instantaneous reply; simply: "Erdische Methode gut, starker Besitzer. Ich bitte, richtig." ("Earth method good, strong possession. Please, right.")

I carried out a second play-in on the same apparatus at Raudive's house on 2 and 3 April 1970. The success we obtained was amazing and really effective. This set-up had put all my others in the shade, so that I naturally discontinued all the previous ones.

4. Postscript

Since that time I have carried out further experiments of the same nature. New discoveries have been made, but they are not yet sufficiently developed to write of them.

I wish once more to confirm that I have grown to recognise in Konstantin Raudive a serious scientist. *I assert that the voices really exist and can no longer be argued away.* The door to a higher dimension has been opened. It is now up to us to come to terms with this reality and to build up the fact with our own experiments.

Unterbalzheim
20 April 1970

The Psychophone. An appliance specially designed for transcendental reception by Ing. Franz Seidl (Vienna)

It is rare indeed for a special area of parapsychological study —as the phenomenon of the voices is—to awaken the interest of serious men of science and researchers to the extent that the source of these voices, which emanate from beings outside the Earth, is studied with the most modern of investigatory methods in universities and research laboratories, with the result that the reality of their existence is established.

Years ago it would probably have been regarded as impossible to make an academic investigation of metaphysical phenomena, since it was axiomatic that nothing could exist which could not be explained by mechanistic or corpuscular physics; recent discoveries in atomic and nuclear physics have, however, changed mental attitudes. Thus, we can read in Grimsehl, *Lehrbuch der Physik* (*Handbook of Physics*), Vol. 4, 15th Edition, for 1968, page 62, published, incidentally, in the G.D.R.: "The formation of pairs represents a materialisation of radiation whereas the destruction of pairs is an annihilation radiation of matter." This almost *spiritistic* recognition of a fact has been further strengthened by the discovery of the antiproton: not only pairs of electrons, but also pairs of protons, that is, atoms can be produced and then scattered. The important word here is *spiritistic*. The discoveries of quantum physics and the quantisation of the states of energy of electromagnetic and gravitation fields leads us, via the neutrino, to the conception of a sub-quantic energy which fills the entire cosmos. It would represent that form of energy, from which all phenomenal forms are constructed by the concentration and retardation of their oscillation, down to the material forms of our visible world. The cosmos would, thus, be regarded as an infinite reservoir of energy in which, in the last analysis, all phenomena find their source and their comprehensible coherence. Perhaps this form of energy is the hypothetical ether, proof of the existence of which eluded both Einstein and Michelson and which was, therefore, "discarded". If these concepts represent a real acceptance, then all paraphysical phenomena would become explicable and all types of phenomenon would constitute a continuous spectral band of oscillatory shapes or planes, such as we partially already know in the field of electromagnetic oscillations, a minute section of which we designate as "Light". Furthermore, materialisation and all paranormal phenomena would be explained and their existence would no longer be an object of wonder. We know from the law of conservation of energy that energy is indestructible, cannot be created from nothing and cannot disintegrate into nothing; it does, on the other hand, change its state; these facts circumscribe the forms that phenomena can assume. When we look at it this way, we are entitled to take up the position that the type and sensitivity of our material existence may be found, not only on the plane of oscillation that is peculiar to us, but also, under certain circumstances, on a higher plane of oscillation in the cosmic spectral band. It is true we may not be able to perceive this higher grade of oscillation with the sole aid of our sense-organs, but this is also true, e.g., of ultra-violet light and radio waves, and we do not therefore contest their existence.

And now we come to the core of our argument, the phenomenon of the voices. It now appears to be more readily comprehensible that a certain frequency band of electromagnetic oscillations can constitute a bridge between various planes. We furthermore know that a signal can be transmitted by a certain change of shape or modulation of such an oscillation; this is the principle on which every wireless transmitter and receiver operate. It is necessary that the latter be in a state to receive the energy beamed from the transmitter and to convert the information, be it speech or music, imposed upon the oscillation into a form which is perceptible by our senses.

It is thus seen that radio frequencies can be used to make audio contact with another oscillatory plane.

This exposition leads us on to the possibility of constructing a type of receiver specially designed to receive the voices, and this invention I have called a "psychophone". This transcendental receiver is so built that it possesses a wide range of high frequencies enabling the beings, whose voices we are hearing, to use a choice of frequencies suitable to their needs and, furthermore, providing for them possibly a source of energy on which they can draw. The type of voice play-in and the registration of psycho-kinetic and psycho-dynamic effects, such as background noise, movements of the indicator needle of the measuring instrument, the working of the magic eye during recording I interpret as follows: the transcendental beings require a certain amount of some form of energy to produce these effects; they get it from the ambient space-field conditions and only after a certain storage period, like that needed for the charging of a capacitor, followed by a sudden discharge. After this brief discharge time of an energy which is now denser, it would be possible for the beings to influence it inductively in order to produce sporadically short phrases or sentences, or other effects. From this we conclude that we ought to try to offer the voices an additional source of energy suitable to them on which they can draw continuously; they would then not have to impart their information in the short periods offered by a breakdown in the field and the release of energy resulting therefrom, but could pursue a continuous stream of conversation.

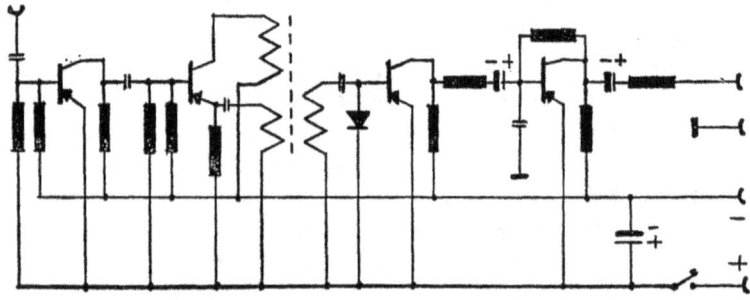

The function of the appliance is evident from the circuit diagram; a matched aerial controls the base of the first transistor which constitutes a high frequency stage working aperiodically. The next transistor is coupled to it and is switched in as a transmitter (oscillator); the radius of oscillation is unscreened and the radiation is diffused into space. A ferrite rod is quite suitable to serve both as a coil former, and a transmitting aerial at many frequencies. The ratio of windings of the collector circuit as a function of the demodulation circuit (the third transistor) should be about 1 : 1. Simple low frequency amplification is then achieved, after a high frequency bandpass filter, through a fourth transistor; the output of the psychophone is passed through a resistor and along a screened cable to the input point of a tape-recorder or an amplifier.

The size of the resistances and capacitors depends on the transistors and working voltage. It can be seen from the circuit diagram that the system works both as a broad band receiver and as a transmitter, as a radiating source of energy. It is optional which frequency is chosen. Experimentation is due to take place ranging from very high frequencies down to very low frequencies. The model used in the test, for example, oscillates in the region of 200 metres; it registers practically no transmitter signal input and does not interfere with other receiving apparatus, for the range in space of the radiating part amounts to about 1 metre. The receiving aerial consists of a short wire, which can be rolled up and which can only give radio reception when a hand is brought near.

One further interesting application of the instrument is, for example, the possibility it offers of locating geopathically sensitive zones. Some additional low frequency stages have to be incorporated for this purpose, and head-phones or a loud-speaker have to be used. When the aerial is directed downwards, the set provides radio reception of the sensitive zones in the medium waveband, but it does not do so for neutral zones.

Further experiments should show whether better results are to be obtained from the use of fields of high potential. Attention must be given to the problem of the continuity of all the phenomena. We must also bear in mind that it appears quite within the realms of possibility to render visible in our range of oscillation events which are taking place in a higher plane of oscillation, by transformation; perhaps also to create material forms out of an artificial ectoplasm. The new Aquarian age will build us these bridges. Today's discoveries will be tomorrow's facts.

Vienna
April 1970

Report by Mr. J. M. Meier-Waltisbühl, physicist (Zürich, Switzerland)

On Saturday, 15th April 1967, my wife and I were guests of Dr. Raudive at his home in Bad Krozingen.

We witnessed two interesting experiments.

I myself had had previous experience of such experiments at Dr. F. Nager's house in Zürich, on 12th July 1966.

1. Two tape-recorders (one the property of Dr. Raudive, the other supplied by me, with a factory-new tape) were placed parallel to a radio-set. The radio was switched on and tuned to a station that we could not hear.

Later, when the tapes were played back, voices became audible against a background of noise, and speech-fragments and sentences spoken in variable pitch and speed, and in several languages (nearly always mixed) could be discerned. The characteristic features of these voices, as well as the texts, make it impossible to presume that they have issued from a radio-station.

2. The two tape-recorders (as above) were connected independently to a microphone each. The persons present conversed in a normal way and at one point their names were read out.

When the tapes were played back, voices other than those of the participants became audible, and words and sentences spoken in various languages (as before) could be distinguished.

I find it impossible to explain in physical terms how these voices—which impressed me as being real—could have been produced. It is a phenomenon that in my opinion deserves the keenest attention.

26th April 1967

Brief Note on Raudive Recordings by Ralph Lovelock, C.Eng., F.I.E.E.

1. The fact that a tape must be run through a machine to obtain the voices is a clear indication that the magnetic track on the tape is the result of currents flowing in the head; and not of direct action of the communicants upon the tape itself.

2. Recordings made by means of currents in the head are the result of currents resulting from an E.M.F. which is periodic at audio frequencies.

3. At much higher frequencies, the tape-recorder would respond to a field without an additional antenna. If such a field was an amplitude modulated carrier then, although the older valve types of recorder would not respond, the newer solid-state instruments, due to the essential non-linearity of the transistors would be capable of rectifying the carrier and passing on the audio modulation component. The fact that better results are obtained with a rectifier across its input, and with a superimposed carrier to traverse the rectifier across its point of maximum curvature, is strong indication that the audio signal is reaching the instrument as an amplified modulated H.F. carrier.

4. The fact that the equipment does not respond when enclosed in a screened enclosure is not only a strong indication that it is an incident field which is responsible for the recordings, but also that this field emanates as a R.P. carrier with modulation from a region outside the enclosure and not from the people with the equipment inside it. Assuming, as seems probable, that the "sensitive" was inside the enclosure, then the radiation at our physical velocity did not originate in the mind of the sensitive, and the reason why such a presence gives a greater probability of success must be due to some other factor. The probability that an enclosure could attenuate a radiation at supra-light velocity which is in a dimension different from and orthogonal to all of our physical dimensions is so small as to represent a virtual impossibility.

5. It is quite feasible for radiation fields emanating in broadcast transmitters and fading due to interaction of multiple paths to produce similar effects to those which have been obtained. From the point of view of our normal experience, this would be the most probable cause of the effects. The sole reason for rejecting this explanation and looking to ESP is the claim that the content of the recordings is such that they could not possibly have resulted from several rapidly fading broadcast signals. It is vitally important, therefore, that a clear analysis of these recordings be made to firmly establish this fact.

6. As an aid to such analysis it should clear the voices of

a fair portion of the superimposed noise and make them more intelligible if they were processed by passing them through a filter with a pass-band of 500 Hz, to 3 kHz. This would be best done on the original tapes, since each recording adds its own modicum of "noise" to that there originally.

7. The presence of a screened enclosure would screen the equipment from all broadcast signals. It would be an experiment of immense value to obtain recordings in some region of the earth's surface where there are no significant levels of broadcast radiation. Such a region would be in the expansive ocean stretches of the southern hemisphere or, maybe, in the middle of the Pacific.

London
6th November 1969

II. THE COLLABORATORS COMMENT

As the reader has observed, participants in the author's experiments have come from many professions and occupations; numbered amongst them are doctors and dentists, teachers and musicians, publishers, writers and a building contractor. Their comments include the following:

Karlis Lidums (Edwardstown, Australia), Building Contractor.

During the month of August 1966, I, Karlis Lidums, had opportunity to witness experiments connected with research into the voice-phenomenon and to be present at recording-sessions. I have heard and personally verified the voices described by the experimenter. Texts of statements recorded on tape correspond to facts. I was particularly impressed by mention of the names of my friends Hutton and Harvey, and by the fact that the voices of my parents became audible. The female voice saying: "Esi parītu te. Mana sirds tev kalpo. Kostja, pažēlo manu dēlu." (Latv.: "Be here the day after tomorrow. My heart serves you. Kostja, have pity for my son.") I found most interesting; and the sentence: "Mēs tevi mīlam, Kārli! Paliec pie Kosti! Paldies! Mēs pateicamies Zentai Maurinai." ("We love you, Karl! Stay with Kosti! Thank you! We thank Zenta Maurina.") impressed me deeply. The recording and the listening-in test were made in my presence. I had a strong impression of reality—so true, so familiar did the voices sound to me.

12th June 1967

Dr. Arnold Reincke (Specialist in internal diseases; Chief Consultant at the Sanatorium Badenweiler-Hof, Badenweiler, Germany).

In the winter of 1966/7 I had the opportunity of taking part in Konstantin Raudive's voice-phenomenon experiments in Bad Krozingen. The phenomenon was of such instant fascination that only later, after one had had time to digest mentally what one had heard, was it possible to try to decide whether it had been reality or only an imagined experience.

It takes prolonged "listening-in" practice before one is able to consider the phenomenon in a dispassionate way. The possibilities arising out of these experiments open up a wide, hitherto unknown field of research. The moment one hears oneself addressed by the voices, one falls under the spell of this strange interrelation between one's own existence in the present on the one hand, and another dimension without time and space, on the other. In three months I listened to and analysed more than seven thousand voices.

As a physician one connects the articulation of words with certain physiological processes. The larynx, the vibrations of the vocal cords and articulation with mouth and tongue are prerequisites to speech, even if it is made audible through technical aids, as happens when the spoken word is broadcast over the radio, or heard through a telephone, a tape-recorder, or diffused by any other means. When words and sounds manifest that cannot be connected to any known source of origin, one's customary way of feeling and thinking receives a severe jolt. Only very slowly, by sorting and sifting all that one has heard and recorded, can the mind adapt itself to the idea of a world so far removed from all our traditional conceptions of time and space.

Our education in natural science sets limits that can, it is true, be extended by mathematicians, physicists and also by psychologists; but accepted formulae and explanations are as solid ground under the feet and one is reluctant to abandon them.

During many long sittings with Konstantin Raudive, I have become convinced that we have contacted a dimension that can expand our mental range considerably, once we have mastered the correlation between that unknown world and the experimenter; especially during the last few weeks of my stay did it strike me how "personal" the relationship between question and answer often is. Konstantin Raudive called this particular aspect of the phenomenon "partnership" between the world of the voices—so difficult for us to comprehend—and the experimenter.

How and where electromagnetic waves come into play—in radio-set or tape-recorder—will only be understood after further long and careful studies, investigations and scientifically conducted technical experiments.

Dr. R. Fatzer (Wädenswil, Switzerland).
Excerpt from a letter to the author:

On 15th and 16th April 1967 I had opportunity, together with members of the Society for Parapsychology, Switzerland, to listen to the voices recorded on tape by your apparatus. I must admit that this process is, as yet, quite incomprehensible to me.

Two possible interpretations spring to mind:

1. According to "animistic" opinion it may be possible that the voices are channelled into the apparatus by some mediumistic process under influences emanating from persons present. The voices can be heard in microphone-recordings as well as in recordings made with the help of a radio-set.

2. According to the Spiritualist theory it could be otherworldly entities (spirits) who are able to "plug into" the vibrations caused by the apparatus, or into the frequencies of radiowaves; in this case, as in the first hypothesis, the presence of a mediumistically gifted participant would be necessary.

I find it impossible to give a final verdict at this stage. Further research is imperative to clarify the matter; above all it should be possible to produce these manifestations in different localities and with quite different participants, in order to create a basis for comparison. This is absolutely necessary if we are to make progress in this investigation. It would also help us to ascertain the meaning behind the phenomena.

19th April 1967.

Dr. Rudolf Zimmermann (Bad Krozingen, Germany).

During 1965 and 1966 I was present on several occasions when experiments were conducted at Dr. Raudive's studio. The procedure was as follows:

1. Our conversations were recorded on tape and the tape then played back and checked for additional voices not previously audible to us. Results were catalogued and carefully re-examined by the participants.

2. In radio-recordings a radio-set was switched on and the same procedure followed as described above. The set was tuned to a frequency where no transmissions could be heard.

Repeated and painstakingly conducted listening-in tests revealed a great number of more or less distinctly audible "voices". I found that "listening-in" usually meant hard, concentrated work. The pitch and strange terseness of sentences, sentence-fragments and words struck me as quite extraordinary; although I could hear the texts spoken in foreign languages, I could not grasp their meaning, but I could follow and understand the words that came over in correct, or slightly modified German.

During these sessions a few meaningful sentences, referring to our conversations, were received.

For instance, in the recording of 22nd February 1966 I heard a voice say: "Mans paldies! Mūsu doctors Zimmermann." ("My thanks! Our Dr. Zimmermann.") and: "Hallo, hundert Toten ab." ("Hallo, one hundred dead."); "Ai, hier sind Strafen!" ("Ah, here are punishments!").

On 4th November 1966 I made a recording by myself with microphone and radio. It produced 80 voices, 35 per cent of which I was able to identify myself. I heard my own name, "Rudolf" called, and after I had said: "I am calling you, let me know if you are present!", a clear answer came: "Call Kosti! Kosti Raudivi!" Another voice said: "We are here." I insisted on contact with the voice-entities and one of them retorted: "Bring Kosti back, you scoundrel!" When I continued: "... but perhaps my near and dear ones...", a voice responded: "Good night, finished talking. Papa, we are ..." The words: "Papa, we are ...", spoken in good, clear German, touched me deeply, for during the recording I had called aloud, as well as in my thoughts, on my little dead son. (All the sentences spoken by voices have here been given in translation.)

Some of the voices referred to Dr. Raudive. He was mentioned by name, or people he had known in life made their presence known to him; for instance: "Raudiv, laid Schulti!" ("Raudiv, let Schulte enter!")

I must confine myself to a simple confirmation of the fact that I have heard the voices; how they are produced is something I cannot explain.

8th March 1967

Mrs. Irma Millere, Educationalist (Stockholm, Sweden).

During my visit to Germany in July 1966, I visited Konstantin Raudive's studio on several occasions and was able to listen to voices, take part in recording-sessions, and to conduct one experiment myself at which Dr. Raudive was not present. This experimental recording produced 123 voices. I was able to hear and verify 60 per cent of these personally.

I could establish the following facts:

1. The voices use a form of speech composed of several languages; for instance: a voice of good audibility, recorded through microphone, says: "Guten Abend med dej. I wishy your bebi Wein." ("Good evening to you. I wish to drink your wine.") I could clearly distinguish the German, Swedish and English words, and the one Spanish word, used in this sentence.

2. The voices could be determined by their texts, and I observed that these often dealt with post-mortal events and contained the names of deceased persons.

3. Several times I was able to hear my own Christian or family name. Some voices referred to me personally; for instance: "Irma Millere. Čakste." (40g: 238) and "Irma te. Māte." (42r: 502) ("Here is Irma. Mother.")

4. Usually the audibility of the voices is so good that anyone with normal hearing can discern them.

5. The listening-in tests demand concentration, a practised ear and an inner calm; only when these preconditions are

fulfilled does it become possible to follow the rapid, rhythmic speech.

6. In my opinion it is difficult to explain the nature of this phenomenon through the hypothesis of the unconscious, or through any theory of the responsibility of physical influences, such as freak radio-sounds or the blending of various languages from different radio-stations. I get the impression that the voices have their own unmistakable characteristics and confront us as individual entities.

The voices are characterised by both rational and emotional texts; but perhaps the work of several generations will be needed to unravel this complicated mystery.

The element of partnership between us and the voices is well illustrated by the voice that observes in the recording I made when alone: "Noslēpi Raudive. Viņš dārzā staigā." (42r: 250) ("You have hidden Raudive. He is walking in the garden.")

Miss Annemarie Morgenthaler, Teacher and Research Assistant (Berne, Switzerland).

During the last two years I have frequently taken part in Konstantin Raudive's voice-phenomenon experiments.

At some of the microphone-recordings I kept record of extraneous noises (ejaculations of participants, whisperings, traffic-noise, noises made by the wind or by animals, etc.), in order to exclude any possible source of error.

To my mind the question of undisturbed, accurate listening-in lies at the centre of the whole problem; "listening-in", by the way, is emotional and spiritual "hard labour" and to enlarge on this I would like to make the following observations:

1. My sense of hearing reacted usually in a set pattern:

    (*a*) hearing of a noise,
    (*b*) isolating it from other noises,
    (*c*) detecting a definite rhythm,
    (*d*) differentiating the vowels,
    (*e*) differentiating the consonants,
    (*f*) understanding the word/words,

(g) a re-examination; that is, a conscious effort to determine whether a different psychological attitude whilst listening may produce a different result,

(h) interpretation of the utterances.

Very often I got stuck somewhere along this eight-point line; as the voices frequently use languages I do not understand, I usually considered it quite satisfactory to reach point five. I would particularly like to stress the importance of point (g), the re-examination. Results of my listening-in tests were 70 per cent to 80 per cent in accord with those of the experimenter.

2. There is a danger that one may "overshoot one's mark" whilst listening-in; by this I mean that—either through fascination and emotional strain caused at times by preoccupation with such phenomena, or through sheer tiredness—one may imagine "words" when in reality there is only a "noise".

I observed, however, that the experimenter and the majority of participants always aimed at the highest objectivity and made their criticisms, when such became necessary, in a detached and dispassionate manner.

Voices recorded via microphone seem, at first hearing, to be more convincing; but some statements received through radio-recordings are most striking. For example: "Raudive, over there is Jesus Christ!" (26r: 630) "You are sick, Koste." (48g: 160) "Sister, where is Kosta?" (45g: 507) "Brother, this is tremendously engaging."—"More softly, Alexej." (44r:232) (All examples given in translation.)

At every renewed contact with the voice-phenomenon I tried to gain deeper insight. I really expected to find in the end that the manifestations rested on some illusion of the senses, or that they could be explained in technical-acoustic terms; but up to date nobody who has studied the matter seriously has been able to bring any evidence to support a refutation of the phenomenon on such grounds.

June 1967.

Mr. Valerij Tarsis, Writer, and Mrs. Hanni Tarsis (Babenhausen, Germany).

On 3rd February 1967 we had the opportunity of conducting our own voice-phenomenon experiment at Bad Krozingen. The experimenter was not present.

When we listened to the first of the resulting tapes we immediately discovered that in the microphone-recording—introduced by Valerij Tarsis—"voices" had appeared between the words he had spoken; quite clearly we heard names mentioned: "Mozarts", "Faustu", "Lorca", "Hitler", "Maurins", "Tarsis", "Kosti", and others. The following words made a strong impact on Valerij Tarsis:

"Ty volnyj drug" (Russian: "You, a free friend"), as he had been able to leave the Soviet Union less than a year before to settle in the West:

"... žalko Wetrow!" (Russian: "(I) ... feel sorry for Wetrow!") Wetrow, a young Russian critic, arrested in 1937, had died in a concentration camp. Valerij Tarsis had loved him dearly. Wetrow was the only Russian critic who had dared to describe Maxim Gorki's book *The Life of Klim Samgin* as being an anti-revolutionary work and had interpreted it as such: this had promptly landed him in a concentration camp. Tarsis had often told friends how sorry he felt for Wetrow.

"Dubka" was the nick-name of one of Valerij Tarsis' drivers during the war, whose real name was Dubkow; Tarsis was particularly fond of him and sometimes called him "Dubok". Dubkow lost his life in 1943.

Back home, on 10th May, we listened to further tapes and found that most of the statements made by the "voices" were phonetically quite distinct, though the meaning of some words was not always clear.

We noted the following points:

1. We could distinguish male and female voices.
2. Some of the voices sounded far-off, others quite near: differentiation in space.
3. All the voices spoke very rapidly in a definite rhythm; syllables were sometimes added to words, or, when necessary, left out; at other times words were given endings belonging to a different language. This led us to the assumption that:

4. A mixture of languages is used; often one, two, or more words in different languages appear in a statement. We could discern German, French, Latin, Latvian, Russian, Swedish. (Swedish spoken in the typical lilt of that language.) It is much more difficult to catch the phonemes of a language one does not understand, than those of a known idiom, and so we had to take far greater pains with words in the languages we have not mastered: Latvian and Swedish.

Naturally, the question of how the voices manage to get on to the tape greatly exercises our minds: they must be radiated out in some way, for it is impossible to hear them until they have been recorded and made audible on tape through microphone, radio and tape-recorder.

As we are only amateurs in these matters we do not wish to speculate about the "how"; we rest content to confirm the acoustically verifiable manifestations of the phenomenon."

18th May 1967.

Mr. Valerij Tarsis and Mrs. Hanni Tarsis (Babenhausen, Germany).

Letter to the experimenter:

We have received the tape containing experimental recordings made here on 10th May and we have listened to it with particular interest. Valerij was a little disappointed, because he missed personal references. "Tarsi-" was mentioned only once, but to my mind that is quite something!

Impressive was also the "answer" to the request our guest made: "... say something", which was given by a microphone-voice: "Nav, ko tev saka!"—"Nothing to tell you!"

The point is, that once one is convinced of the reality of the voice-phenomenon, one concentrates one's whole attention on the meaning of the texts. According to the list you enclosed we understood approximately 95 per cent of the voices; just as before, with the first tape, we found that voices, words, exclamations and quite a few names could be heard (Pushkin, for instance). We heard German, Russian, Latvian—thanks for translation of the Latvian texts; how touching the repeated pleas for forgiveness: "Kosti piedodi!"—"Piedodat man!" Regarding 49g: 219 "Kosti, Kosti, turies!", I am of the opinion that another syllable follows (see experimental recording No. 25: Valerij Tarsis, Hanni Tarsis, Dr. Hildegard Dietrich), but I cannot say for certain, as I do not understand Latvian.

I have been very concerned with the question as to whether the choice of language is in some way connected with the experimenter; such a connection would appear to me to be quite logical, because the voices address you so often directly and therefore choose the languages you understand best.

We are awaiting the publication of your book with the greatest interest.

8th June 1967.

Professor Atis Teichmanis (College of Music, Freiburg Breisgau, Germany).

I have had frequent opportunities to visit Konstantin Raudive's studio and listen to recordings of the voice-phenomenon.

I have noticed that the voices keep the same rhythm throughout their speech; it is possible to recognise and identify a "voice" by this very marked and definite rhythm before one is able to hear what it is actually saying. Swelling and ebbing like a tide, these rhythms are one of the characteristic features of the phenomenon and it is not difficult to understand that, in order to fit into such rigorously imposed tempo, some word-patterns have to be modified.

The volume of the voices can differ greatly. I could distinguish a whole range of sound-volume, from whisperings to clearly audible shouts.

I could hear the voices without help from the experimenter and was able to decipher their words and meaning. In some instances I could correct the experimenter's results; he had, for instance, noted: "Es dzivoj Nonsburgē." (Latv.: "I live in Nonsburgē."), but the word "Nonsburgē" should have been "Nonsburdē"; also, he had heard: "Sava, kungs Atis!", French: "Ça va, M. Atis." ("It's alright, Mr. Atis.") and I could detect another syllable; the above version did not seem to me to fit into the rhythm. Listening carefully, I found the sentence to be: "Ça va, tas kungs Atis!" ("tas" in Latvian means "the").

During several listening-in tests I heard approximately five hundred voices, which coincided—excepting but a few—with those noted by the experimenter. These voices are, without any doubt, an acoustic reality. Considering the many voices I have examined up to date, and judging them by their pitch, intensity, volume and speech-content, I must confirm that in my opinion they cannot be put down to masked sound-effects, but are real word-formations expressing constant and unalterable texts. The human ear has the ability to hear the phenomenon and to determine the voices correctly by the content of their statements.

Mr. Kārlis Bauers, Singer (Basle, Switzerland).

I had my first encounter with Konstantin Raudive's voice-phenomenon experiments in August 1966, and although I felt sceptical at first, I was forced to admit the reality of the phenomenon once I had listened to the voices on tape. I could not hear all the voices on this particular tape, because most of them lay in the "B" and "C" groups; but, to my astonishment, I was able to distinguish many of the "A" and "B" voices without help from the experimenter.

The majority of recorded voices spoke in Latvian. For instance: "Nemociet Kosti!" ("Do not torture Kosti!"), or: "Atceries mūs!" ("Remember us!") "Gribu tevi redzēt." ("I want to see you."); "Te aklie." ("Here are the blind."); or: "Māsa raud." ("[Your] sister cries."). The last two voices I heard before even Dr. Raudive had discerned them.

Some of the microphone-voices I heard: "Man nav vaļas." ("I have no time"); "Solīsi, Kārli?" ("Will you promise me, Karli?"); "Ej savā vietā!" ("Go to your place."); "Gute Nacht." ("Good night."); this, the last word spoken in the recording, was particularly clear.

My second encounter with the voice-phenomenon came in March 1967, when my wife was also present at listening-in tests; she was able to hear many of the voices better than I could. I did, however, discern roughly 70 per cent of 300 recorded voices.

We were both deeply moved and excited by the following incident: on 27th January this year (1967), a relative of my wife had committed suicide by jumping from a bridge. Dr. Raudive could not have had any knowledge of this tragic event.

During a recording-session in our home Dr. Raudive asked my wife to try and contact a person she had known in life and ask a question. After a short hesitation my wife asked for her dead relative, Reinhard; could he indicate his presence? The answer, when the tape was played back, was quite staggering: "For the bridge, Koste."—"Now cemetery."—"Here across the bridge" (given in translation). The words spoken relate perfectly to Reinhard's sad, self-chosen death.

Now, after having listened to Dr. Raudive's recordings with my own ears, I fully believe in the reality of the phenomenon.

Mr. Herwart von Guilleaume, Publisher (Remagen, Germany).

I came across the voice-phenomenon for the first time during a meeting at Bad Krozingen, at which Professor Bender was also present. That evening Friedrich Jürgenson gave an introductory lecture on the subject and demonstrated some of his tapes. To this day the word "Graecola!", spoken in its typical rhythm and strange timbre, remains most vivid in my mind. The conversation that took place among the guests afterwards, was recorded for some minutes via microphone. Examination of the tape revealed several voices of group "B", but they did not seem to have any bearing on the persons present.

Later I had two more opportunities of listening to tape-recordings, together with Mr. Raudive, and to compare my results with his. At first I found it very difficult to identify languages I did not know, but after some time, when my ear had become accustomed to the rhythm of the voices, individual words began to stand out more and more clearly, so that with practice, and intense concentration, I could even understand most of the "B" voices.

At one of the sessions Dr. Raudive left me for a while to record by myself. I first spoke a few words into the microphone and then switched over to radio. My request to be addressed by name from the "other side" was granted. In my opinion it is quite out of the question that this name could have been transmitted at that moment by an ordinary, earthly transmitting-station.

Remagen
31st July 1968

Dr. Wilhelmine C. Hennequin (Kreuzlingen, Switzerland).

I, Wilhelmine Charlotte Hennequin, anaesthetist, confirm that I heard the voice-phenomenon in Dr. Konstantin Raudive's studio in Bad Krozingen, on 11th and 12th November 1967.

I have been able to assure myself of the fact that the investigations are conducted on scientific lines and the results checked by equally strict scientific standards.

I am convinced that other-worldly beings are trying to contact the living through audible manifestations via electro-magnetic waves.

During my visit to Konstantin Raudive's studio I was able to hear voices that had previously been recorded on tape, to be present at a recording-session and finally to take part in a "partnership-voice" experiment.

Of the voices that had already been recorded I could hear every one; my only difficulty was that I could not understand some of the languages spoken, and had to wait for Dr. Raudive's translation, before I could understand the meaning of the words.

The fact that the voices are recorded on tape makes it possible to repeat them at any time and demonstrate them to any interested person. Each voice is registered and numbered and can be listened to, except the voices of group "C" which are not suitable for analysis, as their audibility is too weak.

Amongst the recordings made by Dr. Raudive on 10th October 1967 were several "partnership-voices". They were easily recognised and each one had its own characteristic features of pitch and speech-rhythm. Male and female voices and voices of children could be clearly distinguished.

Voices are either recorded directly through microphone on to the tape, or are received via radio and registered on tape. In radio-recordings the set is tuned to a wavelength that is silent, except for what is termed the "white noise"; it is easier to locate the voices that way, than against a background of music

During a recording Dr. Raudive first contacts a partner in

the "beyond" via microphone, speaking a few words of introduction; he then lets the tape run on for a few minutes. Later, on running the tape back, he can hear the voices through earphones. Voices of good audibility are amplified and re-recorded on to a second tape, and then analysed.

I was able to distinguish all the voices recorded on 28th October 1967, bar one; this was a voice that I could hear, but owing to the speed at which it spoke I could not catch it. It was one of the "partnership-voices" (50r: 257), and apparently said: "Koste plågas, pacieties!"; an "A" voice, speaking in Swedish and Latvian: "Koste is trying hard, have patience!"

At times one can hear conversations amongst voices, as on tape 50r: 385/398. Partner in this case is "Margarete":

386: "Margarete," a "B" voice (female)

388: "Nav Margareta", another female "B" voice; Latvian: "It is not Margarete".

391: "Lāba māte te." A female "A" voice; Latv.: "Your dear mother is here."

394: "Vai tu Mamma?" A female "A" voice; Latv.: "Are you Mama?"

398: "Tev Kostja nepatīk." A male(?) "A" voice; Latv.: "You don't like Kostja."

These are only a few examples taken from over a hundred registered voices.

I have no doubt whatsoever that beings in the beyond are trying to contact us by using our technical devices.

Konstantin Raudive deserves all credit for having made this phenomenon accessible to us. It is to be hoped that by perfecting the technical aids it may become possible to enable anyone to hear the voices and that even the "C" voices will become audible to all.

26th November 1967

III. THE LISTENERS VERIFY

Between February 1966 and June 1968 a series of 43 listening-in tests took place in which about 300 persons participated. The tests included approximately 150 to 200 "voices" each. Participants were not allowed to communicate whilst a test was in progress.

Most of the voices demonstrated during tests belonged to audibility-group "A"; participants had difficulty in hearing "B" voices and with only a few exceptions listed them as "insufficiently audible".

The results of some of the tests have already been mentioned in the commentaries of participants in actual experiments and have therefore been omitted from the following selection:

1. On 21st June 1968 a test took place in Bad Krozingen; 150 voices were demonstrated. Participants in the test were:

Prof. Dr. Hans Bender could hear 50 voices very clearly, 57 clearly and the rest insufficiently clearly. At the end of the test he remarked: "Some of the recordings and particularly those I marked 'very good!' are so clearly audible that the danger of 'projection against a background of noise' seems to be ruled out."

Dr. G. Rönicke, physicist, understood two of the voices very clearly, 48 clearly and the rest insufficiently clearly.

Dr. Arnold Reincke has had great experience in this branch of research and had already listened to many recorded voices. He could understand 65 voices very well, 78 well, and the rest insufficiently well.

Miss Iris Vauchery (USA) could distinguish 58 voices very clearly, 62 clearly and the rest insufficiently clearly. She states: "Some voices were very easy to understand, others were easy to hear, but not so easy to understand, probably because I did not know the appropriate language. Many voices had a certain musical quality, a particular accent of their own. The pitch of the voices, as well as the way in which the various words are accentuated, gives the phenomenon its definite air of authenticity."

Mr. Alson Vaughon, Parapsychological Foundation, U.S.A. heard 51 voices very well, 68 well and the rest insufficiently well. He comments: "They seem to be evidential messages, especially as many of them fit into a context. Further experiments with various different electronic aids may perhaps make it possible to receive longer and more important statements. It seems that at present the energy available does not allow for more than a few words to be passed. The polyglot messages convince one that it is not just a case of random words being picked up from a normal radio-transmission."

Miss Brigitte Rasmus understood 22 voices very well, 66 well, the rest insufficiently well. She writes: "The frequency-transmitter-voices and the diode-voices are the most interesting as far as methods are concerned, and the partnership-voices give the most interesting texts."

2. The same test was applied on 19th June 1968, and this time the participants were:

Dr. Juliane Bieber, Dr. of Philosophy and Psychologist. She heard 106 voices very clearly, the rest clearly. Her comment: "We listened to many voices today in the studio; they have impressed us very much and have confirmed that it is quite possible to explain parapsychological phenomena through scientific investigations."

Mrs. Ilse Tellinghoff, social worker, could understand 98 voices very well, 42 well and the rest insufficiently well. She writes: "Here (in Dr. Raudive's studio) evidence is being obtained by scientific means that the 'world beyond', with which we have had contact for many years through a medium, really does exist."

3. On 22nd June 1968, *Mr. Hans Geisler*, editor, listened to a selection of 37 frequency-transmitter-voices and diode-voices. He understood 9 of them very clearly, 26 clearly and the rest insufficiently clearly; afterwards he said: "If the voices had not been predominantly in Russian and Latvian, one could have given most of them a 'very good' mark."

Mrs. Hilde Dressel, editor, who also took part in this test, heard 19 voices very well, the rest well. She writes: "I am very impressed. A revolutionary scientific discovery."

4. *Miss Rosa Stucki*, Zürich, could verify 75 per cent of the 175 voices she listened to in a test conducted on 15th April 1967.

Mrs. Georgette Fürst, psychologist, proved to have a particularly acute sense of hearing. In the same test she could verify 85 per cent of 250 voices.

5. On 29th June 1967, *Prof. Werner Brunner*, surgeon (Zürich), listened to 100 voices together with *Mrs. Ida Bianchi*, *Mrs. Cornelia Brunner* and *Mr. Peter Rutishauser*. All participants were able to hear—with only a few exceptions—the same voices the experimenter had heard. Mr. Rutishauser heard approximately 50 per cent of the voices demonstrated.

6. On 1st July 1967, *Mr. A. Bieri*, *Mrs. Antoniette Bieri* and *Mrs. Ursula Ruggeri-Bieri* listened to 50 taped voices. They could hear all the voices clearly.

7. *Prof. Alex Schneider* (St. Gallen, Switzerland) heard 95 per cent of the 350 voices he listened to and could understand the texts.

8. The writer and parapsychologist *Peter Andreas* (London) listened to 250 voices (including frequency-transmitter-voices); he was able to understand 70 per cent of the voices very well, 20 per cent fairly well and 10 per cent insufficiently well.

9. *Mr. Raymond A. Donovan* (London) listened to 250 voices and heard 75 per cent of them clearly, 20 per cent he heard fairly well and 5 per cent he heard very faintly.

10. *Mr. Walter Besier*, dentist, could hear 85 per cent of 200 voices very clearly, 15 per cent fairly clearly.

Mrs. Ingeborg Besier could hear 95 per cent of the voices she listened to very well, the rest she could hear only partly.

Mr. and Mrs. Walter Besier wrote the following comment on their visits to Dr. Raudive's studio on 10th, 16th and 24th May 1968:

"Our three visits gave us ample opportunity to study the results of Dr. Raudive's research.

"First we heard a selection of recordings made via microphone, radio and diode; though we were very sceptical to start with, we were soon convinced of the fact that it is really possible to tape-record the voices of the dead. At times these voices are so clear and so easy to understand that it is impossible to doubt their authenticity.

"Our visits, lasting several hours on each occasion, also gave us the opportunity of making our own experimental recording. We used our own tape-recorder and a brand new tape. The fact that we were personally addressed and had our names mentioned, rules out any assumption that the voices may have come from some other sources than from our dead friends."

11. *Mr. Friedhelm Brugmüller*, technician (Cologne, Germany), heard 90 per cent of the 50 voices he listened to very clearly, the rest he heard only partially.

12. On 15th July 1968, 50 "partnership", frequency-transmitter, and diode-voices were demonstrated at a session in Zürich. This test was attended by:

Mrs. N. von Muralt, psychologist and parapsychologist, who understood 45 voices very clearly and 5 clearly. She commented: "I found a great improvement in the audibility of voices, especially diode voices, since I last listened to recordings."

Mrs. Cornelia Brunner, psychologist, who could understand 38 voices very well, 10 well and 2 insufficiently well, said: "I was very tired and therefore found it difficult to concentrate."

Mrs. Susi Stelli (Zürich) heard 24 voices very clearly, 23 clearly and the rest insufficiently clearly.

Miss A. Morgenthaler, teacher (Bern), has taken part in many listening-in tests and has great experience in this type of investigation. She could hear 36 voices perfectly, 13 she could hear well and 1 indistinctly.

Mrs. *Paula Schütz*, medium, heard 16 voices very clearly, 19 clearly, and the rest insufficiently clearly.

On two occasions, when the experimenter was giving lectures, he conducted listening-in tests with people who had had no prior introduction to the phenomenon.

13. The first combined lecture and listening-in test took place in Freiburg, Breisgau (Germany), on 8th December 1967 at which 160 people attended; 40 per cent of these participants heard 100 per cent to 70 per cent of the voices; 30 per cent heard 70 per cent to 20 per cent of the voices and the rest of the audience could not hear the voices sufficiently clearly.

14. The second lecture/listening-in test took place in Munich (Germany) on 21st March 1968. There was an audience of 300; 40 per cent of this audience could understand 100 per cent to 95 per cent of the voices demonstrated; the rest varied between 95 per cent and 20 per cent. (We know that with advancing years the sense of hearing tends to become less acute, especially in people who have no particular opportunity to exercise their hearing-faculty. A normal ear needs roughly 3 months of daily practice before it can discern the voices with any degree of accuracy.)

During the Parapsychological Congress in Freiburg, Breisgau (Germany), 5th to 7th September 1968, several groups of parapsychologists visited Dr. Raudive's studio in Bad Krozingen, and studied the voice-phenomenon. They took part in listening-in tests of four voice-recording methods: microphone, radio, frequency-transmitter and diode recordings.

15. Participants in one of these sessions on 7th September 1968 were:

Dr. Jule Eisenbud (Denver, U.S.A.), who published a book about Ted Serios' "thought-photography". He heard all the 30 voice-texts demonstrated and commented later in just one word: "Fantastic!"

Mrs. Molly Eisenbud, lecturer, also heard all the 30 voices clearly. Her comment: "I have heard the voices and found them very interesting, but could not recognise the personalities behind them."

Prof. Walter H. Uphoff (Boulder, U.S.A.) understood the 30 texts perfectly and remarked: "Very interesting. I very much regret not to have the time to hear the results of a few experimental recordings made by myself."

Mrs. W. Uphoff could hear the texts equally well.

Miss K. M. Goldney, parapsychologist (London), heard 29 of the texts perfectly clearly and one fairly clearly.

16. On the same date, 7th September 1968, a group of Italian parapsychologists met at Dr. Raudive's studio in the evening, and were given the same 30 voices to listen to; they were:

Dr. Guiseppe Crosa, psychiatrist (Director of the Casa di cura e soggiorno, malatie nervose e mentali, Genoa);

Dr. Gastone Boni (Verona);

Prof. Dr. Mengoli.

Dr. Crosa commented on the test: "We have all been able to hear the voices perfectly clearly."

17. The same test was applied on 8th September 1968, when Dr. Karl Osis, psychologist (Research Laboratory, American Society for Psychical Research), visited the studio. He understood 16 of the 30 voices very clearly, 10 clearly and the rest insufficiently clearly. His comment: "Some of the voice-texts could definitely be interpreted as the experimenter had interpreted them; others not. In my opinion two further steps could be taken: (*a*) Voice-impression analyses of frequently recurring words such as, for instance, 'Petrautzka'. (*b*) Checking of voices by an apparatus completely isolated from external influences of electromagnetic waves, and research under conditions in which Dr. Raudive as well as all the necessary apparatus are in an electrically isolated room."

(Dr. Osis is a linguist who understands Russian, Latvian and German as well as English.)

18. On the same date, 8th September 1968, the same test-voices were listened to by:

Dr. Heinz C. Berendt, dentist (member of the Israel Parapsychology Society, Jerusalem). He heard 13 of the 30 voice-texts very clearly, 12 clearly and the rest insufficiently clearly. He declared at the end of the test: "This confirmation can cover no more than the acoustic clarity."

Mr. Jarl Fahler, psychiatrist and author (Helsinki, Finland), who could hear 10 voices very well, 14 well and the rest insufficiently well, commented later: "Most interesting; many thanks for the hour spent on this investigation."

Mr. Erlendur Haraldsson, student of psychology (Iceland). He could hear 7 voices very clearly, 20 clearly, and the rest insufficiently clearly.

Mr. Eckart Brockhaus, psychologist (Freiburg, Germany), could hear 23 voices very clearly and 7 clearly. He commented: "The rhythm of the voices reminds one of African magic formulae and secret languages." He gave a most interesting lecture at the Parapsychological Congress in Freiburg on the possibilities and limits of research in paranormal phenomena in West Africa.

19. On 31st August 1968, 150 voices were demonstrated at a session in Bad Krozingen. This listening-in test was attended by:

Mr. Eckart Wilhelm Wilbertz, editor; he understood 31 voices very well, 66 well and the rest insufficiently well. He commented: "When I visited Dr. Raudive in my capacity as a journalist, I was personally convinced of the existence of the voice-phenomenon. The most impressive voices, I found, were the diode-voices; so far, this method seems to offer the best guarantee against the intrusion of 'earthly transmissions'. In my opinion, science should regard the clarification of this phenomenon as an important task."

Mr. Joachim Hoffmann, healer, who has most acute hearing and understood 133 voices perfectly and the rest clearly enough.

20. On 10th September 1968 the test comprising 30 voices was applied to *Dr. Wladimir Lindenberg*, psychiatrist and author (Berlin). He could hear 23 voices very clearly, 4 clearly and the rest insufficiently clearly. "I have heard nearly all of the voices clearly," he remarked at the end of the test.

IV. EXTRACT FROM ARTICLE BY HOLGER ESS

Appearing in the issue of *Braunschweiger Zeitung*, No. 12 13th February 1966:

Neutron-matter can only be thought of as existing within certain stars where a pressure exists that exceeds by many degrees anything known to man of pressures and of any phenomena connected with pressure. The matter of an ordinary star, of our sun, for instance, consists of a hot plasma; a gas, heated to extreme degrees, which is composed of electrons and ions—atoms, in fact, that have lost their electrons entirely, or at least in part. The source of the colossal energy released by such a star is to be found in thermonuclear processes caused by the collision of high velocity electrons, particularly hydrogen-nuclei. In time the energy radiating from this type of stellar body diminishes in ratio with the amount of hydrogen that is "burnt up". The matter of the star becomes compressed. Density of such matter can then attain very high values, up to hundreds of thousands of tons per ccm.

This can hardly be grasped by the average human intellect. Equally difficult to comprehend is the existence of yet another type of matter—apart from high density neutron-matter—which, expressed in practical terms, is not there but which, theoretically speaking, must exist. If this "anti-matter" were to become visible, it could do so only by a collision with, at least, a part of our visible matter. However, should tangible matter collide with "anti-matter", both would dissolve into nothing under the pressure of unimaginable energies which would be produced; tangible matter and "anti-matter" would disappear—where?

The theory of an "anti-world" sounds, and is, so fantastically difficult a problem, that it took years before a group of eminent physicists, under the leadership of Dr. Leon Ledermann, decided to publish a report which they knew would excite world-wide attention. In it they claim to have succeeded in discovering the so-called "anti-world" which must exist "somewhere in the realm of our life-experience, although we cannot see or feel it". In that world, time runs backwards. If the world in which we live collided with the "anti-world" it would mean the end of everything now in existence. In later publications Dr. Ledermann added: "We must admit to the audacious supposition that this anti-world is peopled with intelligent beings that speculate about our existence in a world positive to us, in the same way as we do about creatures of the anti-world."

Who would not, on reading this, conceive the idea that perhaps the souls of the dead live in this "anti-world", but are, under normal conditions, unable to make contact with us? The simplest interpretation, according to these physicists, would be to think of "anti-matter", including man who must of necessity also have his reflection in that other world, as if, for instance, a human being had a counterpart existing in a "beyond" the existence of which could be proved but which, nevertheless, remained invisible to us unless we possessed the appropriate "mirror" to show us the "anti-world". Consequently, it might be possible to imagine the existence of this "anti-world" as the cause of our decay, our dying—as an inevitable fate—because our world and the "anti-world" are striving, so to speak, to achieve a balance or harmonisation.

Dr. Ledermann was the first to pose the question of "where" this anti-world may exist. It must be amongst us, next to us, in immediate proximity to us; but it could also cut right through our world of physical matter. On the other hand, it could just as well be located at an astronomical distance from our earth. Astronomical distance, however, would be self-contradictory to "anti-matter", as in terms of distance time runs backwards and consequently the sequence of events which, in our world, is tied to a progressive time-element, would cancel itself out.

www.ingramcontent.com/pod-product-compliance
Lightning Source LLC
Chambersburg PA
CBHW031418150426
43191CB00006B/316